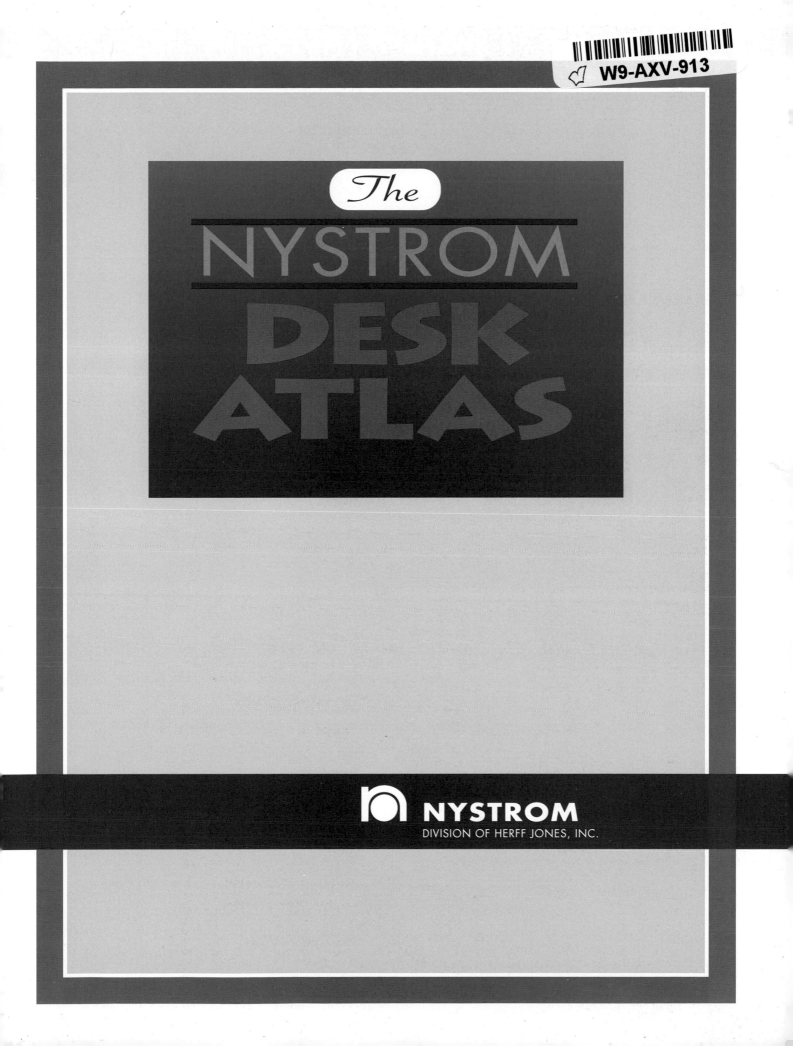

The NYSTROM DESK ATLAS

NYSTROM
DIVISION OF HERFF JONES, INC.

CREDITS

Executive Editor	Charles Novosad
Project Design and Direction	Matthew V. Kania
Project Editor	Joan Pederson
Cartographic Manager	Christine D. Bosacki
Design/Production Manager	Ruth P. Koval
Nystrom Computer Cartography and Graphics	Bonnie Jones, Charlaine Wilkerson
Additional Computer Cartography	Maryland CartoGraphics, Inc.
Additional Nystrom Cartography	Louise Feeney, James Franklin, Phyllis Kawano, Gerald Keefe, Michael Nauert
Map Compilation	Valerie Krejcie, John Chalk, Sharon Knight
Writer	Emily B. Good
Statistical Research	Jennifer Stevens
Photographic Research	Charlotte Goldman
Index	Irene B. Keller, Michael Sweeney
Cover Design	The Quarasan Group, Inc.
Desktop Publishing	Janet Winkler, Jeff Jackson

1999 Edition
Copyright © 1994 **NYSTROM**
Division of Herff Jones, Inc.
3333 Elston Avenue
Chicago, Illinois 60618

For information about ordering this atlas, call toll-free 800-621-8086.

ISBN: 0-7825-0349-7

20 19 18 17 16 15 14 13 12   02 01 00 99
Printed in U.S.A.   9A94

CONTENTS

Introduction 6-7

Maps and Graphics 6
Continents and Oceans 7
Complete Legend 7

World 8-35

Physical Map 8-9
Political Map 10-11
Thematic Maps and Graphs 12-35

North America 36-39

Physical Map 36
Political Map 37
Thematic Maps and Graphs 38-39

Canada 40-51

Physical Map 40-41
Political Map 42-43
Western Canada 44-45
South Central Canada 46-47
Thematic Maps and Graphs 48-51

United States 52-81

Physical Map 52-53
Political Map 54-55
Alaska and Hawaii 57
Southwestern U.S. 58-59
Northwestern U.S. 60-61
North Central U.S. 62-63
Central U.S. 64-65
South Central U.S. 66-67
Southeastern U.S. 68-69
East Central U.S. 70-71
Northeastern U.S. 72-73
Thematic Maps and Graphs 74-81

Middle America 82-87

Physical Map 82-83
Political Map 84-85
Thematic Maps and Graphs 86-87

South America 88-93

Physical Map 88
Political Map 89
Northern South America 90
Thematic Maps and Graphs 90-93

Europe 94-105

Physical Map 94-95
Political Map 96-97
Western Europe 98
Central Europe 99
Former Soviet Union 100-101
Thematic Maps and Graphs 101-105

Africa 106-113

Physical Map 106
Political Map 107
Western Africa 108
South Africa 109
Eastern Africa 110
Thematic Maps and Graphs 108-113

Mediterranean Basin and Persian Gulf 114-117

Political Map 114-115
Thematic Maps and Graphs 116-117

Asia 118-129

Physical Map 118-119
Political Map 120-121
Southern Asia 122
Southeastern Asia 123
China 124
Eastern Asia 125
Thematic Maps and Graphs 122-129

Australia 130-133

Physical Map 130
Political Map 131
Southeastern Australia 133
Thematic Maps and Graphs 132-133

Pacific Rim 134-135

Political Map 134-135
Thematic Maps and Graphs 134-135

Arctic 136

Physical Map 136
Thematic Map 136

Antarctica 137

Physical Map 137
Thematic Maps 137

Geographic Facts and Index 138-176

Map Projections 138-139
Country Tables 140-147
Glossary 148-149
Abbreviations 149
Index 150-176
Pronunciation Key   inside back cover

THEMATIC MAPS AND GRAPHS

Cross Sections

Antarctica 137
Asia 126–127
South America 92
United States 74–75

Culture and History

Africa's Rise to Independence 110
Changing Boundaries
    Europe in 1914 101
    Europe in 1948 101
    Middle East 117
    Soviet Union 100–101
    World 20
European Imperialism 105
Immigration to the U.S. 20
Latin American Languages 87
Major Languages 28
Major Religions 21
Middle East Religions 116
Slave Trade 108
World Migration 21

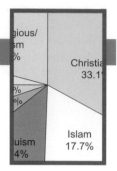

Environmental Concerns

Acid Rain 34
Changing Sahara 112
Domestic Water Use (U.S.) 76
Endangered Species (Africa) 111
Ivory Trade 111
Ozone Depletion 35
Safe Drinking Water 34
Threatened Water Supplies (U.S.) 76
Tropical Rain Forests
    South America 91
    World 35
Wetlands (U.S.) 75

Ethnicity and Indigenous Peoples

Canada 49
Latin America 87
North America 38
Oceania 132
South Africa 109
South America 91
United States 76

Land Use

Africa 113
Asia 128
Australia 133
Canada 48
Europe 103
Middle America 87
North America 39
South America 93
United States 76
World 33

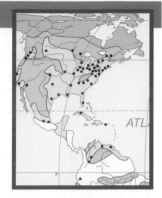

Mineral and Energy Resources

Africa 112
Asia 128
Canada 51
Europe 102
Middle East 117
South America 91
United States 78–79
World 30–31

Natural Vegetation

Africa 112
Asia 127
Australia 132
Europe 103
North America 38
South America 92
United States 75
World 32

Physical World

Climates 14–15
Earthquakes and Volcanoes 12–13
Monsoon Asia 122–123
Ocean Depths and Currents 12–13
Temperature and Precipitation 16–17

Population Density

Africa 113
Asia 129
Australia 133
Canada 49
Europe 104
Middle America 86
North America 39
South America 93
United States 77
World 18

Population Growth and Profiles

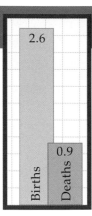

Africa   19
Algeria   110
Brazil   93
Canada   50
China   124
European Union   19
Haiti   86
Iraq   116
New Zealand   132
Nigeria   113
United Kingdom   104
United States   77
Urban Areas   22
World   18–19

Precipitation

Africa   112
Asia   126
Australia   132
Europe   102
North America   38
South America   92
United States   74
World   16

Quality of Life

AIDS   25
Bicycles in China   124
Causes of Death   25
Food
    Availability   22
    Cropland Per Capita   23
    Fisheries   33
    Staple Food Production   23
Leading Automobile Manufacturers   125
Life Expectancy   24
Literacy   29
Persons Per
    Automobile   30
    Newspaper   29
    Physician   24
    Radio   29
    Telephone   29
    Television   29

Relative Location and Travel

Arctic Distances   136
Australia's Isolation   133
Canada's Highways and Airports   50
Speed of Travel   29
Time Zones   28
U.S. Air and Rail Transportation   81
U.S. Regions   56

Size Comparisons

Alaska and U.S.   74
Antarctica and U.S.   137
Canada and U.S.   48
China and U.S.   124
Europe and U.S.   102
Indonesia and U.S.   126
Mexico and U.S.   39
Sahara and U.S.   112
South America and U.S.   90

Trade and Economics

Angola   113
Australia   133
Canada   50–51
Chile   93
China   127
Drug Trade (Americas) 90
Europe   105
Greece   104
India   127
Israel   116
Japan   125
Libya   113
Mexico   86
Nicaragua   87
North America   39
OPEC   117
Poland   104
Saudi Arabia   116
South Africa   109
South Korea   125
United States   79–81
Venezuela   92
World   26–27, 134–135

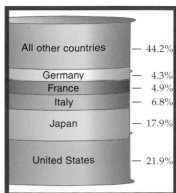

INTRODUCTION

The Nystrom Desk Atlas includes physical and political maps of large areas, regional maps of smaller areas, thematic maps, graphic presentations of data, and illustrative photographs. Each map, graph, and photo is best suited to providing specific kinds of information.

Physical Maps

Physical maps in this atlas are designed so that the names and relative locations of natural features can be seen at a glance. Colors represent water depths and land elevations. Although the emphasis is on natural features, countries and key cities also are named.

Political Maps

Political maps are colored by state, province, or country, making it as easy as possible to tell where one ends and another begins. The names of capitals and other major cities are quickly found because the maps are carefully edited to keep them uncluttered.

Thematic Maps

Thematic maps focus on single topics or themes, and the subject can be anything that is mappable. Among the thematic maps in this atlas are maps of rainfall, land use, and population. Often the patterns on one thematic map become more meaningful when compared to the patterns on another.

Regional Maps

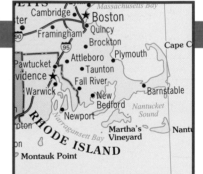

Regional maps in this atlas offer close-up views of areas on the political maps. Because regional maps enlarge the areas shown, they can name more cities while remaining highly readable. Other details also are added, such as the names of landforms, including some not given on the physical maps.

Legends

Legends are provided for all maps. For most of the thematic maps, the legends are simple keys showing what the map colors stand for. The legends for the physical, political, and regional maps are lengthier. To save space, the complete legend for these maps is given only once, on the facing page.

Graphs

Graphs summarize facts in a visual way, making it easier to see trends and make comparisons. Many different topics are presented in a variety of graphic styles. Some topics are graphed only once, while others form strands that run through the whole book.

Photographs

Photographs can portray the characteristics of a place like nothing else can. The photos in this atlas were carefully chosen to illustrate the natural setting and cultural aspects of places around the world. Photographic realism is the perfect complement to the abstract symbolism of maps.

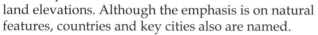
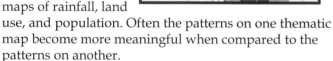

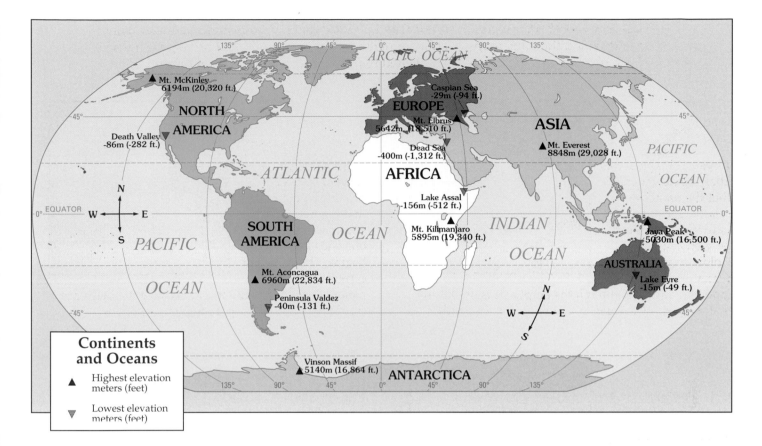

Continents and Oceans

Mt. McKinley 6194m (20,320 ft.)

NORTH AMERICA

Death Valley -86m (-282 ft.)

ATLANTIC

EUROPE

Caspian Sea -29m (-94 ft.)

Mt. Elbrus 5642m (18,510 ft.)

ASIA

Mt. Everest 8848m (29,028 ft.)

PACIFIC OCEAN

Dead Sea -400m (-1,312 ft.)

AFRICA

Lake Assal -156m (-512 ft.)

Mt. Kilimanjaro 5895m (19,340 ft.)

INDIAN OCEAN

Java Peak 5030m (16,500 ft.)

AUSTRALIA

Lake Eyre -15m (-49 ft.)

SOUTH AMERICA

OCEAN

Mt. Aconcagua 6960m (22,834 ft.)

Peninsula Valdez -40m (-131 ft.)

PACIFIC

OCEAN

EQUATOR

Vinson Massif 5140m (16,864 ft.)

ANTARCTICA

Continents and Oceans

▲ Highest elevation meters (feet)

▼ Lowest elevation meters (feet)

Complete Legend

LAND AND WATER FEATURES

River

Canal

Waterfall

Lake

Seasonal or dry lake

Dam

Wetlands

Ice cap, glacier

⋈ Mountain pass

▲ Mountain peak

▼ Depression

⟨90⟩ U.S. Interstate highway

⟨17⟩⟨10⟩ Principal Canadian intercity highway

LETTERING STYLES

ASIA **ASIA**   Continent

PARAGUAY   Country

Great Plains   Land feature

ARCTIC OCEAN   Water feature

Saskatchewan R.   Water feature

Odessa   City

(U.S.)   Possession

POLITICAL BOUNDARIES

International boundary

Internal boundary (state, province, republic)

Other boundary (disputed or undefined)

■ Small country or possession

ELEVATION

Meters		Feet
Over 6000		Over 20,000
3000 to 6000		10,000 to 20,000
1500 to 3000		5,000 to 10,000
600 to 1500		2,000 to 5,000
300 to 600		1,000 to 2,000
150 to 300		500 to 1,000
0 to 150		0 to 500
Below sea level		Below sea level

WATER DEPTH

Less than 200		Less than 600
Greater than 200		Greater than 600

Metric numbers are rounded.

CITIES

• Bombay

· Vladivostok

· Mecca

A city's relative size is shown by the size of its symbol and lettering.

⊛ Tokyo   National capital

★ Hartford   Internal capital (state, province, territory, republic)

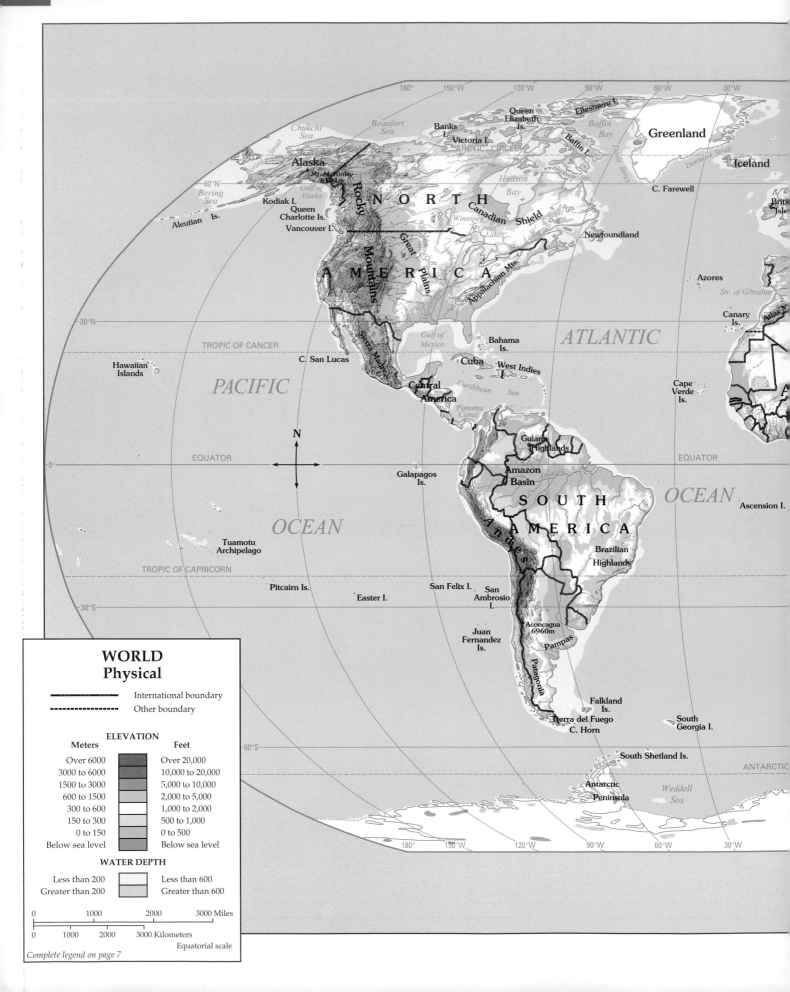

WORLD
Physical

———————	International boundary
- - - - - - - -	Other boundary

ELEVATION

Meters		Feet
Over 6000		Over 20,000
3000 to 6000		10,000 to 20,000
1500 to 3000		5,000 to 10,000
600 to 1500		2,000 to 5,000
300 to 600		1,000 to 2,000
150 to 300		500 to 1,000
0 to 150		0 to 500
Below sea level		Below sea level

WATER DEPTH

Less than 200		Less than 600
Greater than 200		Greater than 600

0   1000   2000   3000 Miles

0   1000   2000   3000 Kilometers

Equatorial scale

Complete legend on page 7

Chukchi Sea
Beaufort Sea
Queen Elizabeth Is.
Ellesmere I.
Banks I.
Victoria I.
Baffin Bay
Baffin I.
Greenland
Iceland
ARCTIC CIRCLE
Bering Strait
Alaska
Mt. McKinley 6194m
Hudson Str.
Denmark Strait
Brit. Isle
60°N
Bering Sea
Gulf of Alaska
Rocky Mountains
Hudson Bay
C. Farewell
Kodiak I.
Queen Charlotte Is.
Vancouver I.
NORTH AMERICA
Canadian Shield
Great Lakes
Winnipeg
Lawrence R.
Newfoundland
Aleutian Is.
Great Plains
Appalachian Mts.
Azores
Str. of Gibraltar
30°N
Atlas M
TROPIC OF CANCER
C. San Lucas
Sierra Madre
Gulf of Mexico
Bahama Is.
ATLANTIC
Canary Is.
Hawaiian Islands
PACIFIC
Cuba
West Indies
Cape Verde Is.
Central America
Caribbean Sea
Panama Canal
Guiana Highlands
N
EQUATOR
Galapagos Is.
Amazon Basin
Amazon R.
SOUTH AMERICA
EQUATOR
Ascension I.
OCEAN
Andes
Brazilian Highlands
Tuamotu Archipelago
TROPIC OF CAPRICORN
Pitcairn Is.
San Felix I.
San Ambrosio I.
Easter I.
Aconcagua 6960m
Juan Fernandez Is.
Pampas
30°S
Patagonia
Falkland Is.
South Georgia I.
Tierra del Fuego
C. Horn
South Shetland Is.
60°S
ANTARCTIC
Antarctic Peninsula
Weddell Sea
180°   150°W   120°W   90°W   60°W   30°W

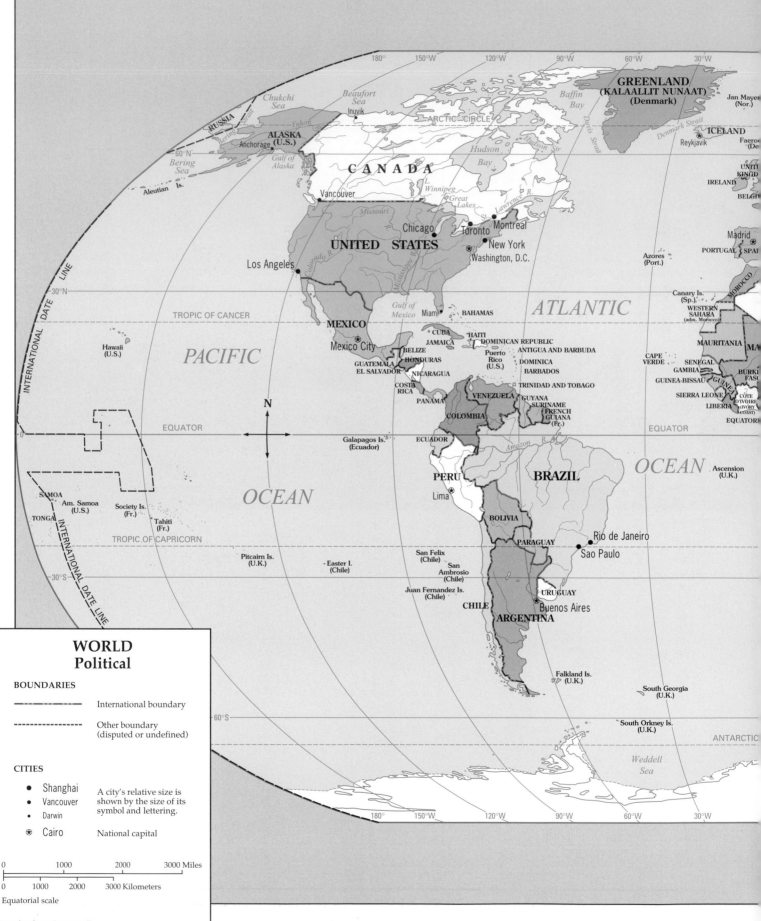

WORLD
Political

BOUNDARIES

——————— International boundary

- - - - - - - - Other boundary
(disputed or undefined)

CITIES

● Shanghai   A city's relative size is
● Vancouver   shown by the size of its
  Darwin   symbol and lettering.

⊛ Cairo   National capital

0	1000	2000	3000 Miles

0	1000	2000	3000 Kilometers

Equatorial scale

Complete legend on page 7

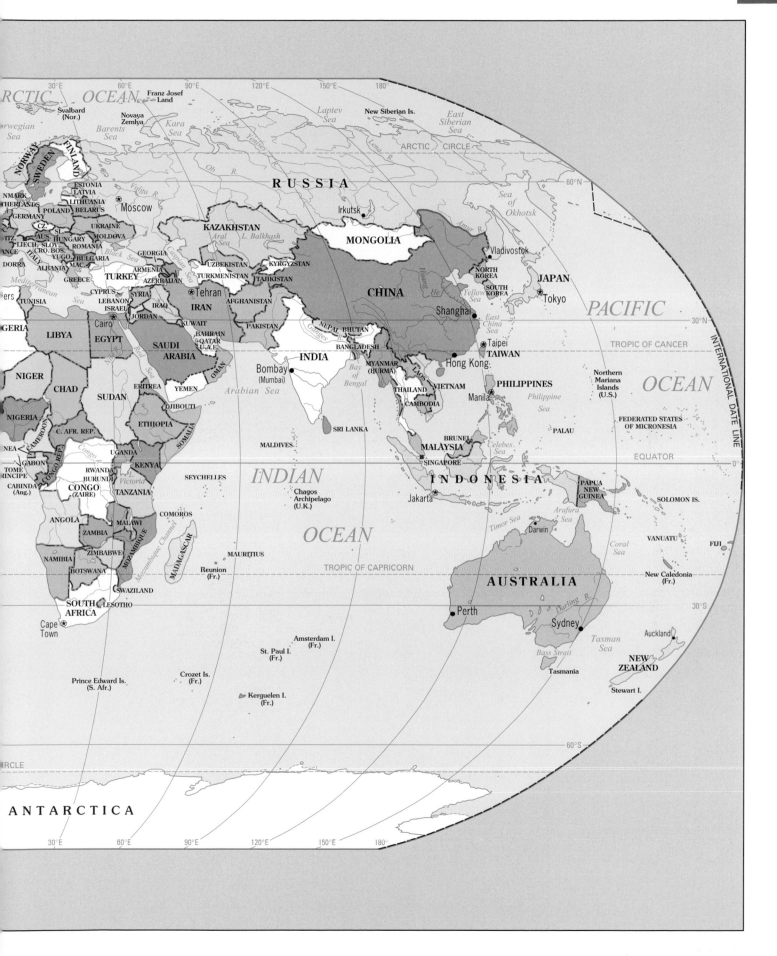

ARCTIC OCEAN
Franz Josef Land
Svalbard (Nor.)
Novaya Zemlya
New Siberian Is.
Laptev Sea
East Siberian Sea
ARCTIC CIRCLE

NORWAY
SWEDEN
FINLAND
Norwegian Sea
Barents Sea
Kara Sea
Yenisey R.

NMARK
NETHERLANDS
GERMANY
ESTONIA
LATVIA
LITHUANIA
BELARUS
Moscow
Volga R.
Ob R.

RUSSIA

Sea of Okhotsk
60°N

POLAND
CZ.
AUS.
SL.
HUNGARY
ROMANIA
UKRAINE
MOLDOVA
KAZAKHSTAN
Aral Sea
L. Balkhash
Irkutsk
Amur R.

Vladivostok

LIECH.
SLOV.
CRO. BOS.
YUGO.
MAC.
BULGARIA
GEORGIA
Black Sea
Caspian Sea
UZBEKISTAN
KYRGYZSTAN

MONGOLIA

NORTH KOREA
JAPAN

DORRA
ITALY
ALBANIA
GREECE
ARMENIA
AZERBAIJAN
TURKMENISTAN
TAJIKISTAN
Hwang He
SOUTH KOREA
Tokyo
PACIFIC

TURKEY
CYPRUS
SYRIA
LEBANON
ISRAEL
IRAQ
JORDAN
IRAN
AFGHANISTAN
CHINA
Shanghai
Yellow Sea
East China Sea
30°N

Mediterranean Sea
TUNISIA
Cairo
KUWAIT
BAHRAIN
QATAR
U.A.E.
PAKISTAN
NEPAL
BHUTAN
Ganges
Taipei
TAIWAN
TROPIC OF CANCER

GERIA
LIBYA
EGYPT
SAUDI ARABIA
OMAN
Nile
Red Sea
BANGLADESH
Hong Kong
OCEAN

NIGER
CHAD
SUDAN
ERITREA
YEMEN
Arabian Sea
INDIA
Bombay (Mumbai)
Bay of Bengal
MYANMAR (BURMA)
THAILAND
LAOS
VIETNAM
PHILIPPINES
Manila
Northern Mariana Islands (U.S.)

NIGERIA
C. AFR. REP.
DJIBOUTI
ETHIOPIA
SOMALIA
CAMBODIA
SRI LANKA
BRUNEI
MALAYSIA
Philippine Sea
PALAU
FEDERATED STATES OF MICRONESIA

NEA
TOME PRINCIPE
GABON
CONGO REP.
Congo R.
UGANDA
RWANDA
BURUNDI
KENYA
L. Victoria
MALDIVES
SINGAPORE
Celebes Sea
EQUATOR

CABINDA (Ang.)
CONGO (ZAIRE)
TANZANIA
SEYCHELLES
INDIAN
Chagos Archipelago (U.K.)
INDONESIA
Jakarta
PAPUA NEW GUINEA
SOLOMON IS.

ANGOLA
ZAMBIA
MALAWI
MOZAMBIQUE
COMOROS
MADAGASCAR
OCEAN
Timor Sea
Arafura Sea
Darwin
Coral Sea
VANUATU
FIJI

NAMIBIA
ZIMBABWE
BOTSWANA
Mozambique Channel
MAURITIUS
Reunion (Fr.)
TROPIC OF CAPRICORN
New Caledonia (Fr.)

SOUTH AFRICA
SWAZILAND
LESOTHO
Cape Town
AUSTRALIA
Perth
Darling R.
Sydney
Auckland
30°S

Amsterdam I. (Fr.)
St. Paul I. (Fr.)
Tasman Sea
Bass Strait
Tasmania
NEW ZEALAND

Prince Edward Is. (S. Afr.)
Crozet Is. (Fr.)
Kerguelen I. (Fr.)
Stewart I.

60°S

RCLE

ANTARCTICA

30°E
60°E
90°E
120°E
150°E
180°

International Date Line

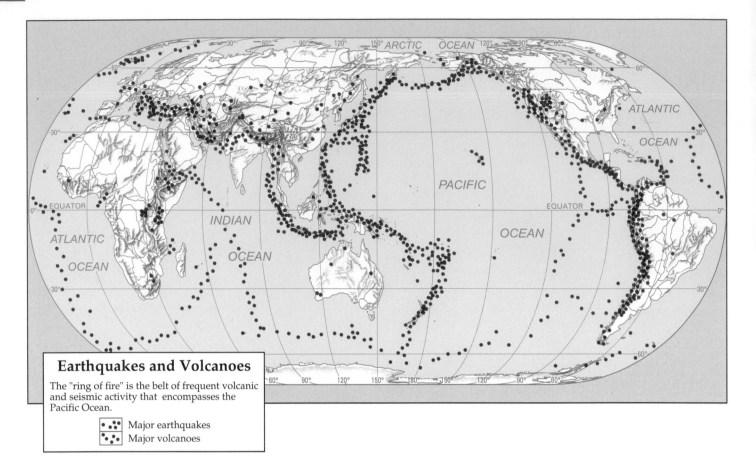

Earthquakes and Volcanoes

The "ring of fire" is the belt of frequent volcanic and seismic activity that encompasses the Pacific Ocean.

Major earthquakes
Major volcanoes

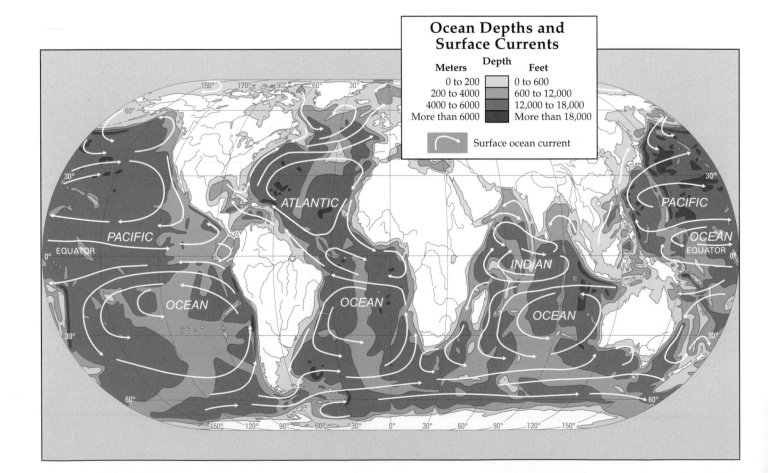

Ocean Depths and Surface Currents

Depth

Meters		Feet
0 to 200		0 to 600
200 to 4000		600 to 12,000
4000 to 6000		12,000 to 18,000
More than 6000		More than 18,000

Surface ocean current

Notable Earthquakes

Earthquake	Date	Magnitude (Richter Scale)	Deaths
Central India	Sept. 30, 1993	6.4	22,000
Northwestern Iran	June 21, 1990	7.7	40,000+
Loma Prieta, CA, U.S.	October 17, 1989	6.9	62
Northwestern Armenia	December 7, 1988	6.8	55,000+
Mexico City, Mexico	Sept. 19-21, 1985	8.1	4,200+
Tangshan, China	July 28, 1976	7.6	242,000
Guatemala	February 4, 1976	7.5	22,778
San Fernando, CA, U.S.	February 9, 1971	6.5	65
Northern Peru	May 31, 1970	7.8	66,794
Kenai Pen., AK, U.S.	March 28, 1964	8.6	131
Nan-Shan, China	May 22, 1927	8.3	200,000
Yokohama, Japan	September 1, 1923	8.3	143,000
Gansu, China	December 16, 1920	8.6	100,000
Messina, Italy	December 28, 1908	7.5	83,000
San Francisco, CA, U.S.	April 18, 1906	8.3	700
New Madrid, MO, U.S.	December 16, 1811- February 7, 1812	8.7	unknown
Calcutta, India	October 11, 1737	---	300,000
Shemaka, Azerbaijan	November 1667	---	80,000
Shaanxi, China	January 24, 1556	---	830,000
Antioch, Syria	May 20, 526	---	250,000

Notable Volcanic Eruptions

Volcano	Place	Year	Deaths
Kilauea	Hawaii, U.S.	1983-present	1
Pinatubo	Philippines	1992	200+
Redoubt	Alaska, U.S.	1989-1990	0
Nevada del Ruiz	Colombia	1985	22,940
Mauna Loa	Hawaii, U.S.	1984	0
El Chicon	Mexico	1982	100+
St. Helens	Washington, U.S.	1980	57
Erebus	Ross I., Antarctica	1970-1980	0
Surtsey	N. Atlantic Ocean	1963-1967	0
Paricutin	Mexico	1943-1952	1,000
Kelud	Java, Indonesia	1919	5,000
Pelee	Martinique	1902	26,000
Krakatoa	Sumatra, Indonesia	1883	36,000
Tambora	Sumbawa, Indonesia	1815	56,000
Unzen	Japan	1792	10,400
Etna	Sicily, Italy	1669	20,000
Kelud	Java, Indonesia	1586	10,000
Etna	Sicily, Italy	1169	15,000
Vesuvius	Italy	79	16,000
Thera (Santorini)	Aegean Sea	1645 B.C.	thousands

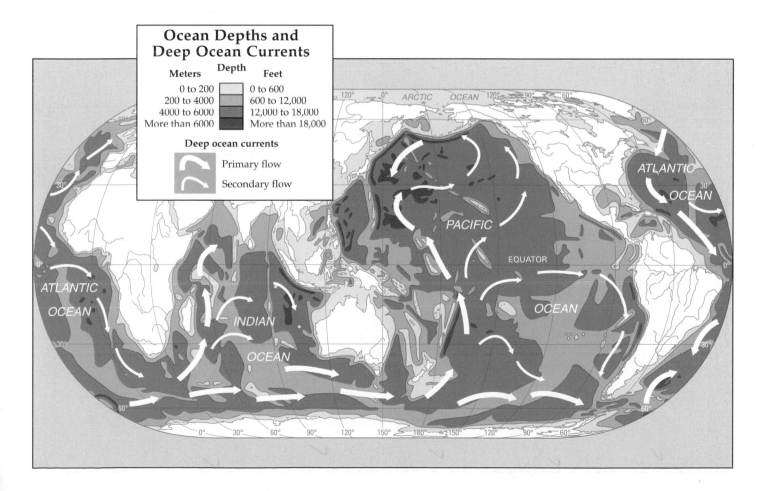

Ocean Depths and Deep Ocean Currents

Depth

Meters	Feet
0 to 200	0 to 600
200 to 4000	600 to 12,000
4000 to 6000	12,000 to 18,000
More than 6000	More than 18,000

Deep ocean currents

Primary flow

Secondary flow

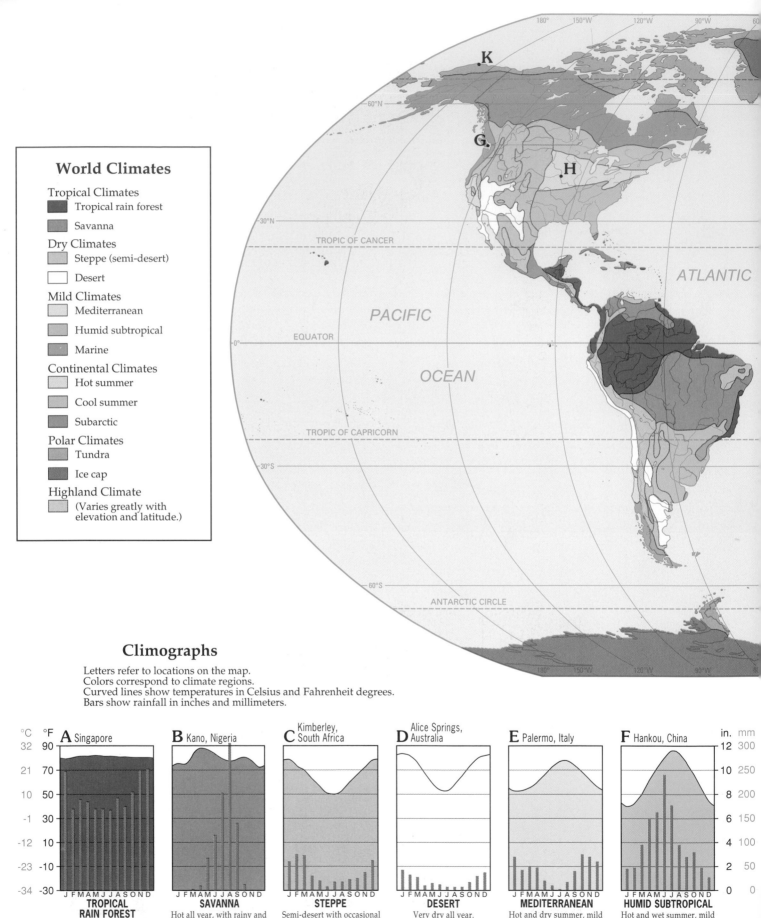

World Climates

Tropical Climates
Tropical rain forest
Savanna

Dry Climates
Steppe (semi-desert)
Desert

Mild Climates
Mediterranean
Humid subtropical
Marine

Continental Climates
Hot summer
Cool summer
Subarctic

Polar Climates
Tundra
Ice cap

Highland Climate
(Varies greatly with elevation and latitude.)

Climographs

Letters refer to locations on the map.
Colors correspond to climate regions.
Curved lines show temperatures in Celsius and Fahrenheit degrees.
Bars show rainfall in inches and millimeters.

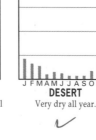

A Singapore
TROPICAL RAIN FOREST
Hot and rainy all year.

B Kano, Nigeria
SAVANNA
Hot all year, with rainy and dry seasons.

C Kimberley, South Africa
STEPPE
Semi-desert with occasional rain.

D Alice Springs, Australia
DESERT
Very dry all year.

E Palermo, Italy
MEDITERRANEAN
Hot and dry summer, mild and rainy winter.

F Hankou, China
HUMID SUBTROPICAL
Hot and wet summer, mild and damp winter.

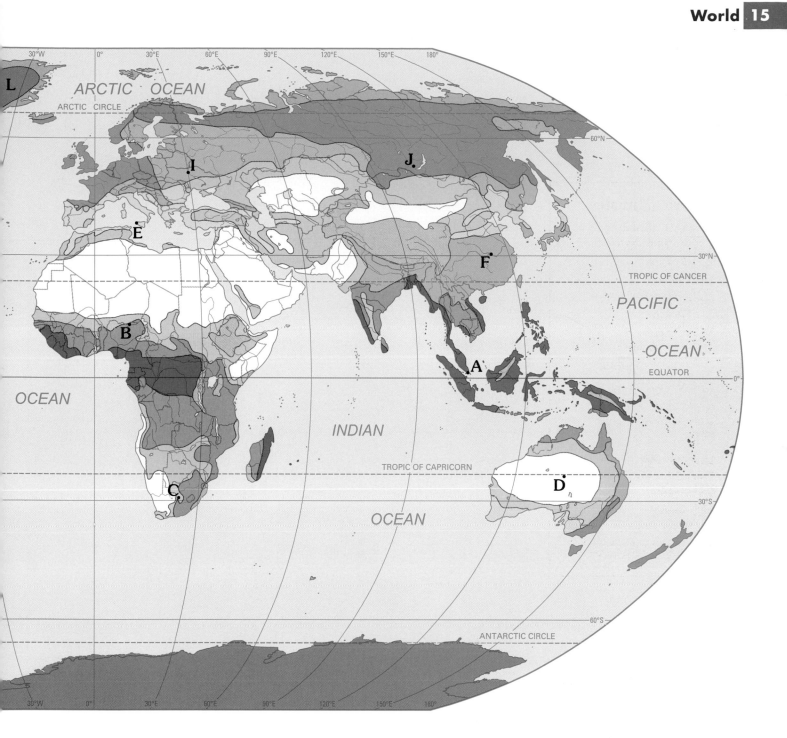

ARCTIC OCEAN
ARCTIC CIRCLE

L

60°N

J

I

E

F

30°N

TROPIC OF CANCER

PACIFIC

B

OCEAN

A

OCEAN

EQUATOR

0°

INDIAN

C

D

TROPIC OF CAPRICORN

OCEAN

30°S

60°S

ANTARCTIC CIRCLE

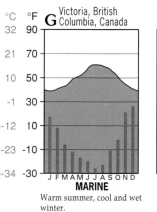

°C °F   **G** Victoria, British
32   90   Columbia, Canada
21   70
10   50
-1   30
-12 10
-23 -10
-34 -30   J FMAM J J A S O N D
              MARINE
           Warm summer, cool and wet
           winter.

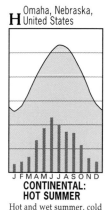

H Omaha, Nebraska,
      United States

J FMAM J J A S O N D
CONTINENTAL:
HOT SUMMER
Hot and wet summer, cold
and snowy winter.

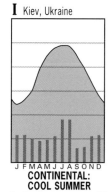

I Kiev, Ukraine

J FMAM J J A S O N D
CONTINENTAL:
COOL SUMMER
Cool and wet summer, cold
and very snowy winter.

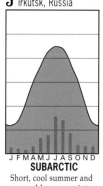

J Irkutsk, Russia

J FMAM J J A S O N D
SUBARCTIC
Short, cool summer and
very cold, snowy winter.

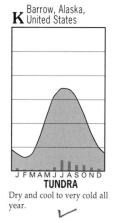

K Barrow, Alaska,
      United States

J FMAM J J A S O N D
TUNDRA
Dry and cool to very cold all
year.

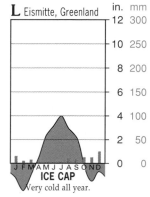

L Eismitte, Greenland   in. mm
                              12 300
                              10 250
                               8 200
                               6 150
                               4 100
                               2   50
                               0   0
J FMAM J J A S O N D
ICE CAP
Very cold all year.

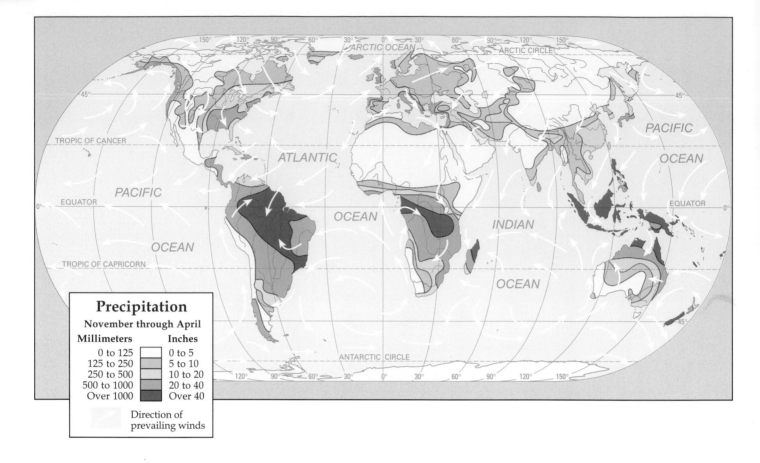

Precipitation

November through April

Millimeters		Inches
0 to 125		0 to 5
125 to 250		5 to 10
250 to 500		10 to 20
500 to 1000		20 to 40
Over 1000		Over 40

Direction of prevailing winds

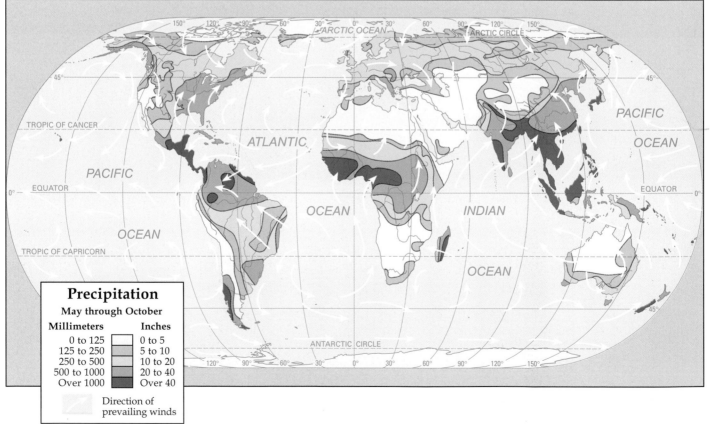

Precipitation

May through October

Millimeters		Inches
0 to 125		0 to 5
125 to 250		5 to 10
250 to 500		10 to 20
500 to 1000		20 to 40
Over 1000		Over 40

Direction of prevailing winds

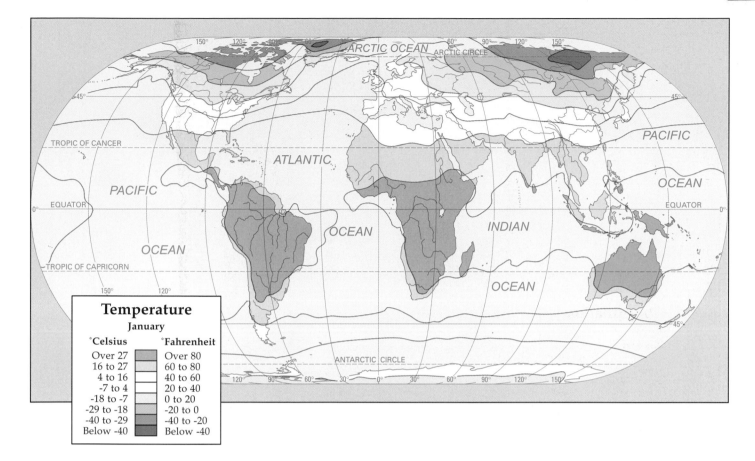

Temperature

January

°Celsius		°Fahrenheit
Over 27		Over 80
16 to 27		60 to 80
4 to 16		40 to 60
-7 to 4		20 to 40
-18 to -7		0 to 20
-29 to -18		-20 to 0
-40 to -29		-40 to -20
Below -40		Below -40

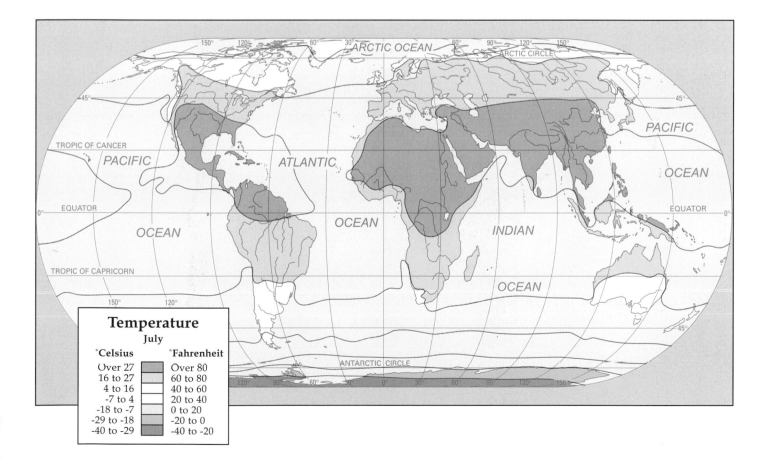

Temperature

July

°Celsius		°Fahrenheit
Over 27		Over 80
16 to 27		60 to 80
4 to 16		40 to 60
-7 to 4		20 to 40
-18 to -7		0 to 20
-29 to -18		-20 to 0
-40 to -29		-40 to -20

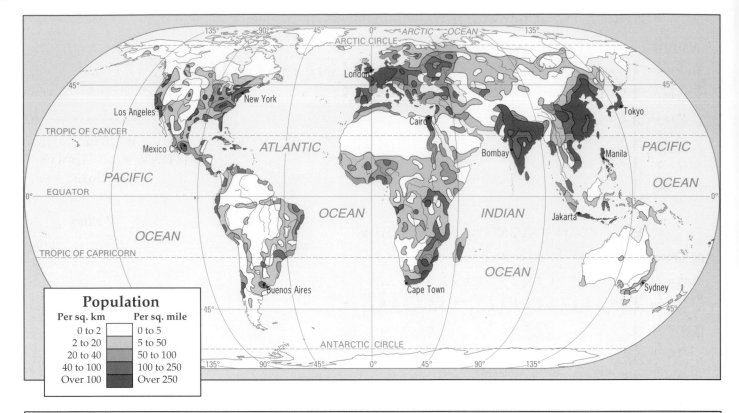

Population

Per sq. km	Per sq. mile
0 to 2	0 to 5
2 to 20	5 to 50
20 to 40	50 to 100
40 to 100	100 to 250
Over 100	Over 250

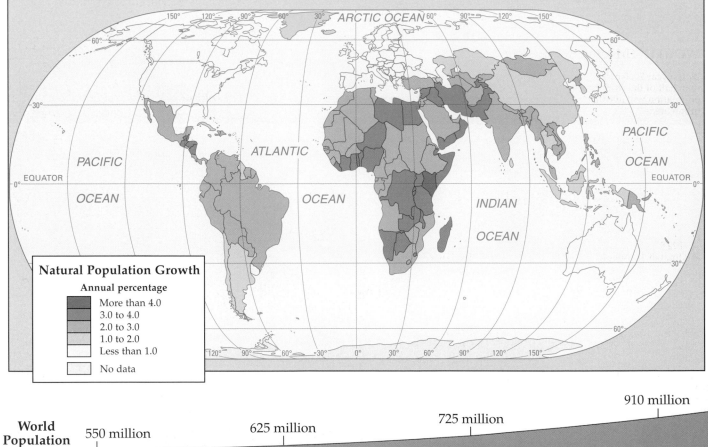

Natural Population Growth

Annual percentage

- More than 4.0
- 3.0 to 4.0
- 2.0 to 3.0
- 1.0 to 2.0
- Less than 1.0
- No data

World Population

550 million — 625 million — 725 million — 910 million

Year 1650 — 1700 — 1750 — 1800

AFRICA Population Profile

Age Group   **Number per 100 People**

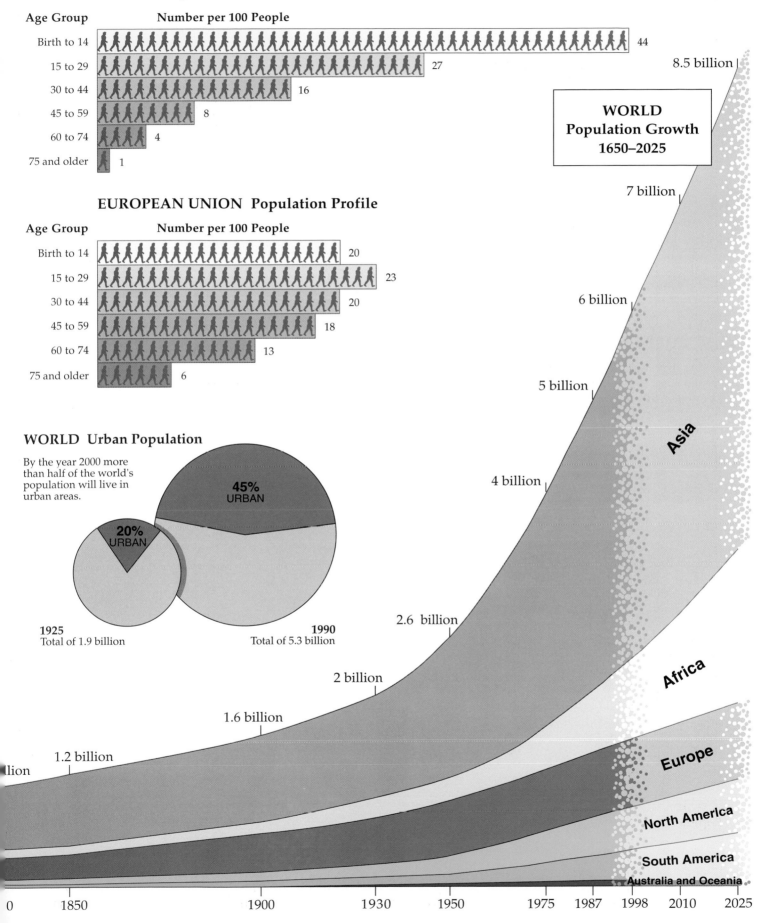

Age Group	Number per 100 People
Birth to 14	44
15 to 29	27
30 to 44	16
45 to 59	8
60 to 74	4
75 and older	1

EUROPEAN UNION Population Profile

Age Group   **Number per 100 People**

Age Group	Number per 100 People
Birth to 14	20
15 to 29	23
30 to 44	20
45 to 59	18
60 to 74	13
75 and older	6

WORLD Urban Population

By the year 2000 more than half of the world's population will live in urban areas.

20% URBAN

45% URBAN

1925
Total of 1.9 billion

1990
Total of 5.3 billion

WORLD
Population Growth
1650–2025

8.5 billion

7 billion

6 billion

5 billion

4 billion

Asia

2.6 billion

2 billion

1.6 billion

1.2 billion

...lion

Africa

Europe

North America

South America

Australia and Oceania

0   1850   1900   1930   1950   1975   1987   1998   2010   2025

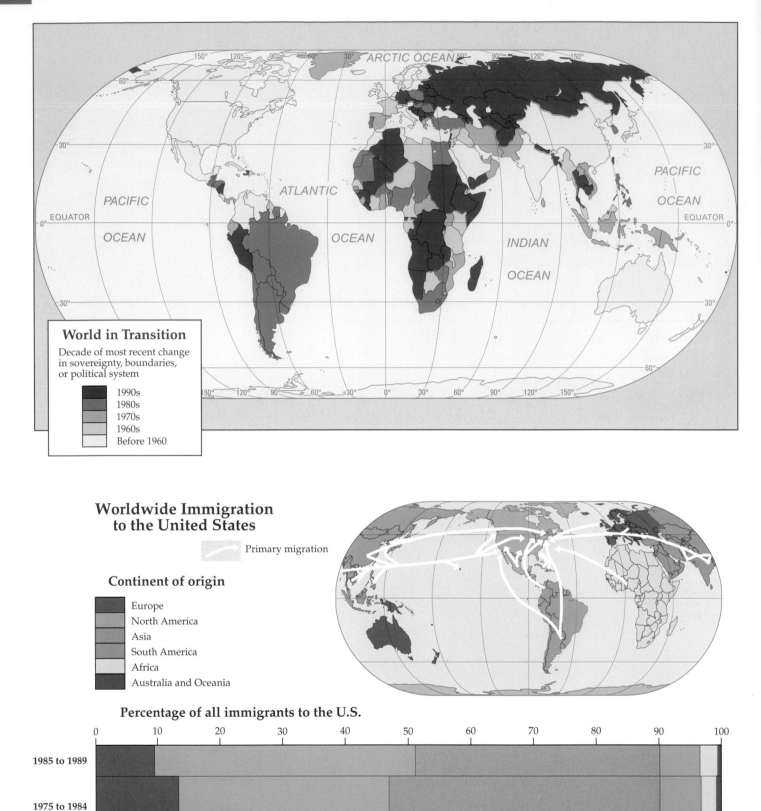

World in Transition

Decade of most recent change in sovereignty, boundaries, or political system

- 1990s
- 1980s
- 1970s
- 1960s
- Before 1960

Worldwide Immigration to the United States

Primary migration

Continent of origin

- Europe
- North America
- Asia
- South America
- Africa
- Australia and Oceania

Percentage of all immigrants to the U.S.

	0	10	20	30	40	50	60	70	80	90	100

1985 to 1989

1975 to 1984

1965 to 1974

1955 to 1964

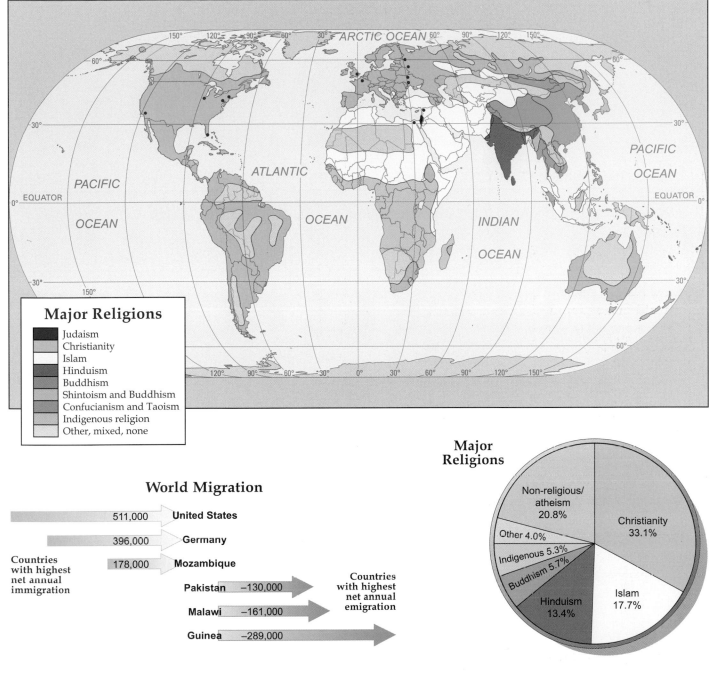

Major Religions

- Judaism
- Christianity
- Islam
- Hinduism
- Buddhism
- Shintoism and Buddhism
- Confucianism and Taoism
- Indigenous religion
- Other, mixed, none

World Migration

Countries with highest net annual immigration

511,000	**United States**
396,000	**Germany**
178,000	**Mozambique**

Pakistan	−130,000
Malawi	−161,000
Guinea	−289,000

Countries with highest net annual emigration

Major Religions

- Christianity 33.1%
- Islam 17.7%
- Hinduism 13.4%
- Buddhism 5.7%
- Indigenous 5.3%
- Other 4.0%
- Non-religious/atheism 20.8%

European immigrants were sworn in as citizens at New York's Ellis Island in the early 1900s. By then, laws restricted the number of aliens admitted into the United States.

Hispanic residents become U.S. citizens in a mass naturalization ceremony at a Miami stadium. Many immigrants are political or economic refugees from countries in turmoil.

World's Fastest Growing Urban Areas

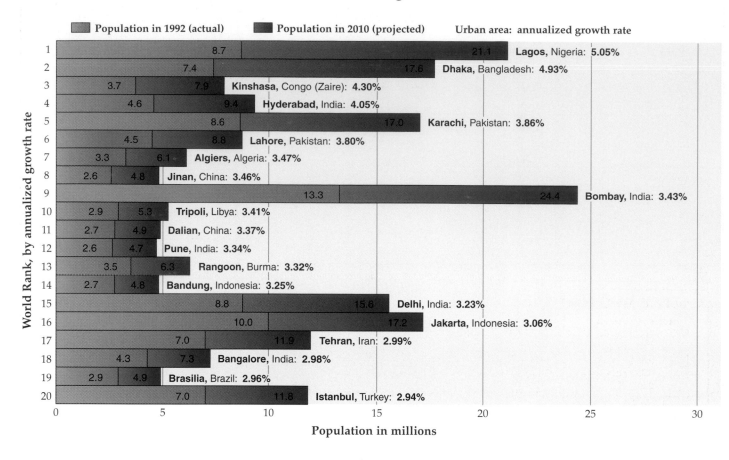

Population in 1992 (actual)   Population in 2010 (projected)   Urban area: annualized growth rate

World Rank, by annualized growth rate	1992	2010	City
1	8.7	21.1	**Lagos**, Nigeria: **5.05%**
2	7.4	17.6	**Dhaka**, Bangladesh: **4.93%**
3	3.7	7.9	**Kinshasa**, Congo (Zaire): **4.30%**
4	4.6	9.4	**Hyderabad**, India: **4.05%**
5	8.6	17.0	**Karachi**, Pakistan: **3.86%**
6	4.5	8.8	**Lahore**, Pakistan: **3.80%**
7	3.3	6.1	**Algiers**, Algeria: **3.47%**
8	2.6	4.8	**Jinan**, China: **3.46%**
9	13.3	24.4	**Bombay**, India: **3.43%**
10	2.9	5.3	**Tripoli**, Libya: **3.41%**
11	2.7	4.9	**Dalian**, China: **3.37%**
12	2.6	4.7	**Pune**, India: **3.34%**
13	3.5	6.3	**Rangoon**, Burma: **3.32%**
14	2.7	4.8	**Bandung**, Indonesia: **3.25%**
15	8.8	15.6	**Delhi**, India: **3.23%**
16	10.0	17.2	**Jakarta**, Indonesia: **3.06%**
17	7.0	11.9	**Tehran**, Iran: **2.99%**
18	4.3	7.3	**Bangalore**, India: **2.98%**
19	2.9	4.9	**Brasilia**, Brazil: **2.96%**
20	7.0	11.8	**Istanbul**, Turkey: **2.94%**

Population in millions

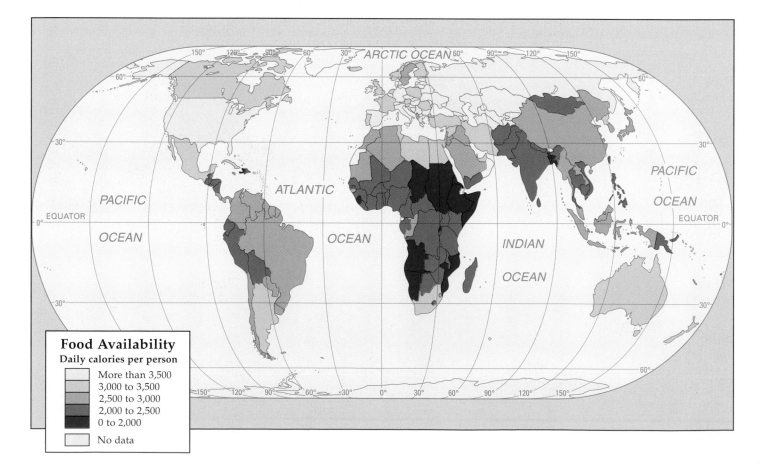

Food Availability
Daily calories per person

- More than 3,500
- 3,000 to 3,500
- 2,500 to 3,000
- 2,000 to 2,500
- 0 to 2,000
- No data

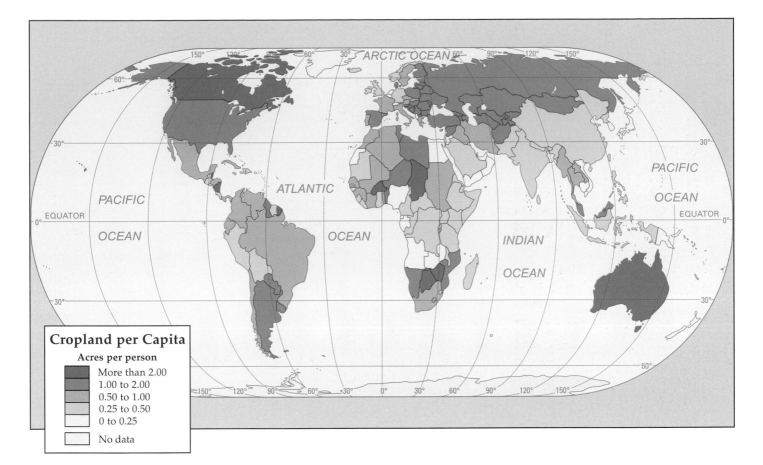

Cropland per Capita

Acres per person

More than 2.00
1.00 to 2.00
0.50 to 1.00
0.25 to 0.50
0 to 0.25

No data

Staple Food Production

Grains are the main source of food for most of the world's population. Many grains are also used in processed foods and livestock feed. Grain producers range from large commercial farms that export their harvest to small farms that grow grains for regional consumption.

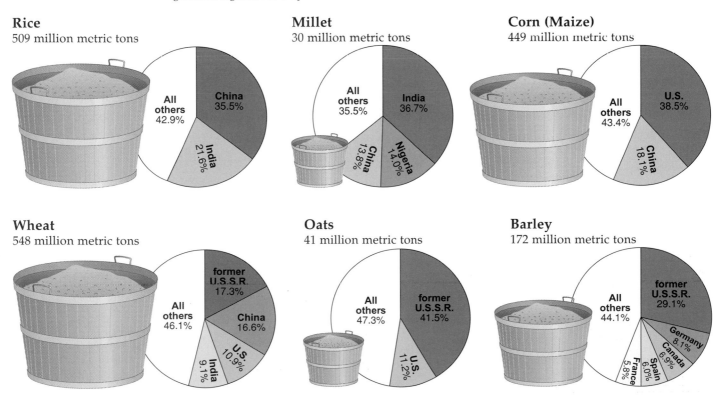

Rice
509 million metric tons

All others 42.9%
China 35.5%
India 21.6%

Millet
30 million metric tons

All others 35.5%
India 36.7%
China 13.8%
Nigeria 14.0%

Corn (Maize)
449 million metric tons

All others 43.4%
U.S. 38.5%
China 18.1%

Wheat
548 million metric tons

former U.S.S.R. 17.3%
All others 46.1%
China 16.6%
U.S. 10.9%
India 9.1%

Oats
41 million metric tons

All others 47.3%
former U.S.S.R. 41.5%
U.S. 11.2%

Barley
172 million metric tons

All others 44.1%
former U.S.S.R. 29.1%
Germany 8.1%
Canada 6.9%
Spain 6.0%
France 5.8%

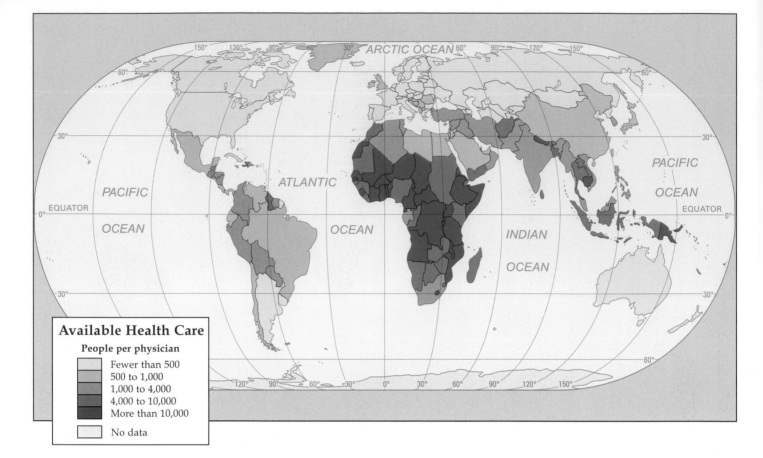

Available Health Care

People per physician

- Fewer than 500
- 500 to 1,000
- 1,000 to 4,000
- 4,000 to 10,000
- More than 10,000

- No data

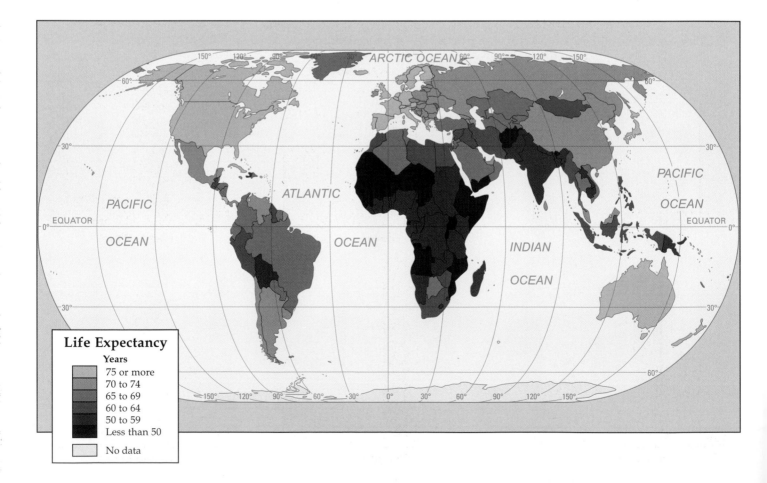

Life Expectancy

Years

- 75 or more
- 70 to 74
- 65 to 69
- 60 to 64
- 50 to 59
- Less than 50

- No data

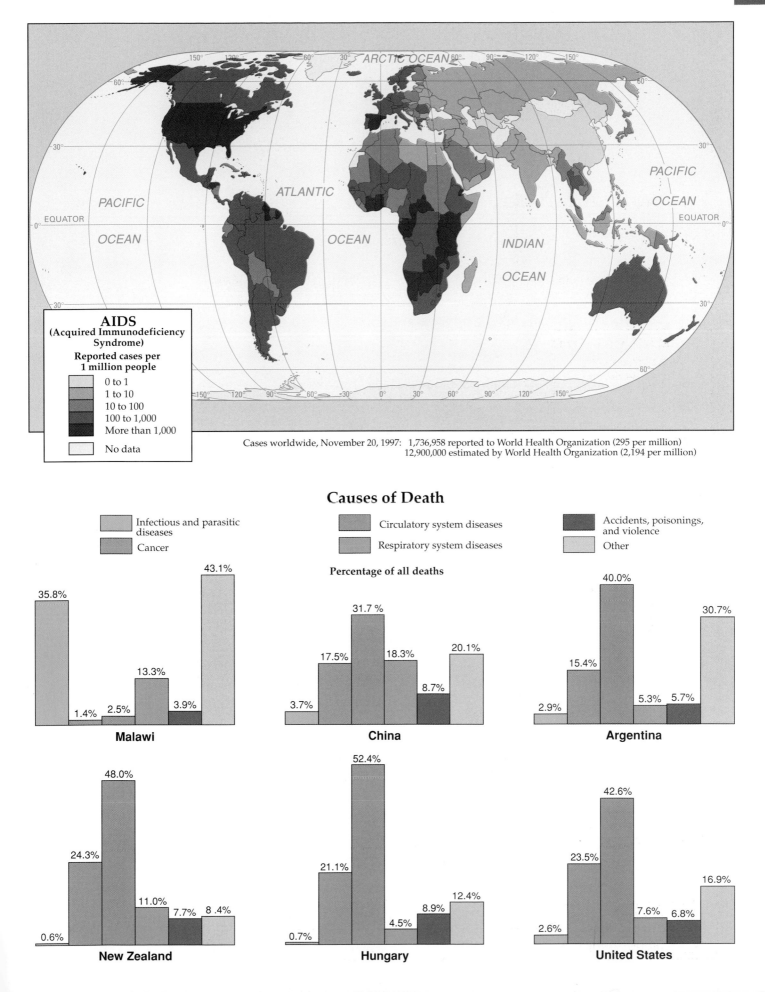

AIDS
(Acquired Immunodeficiency Syndrome)
Reported cases per 1 million people

- 0 to 1
- 1 to 10
- 10 to 100
- 100 to 1,000
- More than 1,000
- No data

Cases worldwide, November 20, 1997: 1,736,958 reported to World Health Organization (295 per million)
12,900,000 estimated by World Health Organization (2,194 per million)

Causes of Death

- Infectious and parasitic diseases
- Cancer
- Circulatory system diseases
- Respiratory system diseases
- Accidents, poisonings, and violence
- Other

Percentage of all deaths

Malawi
35.8% 1.4% 2.5% 13.3% 3.9% 43.1%

China
3.7% 17.5% 31.7% 18.3% 8.7% 20.1%

Argentina
2.9% 15.4% 40.0% 5.3% 5.7% 30.7%

New Zealand
0.6% 24.3% 48.0% 11.0% 7.7% 8.4%

Hungary
0.7% 21.1% 52.4% 4.5% 8.9% 12.4%

United States
2.6% 23.5% 42.6% 7.6% 6.8% 16.9%

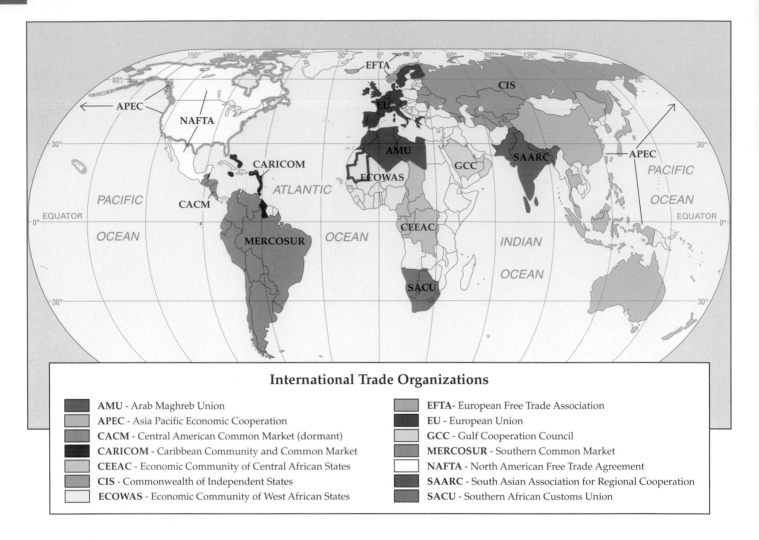

International Trade Organizations

AMU - Arab Maghreb Union	**EFTA** - European Free Trade Association
APEC - Asia Pacific Economic Cooperation	**EU** - European Union
CACM - Central American Common Market (dormant)	**GCC** - Gulf Cooperation Council
CARICOM - Caribbean Community and Common Market	**MERCOSUR** - Southern Common Market
CEEAC - Economic Community of Central African States	**NAFTA** - North American Free Trade Agreement
CIS - Commonwealth of Independent States	**SAARC** - South Asian Association for Regional Cooperation
ECOWAS - Economic Community of West African States	**SACU** - Southern African Customs Union

Single-Commodity Economies

Many countries rely on only one natural resource to support 75% or more of their export economies.

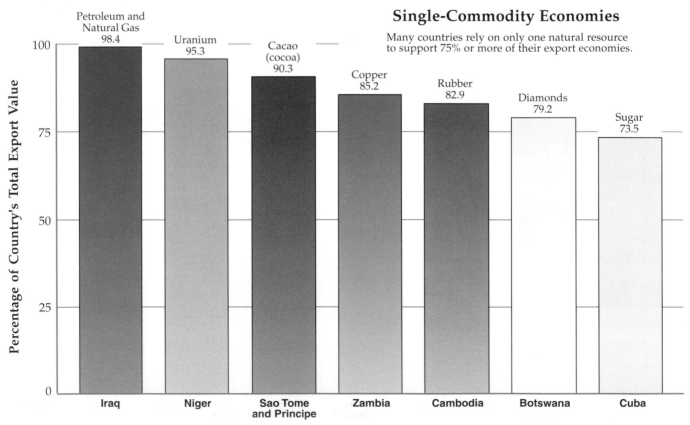

Percentage of Country's Total Export Value

- Iraq — Petroleum and Natural Gas — 98.4
- Niger — Uranium — 95.3
- Sao Tome and Principe — Cacao (cocoa) — 90.3
- Zambia — Copper — 85.2
- Cambodia — Rubber — 82.9
- Botswana — Diamonds — 79.2
- Cuba — Sugar — 73.5

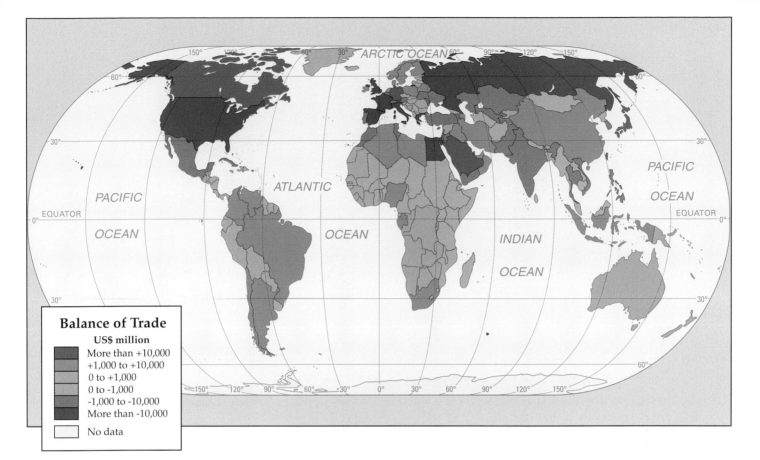

Balance of Trade

US$ million

- More than +10,000
- +1,000 to +10,000
- 0 to +1,000
- 0 to -1,000
- -1,000 to -10,000
- More than -10,000
- No data

Disparity of Income

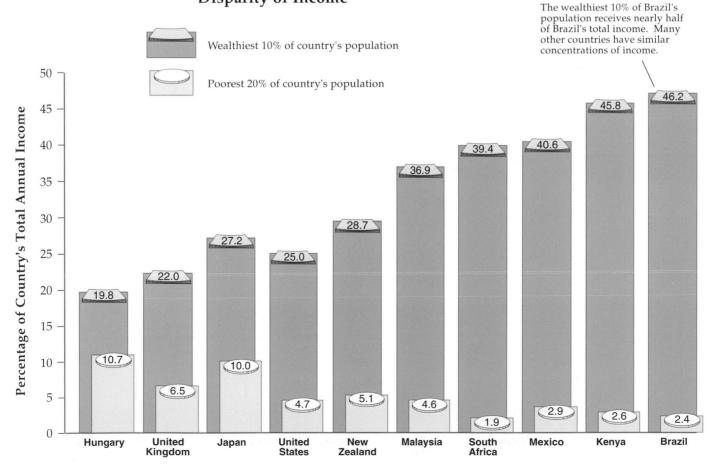

Wealthiest 10% of country's population

Poorest 20% of country's population

The wealthiest 10% of Brazil's population receives nearly half of Brazil's total income. Many other countries have similar concentrations of income.

Percentage of Country's Total Annual Income

Country	Wealthiest 10%	Poorest 20%
Hungary	19.8	10.7
United Kingdom	22.0	6.5
Japan	27.2	10.0
United States	25.0	4.7
New Zealand	28.7	5.1
Malaysia	36.9	4.6
South Africa	39.4	1.9
Mexico	40.6	2.9
Kenya	45.8	2.6
Brazil	46.2	2.4

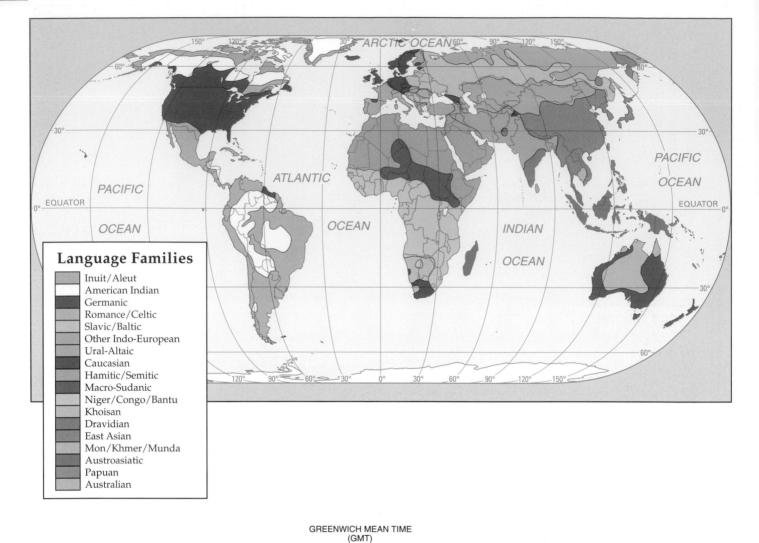

Language Families

- Inuit/Aleut
- American Indian
- Germanic
- Romance/Celtic
- Slavic/Baltic
- Other Indo-European
- Ural-Altaic
- Caucasian
- Hamitic/Semitic
- Macro-Sudanic
- Niger/Congo/Bantu
- Khoisan
- Dravidian
- East Asian
- Mon/Khmer/Munda
- Austroasiatic
- Papuan
- Australian

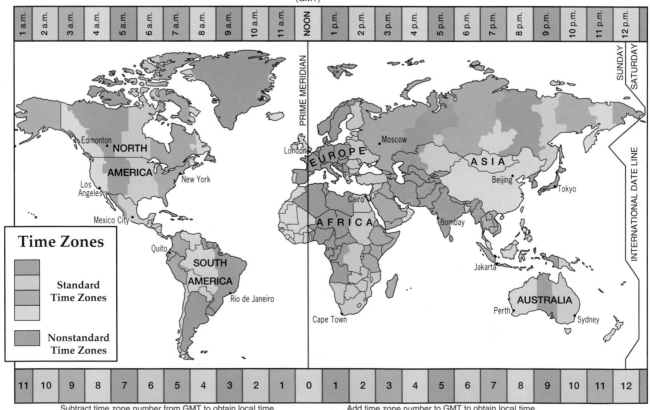

GREENWICH MEAN TIME
(GMT)

1 a.m. | 2 a.m. | 3 a.m. | 4 a.m. | 5 a.m. | 6 a.m. | 7 a.m. | 8 a.m. | 9 a.m. | 10 a.m. | 11 a.m. | NOON | 1 p.m. | 2 p.m. | 3 p.m. | 4 p.m. | 5 p.m. | 6 p.m. | 7 p.m. | 8 p.m. | 9 p.m. | 10 p.m. | 11 p.m. | 12 p.m.

Time Zones

Standard Time Zones

Nonstandard Time Zones

11 | 10 | 9 | 8 | 7 | 6 | 5 | 4 | 3 | 2 | 1 | 0 | 1 | 2 | 3 | 4 | 5 | 6 | 7 | 8 | 9 | 10 | 11 | 12

Subtract time zone number from GMT to obtain local time.   Add time zone number to GMT to obtain local time.

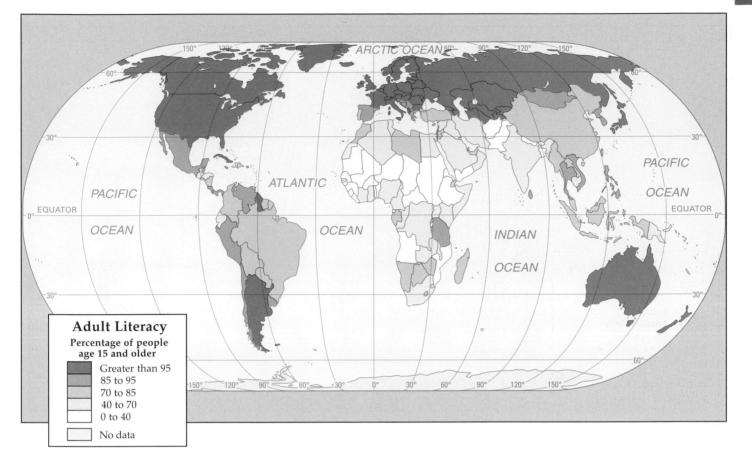

Adult Literacy

Percentage of people age 15 and older

- Greater than 95
- 85 to 95
- 70 to 85
- 40 to 70
- 0 to 40
- No data

Persons per Newspaper

Daily circulation	Country	Persons
25,200,000	United Kingdom	2.5
62,700,000	United States	4.0
11,300,000	Mexico	7.0
16,700,000	India	46.2

Persons per Telephone

Telephones owned	Country	Persons
181,000,000	United States	1.3
14,000,000	Brazil	10
77,000	Angola	123
26,000	Nepal	412

Persons per Radio

Radios owned	Country	Persons
520,000,000	United States	0.5
7,200,000	Australia	1.9
7,000,000	Vietnam	9.5
400,000	Somalia	19

Persons per Television

Televisions owned	Country	Persons
200,000,000	United States	1.2
31,500,000	Japan	2.4
200,000	Nicaragua	18
20,000	Congo (Zaire)	1,708

Speed of Travel

Route	Year	Means of travel	Length of time
New York to Europe via air	1978	Concorde SST – supersonic jet	3.5 hours
	1950	Intercontinental jet – twin engine jet	10 hours
	1927	*Spirit of St. Louis* – single engine aircraft	33.5 hours
New York to Europe via ocean	1993	*Queen Elizabeth II* – ocean liner	5 days
	1898	*Lucania* – steamer	5.5 days
	1497	John Cabot – sailing vessel	43 days

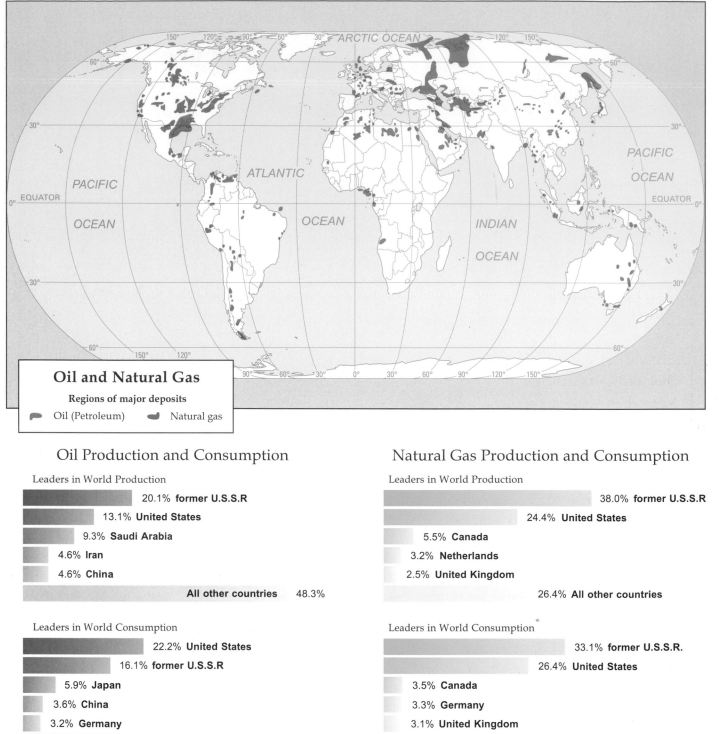

Oil and Natural Gas

Regions of major deposits

Oil (Petroleum)   Natural gas

Oil Production and Consumption

Leaders in World Production

- 20.1% **former U.S.S.R**
- 13.1% **United States**
- 9.3% **Saudi Arabia**
- 4.6% **Iran**
- 4.6% **China**
- **All other countries** 48.3%

Leaders in World Consumption

- 22.2% **United States**
- 16.1% **former U.S.S.R**
- 5.9% **Japan**
- 3.6% **China**
- 3.2% **Germany**
- **All other countries** 49.0%

Natural Gas Production and Consumption

Leaders in World Production

- 38.0% **former U.S.S.R**
- 24.4% **United States**
- 5.5% **Canada**
- 3.2% **Netherlands**
- 2.5% **United Kingdom**
- 26.4% **All other countries**

Leaders in World Consumption

- 33.1% **former U.S.S.R.**
- 26.4% **United States**
- 3.5% **Canada**
- 3.3% **Germany**
- 3.1% **United Kingdom**
- 30.6% **All other countries**

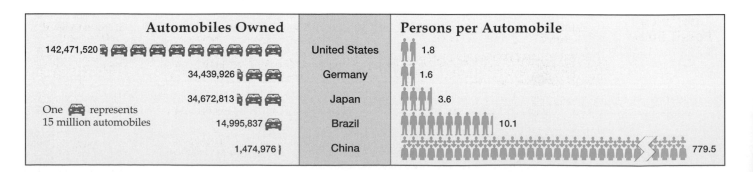

Automobiles Owned		**Persons per Automobile**
142,471,520	United States	1.8
34,439,926	Germany	1.6
34,672,813	Japan	3.6
14,995,837	Brazil	10.1
1,474,976	China	779.5

One represents 15 million automobiles

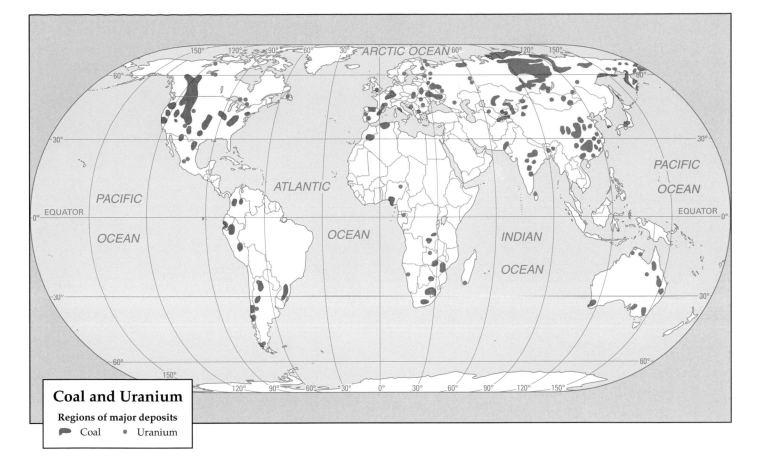

Coal and Uranium

Regions of major deposits

🐖 Coal • Uranium

Coal Production and Consumption

Leaders in World Production

29.3% **China**
23.1% **United States**
16.2% **former U.S.S.R.**
5.6% **India**
5.0% **South Africa**
20.8% **All other countries**

Leaders in World Consumption

28.9% **China**
20.8% **United States**
15.5% **former U.S.S.R.**
5.7% **India**
4.1% **Poland**
25.0% **All other countries**

Uranium Production and Consumption*

Leaders in World Production

30.3% **Canada**
17.9% **South Africa**
12.9% **United States**
10.0% **Australia**
8.9% **France**
20.0% **All other countries**

Leaders in World Consumption

28.9% **United States**
15.7% **France**
9.9% **Japan**
8.4% **Germany**
6.2% **former U.S.S.R.**
30.9% **All other countries**

*Includes only uranium used to generate electricity.

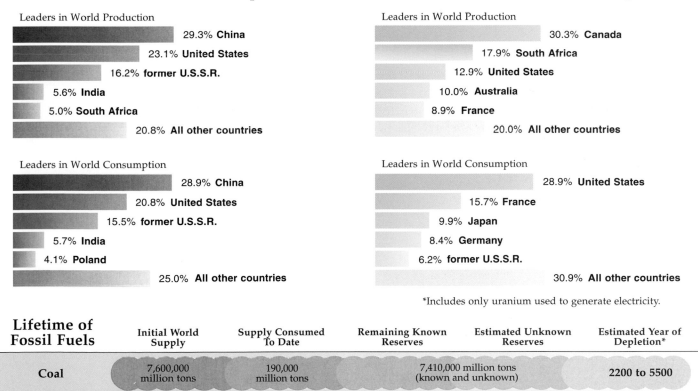

Lifetime of Fossil Fuels	Initial World Supply	Supply Consumed To Date	Remaining Known Reserves	Estimated Unknown Reserves	Estimated Year of Depletion*
Coal	7,600,000 million tons	190,000 million tons	7,410,000 million tons (known and unknown)		2200 to 5500
Oil (petroleum)	1,721,000 million barrels	560,320 million barrels	535,380 million barrels	525,300 million barrels	2035
Natural gas	255,400,000 million cubic meters	36,400,000 million cubic meters	97,300,000 million cubic meters	121,800,000 million cubic meters	2050

*given present rates of use

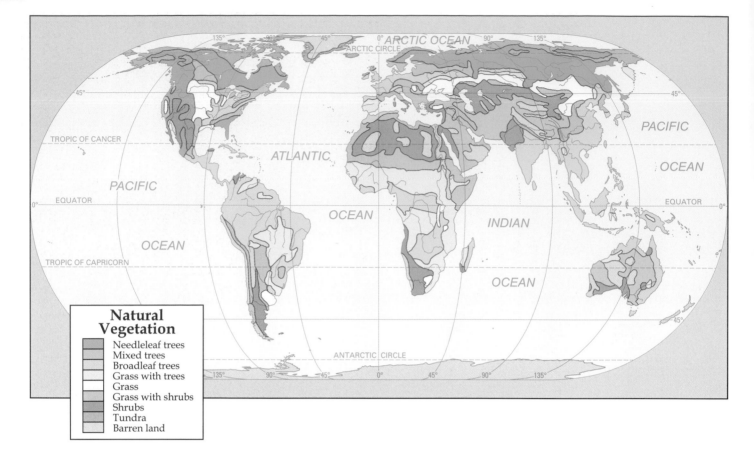

Natural Vegetation

Needleleaf trees
Mixed trees
Broadleaf trees
Grass with trees
Grass
Grass with shrubs
Shrubs
Tundra
Barren land

Natural Vegetation

The world can be divided into zones of natural vegetation. Several categories of vegetation are mapped above.

Most of the categories can be subdivided. For example, there are several kinds of broadleaf trees: maples, oaks, birches, sycamores, cottonwoods, and so on.

Seven types of vegetation listed in the map key are shown here.

needleleaf trees

mixed trees

broadleaf trees

grass with trees

grass

shrubs

tundra

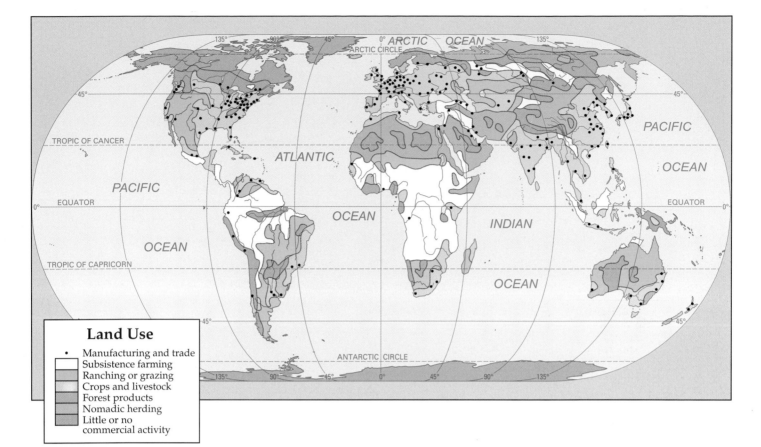

Land Use

- • Manufacturing and trade
- Subsistence farming
- Ranching or grazing
- Crops and livestock
- Forest products
- Nomadic herding
- Little or no commercial activity

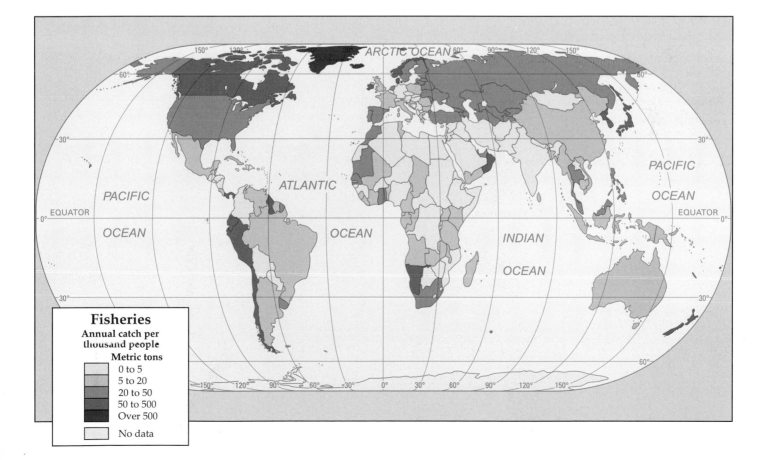

Fisheries

Annual catch per thousand people

Metric tons

- 0 to 5
- 5 to 20
- 20 to 50
- 50 to 500
- Over 500
- No data

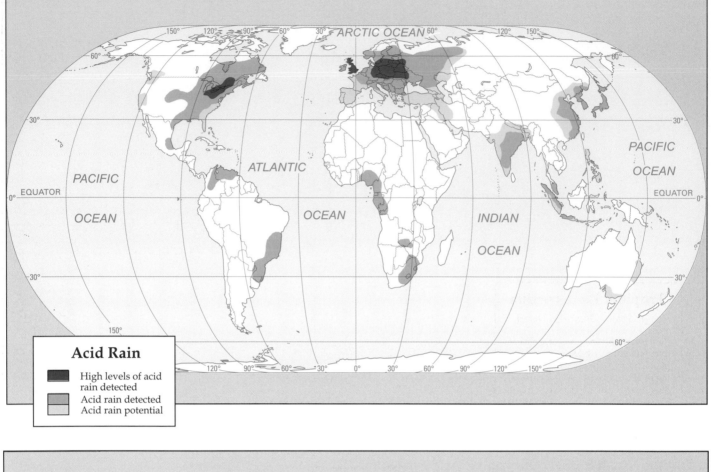

Acid Rain

- High levels of acid rain detected
- Acid rain detected
- Acid rain potential

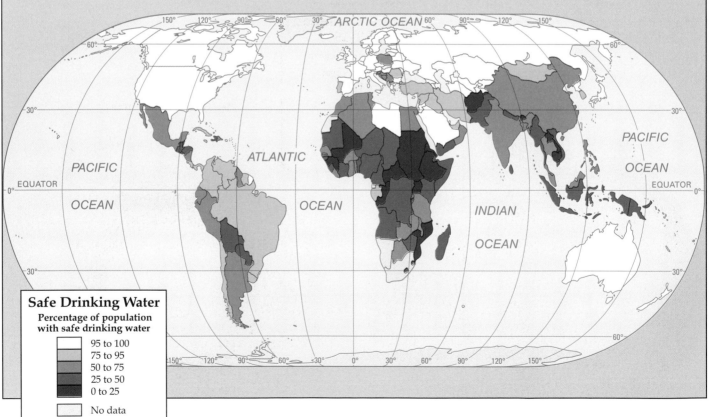

Safe Drinking Water

Percentage of population with safe drinking water

- 95 to 100
- 75 to 95
- 50 to 75
- 25 to 50
- 0 to 25
- No data

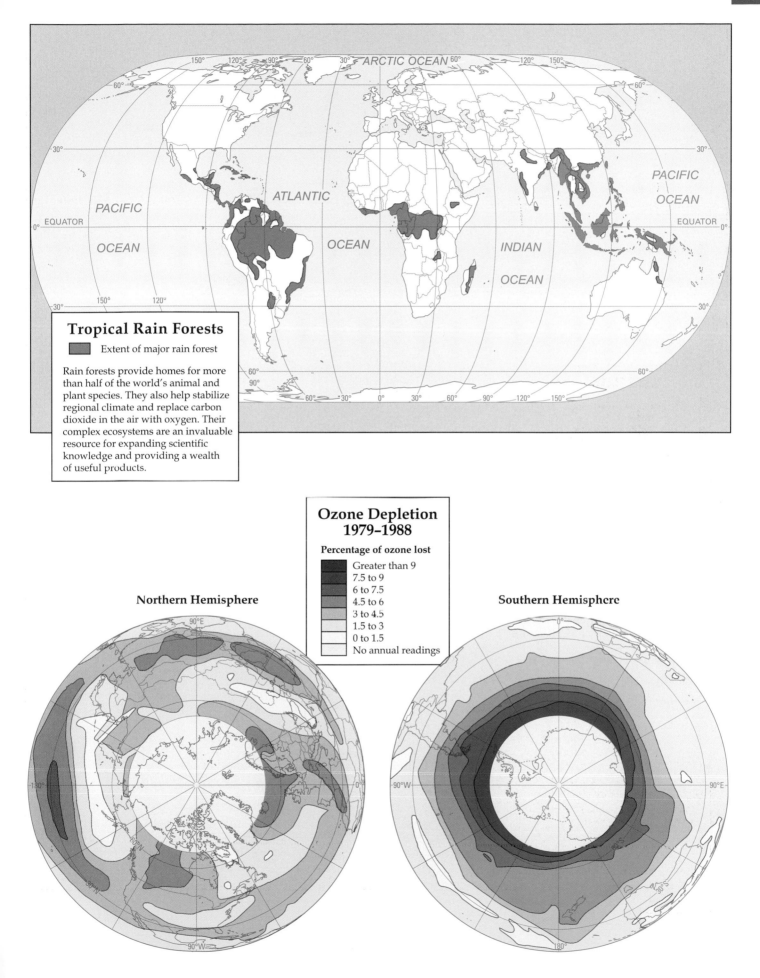

Tropical Rain Forests

Extent of major rain forest

Rain forests provide homes for more than half of the world's animal and plant species. They also help stabilize regional climate and replace carbon dioxide in the air with oxygen. Their complex ecosystems are an invaluable resource for expanding scientific knowledge and providing a wealth of useful products.

Ozone Depletion 1979–1988

Percentage of ozone lost

Greater than 9
7.5 to 9
6 to 7.5
4.5 to 6
3 to 4.5
1.5 to 3
0 to 1.5
No annual readings

Northern Hemisphere

Southern Hemisphere

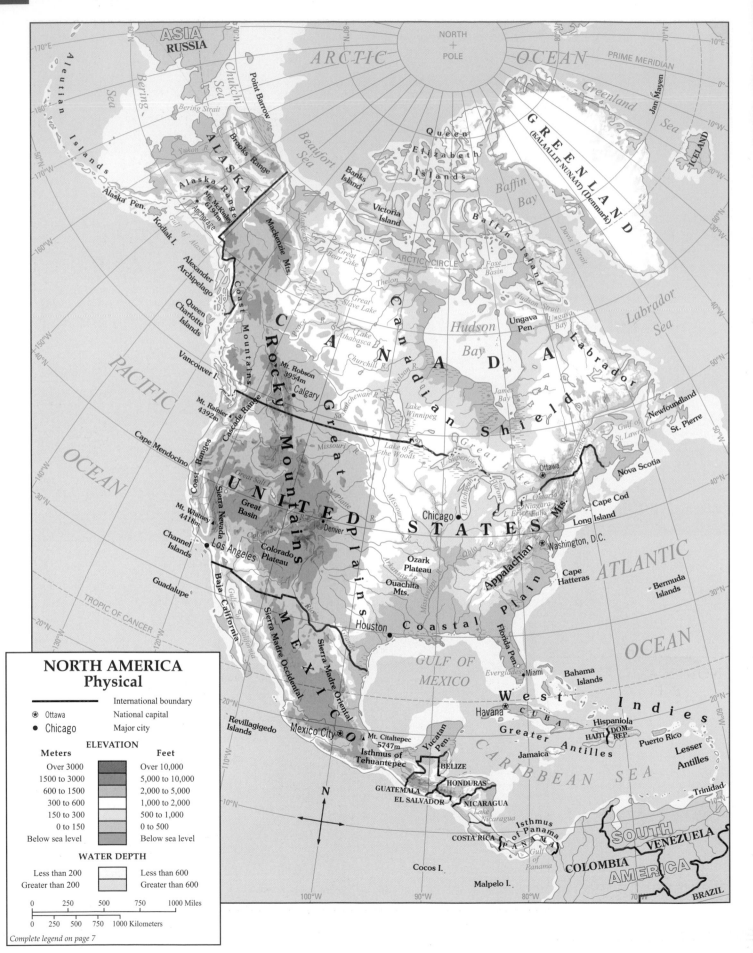

NORTH AMERICA
Physical

⎯⎯⎯	International boundary
⊛ Ottawa	National capital
● Chicago	Major city

ELEVATION

Meters		Feet
Over 3000		Over 10,000
1500 to 3000		5,000 to 10,000
600 to 1500		2,000 to 5,000
300 to 600		1,000 to 2,000
150 to 300		500 to 1,000
0 to 150		0 to 500
Below sea level		Below sea level

WATER DEPTH

Less than 200		Less than 600
Greater than 200		Greater than 600

```
0    250   500   750   1000 Miles
0  250  500  750  1000 Kilometers
```

Complete legend on page 7

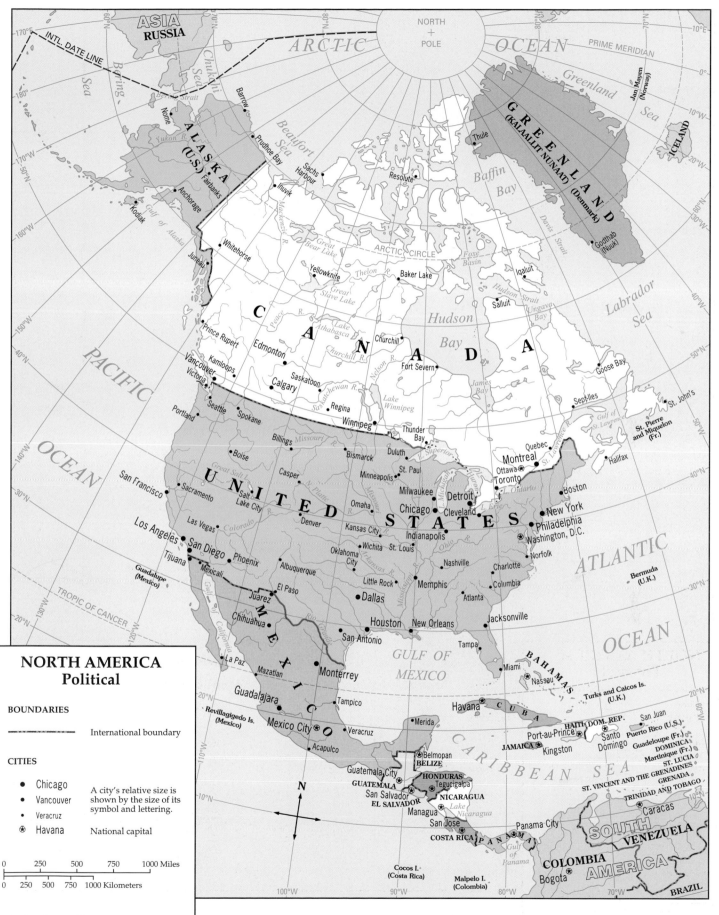

NORTH AMERICA
Political

BOUNDARIES

―――――― International boundary

CITIES

● **Chicago**

● Vancouver   A city's relative size is
                     shown by the size of its
· Veracruz   symbol and lettering.

⊛ **Havana**   National capital

0   250   500   750   1000 Miles

0   250   500   750   1000 Kilometers

Complete legend on page 7

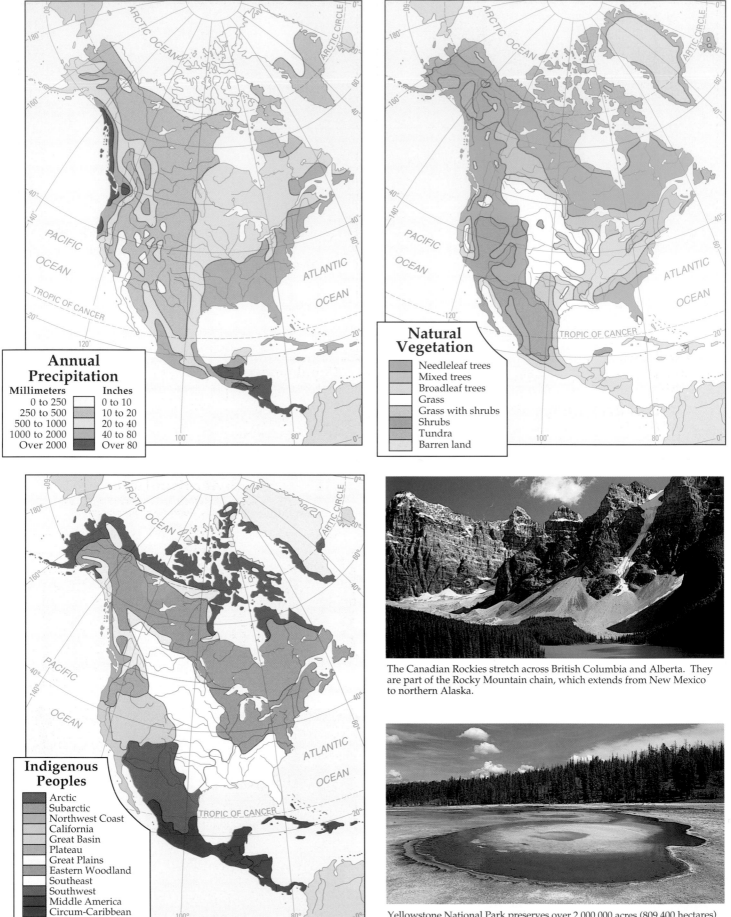

Annual Precipitation

Millimeters	Inches
0 to 250	0 to 10
250 to 500	10 to 20
500 to 1000	20 to 40
1000 to 2000	40 to 80
Over 2000	Over 80

Natural Vegetation

- Needleleaf trees
- Mixed trees
- Broadleaf trees
- Grass
- Grass with shrubs
- Shrubs
- Tundra
- Barren land

Indigenous Peoples

- Arctic
- Subarctic
- Northwest Coast
- California
- Great Basin
- Plateau
- Great Plains
- Eastern Woodland
- Southeast
- Southwest
- Middle America
- Circum-Caribbean
- Few, unknown, or none predominant

The Canadian Rockies stretch across British Columbia and Alberta. They are part of the Rocky Mountain chain, which extends from New Mexico to northern Alaska.

Yellowstone National Park preserves over 2,000,000 acres (809 400 hectares) of evergreen forests and mountain meadows. Its natural wonders include 3,000 geysers and hot springs.

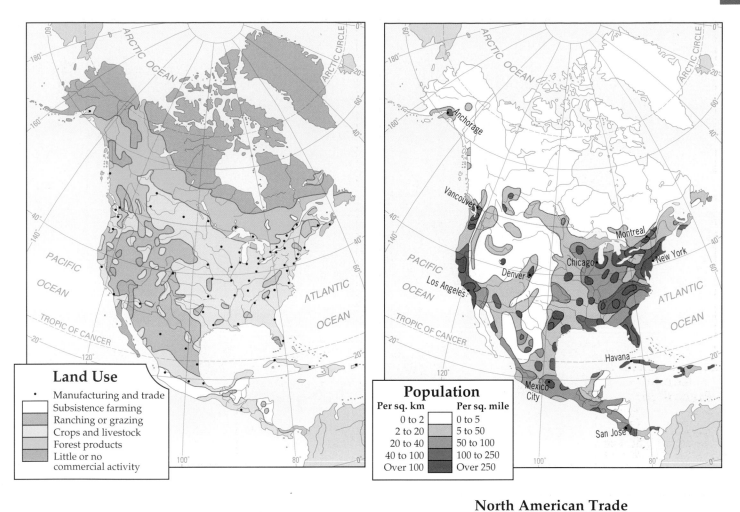

Land Use

- Manufacturing and trade
- Subsistence farming
- Ranching or grazing
- Crops and livestock
- Forest products
- Little or no commercial activity

Population

Per sq. km	Per sq. mile
0 to 2	0 to 5
2 to 20	5 to 50
20 to 40	50 to 100
40 to 100	100 to 250
Over 100	Over 250

MEXICO
Area Comparison

Mexico is about one-fourth the size of the United States. Even though both countries have vast deserts and rugged mountains, Mexico has nearly twice as many people per square mile as the United States.

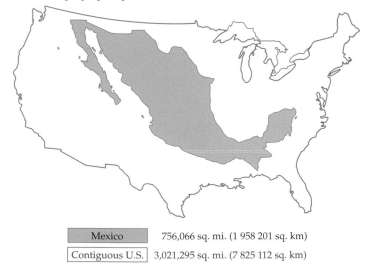

Mexico	756,066 sq. mi. (1 958 201 sq. km)
Contiguous U.S.	3,021,295 sq. mi. (7 825 112 sq. km)

North American Trade

The United States accounts for at least half of all imports to and/or exports from many North American countries.

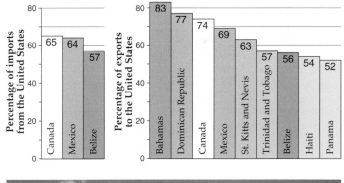

Percentage of imports from the United States:
- Canada: 65
- Mexico: 64
- Belize: 57

Percentage of exports to the United States:
- Bahamas: 83
- Dominican Republic: 77
- Canada: 74
- Mexico: 69
- St. Kitts and Nevis: 63
- Trinidad and Tobago: 57
- Belize: 56
- Haiti: 54
- Panama: 52

North America--the world's breadbasket--is the leading producer and exporter of wheat.

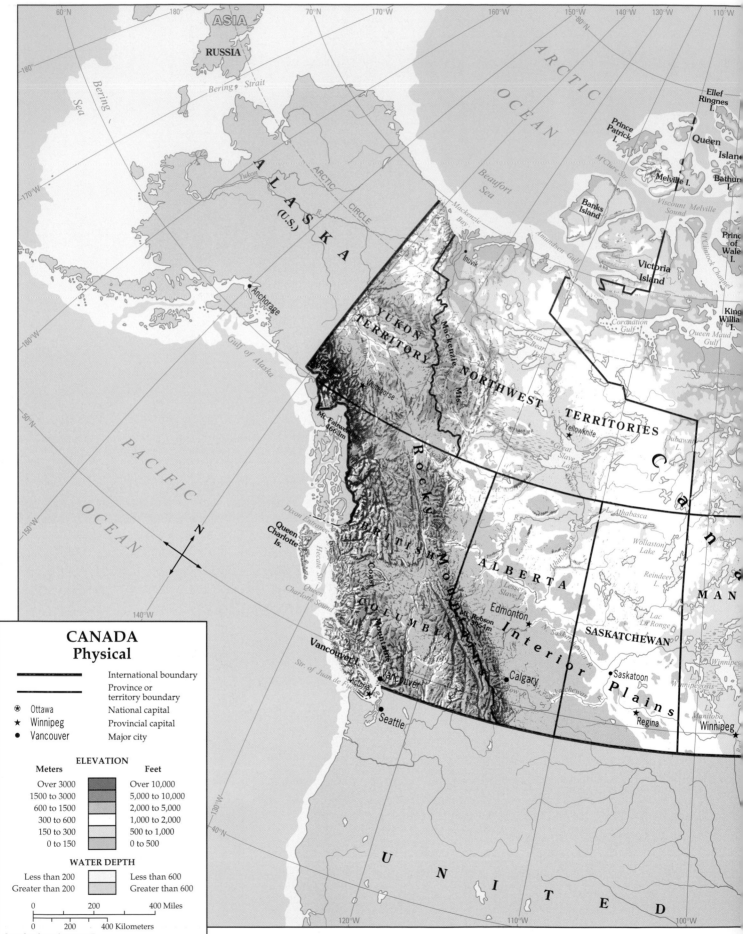

ASIA

RUSSIA

Bering Strait

Bering Sea

ARCTIC OCEAN

Ellef Ringnes I.

Prince Patrick I.

Queen

Islane

Melville I.

Bathur

Viscount Melville

Banks Island

Amundsen Gulf

M'Clure Str.

Princ of Wale I.

Beaufort Sea

Mackenzie Bay

Inuvik

ALASKA (U.S.)

Yukon

ARCTIC CIRCLE

Anchorage

Gulf of Alaska

YUKON TERRITORY

Whitehorse

Mt. Fairweather 4663m

Mackenzie Mts.

NORTHWEST

Great Bear Lake

Victoria Island

Coronation Gulf

Queen Maud Gulf

King Willia I.

M'Clintock Channel

TERRITORIES

Yellowknife

Great Slave Lake

C

Dubawn L.

PACIFIC OCEAN

N

Dixon Entrance

Queen Charlotte Is.

Hecate Str.

Queen Charlotte Sound

Rocky

BRITISH

COLUMBIA

Coast Mountains

Vancouver I.

Str. of Juan de Fuca

Victoria

Vancouver

Seattle

Mts.

Mt. Robson 3954m

ALBERTA

Edmonton

Calgary

Interior

L. Athabasca

Lesser Slave L.

N. Saskatchewan R.

Bow R.

S. Saskatchewan R.

Plains

Wollaston Lake

Reindeer L.

Lac La Ronge

SASKATCHEWAN

Saskatoon

Regina

Winnipegosis

L. Winnipeg

L. Manitoba

MAN

Winnipeg

UNITED

CANADA
Physical

International boundary

Province or territory boundary

⊛ Ottawa   National capital

★ Winnipeg   Provincial capital

● Vancouver   Major city

ELEVATION

Meters		Feet
Over 3000		Over 10,000
1500 to 3000		5,000 to 10,000
600 to 1500		2,000 to 5,000
300 to 600		1,000 to 2,000
150 to 300		500 to 1,000
0 to 150		0 to 500

WATER DEPTH

Less than 200		Less than 600
Greater than 200		Greater than 600

0   200   400 Miles

0   200   400 Kilometers

Complete legend on page 7

Axel
Heiberg I.

Ellesmere Island

zabeth

Kane
Basin

Devon Island

Lancaster Sound

merset
I.

othia
en.

GREENLAND
(KALAALLIT NUNAAD) (Denmark)

ARCTIC CIRCLE

ICELAND

Denmark

Baffin

Bay

Denmark Strait

ATLANTIC

OCEAN

Baffin
Island

Cumberland Sd.

Melville
Peninsula

N U N A V U T

Foxe

Davis Strait

Cape Farewell

Iqaluit

Foxe
Peninsula

Frobisher Bay

Chesterfield Inlet

Foxe
Basin

Foxe Channel

Southampton
I.

Hudson

Strait

Labrador

Sea

Cape
Chidley

Coats
I.

Mansel
I.

Ungava
Peninsula

Ungava
Bay

Torngat Mts.

Hudson

Bay

James
Bay

Belcher
Is.

L a b r a d o r

Happy Valley-
Goose Bay

NEWFOUNDLAND

Smallwood

Churchill R.

St. John's

OBA

n

Albany R.

Severn R.

Winisk R.

Attawapiskat R.

Eastmain R.

S h i e l d

C a n a d i a n

ONTARIO

Lake of
the Woods

Thunder
Bay

Superior

Sault Ste.
Marie

L. Nipigon

L.
Mistassini

L.
Nipissing

QUEBEC

St. Lawrence R.

Gaspé Pen.

Quebec

Georgian
Bay

L. Huron

Ottawa

Montreal

NEW
BRUNSWICK

Fredericton

Anticosti
I.

Gulf of
St. Lawrence

Strait of Belle Isle

Newfoundland

Cape Race

Miquelon
(Fr.)

St.-Pierre
(Fr.)

PRINCE
EDWARD
ISLAND

Cape
Breton
Island

NOVA

SCOTIA

Halifax

Sable I.

Cape Sable

Bay of Fundy

L. Simcoe

Toronto

L. Ontario

Detroit

Windsor

L. Erie

Niagara
Falls

S T A T E S

ATLANTIC

OCEAN

U N I T E D

ASIA

RUSSIA

INTERNATIONAL DATE LINE

Bering Strait

Bering Sea

A L A S K A (U.S.)

ARCTIC CIRCLE

ARCTIC OCEAN

Beaufort Sea

Mackenzie Bay

Anchorage

Gulf of Alaska

PACIFIC OCEAN

Yukon R.

• Old Crow

• Inuvik

Sachs Harbour

Banks I.

Amundsen Gulf

Victoria Island

Prince Patrick I.

Ellef Ringnes I.

Queen Island

Melville I.

Viscount Melville Sound

M'Clure Str.

M'Clintock Channel

Prin or Wal

Queen Maud Gulf

Coronation Gulf

Cambridge Bay

K Wil

Bath

Y U K O N

T E R R I T O R Y

• Dawson

• Pelly Crossing

★ Whitehorse

Yukon R.

• Watson Lake

Juneau

Dixon Entrance

Queen Charlotte Is.

Prince Rupert

Skeena R.

Hecate Str.

Kitimat

Queen Charlotte Sound

Norman Wells •

Great Bear Lake

N O R T H W E S T   T E R R I T O R I E S

Mackenzie R.

Fort Simpson •

★ Yellowknife

Great Slave Lake

Hay River •

Fort Smith

Slave R.

Dubawnt L.

L. Athabasca

Fort Nelson •

B R I T I S H

C O L U M B I A

Liard R.

Williston Lake

Dawson Creek •

Prince George •

Fraser R.

Peace R.

Peace River •

Grande Prairie •

A L B E R T A

Athabasca R.

Fort McMurray •

Lesser Slave L.

Edmonton ★

Red Deer •

Buffalo Narrows •

Wollaston Lake

Reindeer L.

Lac La Ronge

Prince Albert •

S A S K A T C H E W A N

N. Saskatchewan R.

Saskatoon •

Thompson •

Flin Flon •

M A N

L. Winnip

Winnipegosis

Vancouver I.

Str. of Juan de Fuca

Victoria ★

Vancouver •

Kamloops •

Columbia R.

Calgary •

Bow R.

S. Saskatchewan R.

Medicine Hat •

Moose Jaw •

Regina ★

L. Manito

Winnipeg

Brandon •

Seattle •

Lethbridge •

Portland •

U N I T E D

E D

D

N

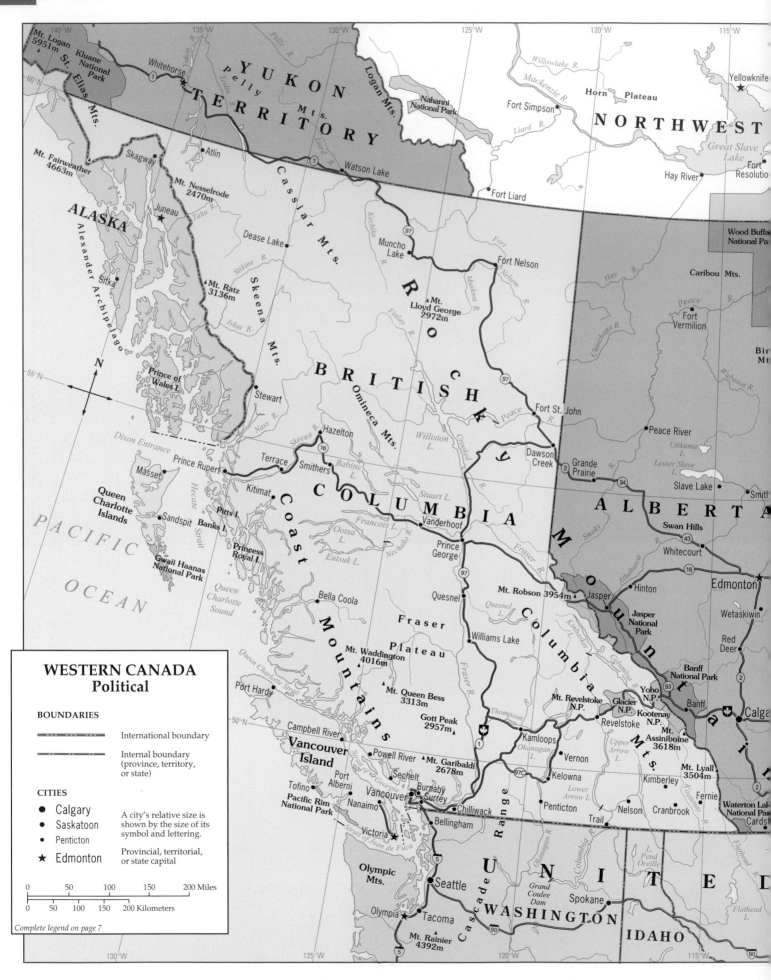

WESTERN CANADA
Political

BOUNDARIES

———————— International boundary

———————— Internal boundary
(province, territory,
or state)

CITIES

● Calgary

● Saskatoon

• Penticton

★ Edmonton

A city's relative size is
shown by the size of its
symbol and lettering.

Provincial, territorial,
or state capital

0	50	100	150	200 Miles
0	50	100	150	200 Kilometers

Complete legend on page 7

Map labels

YUKON TERRITORY

NORTHWEST

Mt. Logan 5951m
Kluane National Park
St. Elias Mts.
Whitehorse
Pelly R.
Pelly Mts.
Yukon R.
Teslin
Logan Mts.
Nahanni National Park
Yellowknife
Fort Simpson
Horn Plateau
Mackenzie R.
Willowlake R.
Liard R.

Mt. Fairweather 4663m
Skagway
Atlin
Mt. Nesselrode 2470m
Cassiar Mts.
Watson Lake
Liard R.
Fort Liard
Hay River
Fort Resolutio
Great Slave Lake
Wood Buffa National Pa

ALASKA
Juneau
Taku R.
Dease Lake
Stikine R.
Skeena Mts.
Iskut R.
Muncho Lake
Fort Nelson
Muskwa R.
Fort Nelson R.
Fort Vermilion
Caribou Mts.
Peace R.
Chinchaga R.
Bir Mt

Sitka
Alexander Archipelago
Mt. Ratz 3136m
ROCKY
Mt. Lloyd George 2972m
Finlay R.
Fort St. John
Peace R.
Peace River
Utikuma L.
Lesser Slave

Prince of Wales I.
Stewart
Nass R.
Skeena R.
Omineca Mts.
Williston L.
Crooked R.
Peace R.
Dawson Creek
Grande Prairie
Swan Hills
Slave Lake
Lesser Slave Smith

Dixon Entrance
Prince Rupert
Hazelton
Terrace
Smithers
Babine L.
BRITISH COLUMBIA
Stuart L.
Vanderhoof
Whitecourt
Smoky R.
ALBERTA

Masset
Queen Charlotte Islands
Kitimat
Pitts I.
Banks I.
Francois L.
Nechako R.
Stuart L.
Prince George
Fraser R.
Jasper
Hinton
Edmonton
Swan Hills

Sandspit
Princess Royal I.
Ootsa L.
Eutsuk L.
Mt. Robson 3954m
Jasper National Park
Wetaskiwin

Gwaii Haanas National Park
Hecate Strait
Coast
Bella Coola
Quesnel
Quesnel L.
Kinbasket L.
Columbia R.
Red Deer

PACIFIC OCEAN
Queen Charlotte Sound
Fraser Plateau
Williams Lake
Fraser R.
Mt. Revelstoke N.P.
Glacier N.P.
Yoho N.P.
Banff National Park
Banff
Calga

Mountains
Mt. Waddington 4016m
Mt. Queen Bess 3313m
Kootenay N.P.
Revelstoke
Mt. Assiniboine 3618m
Mt. Lyall 3504m

Port Hardy
Queen Charlotte Strait
Gott Peak 2957m
Thompson R.
Kamloops
Okanagan L.
Upper Arrow L.
Kimberley
Waterton Lake National Par
Cards

Campbell River
Mt. Garibaldi 2678m
Powell River
Sechelt
Vernon
Kelowna
Lower Arrow L.
Fernie
Cranbrook

Vancouver Island
Port Alberni
Burnaby
Surrey
Penticton
Nelson
Trail
Kootenay R.

Tofino
Nanaimo
Vancouver
Strait of Georgia
Chilliwack
Bellingham

Pacific Rim National Park
Victoria
Strait of Juan de Fuca
Cascade Range
L. Pend Oreille

Olympic Mts.
Seattle
Grand Coulee Dam
Columbia R.
Spokane
Flathea

Olympia
Tacoma
WASHINGTON
UNITED
IDAHO
Okanogan R.
Pend Oreille R.
Flathead R.

Mt. Rainier 4392m

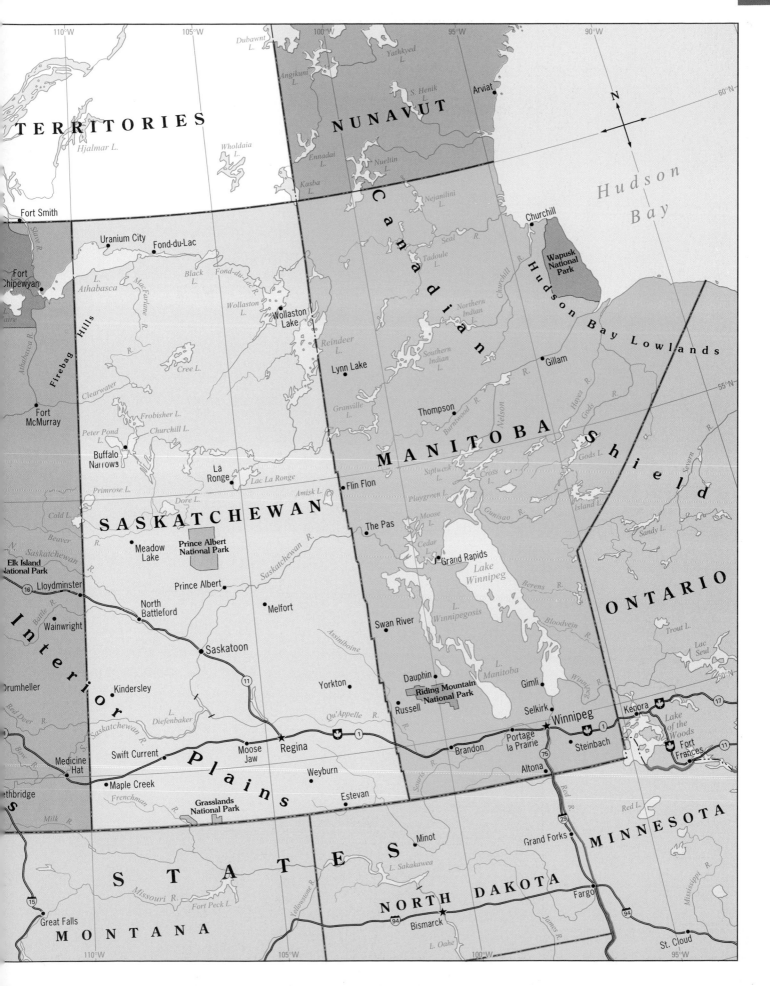

110°W 105°W 100°W 95°W 90°W

TERRITORIES

Hjalmar L.

Dubawnt L.

Wholdaia L.

NUNAVUT

Yathkyed L.

Angikuni L.

S. Henik L.

Arviat

60°N

N

Ennadai L.

Kasba L.

Nueltin L.

Nejanilini L.

Hudson Bay

Fort Smith

Churchill

Canadian

Uranium City

Fond-du-Lac

Seal R.

Tadoule L.

Wapusk National Park

Fort Chipewyan

L. Athabasca

MacFarlane R.

Black L.

Fond-du-Lac R.

Wollaston L.

Wollaston Lake

Northern Indian L.

Churchill R.

Hudson Bay Lowlands

Firebag Hills

Clearwater R.

Reindeer L.

Southern Indian L.

Gillam

55°N

Fort McMurray

Frobisher L.

Cree L.

Lynn Lake

Granville L.

Thompson

Barnwood R.

Nelson R.

Gods R.

Hayes R.

Severn R.

Peter Pond L.

Churchill R.

MANITOBA

Sandy L.

Buffalo Narrows

Primrose L.

Dore L.

La Ronge

Lac La Ronge

Amisk L.

Flin Flon

Siptwesk L.

Cross L.

Island L.

S a s k a t c h e w a n   S h i e l d

Cold L.

Beaver R.

SASKATCHEWAN

Saskatchewan R.

The Pas

Moose L.

Playgreen L.

Gunisao R.

Elk Island National Park

Saskatchewan R.

Meadow Lake

Prince Albert National Park

Cedar L.

Grand Rapids

Lake Winnipeg

Berens R.

ONTARIO

Lloydminster

16

Prince Albert

Melfort

L. Winnipegosis

Bloodvein R.

Trout L.

North Battleford

Assiniboine R.

Swan River

Lac Seul

Wainwright

I n t e r i o r

Saskatoon

11

L. Manitoba

Winnipeg R.

50°N

Drumheller

Kindersley

L. Diefenbaker

Yorkton

Dauphin

Riding Mountain National Park

Gimli

Kenora

Lake of the Woods

17

Russell

Selkirk

Winnipeg

P l a i n s

Qu'Appelle R.

Moose Jaw

Regina

1

Brandon

Portage la Prairie

Steinbach

1

Fort Frances

11

Swift Current

75

Medicine Hat

Souris R.

Altona

ethbridge

Maple Creek

Frenchman R.

Weyburn

Estevan

Red R.

Red L.

Milk R.

Grasslands National Park

29

Minot

Grand Forks

MINNESOTA

15

S T A T E S

Missouri R.

L. Sakakawea

NORTH DAKOTA

Fargo

Mississippi R.

94

Great Falls

MONTANA

Fort Peck L.

Yellowstone R.

Bismarck

James R.

St. Cloud

L. Oahe

110°W 105°W 100°W 95°W

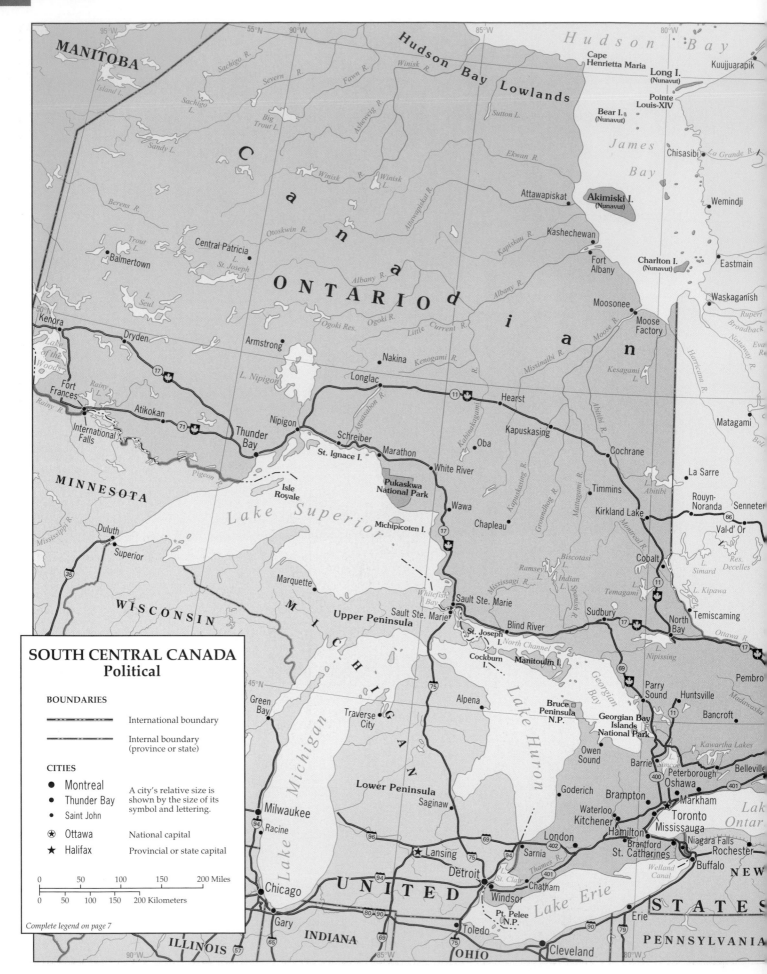

MANITOBA

Hudson Bay Lowlands

Hudson Bay

Cape Henrietta Maria

Long I. (Nunavut)

Kuujjuarapik

Sachigo R.
Island L.
Sandy L.
Big Trout L.
Severn R.
Fawn R.
Winisk R.

Bear I. (Nunavut)

Pointe Louis-XIV

James Bay

Chisasibi

La Grande R.

Akimiski I. (Nunavut)

Wemindji

C a n a d i a n

O N T A R I O

Central Patricia

Balmertown

Trout L.
St. Joseph L.
L. Seul
Otoskwin R.
Berens R.
Winisk R.
Winisk L.

Attawapiskat

Kashechewan

Fort Albany

Charlton I. (Nunavut)

Eastmain

Waskaganish

Rupert R.
Broadback R.

Albany R.
Ogoki Res.
Ogoki R.
Little Current R.
Kapiskau R.

Moosonee

Moose Factory

Moose R.
Broadback R.
Notaway R.
Eva R.

Kenora

Dryden

Armstrong

Nakina

L. Nipigon
Kenogami R.
Albany R.
Missinaibi R.
Kesagami L.
Hurricana R.

Longlac

Hearst

Matagami

17

Fort Frances

Atikokan

Nipigon

Schreiber

Kapuskasing

Cochrane

Rainy L.
Rainy R.
71

International Falls

Thunder Bay

St. Ignace I.

Marathon

Oba

White River

Kabinakagami R.
Kapuskasing R.
Groundhog R.

Timmins

La Sarre

Rouyn-Noranda

Senneter

Pigeon R.

Pukaskwa National Park

Wawa

Chapleau

Mattagami R.

Kirkland Lake

L. Abitibi

66

MINNESOTA

Isle Royale

Lake Superior

Michipicoten I.

17

Mississagi R.
Biscotasi L.
Ramsey L.
Indian L.
Spanish R.

Cobalt

Val-d' Or

L. Simard
Res. Decelles

Duluth

Superior

Marquette

Mississippi R.

35

Whitefish Bay

Sault Ste. Marie

Sault Ste. Marie

Blind River

Sudbury

Temagami L.

North Bay

L. Kipawa

Temiscaming

11

17

WISCONSIN

M I C H I G A N

Upper Peninsula

St. Joseph I.

North Channel

Cockburn I.

Manitoulin I.

Ottawa R.
L. Nipissing

SOUTH CENTRAL CANADA
Political

BOUNDARIES

――――――― International boundary

――――――― Internal boundary (province or state)

CITIES

● Montreal

● Thunder Bay

• Saint John

⊛ Ottawa   National capital

★ Halifax   Provincial or state capital

A city's relative size is shown by the size of its symbol and lettering.

Green Bay

Traverse City

Alpena

Georgian Bay

69

Bruce Peninsula N.P.

Parry Sound

Huntsville

Madawaska R.

Bancroft

Pembro

Georgian Bay Islands National Park

11

Lake Michigan

Lake Huron

Owen Sound

Barrie

400

Peterborough

Kawartha Lakes

Belleville

L. Simcoe

Lower Peninsula

Saginaw

Goderich

Owen Sound

Brampton

Waterloo

Kitchener

Oshawa

Markham

Toronto

Mississauga

Lake Ontar

0   50   100   150   200 Miles
0   50   100   150   200 Kilometers

Milwaukee

Racine

94

London

Hamilton

Brantford

St. Catharines

Niagara Falls

Rochester

96

Lansing

★

75

Sarnia

402

Thames R.

401

Welland Canal

Buffalo

NEW

Detroit

St. Clair

Chatham

Windsor

Erie

80 90

Lake Erie

Chicago

Gary

UNITED

Pt. Pelee N.P.

Toledo

Cleveland

90

79

STATES

PENNSYLVANIA

65   57

ILLINOIS

INDIANA

OHIO

Complete legend on page 7

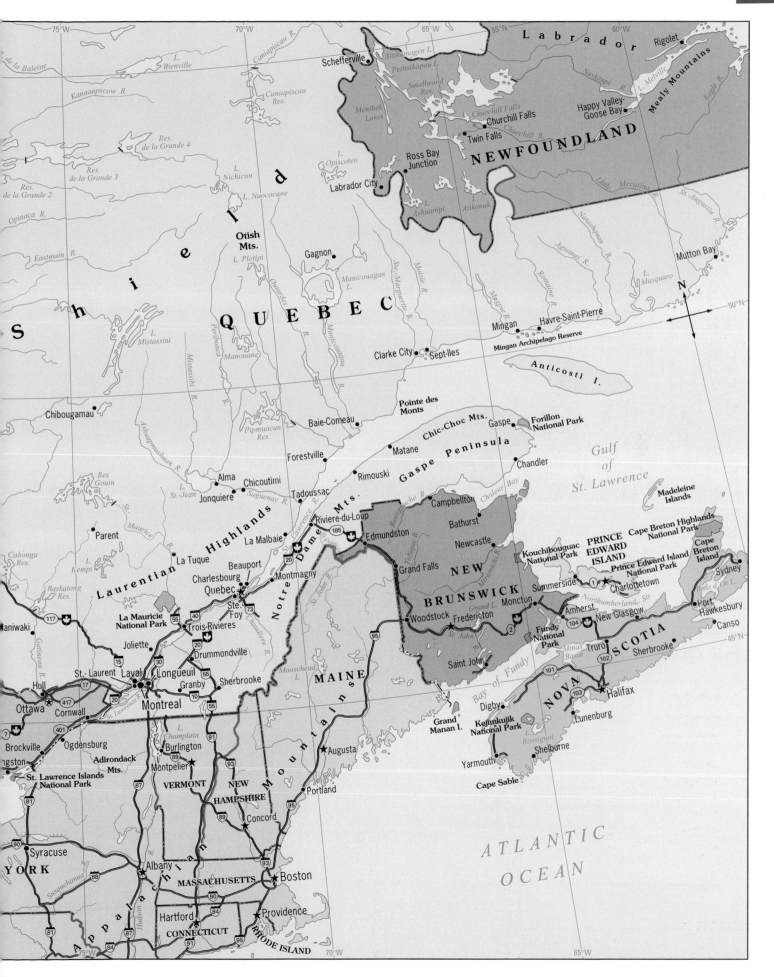

75°W · 70°W · 65°W · 55°N · 60°W

L a b r a d o r · Rigolet

de la Baleine · L. Bienville · Caniapiscau R. · Scefferville · Attikamagen L. · Niskaupi R. · L. Melville · Mealy Mountains

Kanaaupscow R. · Petitsikapau L. · Smallwood Res. · Happy Valley-Goose Bay · Eagle R.

Res. de la Grande 4 · Caniapiscau Res. · L. Opiscoteo · Churchill Falls · Churchill Falls · **NEWFOUNDLAND**

Res. de la Grande 3 · L. Nichicun · Twin Falls · Churchill R.

Res. de la Grande 2 · L. Naococane · Ross Bay Junction

Opinaca R. · Eastmain R. · Labrador City · L. Ashuanipi · L. Atikonak · St-Augustin R. · Mutton Bay

Otish Mts. · L. Pletipi · Gagnon · Aguanus R. · Romaine R. · L. Musquaro

S h i e l d · L. Mistassini · **QUEBEC** · Manicouagan L. · Ste-Marguerite R. · Moisie R. · Magpie R. · Nataashquan R. · N

Mistassibi R. · Perbonca R. · Manouane · Manicouagan R. · Mingan · Havre-Saint-Pierre · 50°N

Chibougamau · Pipmuacan Res. · Clarke City · Sept-Iles · Mingan Archipelago Reserve · Anticosti I.

Ashuapmushuan R. · **Pointe des Monts** · A n t i c o s t i I.

Res. Gouin · Baie-Comeau · **Chic-Choc Mts.** · Gaspe · Forillon National Park

L. St.-Jean · Alma · Chicoutimi · Forestville · Matane · G a s p e P e n i n s u l a · Chandler · Gulf of St. Lawrence

Parent · Jonquiere · Saguenay R. · Tadoussac · Rimouski · Restigouche R. · Chaleur Bay · Madeleine Islands

Cabonga Res. · St. Maurice · La Malbaie · N o t r e D a m e M t s. · Riviere-du-Loup · Campbellton · Cape Breton Highlands National Park

L a u r e n t i a n H i g h l a n d s · La Tuque · Beauport · 185 · Edmundston · Bathurst · **PRINCE EDWARD ISLAND** · Cape Breton Island

Kempt · Charlesbourg · Quebec · Montmagny · Grand Falls · Newcastle · Kouchibouguac National Park · Prince Edward Island National Park · Sydney

Baskatong Res. · 117 · Ste. Foy · 73 · St. John R. · **NEW BRUNSWICK** · Summerside · 1 · Charlottetown · Bras d'Or L.

La Mauricie National Park · 40 · 20 · Notre Dame Mts. · Chaudiere R. · Miramichi R. · Northumberland Str. · Port Hawkesbury

Maniwaki · Trois-Rivieres · 55 · Woodstock · Fredericton · Moncton · Amherst · New Glasgow · Canso

Joliette · 20 · Drummondville · 95 · Grand L. · St. John · 104 · 2 · **NOVA** · 45°N

Gatineau R. · 30 · St.-Laurent · Laval · Longueuil · Sherbrooke · Fundy National Park · Truro · Minas Basin · **SCOTIA** · Sherbrooke

Hull · 15 · Granby · Mooshead L. · **MAINE** · Saint John · Minas Basin · 102

Ottawa · 17 · **Montreal** · 10 · 55 · Bay of Fundy · 101 · Halifax

417 · 20 · St. Lawrence R. · Digby · **NOVA** · 103

Cornwall · 401 · Grand Manan I. · 7 · Brockville · Ogdensburg · L. Champlain · Burlington · Kejimkujik National Park · Lunenburg

Kingston · St. Lawrence Islands National Park · **Adirondack Mts.** · Montpelier · 93 · L. Rossignol · Shelburne

81 · 87 · 89 · Augusta · Yarmouth · Cape Sable

90 · Syracuse · **VERMONT** · **NEW HAMPSHIRE** · 95 · Portland

YORK · Albany · 88 · 93 · 89 · Concord · **A T L A N T I C**

MASSACHUSETTS · Boston · **O C E A N**

90 · Hartford · 84 · Providence

81 · 84 · 87 · 91 · **CONNECTICUT** · **RHODE ISLAND** · 95

70°W · 65°W

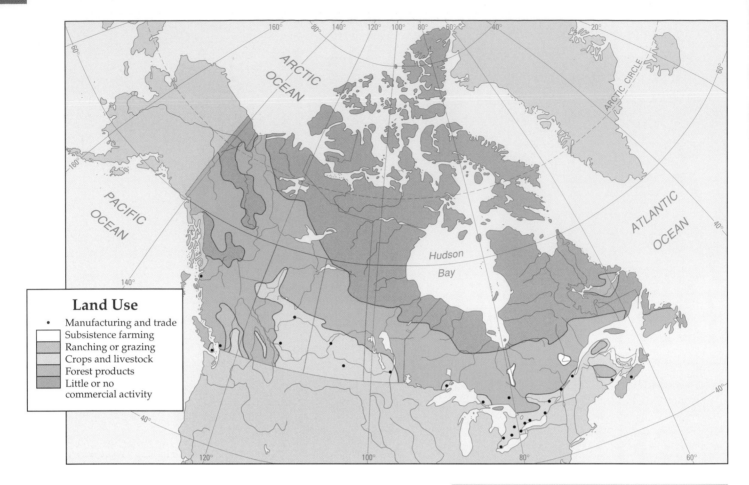

Land Use

- • Manufacturing and trade
- ☐ Subsistence farming
- ☐ Ranching or grazing
- ☐ Crops and livestock
- ☐ Forest products
- ☐ Little or no commercial activity

CANADA
Area Comparison

Canada is the largest country in the Western Hemisphere. Texas could easily fit within Hudson Bay, Canada's largest body of water.

Canada	3,849,674 sq. mi. (9 970 610 sq. km)
Contiguous U.S.	3,021,295 sq. mi. (7 825 112 sq. km)

Vancouver, Canada's third-largest metropolitan area, is a major center for commerce and transportation. Known as the Gateway to the Pacific, it has the busiest seaport in Canada.

Fishing has been an important industry in Canada's Maritime Provinces since the late 1400s. The region's picturesque seacoast also attracts many tourists.

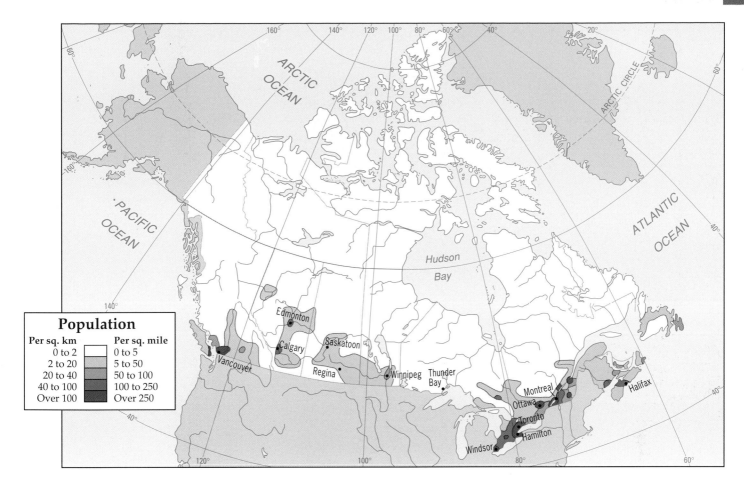

Population

Per sq. km	Per sq. mile
0 to 2	0 to 5
2 to 20	5 to 50
20 to 40	50 to 100
40 to 100	100 to 250
Over 100	Over 250

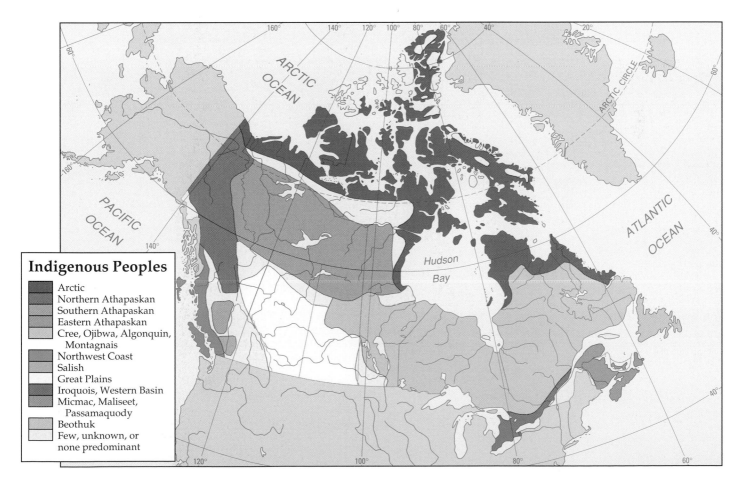

Indigenous Peoples

- Arctic
- Northern Athapaskan
- Southern Athapaskan
- Eastern Athapaskan
- Cree, Ojibwa, Algonquin, Montagnais
- Northwest Coast
- Salish
- Great Plains
- Iroquois, Western Basin
- Micmac, Maliseet, Passamaquody
- Beothuk
- Few, unknown, or none predominant

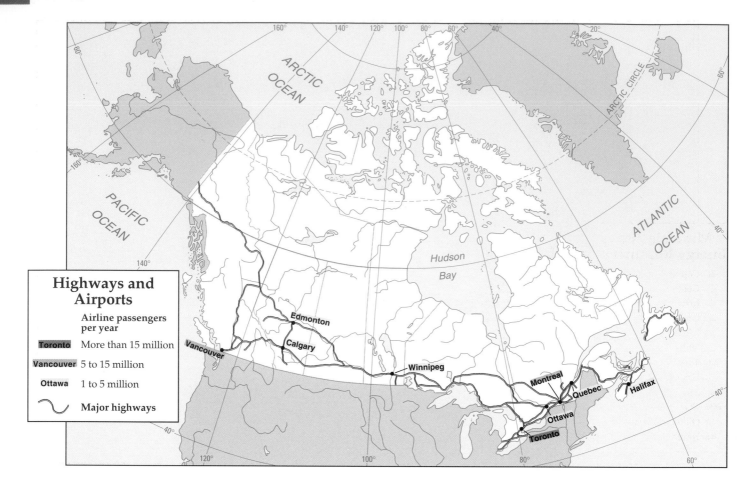

Highways and Airports

Airline passengers per year

Toronto	More than 15 million
Vancouver	5 to 15 million
Ottawa	1 to 5 million
〰	Major highways

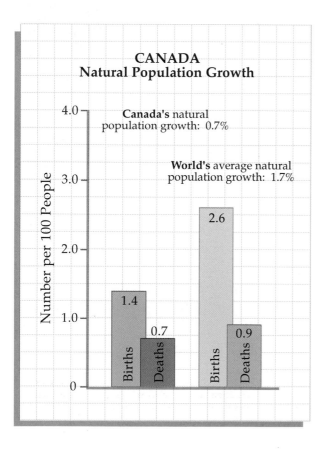

CANADA
Natural Population Growth

Canada's natural population growth: 0.7%

World's average natural population growth: 1.7%

Number per 100 People

- 1.4 Births
- 0.7 Deaths
- 2.6 Births
- 0.9 Deaths

CANADA
Balance of Trade

Exports total US$118.5 billion

Imports total US$113.8 billion

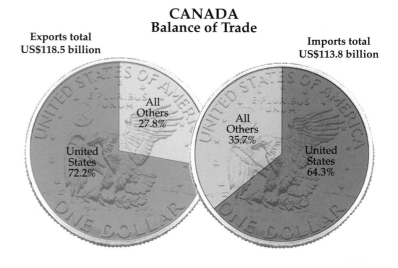

All Others 27.8%
United States 72.2%

All Others 35.7%
United States 64.3%

Export Destinations	
United States	72.2%
Japan	6.2%
United Kingdom	2.4%
China	1.3%
Germany	1.2%
South Korea	1.0%
Netherlands	1.0%
All others	14.7%

Import Sources	
United States	64.3%
Japan	7.1%
United Kingdom	3.4%
Germany	2.8%
South Korea	1.7%
Taiwan	1.7%
France	1.6%
All others	17.4%

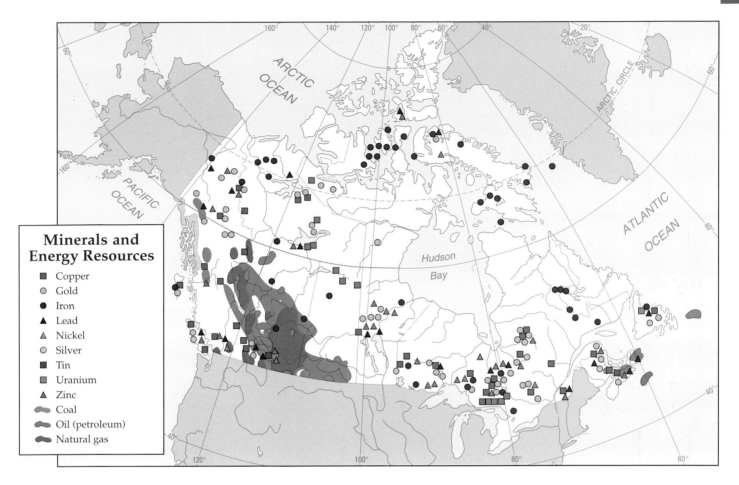

Minerals and Energy Resources

- ■ Copper
- ● Gold
- ● Iron
- ▲ Lead
- ▲ Nickel
- ● Silver
- ■ Tin
- ■ Uranium
- ▲ Zinc
- Coal
- Oil (petroleum)
- Natural gas

Forestry Exports

More of Canada's forest products are exported to the United States than to any other country.

Export Products

- Pulp 23.9 %
- Lumber 28.5 %
- Newsprint 31.6 %
- Other wood 6.9 %
- Other paper 9.1 %

Export Destinations

- United States 67 %
- All others 20 %
- United Kingdom 6%
- Japan 7 %

Quebec's growing industrial strength is partly due to its hydro-electric power. High-voltage lines carry electricity from dams in the north to cities near the St. Lawrence River.

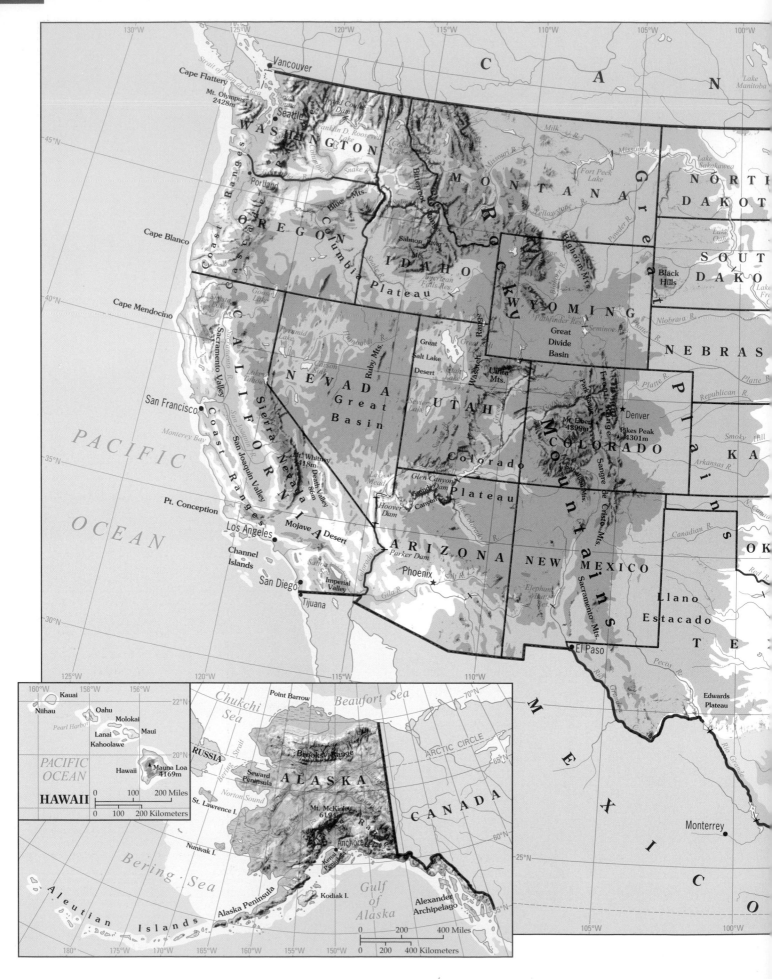

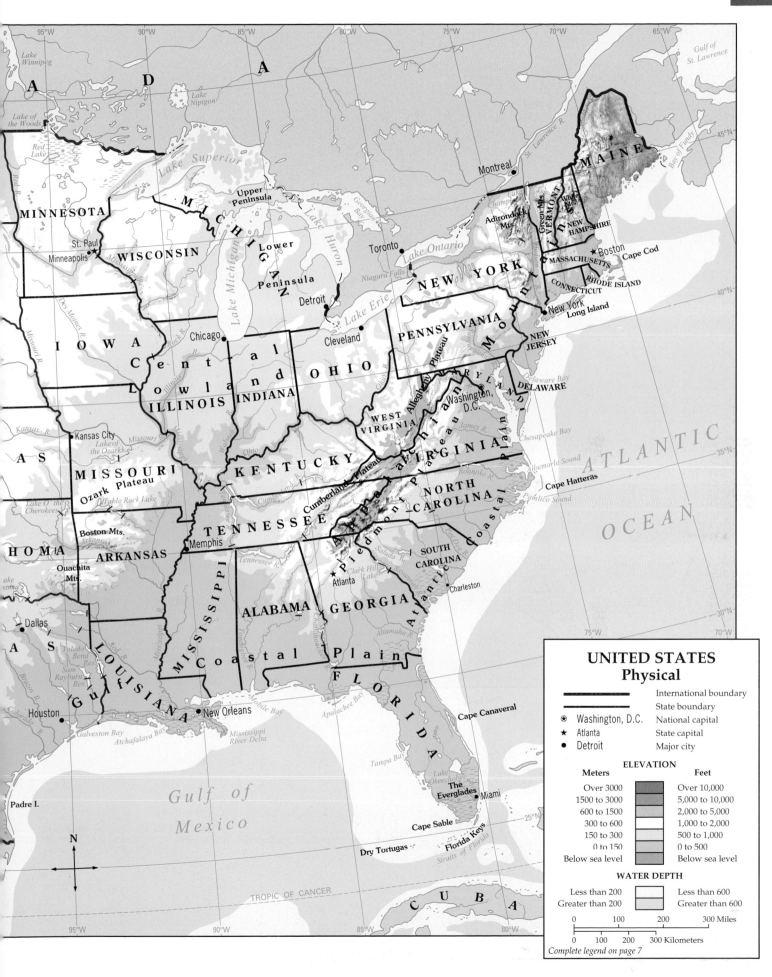

CANADA

Lake Winnipeg
Lake of the Woods
Red Lake
Red R.
MINNESOTA
St. Paul
Minneapolis
Mississippi R.
IOWA
Des Moines R.
Missouri R.
KANSAS
Kansas R.
Kansas City
Lake of the Ozarks
MISSOURI
Ozark Plateau
Table Rock Lake
Lake O' the Cherokees
Boston Mts.
OKLAHOMA
Ouachita Mts.
Lake Texoma
ARKANSAS
Ouachita R.
TEXAS
Dallas
Toledo Bend Res.
Sam Rayburn Res.
Colorado R.
Brazos R.
Houston
Galveston Bay
Padre I.

Lake Superior
Lake Nipigon
MICHIGAN
Upper Peninsula
Lower Peninsula
Lake Michigan
Lake Huron
Georgian Bay
WISCONSIN
Central Lowland
ILLINOIS
Chicago
Rock R.
INDIANA
Wabash R.
KENTUCKY
Ohio R.
Cumberland Plateau
Cumberland R.
TENNESSEE
Memphis
Tennessee R.
MISSISSIPPI
ALABAMA
Tombigbee R.
Coastal Plain
LOUISIANA
New Orleans
Mobile Bay
Atchafalaya Bay
Mississippi River Delta

Lake Erie
Detroit
Cleveland
OHIO
WEST VIRGINIA
Allegheny Plateau
Allegheny Mts.
Cumberland Plateau
Appalachian Mountains
Niagara Falls
Lake Ontario
Toronto
Montreal
St. Lawrence R.
NEW YORK
Adirondack Mts.
Lake Champlain
Green Mts.
VERMONT
White Mts.
NEW HAMPSHIRE
MAINE
Bay of Fundy
Gulf of St. Lawrence
PENNSYLVANIA
Piedmont
MARYLAND
Washington, D.C.
Potomac R.
James R.
VIRGINIA
NORTH CAROLINA
SOUTH CAROLINA
Saluda R.
Savannah R.
Clark Hill Lake
Atlanta
GEORGIA
Altamaha R.
Charleston
Roanoke R.
Albemarle Sound
Pamlico Sound
Cape Hatteras
Chesapeake Bay
Delaware Bay
DELAWARE
NEW JERSEY
New York
Long Island
CONNECTICUT
RHODE ISLAND
MASSACHUSETTS
Boston
Cape Cod
Atlantic Coastal Plain

ATLANTIC OCEAN

FLORIDA
Apalachee Bay
Cape Canaveral
Tampa Bay
Lake Okeechobee
The Everglades
Miami
Cape Sable
Florida Keys
Dry Tortugas
Straits of Florida

Gulf of Mexico

CUBA

TROPIC OF CANCER

N

UNITED STATES
Physical

———————— International boundary

———————— State boundary

⊛ Washington, D.C.   National capital

★ Atlanta   State capital

● Detroit   Major city

ELEVATION

Meters	Feet
Over 3000	Over 10,000
1500 to 3000	5,000 to 10,000
600 to 1500	2,000 to 5,000
300 to 600	1,000 to 2,000
150 to 300	500 to 1,000
0 to 150	0 to 500
Below sea level	Below sea level

WATER DEPTH

Less than 200	Less than 600
Greater than 200	Greater than 600

| 0 | 100 | 200 | 300 Miles |

| 0 | 100 | 200 | 300 Kilometers |

Complete legend on page 7

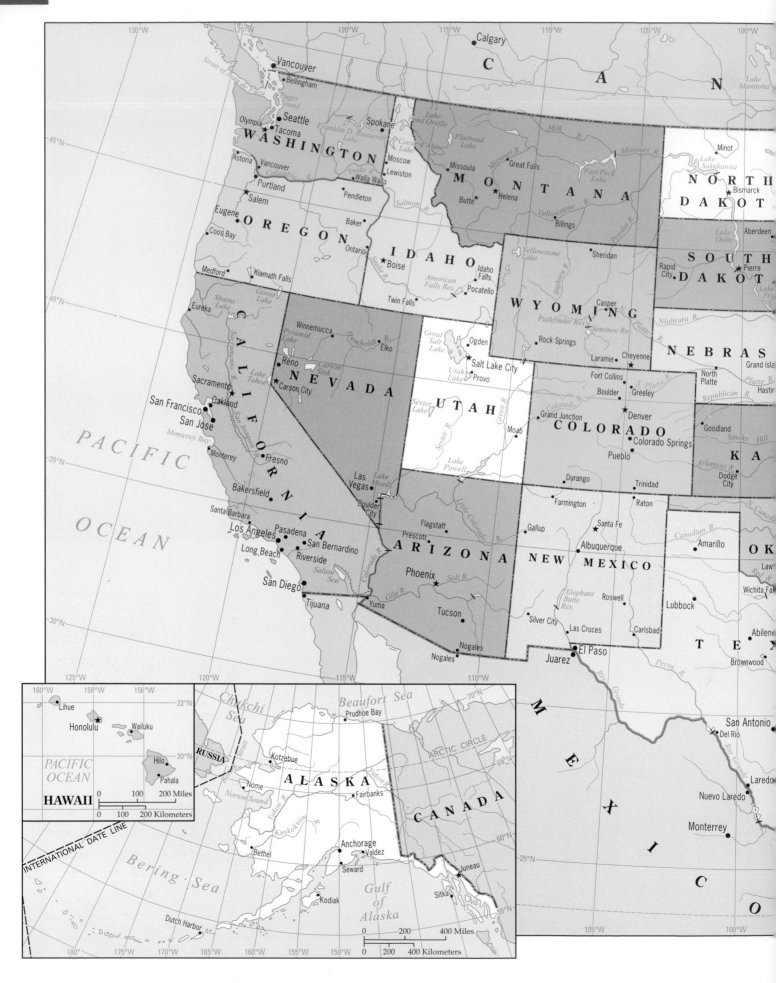

UNITED STATES
Political

BOUNDARIES

—————————— International boundary

—————— State boundary

CITIES

● Chicago

● Anchorage

• Boulder   A city's relative size is shown by the size of its symbol and lettering.

⊛ Washington, D.C.   National capital

★ Honolulu   State capital

0   100   200   300 Miles

0   100   200   300 Kilometers

Complete legend on page 7

Traditional Regions and Regional Names

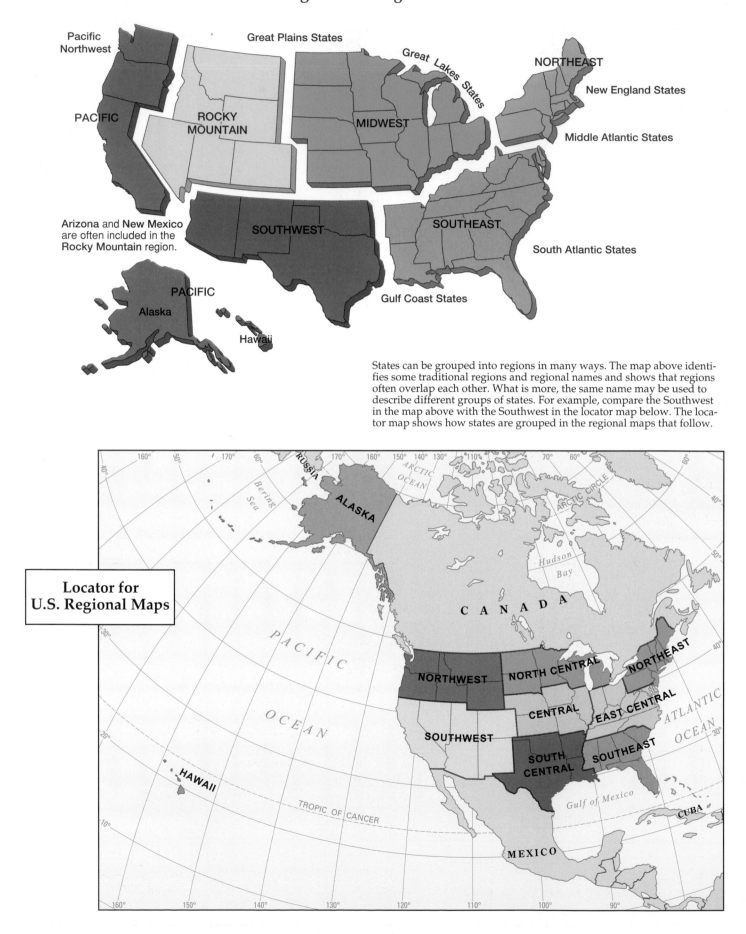

Pacific Northwest

Great Plains States

Great Lakes States

NORTHEAST

New England States

PACIFIC

ROCKY MOUNTAIN

MIDWEST

Middle Atlantic States

Arizona and **New Mexico** are often included in the Rocky Mountain region.

SOUTHWEST

SOUTHEAST

South Atlantic States

PACIFIC

Alaska

Hawaii

Gulf Coast States

States can be grouped into regions in many ways. The map above identifies some traditional regions and regional names and shows that regions often overlap each other. What is more, the same name may be used to describe different groups of states. For example, compare the Southwest in the map above with the Southwest in the locator map below. The locator map shows how states are grouped in the regional maps that follow.

Locator for U.S. Regional Maps

RUSSIA

ARCTIC OCEAN

ALASKA

ARCTIC CIRCLE

Bering Sea

Hudson Bay

C A N A D A

PACIFIC OCEAN

NORTHWEST

NORTH CENTRAL

NORTHEAST

CENTRAL

EAST CENTRAL

ATLANTIC OCEAN

SOUTHWEST

SOUTH CENTRAL

SOUTHEAST

HAWAII

TROPIC OF CANCER

Gulf of Mexico

CUBA

MEXICO

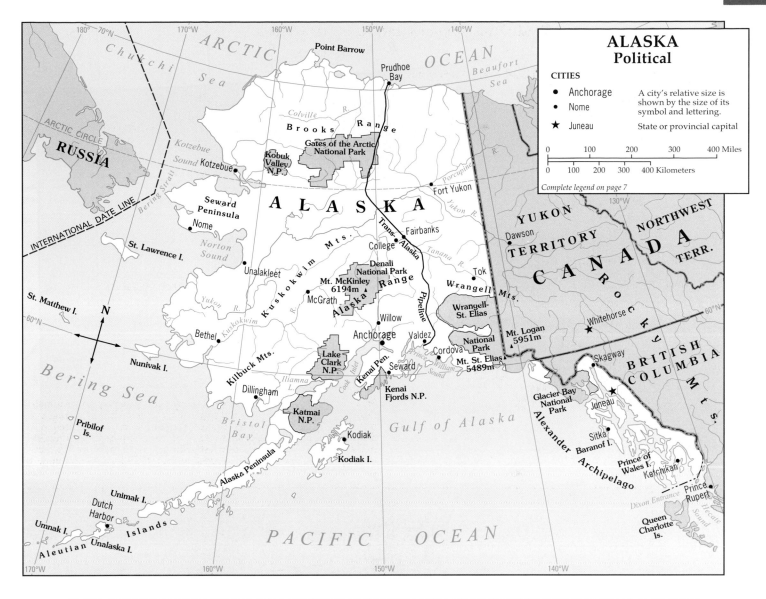

**ALASKA
Political**

CITIES

● Anchorage A city's relative size is shown by the size of its symbol and lettering.

● Nome

★ Juneau State or provincial capital

0 100 200 300 400 Miles

0 100 200 300 400 Kilometers

Complete legend on page 7

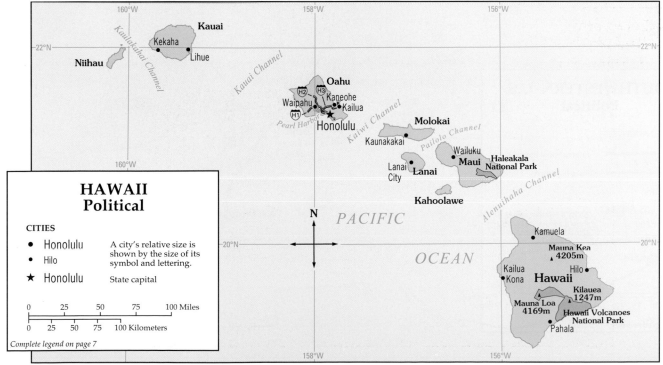

**HAWAII
Political**

CITIES

● Honolulu A city's relative size is shown by the size of its symbol and lettering.

● Hilo

★ Honolulu State capital

0 25 50 75 100 Miles

0 25 50 75 100 Kilometers

Complete legend on page 7

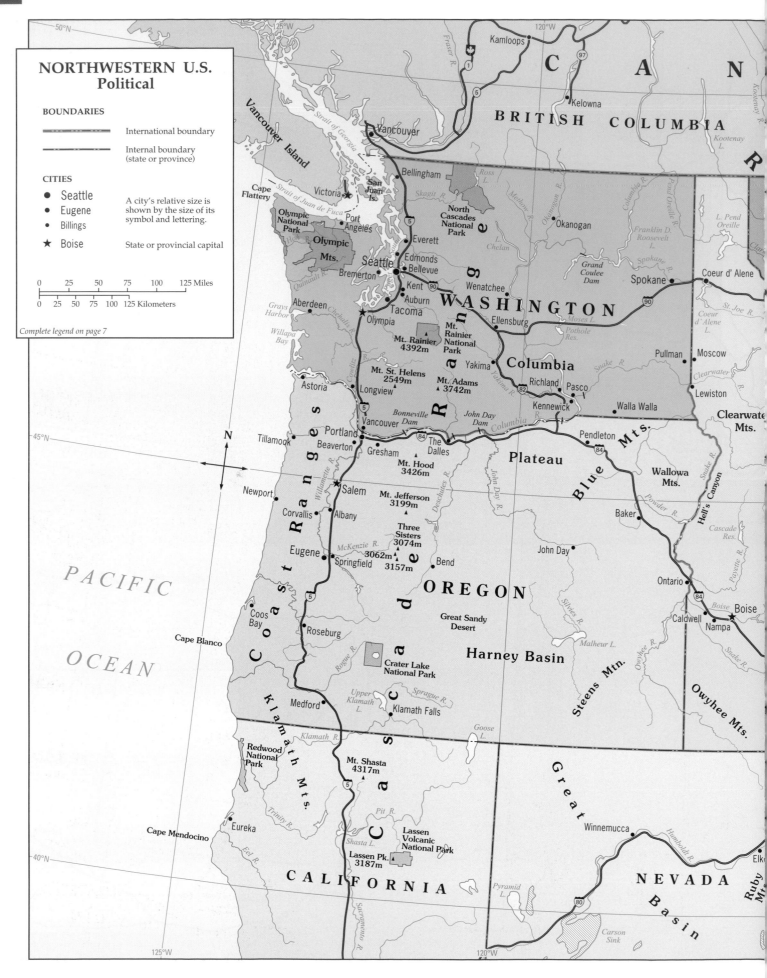

NORTHWESTERN U.S.
Political

BOUNDARIES

International boundary

Internal boundary
(state or province)

CITIES

● Seattle

● Eugene

• Billings

★ Boise

A city's relative size is
shown by the size of its
symbol and lettering.

State or provincial capital

0   25   50   75   100   125 Miles

0   25   50   75   100   125 Kilometers

Complete legend on page 7

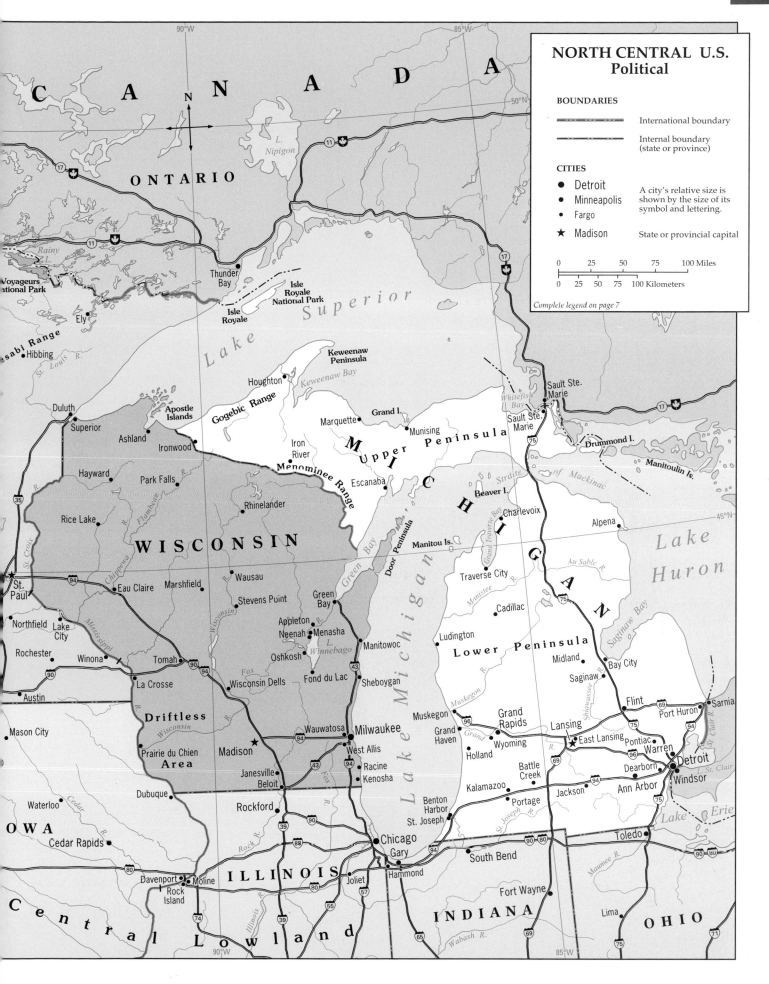

NORTH CENTRAL U.S.
Political

BOUNDARIES

International boundary

Internal boundary
(state or province)

CITIES

● Detroit   A city's relative size is
● Minneapolis   shown by the size of its
• Fargo   symbol and lettering.

★ Madison   State or provincial capital

0   25   50   75   100 Miles

0   25   50   75   100 Kilometers

Complete legend on page 7

CANADA

ONTARIO

L. Nipigon

Rainy L.

Voyageurs National Park

Ely

Thunder Bay

Isle Royale National Park

Isle Royale

Lake Superior

Keweenaw Peninsula

Keweenaw Bay

Houghton

Whitefish Bay

Sault Ste. Marie

Sault Ste. Marie

Mesabi Range

Hibbing

St. Louis R.

Duluth

Superior

Ashland

Apostle Islands

Gogebic Range

Marquette

Grand I.

Munising

MICHIGAN

Upper Peninsula

Drummond I.

Manitoulin Is.

Ironwood

Iron River

Menominee Range

Escanaba

Straits of Mackinac

Beaver I.

Hayward

Park Falls

Rhinelander

Charlevoix

Alpena

Rice Lake

WISCONSIN

Flambeau R.

Chippewa R.

Green Bay

Door Peninsula

Manitou Is.

Traverse City

Grand Traverse Bay

Lake Huron

Au Sable R.

Manistee R.

St. Paul

Eau Claire

Marshfield

Wausau

Stevens Point

Green Bay

Lake Michigan

Cadillac

Northfield

Lake City

Appleton

Neenah Menasha

Oshkosh

L. Winnebago

Manitowoc

Ludington

Midland

Bay City

Rochester

Winona

Tomah

Wisconsin Dells

Fond du Lac

Sheboygan

Muskegon R.

Grand Rapids

Saginaw

Saginaw Bay

Flint

Sarnia

Austin

La Crosse

Fox R.

Driftless

Wisconsin R.

Wauwatosa

Milwaukee

Muskegon

Grand Haven

Wyoming

Lansing

Shiawassee R.

East Lansing

Pontiac

Port Huron

St. Clair R.

Warren

Mason City

Prairie du Chien

Area

Madison

West Allis

Racine

Holland

Battle Creek

Kalamazoo

Jackson

Dearborn

Ann Arbor

Detroit

Windsor

L. St. Clair

Janesville

Beloit

Kenosha

Portage

Benton Harbor

St. Joseph

St. Joseph R.

Waterloo

Cedar R.

Dubuque

Rockford

IOWA

Cedar Rapids

Lake Erie

Toledo

Davenport Moline

Rock Island

ILLINOIS

Joliet

Chicago

Gary

Hammond

South Bend

Maumee R.

INDIANA

Fort Wayne

Lima

OHIO

Central Lowland

Wabash R.

Mississippi R.

St. Croix R.

45°N

45°N

50°N

90°W

90°W

85°W

85°W

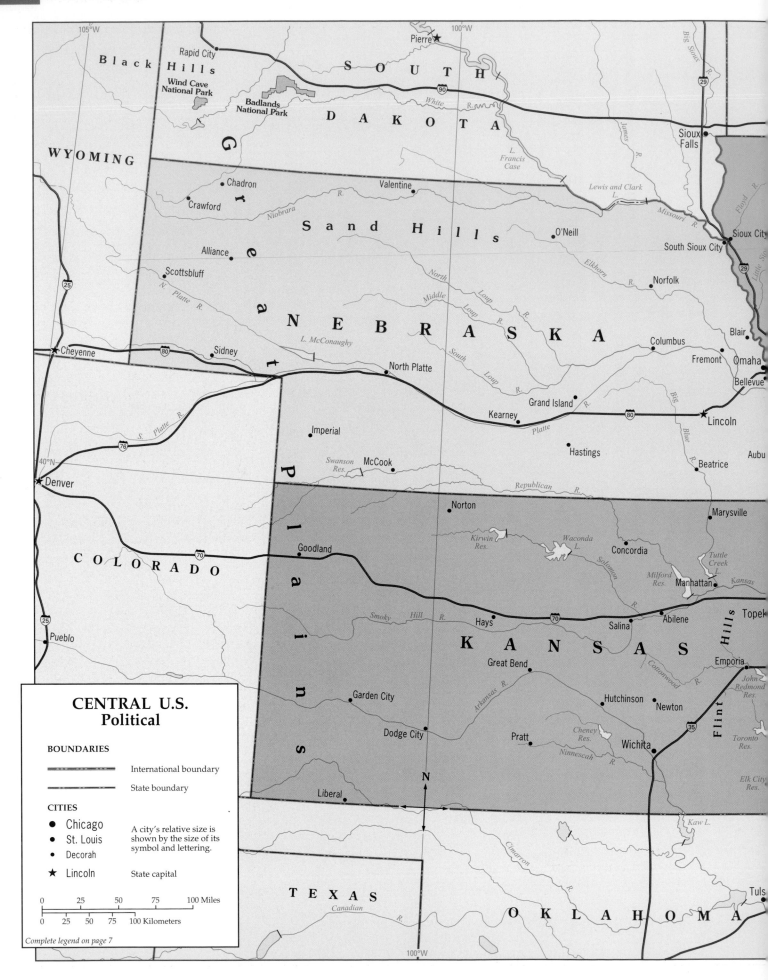

105°W

100°W

Black Hills

Rapid City

Wind Cave National Park

Badlands National Park

SOUTH DAKOTA

Pierre ★

I-90

I-29

White R.

James R.

L. Francis Case

Sioux Falls

WYOMING

G r e a t

Chadron

Crawford

Niobrara R.

Valentine

Sand Hills

O'Neill

Lewis and Clark L.

Missouri R.

Sioux City

South Sioux City

Alliance

Scottsbluff

N. Platte R.

North Loup R.

Middle Loup

Elkhorn R.

Norfolk

N E B R A S K A

Blair

Cheyenne

I-80

Sidney

L. McConaughy

South Loup R.

Columbus

Fremont

Omaha

North Platte

Bellevue

P l a i n s

Grand Island

Platte R.

I-80

Lincoln ★

Kearney

S. Platte R.

I-76

Imperial

Hastings

Beatrice

Aubu

40°N

Denver ★

Swanson Res.

McCook

Republican R.

COLORADO

I-70

Norton

Marysville

Kirwin Res.

Waconda L.

Concordia

Tuttle Creek L.

Goodland

Solomon R.

Milford Res.

Manhattan

Kansas R.

Pueblo

I-25

Smoky Hill R.

Hays

I-70

Salina

Abilene

Topek

K A N S A S

Flint Hills

Emporia

CENTRAL U.S.
Political

Great Bend

John 2 Redmond Res.

Garden City

Arkansas R.

Hutchinson

Newton

I-35

BOUNDARIES

International boundary

State boundary

Dodge City

Pratt

Cheney Res.

Wichita

Ninnescah R.

Cottonwood R.

Toronto Res.

Flint

CITIES

● Chicago

● St. Louis

● Decorah

★ Lincoln

A city's relative size is shown by the size of its symbol and lettering.

State capital

N

Liberal

Elk City Res.

0 25 50 75 100 Miles

0 25 50 75 100 Kilometers

Kaw L.

Complete legend on page 7

T E X A S

Canadian R.

Cimarron R.

O K L A H O M A

Tuls

100°W

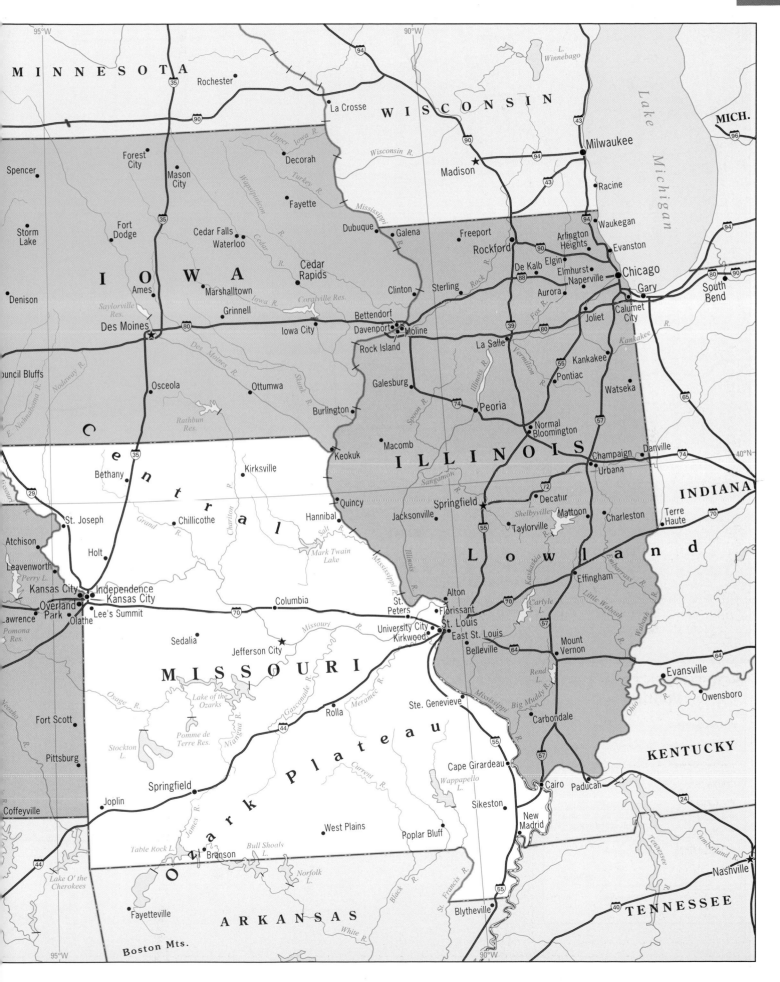

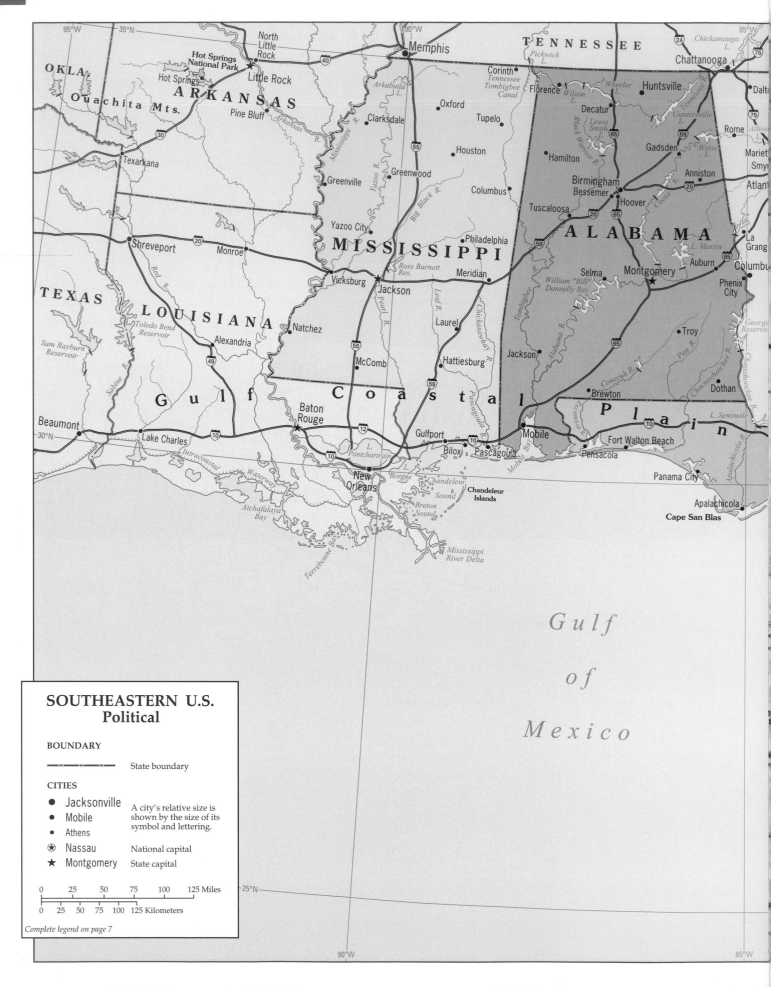

SOUTHEASTERN U.S.
Political

BOUNDARY

———————— State boundary

CITIES

● Jacksonville   A city's relative size is
● Mobile   shown by the size of its
• Athens   symbol and lettering.
⊛ Nassau   National capital
★ Montgomery   State capital

0   25   50   75   100   125 Miles

0   25 50 75 100 125 Kilometers

Complete legend on page 7

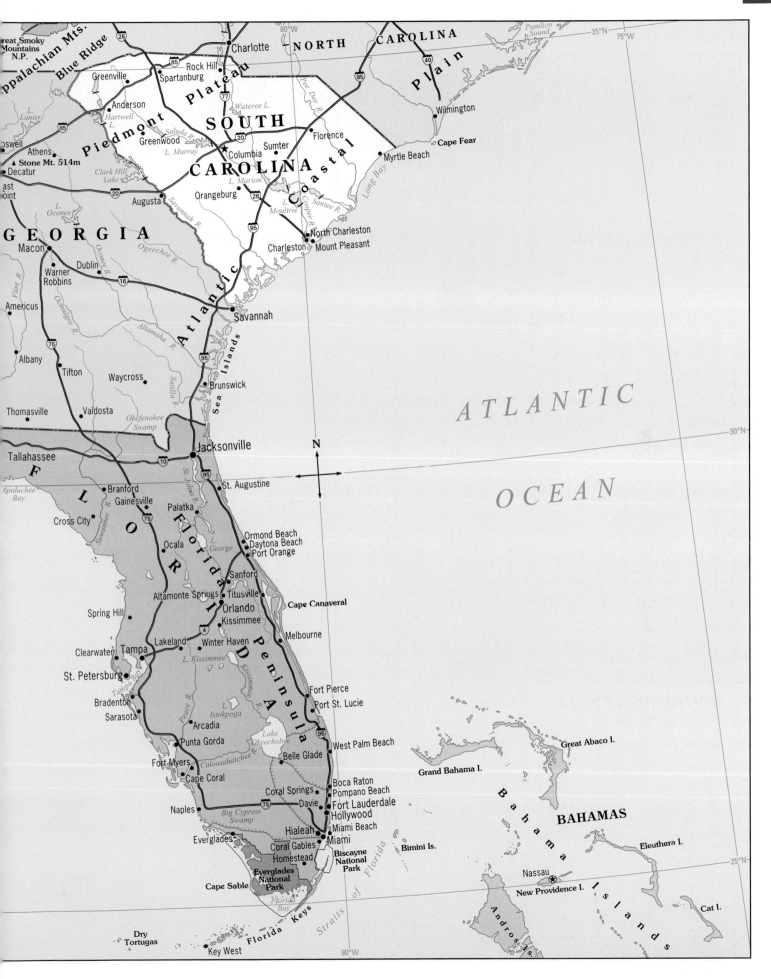

Great Smoky Mountains N.P.
Appalachian Mts.
Blue Ridge
Piedmont Plateau
Charlotte
NORTH **CAROLINA** **Plain**
Rock Hill
Greenville
Spartanburg
Anderson
L. Lanier
Hartwell L.
Wateree L.
Wilmington
SOUTH
Roswell
Athens
Stone Mt. 514m
Decatur
East Point
Greenwood
L. Murray
Columbia
Sumter
Florence
Cape Fear
Myrtle Beach
CAROLINA Coastal
GEORGIA
L. Oconee
Clark Hill Lake
Augusta
Orangeburg
L. Marion
L. Moultrie
Santee R.
Long Bay
Macon
Warner Robbins
Dublin
Ogeechee R.
North Charleston
Charleston
Mount Pleasant
Americus
Flint R.
Oconee R.
Altamaha R.
Savannah R.
Cooper R.
Atlantic
Albany
Tifton
Waycross
Sea Islands
Savannah
ATLANTIC
Thomasville
Valdosta
Okefenokee Swamp
Satilla R.
Brunswick
Coastal
OCEAN
Tallahassee
Apalachee Bay
FLORIDA
Branford
Gainesville
Palatka
St. Johns R.
Jacksonville
St. Augustine
N
Cross City
Suwannee R.
Ocala
L. George
Ormond Beach
Daytona Beach
Port Orange
Florida
Spring Hill
Altamonte Springs
Sanford
Titusville
Orlando
Kissimmee
Cape Canaveral
Clearwater
Tampa
Lakeland
Winter Haven
Melbourne
Peninsula
St. Petersburg
L. Kissimmee
Kissimmee R.
Peace R.
Bradenton
Sarasota
Arcadia
L. Istokpoga
Fort Pierce
Port St. Lucie
Tampa Bay
Punta Gorda
Caloosahatchee R.
Lake Okeechobee
West Palm Beach
Fort Myers
Cape Coral
Belle Glade
Boca Raton
Naples
Coral Springs
Pompano Beach
Big Cypress Swamp
Davie
Fort Lauderdale
Hollywood
Hialeah
Miami Beach
Everglades
Coral Gables
Miami
Homestead
Biscayne National Park
Everglades National Park
Cape Sable
Florida Bay
Straits of Florida
Dry Tortugas
Florida Keys
Key West

ATLANTIC

OCEAN

Great Abaco I.
Grand Bahama I.
BAHAMAS
Bimini Is.
Eleuthera I.
Bahama Islands
Nassau
New Providence I.
Cat I.
Androvs I.

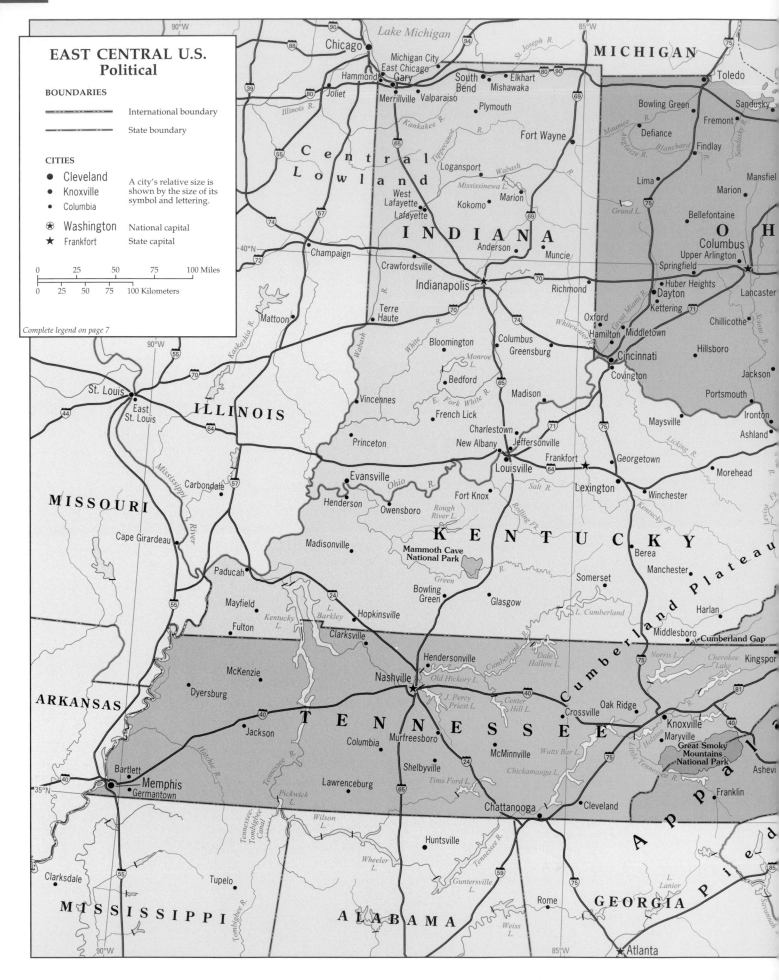

EAST CENTRAL U.S.
Political

BOUNDARIES

International boundary

State boundary

CITIES

● Cleveland

● Knoxville

○ Columbia

A city's relative size is shown by the size of its symbol and lettering.

⊛ Washington   National capital

★ Frankfort   State capital

| 0 | 25 | 50 | 75 | 100 Miles |

| 0 | 25 | 50 | 75 | 100 Kilometers |

Complete legend on page 7

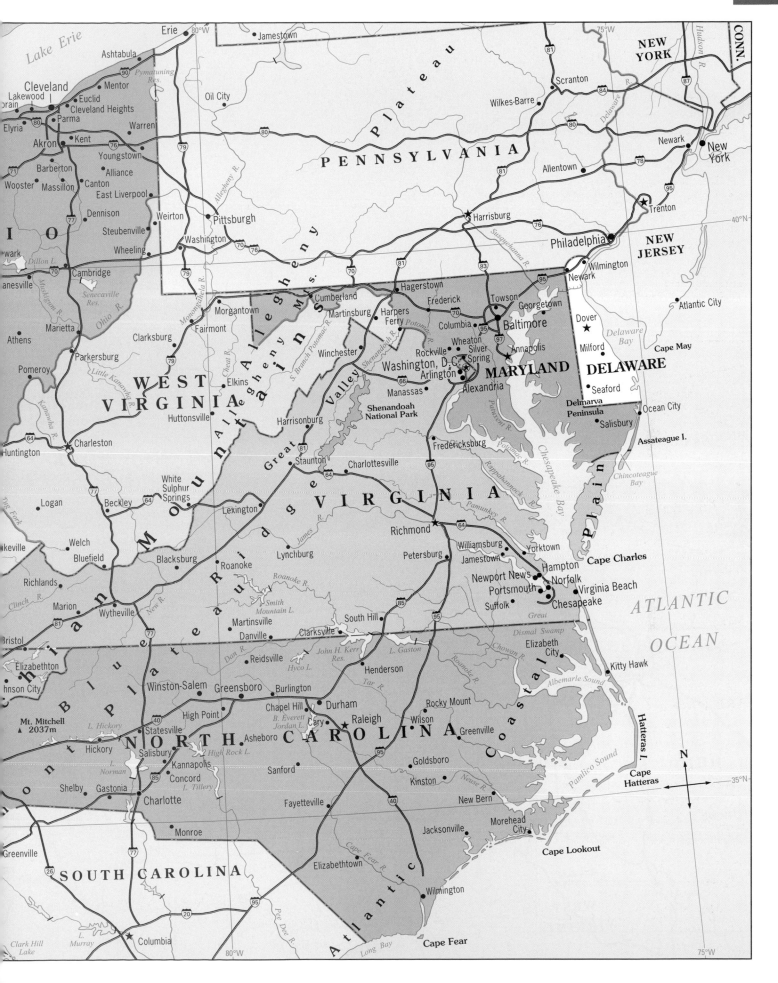

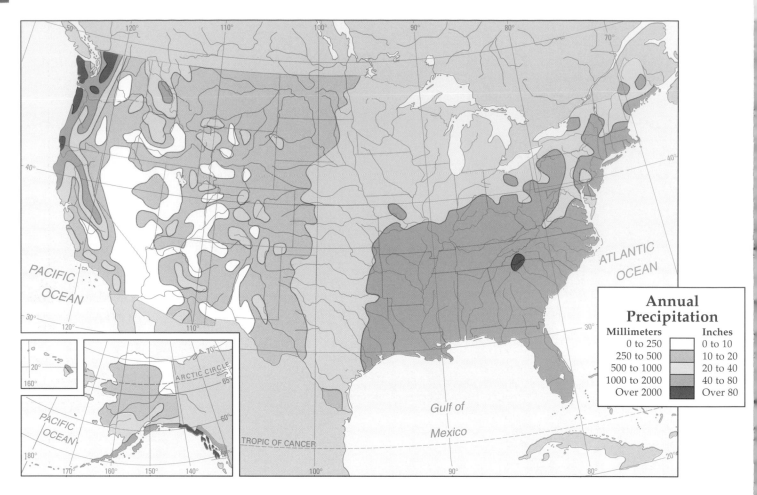

Annual Precipitation

Millimeters		Inches
0 to 250		0 to 10
250 to 500		10 to 20
500 to 1000		20 to 40
1000 to 2000		40 to 80
Over 2000		Over 80

ALASKA
Area Comparison

Alaska is one-fifth the size of the first 48 states combined. It is twice as big as Texas, which is the second-largest state.

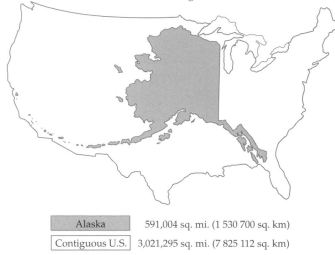

Alaska	591,004 sq. mi. (1 530 700 sq. km)
Contiguous U.S.	3,021,295 sq. mi. (7 825 112 sq. km)

Bryce Canyon's rock formations are a spectacular example of the rugged terrain that is found in the desert areas of the Southwest.

Cross Section of the United States

ELEVATION

Meters		Feet
Over 3000		Over 10,000
1500 to 3000		5,000 to 10,000
600 to 1500		2,000 to 5,000
300 to 600		1,000 to 2,000
150 to 300		500 to 1,000
0 to 150		0 to 500
Below sea level		Below sea level

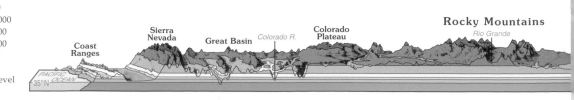

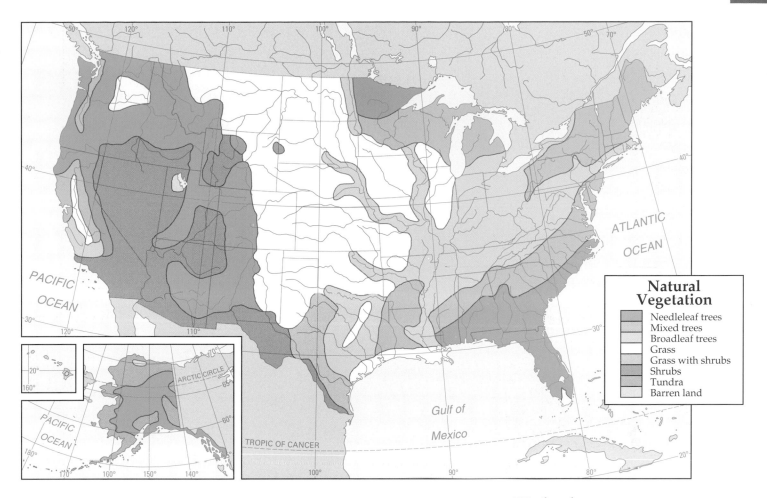

Natural Vegetation

- Needleleaf trees
- Mixed trees
- Broadleaf trees
- Grass
- Grass with shrubs
- Shrubs
- Tundra
- Barren land

Wetlands

Wetlands are an important natural resource that provides habitat for wildlife, controls floods, and produces clean fresh water. During the past 200 years, however, more than half the wetlands in the United States have been drained, filled, or paved to develop agricultural land or to expand urban areas.

Florida's Everglades is a unique tropical savanna dominated by saltwater marshes and mangrove swamps. These wetlands are home to a great variety of birds and other animals.

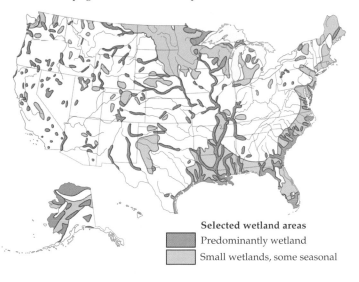

Selected wetland areas
- Predominantly wetland
- Small wetlands, some seasonal

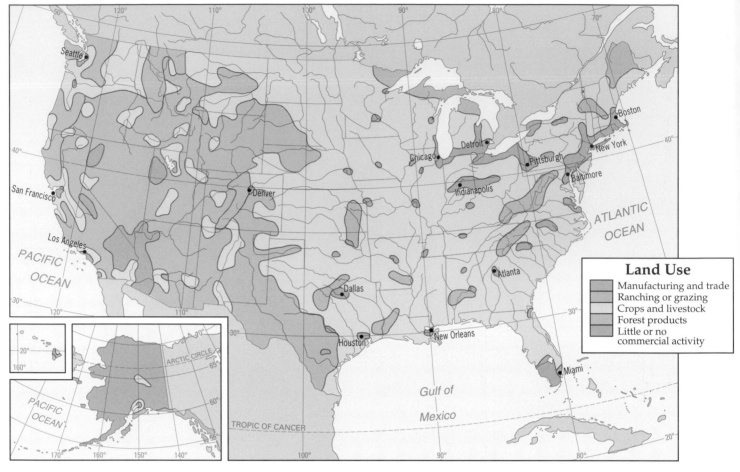

Land Use
- Manufacturing and trade
- Ranching or grazing
- Crops and livestock
- Forest products
- Little or no commercial activity

Domestic Water Use

In the United States, an average family of four uses 240 gallons of water each day. Only ten gallons, or four percent, are used for preparing food or drinking.

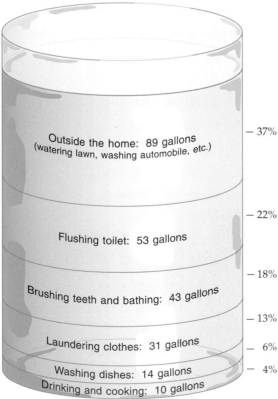

Outside the home: 89 gallons
(watering lawn, washing automobile, etc.) — 37%

Flushing toilet: 53 gallons — 22%

Brushing teeth and bathing: 43 gallons — 18%

Laundering clothes: 31 gallons — 13%

Washing dishes: 14 gallons — 6%

Drinking and cooking: 10 gallons — 4%

Ethnic Composition
(based on responses to 1990 U.S. census)

Population: 248,709,873

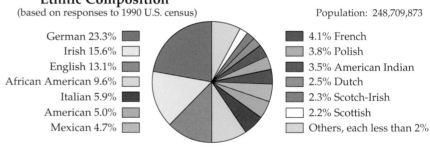

- German 23.3%
- Irish 15.6%
- English 13.1%
- African American 9.6%
- Italian 5.9%
- American 5.0%
- Mexican 4.7%

- 4.1% French
- 3.8% Polish
- 3.5% American Indian
- 2.5% Dutch
- 2.3% Scotch-Irish
- 2.2% Scottish
- Others, each less than 2%

Threatened Water Supplies

Rivers and aquifers in the arid regions of the West and Great Plains are being drained to supply water for farm and ranch irrigation, hydroelectric plants, flood-control dams, and industrial and residential needs.

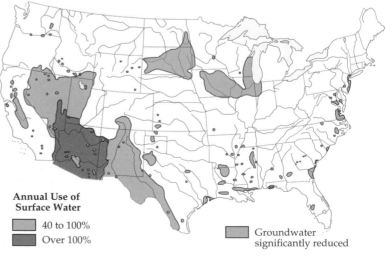

Annual Use of Surface Water
- 40 to 100%
- Over 100%
- Groundwater significantly reduced

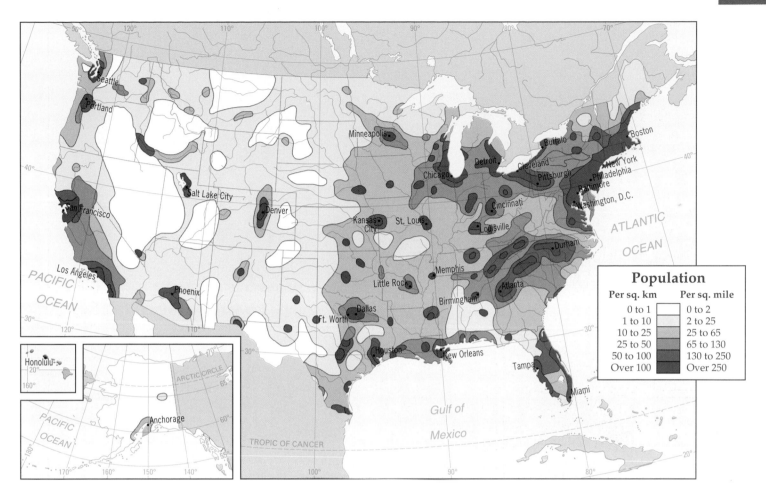

Population

Per sq. km	Per sq. mile
0 to 1	0 to 2
1 to 10	2 to 25
10 to 25	25 to 65
25 to 50	65 to 130
50 to 100	130 to 250
Over 100	Over 250

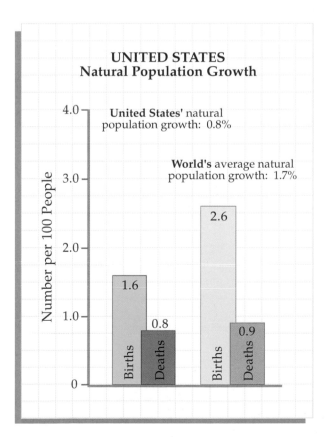

UNITED STATES
Natural Population Growth

United States' natural population growth: 0.8%

World's average natural population growth: 1.7%

Number per 100 People

4.0

3.0

2.0 — 2.6

1.6

1.0

0.8 0.9

0

Births Deaths Births Deaths

Center of Population

1790
1850
1900
1950
1990

Equal numbers of U.S. residents live north, south, east, and west of the center of population. Westward movement of the center of population has followed the historical expansion and settlement of the country; the center's slightly southerly trend in recent decades reflects urban growth in the Sunbelt.

• **Center of population**

Based on decennial census from 1790 to 1990

New York, New York

Petaluma, California

Bumper-to-bumper traffic is a way of life in big cities, while small towns face few problems with congestion. Towns, however, may have their economic base eroded by the loss of population to the cities.

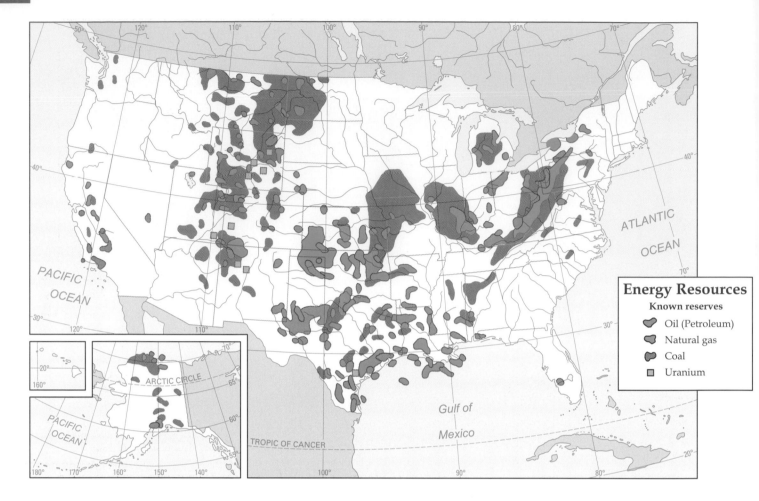

Energy Resources
Known reserves
- Oil (Petroleum)
- Natural gas
- Coal
- Uranium

Energy in the United States
1950 and 1990

Coal
41.3%

Natural gas
19.1%

Petroleum
35.2%

Hydroelectric
4.4%

Sources of Consumed Energy: 1950

Other
0.3%

Coal
23.3%

Nuclear 7.0%

Petroleum
42.1%

Natural gas
23.8%

Hydroelectric
3.5%

Sources of Consumed Energy: 1990

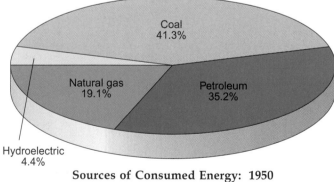

| Industrial 48.7% | Transportation 27.7% | Residential-Commercial 23.6% |

Uses of Consumed Energy: 1950

| Industrial 36.2% | Transportation 27.5% | Residential 20.5% | Commercial 15.8% |

Uses of Consumed Energy: 1990

Barges offer an inexpensive way to deliver coal to factories along rivers in the Midwest and Northeast.

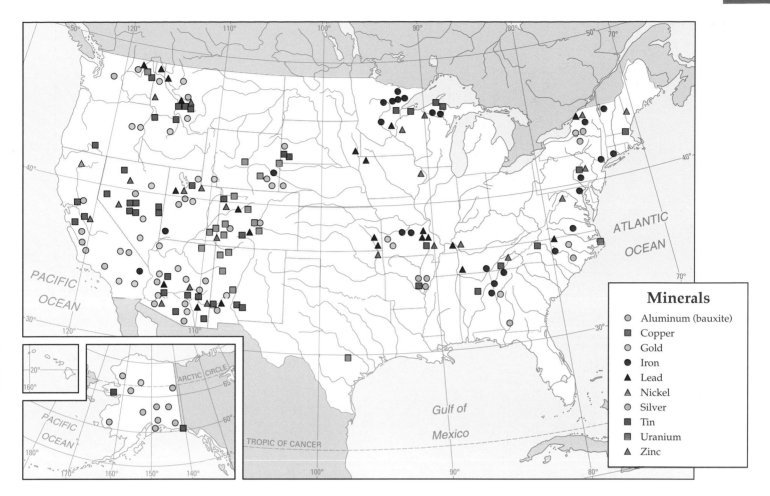

Minerals

- ⦿ Aluminum (bauxite)
- ▪ Copper
- ⦿ Gold
- ● Iron
- ▲ Lead
- ▲ Nickel
- ⦿ Silver
- ▪ Tin
- ▪ Uranium
- ▲ Zinc

Two-thirds of the steel produced in the United States comes from the Midwest. But competition from other countries has reduced steel production and forced the closing of many plants.

More than half of the aluminum cans used in the United States are recycled into new cans and other metal products.

Productivity in the United States

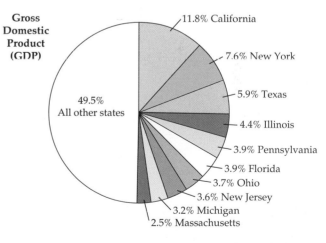

Gross Domestic Product (GDP)

- 49.5% All other states
- 11.8% California
- 7.6% New York
- 5.9% Texas
- 4.4% Illinois
- 3.9% Pennsylvania
- 3.9% Florida
- 3.7% Ohio
- 3.6% New Jersey
- 3.2% Michigan
- 2.5% Massachusetts

The United States has the highest GDP in the world: US$ 5,439.4 billion. If individual states were compared with other countries, two would rank in the world's top 10, and ten in the world's top 30.

Rank	Country or state	GDP or GNP (US$ billion)
1	Japan	3,154.1
2	Germany	1,398.6
3	France	1,090.2
4	Italy	970.7
5	United Kingdom	911.4
6	**California**	**642.7**
7	Canada	535.6
8	Russia	480.1
9	Spain	426.7
10	**New York**	**415.3**

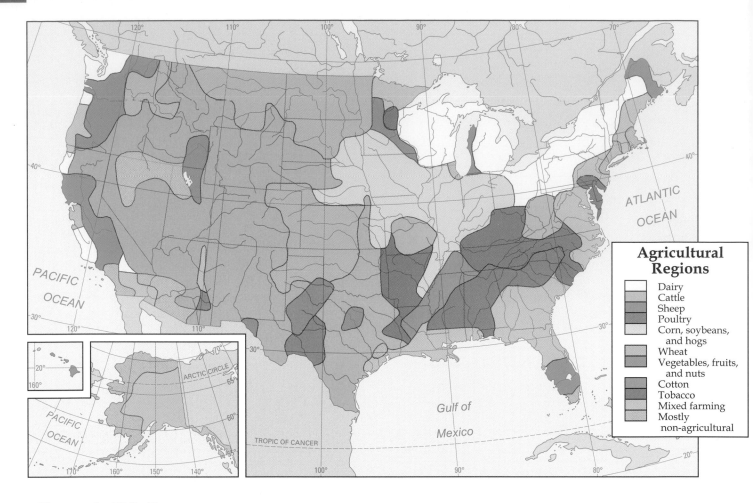

Agricultural Regions

- Dairy
- Cattle
- Sheep
- Poultry
- Corn, soybeans, and hogs
- Wheat
- Vegetables, fruits, and nuts
- Cotton
- Tobacco
- Mixed farming
- Mostly non-agricultural

Change in U.S. Farms

	1910	1930	1950	1970	1990
Number of people engaged in farming = 1 million	32.1 million	30.5 million	23.3 million	9.7 million	4.6 million
Farmers, as a percentage of U.S. population = percentage	34.3%	24.7%	15.5%	4.8%	1.9%
Number of farms = 1 million farms	6.4 million	6.3 million	5.4 million	2.9 million	2.1 million
Average farm size = 100 acres	138 acres	157 acres	215 acres	374 acres	445 acres

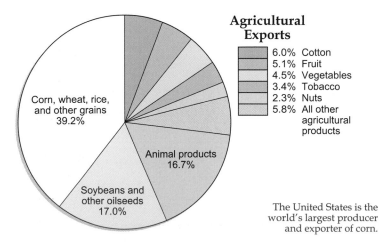

Agricultural Exports

- Corn, wheat, rice, and other grains 39.2%
- Animal products 16.7%
- Soybeans and other oilseeds 17.0%
- 6.0% Cotton
- 5.1% Fruit
- 4.5% Vegetables
- 3.4% Tobacco
- 2.3% Nuts
- 5.8% All other agricultural products

The United States is the world's largest producer and exporter of corn.

UNITED STATES
Balance of Trade

Exports total
US$359.9 billion

Imports total
US$458 billion

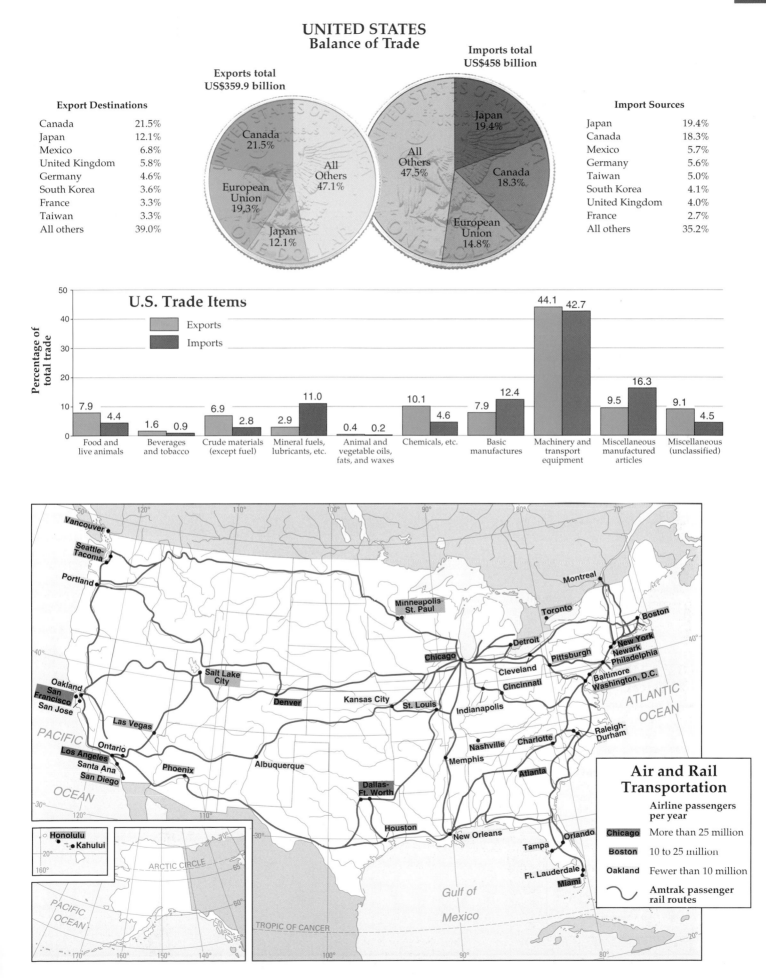

Export Destinations

Canada	21.5%
Japan	12.1%
Mexico	6.8%
United Kingdom	5.8%
Germany	4.6%
South Korea	3.6%
France	3.3%
Taiwan	3.3%
All others	39.0%

Import Sources

Japan	19.4%
Canada	18.3%
Mexico	5.7%
Germany	5.6%
Taiwan	5.0%
South Korea	4.1%
United Kingdom	4.0%
France	2.7%
All others	35.2%

U.S. Trade Items

Percentage of total trade

Exports / Imports

Item	Exports	Imports
Food and live animals	7.9	4.4
Beverages and tobacco	1.6	0.9
Crude materials (except fuel)	6.9	2.8
Mineral fuels, lubricants, etc.	2.9	11.0
Animal and vegetable oils, fats, and waxes	0.4	0.2
Chemicals, etc.	10.1	4.6
Basic manufactures	7.9	12.4
Machinery and transport equipment	44.1	42.7
Miscellaneous manufactured articles	9.5	16.3
Miscellaneous (unclassified)	9.1	4.5

Air and Rail Transportation

Airline passengers per year

Chicago	More than 25 million
Boston	10 to 25 million
Oakland	Fewer than 10 million
∿	Amtrak passenger rail routes

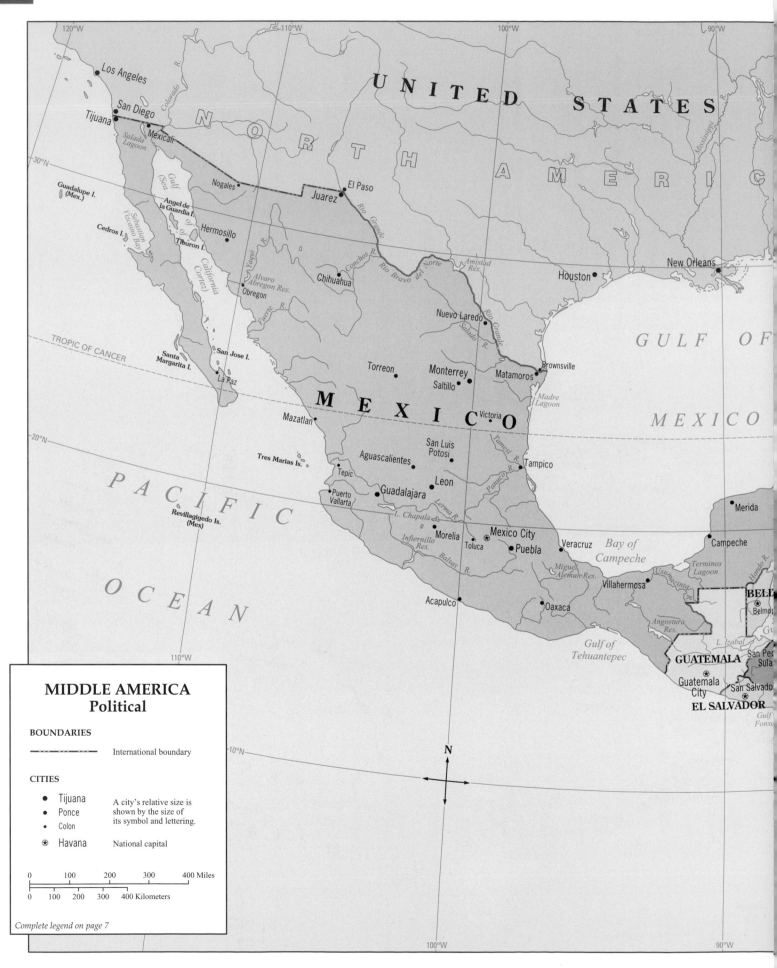

UNITED STATES

Los Angeles
San Diego
Tijuana
Mexicali
Salada Lagoon
Gulf (Sea)
Guadalupe I. (Mex.)
Nogales
El Paso
Juarez
Angel de la Guardia I.
Hermosillo
Cedros I.
Sebastian Vizcaino Bay
Tiburon I.
Alvaro Abregon Res.
Obregon
Chihuahua
Rio Grande
Rio Bravo del Norte
Amistad Res.
Houston
New Orleans
Santa Margarita I.
San Jose I.
La Paz
Nuevo Laredo
Salado R.
Rio Grande
GULF OF
TROPIC OF CANCER
Torreon
Monterrey
Saltillo
Matamoros
Brownsville
Madre Lagoon
MEXICO
Victoria
MEXICO
Mazatlan
San Luis Potosi
Tres Marias Is.
Aguascalientes
Tepic
Leon
Tampico
Puerto Vallarta
Guadalajara
L. Chapala
Lerma R.
Panuco R.
Revillagigedo Is. (Mex.)
Infiernillo Res.
Morelia
Toluca
Mexico City
Puebla
Veracruz
Merida
Bay of Campeche
Campeche
PACIFIC
Balsas R.
Miguel Aleman Res.
Terminos Lagoon
Villahermosa
Usumacinta R.
Hondo R.
OCEAN
Acapulco
Oaxaca
Angostura Res.
BELI
Belmop
L. Izabal
Gulf of Tehuantepec
GUATEMALA
San Pe Sula
Guatemala City
San Salvador
EL SALVADOR
Gulf Fonse

NORTH AMERICA

GULF OF MEXICO

N

MIDDLE AMERICA
Political

BOUNDARIES

–––––––––––– International boundary

CITIES

● Tijuana

● Ponce   A city's relative size is

• Colon   shown by the size of
      its symbol and lettering.

⊛ Havana   National capital

| 0 | 100 | 200 | 300 | 400 Miles |

| 0 | 100 | 200 | 300 | 400 Kilometers |

Complete legend on page 7

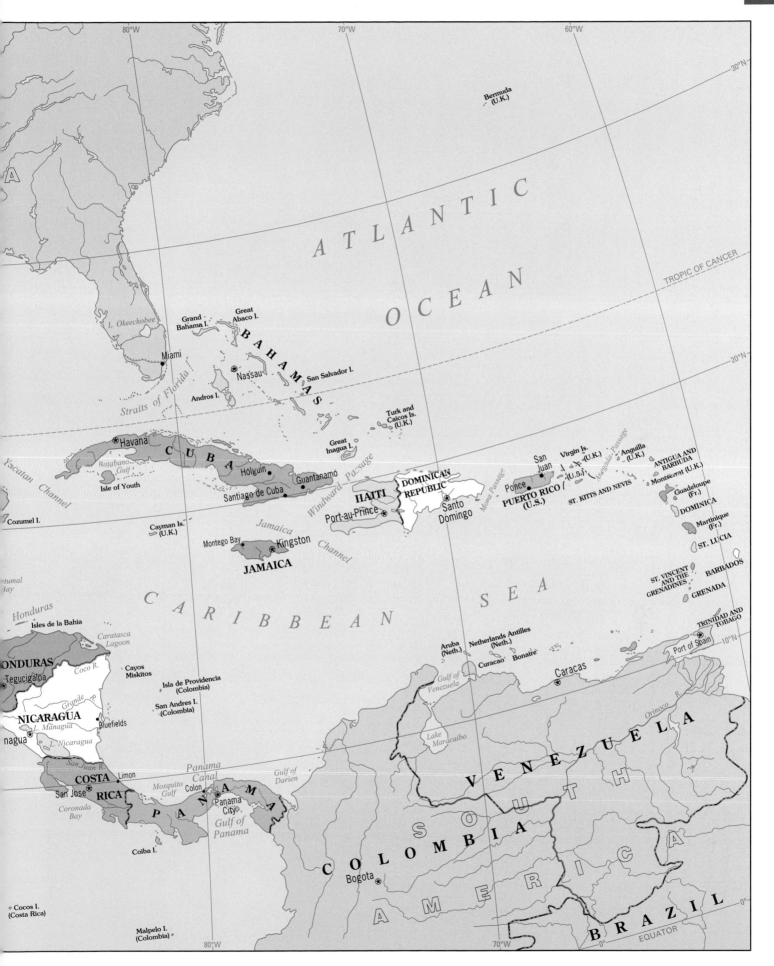

ATLANTIC

OCEAN

TROPIC OF CANCER

Bermuda
(U.K.)

30°N

20°N

L. Okeechobee

Grand
Bahama I.

Great
Abaco I.

Miami

B
A
H
A
M
A
S

Nassau

San Salvador I.

Straits of Florida

Andros I.

Turk and
Caicos Is.
(U.K.)

Yucatan Channel

Havana

C U B A

*Batabano
Gulf*

Holguin

Isle of Youth

Santiago de Cuba

Guantanamo

Great
Inagua I.

Windward Passage

Cozumel I.

Cayman Is.
(U.K.)

*Jamaica
Channel*

Montego Bay

Kingston

JAMAICA

HAITI

Port-au-Prince

DOMINICAN
REPUBLIC

Santo
Domingo

Mona Passage

San
Juan

Ponce

PUERTO RICO
(U.S.)

Virgin Is.
(U.K.)
(U.S.)

Anegada Passage

Anguilla
(U.K.)

ANTIGUA AND
BARBUDA

Montserrat (U.K.)

ST. KITTS AND NEVIS

Guadeloupe
(Fr.)

DOMINICA

Martinique
(Fr.)

ST. LUCIA

ST. VINCENT
AND THE
GRENADINES

BARBADOS

GRENADA

*Portumal
Bay*

Honduras

Isles de la Bahia

*Caratasca
Lagoon*

C A R I B B E A N   S E A

HONDURAS

Tegucigalpa

Coco R.

Cayos
Miskitos

Isla de Providencia
(Colombia)

San Andres I.
(Colombia)

Grande

NICARAGUA

L. Managua

nagua

Bluefields

L. Nicaragua

San Juan R.

COSTA

Limon

RICA

San Jose

PANAMA

Colon

Panama
Canal

*Mosquito
Gulf*

Gulf of
Darien

Aruba
(Neth.)

Netherlands Antilles
(Neth.)

Curacao

Bonaire

Caracas

Gulf of
Venezuela

TRINIDAD AND
TOBAGO

Port of Spain

10°N

V E N E Z U E L A

Lake
Maracaibo

Orinoco R.

*Coronada
Bay*

Panama
City

Gulf of
Panama

Coiba I.

C O L O M B I A

S
O
U
T
H

A
M
E
R
I
C
A

Bogota

B R A Z I L

Cocos I.
(Costa Rica)

Malpelo I.
(Colombia)

EQUATOR

0°

80°W

70°W

60°W

80°W

70°W

0°

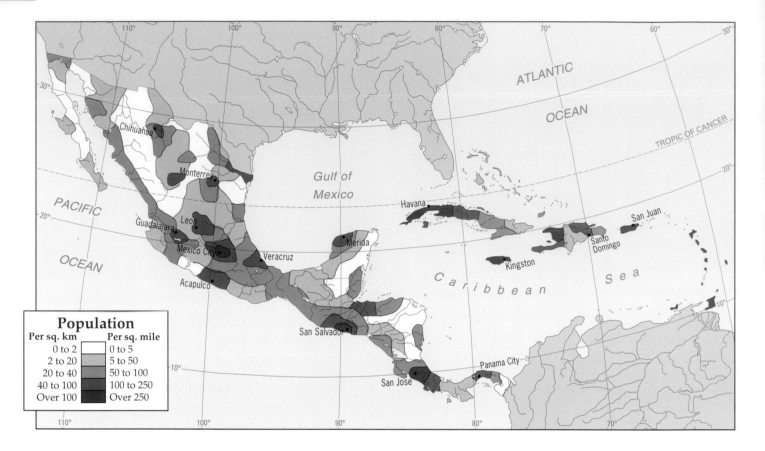

Population

Per sq. km	Per sq. mile
0 to 2	0 to 5
2 to 20	5 to 50
20 to 40	50 to 100
40 to 100	100 to 250
Over 100	Over 250

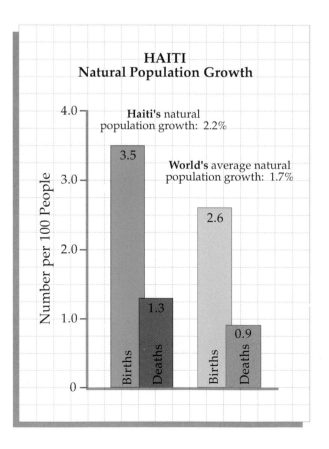

HAITI
Natural Population Growth

Haiti's natural population growth: 2.2%

World's average natural population growth: 1.7%

Number per 100 People

3.5 Births
1.3 Deaths
2.6 Births
0.9 Deaths

MEXICO
Balance of Trade

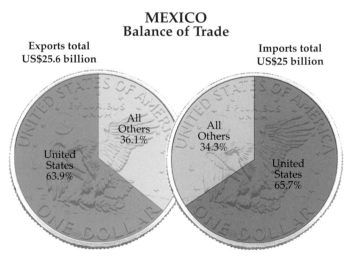

Exports total US$25.6 billion

All Others 36.1%

United States 63.9%

Imports total US$25 billion

All Others 34.3%

United States 65.7%

Mexico City's Population Growth

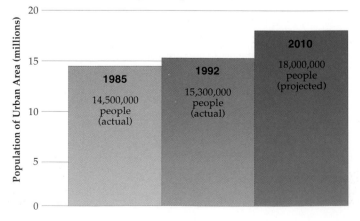

Population of Urban Area (millions)

1985 14,500,000 people (actual)

1992 15,300,000 people (actual)

2010 18,000,000 people (projected)

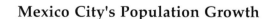

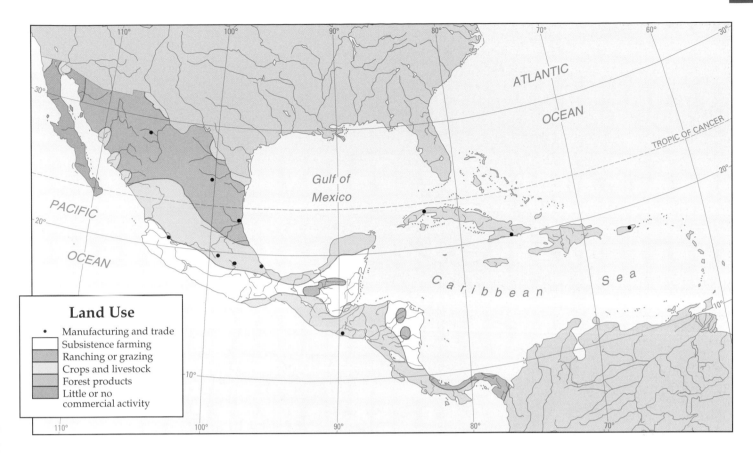

Land Use

- Manufacturing and trade
- Subsistence farming
- Ranching or grazing
- Crops and livestock
- Forest products
- Little or no commercial activity

NICARAGUA
Balance of Trade

Exports total
US$287 million

European Union
21.8%

All Others
60.9%

United States
17.3%

Imports total
US$708 million

United States
22.2%

All Others
67.7%

Russia
10.1%

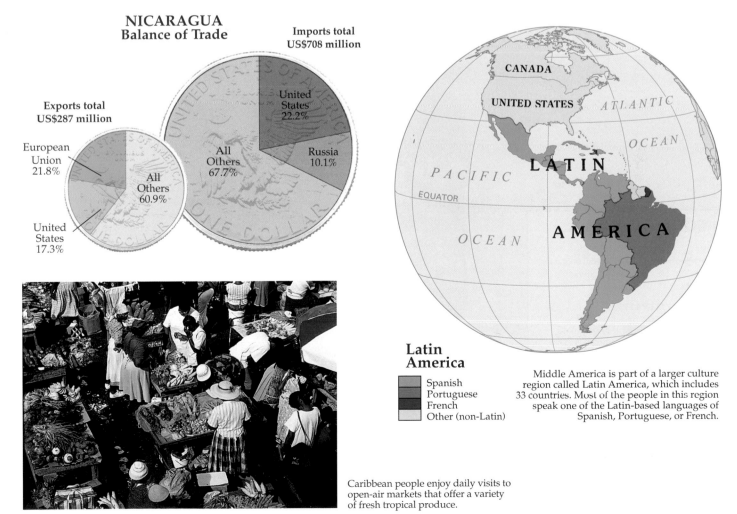

Latin America

- Spanish
- Portuguese
- French
- Other (non-Latin)

Middle America is part of a larger culture region called Latin America, which includes 33 countries. Most of the people in this region speak one of the Latin-based languages of Spanish, Portuguese, or French.

Caribbean people enjoy daily visits to open-air markets that offer a variety of fresh tropical produce.

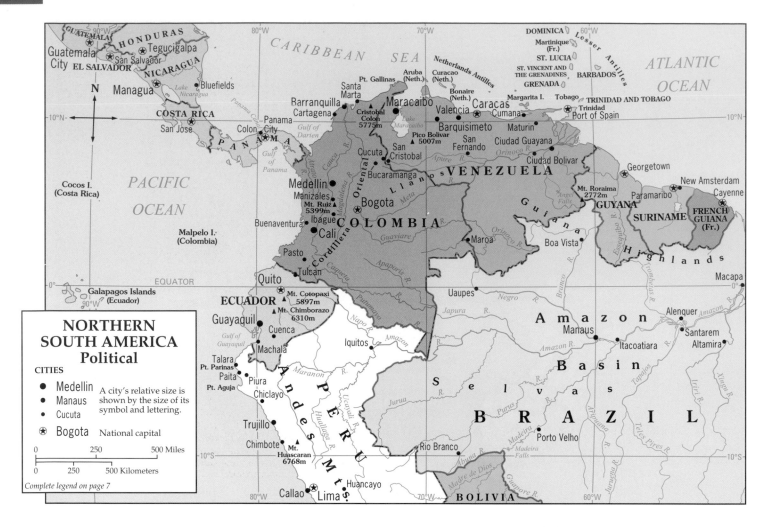

NORTHERN SOUTH AMERICA Political

CITIES

● Medellin — A city's relative size is
● Manaus — shown by the size of its
• Cucuta — symbol and lettering.

⊛ Bogota — National capital

0   250   500 Miles
0   250   500 Kilometers

Complete legend on page 7

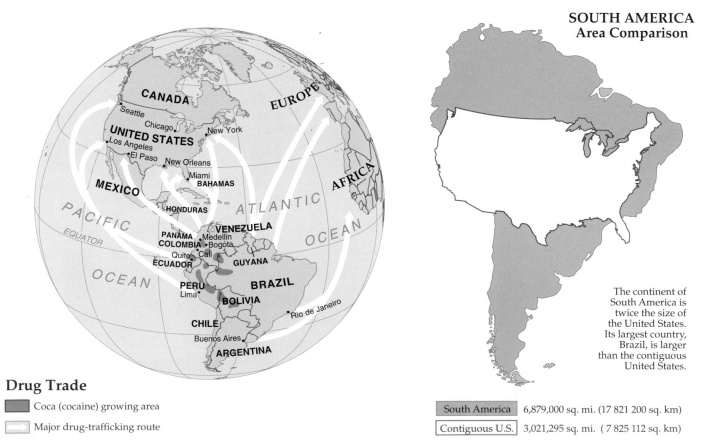

Drug Trade

▨ Coca (cocaine) growing area

▢ Major drug-trafficking route

SOUTH AMERICA
Area Comparison

The continent of
South America is
twice the size of
the United States.
Its largest country,
Brazil, is larger
than the contiguous
United States.

South America	6,879,000 sq. mi. (17 821 200 sq. km)
Contiguous U.S.	3,021,295 sq. mi. (7 825 112 sq. km)

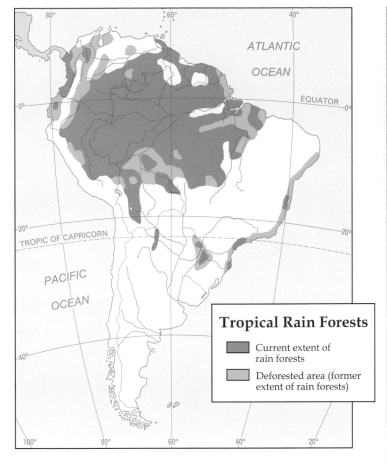

Tropical Rain Forests

- Current extent of rain forests
- Deforested area (former extent of rain forests)

Brazil's economic development often comes at the expense of the Amazon rain forest. Deforestation increases annually as trees are cut down to make way for farms and highways.

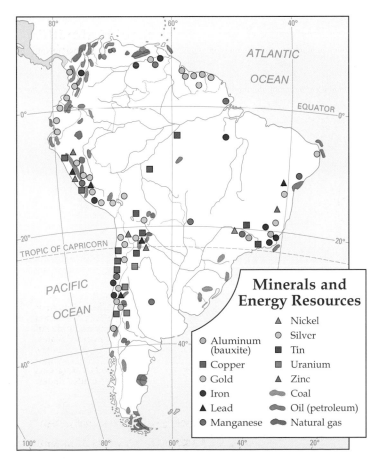

Minerals and Energy Resources

- Aluminum (bauxite)
- Copper
- Gold
- Iron
- Lead
- Manganese
- Nickel
- Silver
- Tin
- Uranium
- Zinc
- Coal
- Oil (petroleum)
- Natural gas

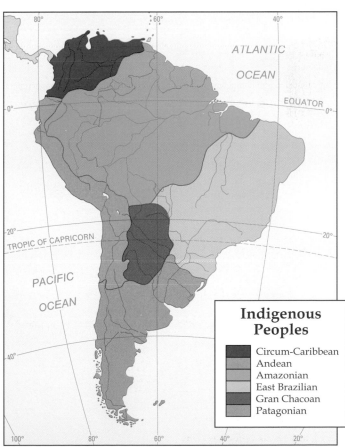

Indigenous Peoples

- Circum-Caribbean
- Andean
- Amazonian
- East Brazilian
- Gran Chacoan
- Patagonian

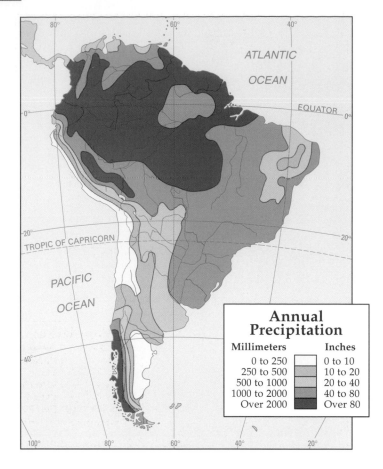

Annual Precipitation

Millimeters	Inches
0 to 250	0 to 10
250 to 500	10 to 20
500 to 1000	20 to 40
1000 to 2000	40 to 80
Over 2000	Over 80

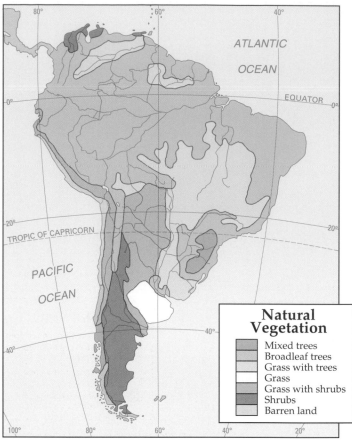

Natural Vegetation

Mixed trees
Broadleaf trees
Grass with trees
Grass
Grass with shrubs
Shrubs
Barren land

Brazil's urban population is a diverse mixture of European, African, and Indian ancestry.

VENEZUELA
Balance of Trade

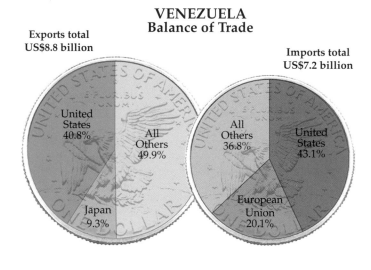

Exports total
US$8.8 billion

United States 40.8%
All Others 49.9%
Japan 9.3%

Imports total
US$7.2 billion

All Others 36.8%
United States 43.1%
European Union 20.1%

Cross Section of South America

ELEVATION

Meters	Feet
Over 6000	Over 20,000
3000 to 6000	10,000 to 20,000
1500 to 3000	5,000 to 10,000
600 to 1500	2,000 to 5,000
300 to 600	1,000 to 2,000
150 to 300	500 to 1,000
0 to 150	0 to 500
Below sea level	Below sea level

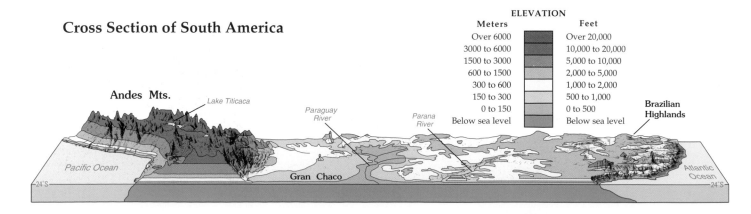

Andes Mts.
Lake Titicaca
Paraguay River
Parana River
Brazilian Highlands
Pacific Ocean
Gran Chaco
Atlantic Ocean

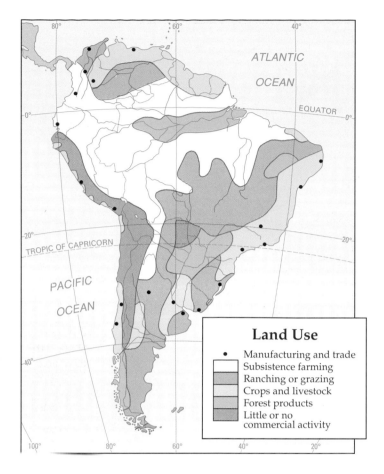

Land Use

- • Manufacturing and trade
- Subsistence farming
- Ranching or grazing
- Crops and livestock
- Forest products
- Little or no commercial activity

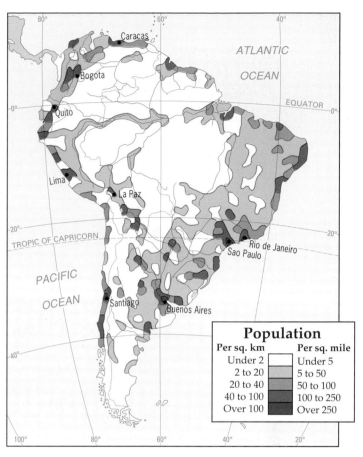

Population

Per sq. km	Per sq. mile
Under 2	Under 5
2 to 20	5 to 50
20 to 40	50 to 100
40 to 100	100 to 250
Over 100	Over 250

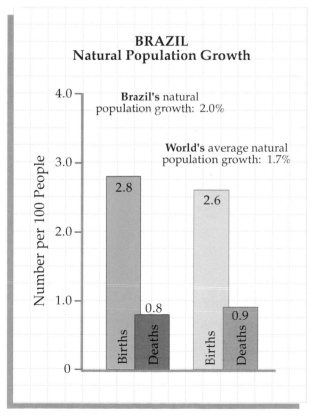

BRAZIL
Natural Population Growth

Brazil's natural population growth: 2.0%

World's average natural population growth: 1.7%

Number per 100 People

- 4.0
- 3.0
- 2.8 Births
- 2.6 Births
- 2.0
- 1.0
- 0.8 Deaths
- 0.9 Deaths
- 0

CHILE
Balance of Trade

Exports total US$6.9 billion

Imports total US$5.3 billion

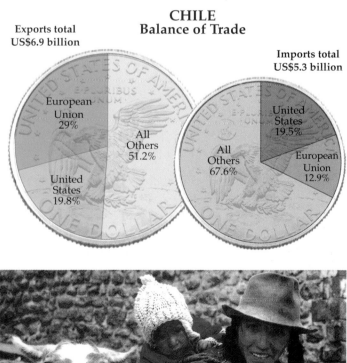

European Union 29%
United States 19.8%
All Others 51.2%

United States 19.5%
European Union 12.9%
All Others 67.6%

More Indians live in Peru than in any other South American country. Many still farm and bring goods to market in the highlands where their ancestors, the Incas, once reigned.

EUROPE
Political

BOUNDARIES

——————————— International boundary

——·——·——·—— Internal boundary

- - - - - - - - - - Other boundary
(disputed or undefined)

CITIES

● Barcelona   A city's relative size is
● Glasgow   shown by the size of
· Constanta   its symbol and lettering.

⊛ Moscow   National capital

0   100   200   300   400   500 Miles
0 100 200 300 400 500 Kilometers

Complete legend on page 7

OCEAN

Barents Sea

Novaya Zemlya

Kolguyev I.

mmerfest

Vardo

L. Inari

Kiruna

Murmansk

White Sea

Arkhangelsk

Syktyvkar

RUSSIA

Oulu

FINLAND

Vaasa

L. Saimaa

L. Onega

Onega R.

Northern Dvina R.

Sukhona R.

Ob R.

Pechora R.

Tampere

Turku

Helsinki

Gulf of Finland

Lake Ladoga

St. Petersburg
(Leningrad)

Tallinn

ESTONIA

L. Peipus

Pskov

Riga

LATVIA

LITHUANIA

Neman R.

Vilnius

Minsk

BELARUS

Pripyat
Marshes

Pripyat R.

Bug R.

Chernobyl

Kiev

Lviv

UKRAINE

Dnepr R.

Kharkiv

Donets R.

Donetsk

Dnipropetrovsk

MOLDOVA

Chisinau

Cluj-Napoca

Dnestr R.

Prut R.

OMANIA

Bucharest

Danube

Odessa

Sea of Azov

Kerch

Novorossiysk

Sevastopol

Constanta

Varna

Sofia

BULGARIA

Plovdiv

Black Sea

Bosporus

E

alonika

Dardanelles

Euboea

Athens

Crete (Greece)

SEA

Aegean Sea

Sea of Marmara

Istanbul

Ankara

L. Tuz

TURKEY

Nicosia

CYPRUS

LEBANON

SYRIA

IRAQ

Yaroslavl

Gorki
Res.

Rybinsk
Res.

Volga R.

Moscow

Nizhniy
Novgorod

Kazan

Vyatka R.

Kama R.

Ufa

Perm

Kamskoye
Res.

Kuybyshev
Res.

Samara

Oka R.

Tula

Bryansk

Orel

Voronezh

Saratov

Volgograd
Res.

Volgograd

Don R.

Rostov-na-Donu

Krasnodar

Astrakhan

Volga R. Delta

Grozny

GEORGIA

Tbilisi

ARMENIA

Yerevan

AZERBAIJAN

Baku

Lake
Van

Lake Urmia

Tehran

IRAN

Orenburg

Ural R.

Oral

KAZAKHSTAN

A S I A

Syr Darya

Aral
Sea

UZBEKISTAN

Amu Darya

TURKMENISTAN

Ashgabat

Caspian Sea

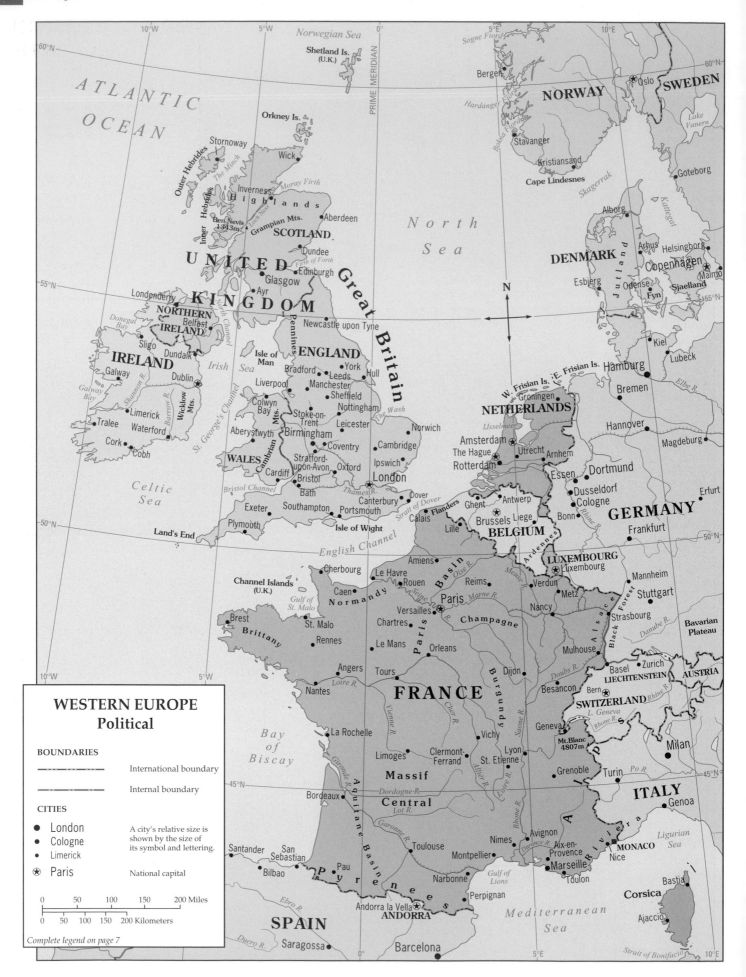

WESTERN EUROPE
Political

BOUNDARIES

———————— International boundary

———————— Internal boundary

CITIES

● London

• Cologne

· Limerick

⍟ Paris   National capital

A city's relative size is shown by the size of its symbol and lettering.

0   50   100   150   200 Miles

0 50 100 150 200 Kilometers

Complete legend on page 7

**CENTRAL EUROPE
Political**

BOUNDARIES

International boundary

Internal boundary
(republic or territory)

CITIES

● Milan

● Leipzig

• Salzburg

⊛ Warsaw

A city's relative size is
shown by the size of its
symbol and lettering.

National capital

0   50   100   150   200 Miles

0   50 100 150 200 Kilometers

Complete legend on page 7

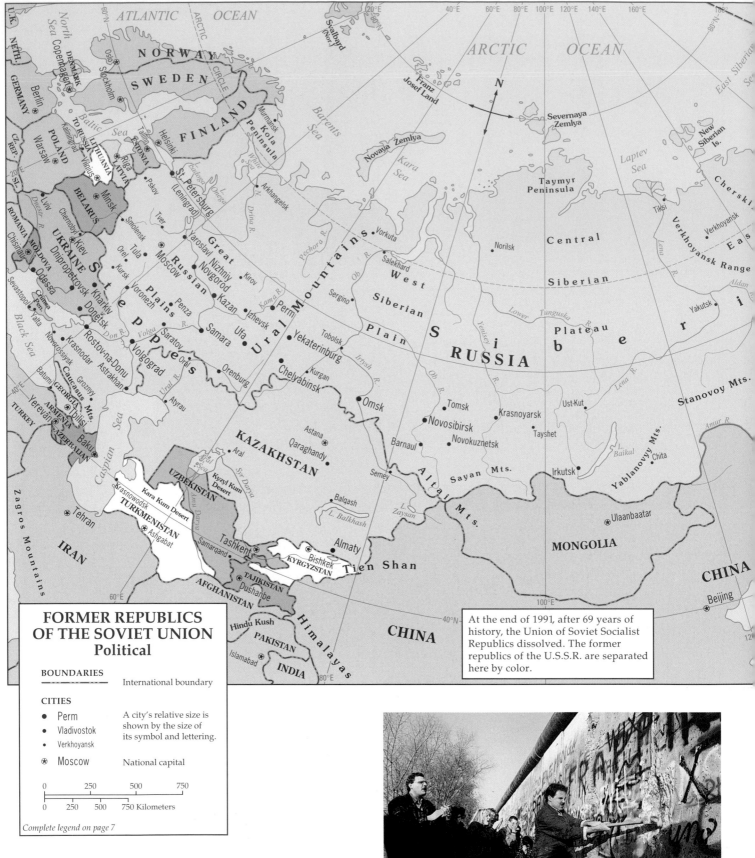

ATLANTIC OCEAN

ARCTIC OCEAN

U.K.
NETH.
GERMANY
North Sea
Copenhagen
DENMARK
Berlin
CZ. REP.
SL.
POLAND
Warsaw
Baltic Sea
TO RUSSIA
Kaliningrad
LITHUANIA
Vilnius
Oslo
Stockholm
NORWAY
SWEDEN
FINLAND
Helsinki
Tallinn
ESTONIA
Riga
LATVIA
Pskov
BELARUS
Minsk
Smolensk
St. Petersburg (Leningrad)
Murmansk
Kola Peninsula
Arkhangelsk
White Sea
Barents Sea
Svalbard (Nor.)
Novaya Zemlya
Kara Sea
Franz Josef Land
N
Severnaya Zemlya
ARCTIC OCEAN
East Siberian
New Siberian Is.
Taymyr Peninsula
Laptev Sea
Cherski
Tiksi
Verkhoyansk
Verkhoyansk Range
E a s

ROMANIA
Chişinău
MOLDOVA
Odessa
UKRAINE
Kiev
Lviv
Chernobyl
Dnipropetrovsk
Kharkiv
Donetsk
Sevastopol
Crimea
Yalta
Black Sea
Novorossiysk
Krasnodar
Rostov-na-Donu
Batumi
GEORGIA
Tbilisi
Grozny
Caucasus Mts.
ARMENIA
Yerevan
AZERBAIJAN
Baku
TURKEY
Dniester
Dnipro R.
Odessa
Tula
Orel
Kursk
Voronezh
Penza
Moscow
Yaroslavl
Nizhniy Novgorod
Kazan
Izhevsk
Samara
Saratov
Volgograd
Astrakhan
Volga
Don
Great Russian Plains
S t e p p e s
Ufa
Perm
Kirov
Kama R.
Ural Mountains
Ural R.
Atyrau
Caspian Sea
Orenburg
Yekaterinburg
Chelyabinsk
Kurgan
Tobolsk
Irtysh R.
Omsk
Astana
Qaraghandy
KAZAKHSTAN
Aral
Aral
Kyzyl Kum Desert
Syr Darya
Amu Darya
UZBEKISTAN
Tashkent
Samarqand
Kara Kum Desert
Krasnowodsk
TURKMENISTAN
Ashgabat
IRAN
Tehran
Zagros Mountains
Balqash
L. Balkhash
L. Zaysan
Almaty
Bishkek
KYRGYZSTAN
TAJIKISTAN
Dushanbe
Tien Shan
AFGHANISTAN
Hindu Kush
Himalayas
PAKISTAN
Islamabad
INDIA
Sergino
Salekhard
Vorkuta
Pechora R.
West Siberian Plain
Ob R.
Ob R.
Yenisey
Norilsk
Central Siberian Plateau
RUSSIA
Lower Tunguska
Aldan R.
Yakutsk
Lena R.
Tomsk
Novosibirsk
Barnaul
Novokuznetsk
Semey
Krasnoyarsk
Tayshet
Ust-Kut
Irkutsk
Chita
L. Baikal
Sayan Mts.
Altai Mts.
Yablonovyy Mts.
Stanovoy Mts.
Amur R.
Ulaanbaatar
MONGOLIA
CHINA
Beijing
CHINA
S i b e r i

Complete legend on page 7

FORMER REPUBLICS OF THE SOVIET UNION
Political

BOUNDARIES

International boundary

CITIES

● Perm

● Vladivostok

· Verkhoyansk

⊛ Moscow — National capital

A city's relative size is shown by the size of its symbol and lettering.

0 250 500 750

0 250 500 750 Kilometers

At the end of 1991, after 69 years of history, the Union of Soviet Socialist Republics dissolved. The former republics of the U.S.S.R. are separated here by color.

In November 1989, Germans tore down the Berlin Wall. It was an event that symbolized the collapse of over 40 years of Communist rule in Eastern Europe.

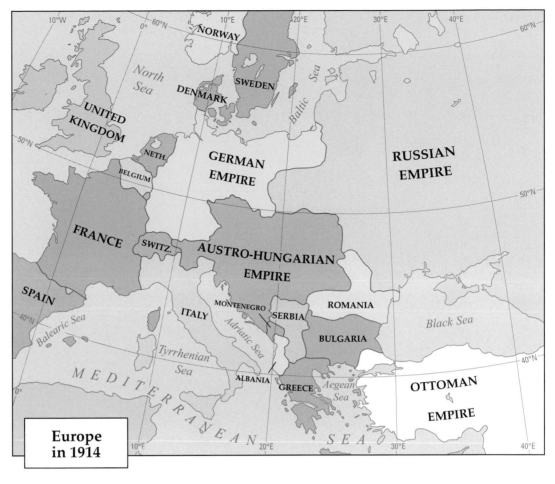

Europe in 1914

Twentieth-century Europe has seen radical changes in governments and boundaries. World War I brought the break-up of imperialistic monarchies and the formation of new, smaller states. Some of these, like Czechoslovakia, acquired democratic governments only to fall to Communism after World War II. Then, between 1989 and 1992, all the Communist governments of Europe were overthrown, and again new nations were formed.

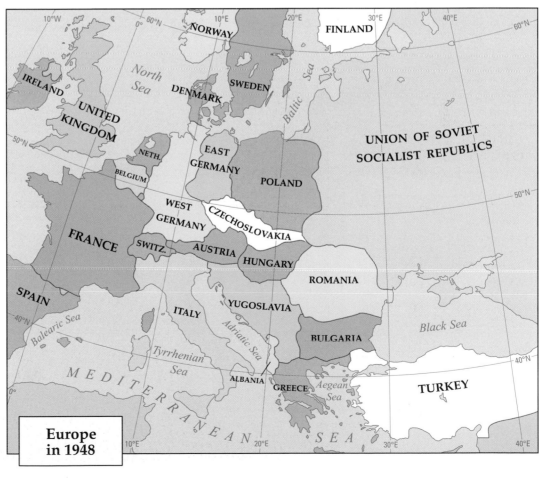

Europe in 1948

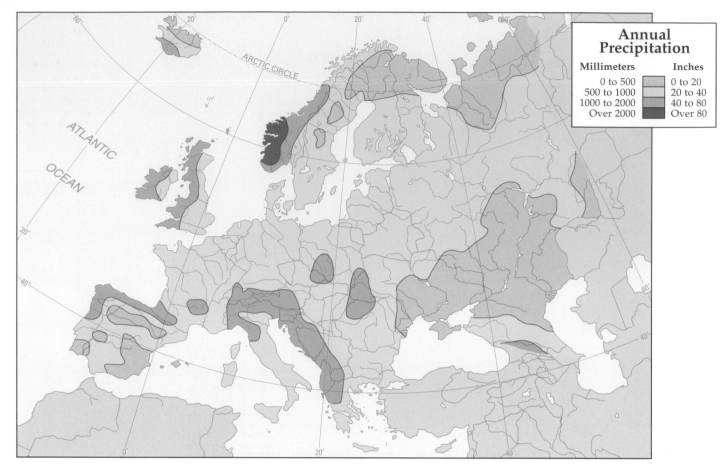

Annual Precipitation

Millimeters
0 to 500
500 to 1000
1000 to 2000
Over 2000

Inches
0 to 20
20 to 40
40 to 80
Over 80

Sources of Electrical Energy

Each country's position on the triangle shows its relative reliance on three sources of electrical energy. For example, Hungary gets about as much electricity from fossil fuel as from nuclear power and none from hydroelectricity.

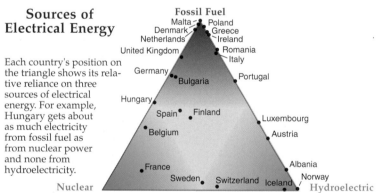

Fossil Fuel
Malta
Denmark
Netherlands
United Kingdom
Germany
Bulgaria
Hungary
Spain
Belgium
Finland
France
Sweden
Switzerland
Iceland
Nuclear
Poland
Greece
Ireland
Romania
Italy
Portugal
Luxembourg
Austria
Albania
Norway
Hydroelectric

EUROPE Area Comparison

Although the entire continent of Europe is larger than the United States, the British Isles are smaller than America's Great Basin.

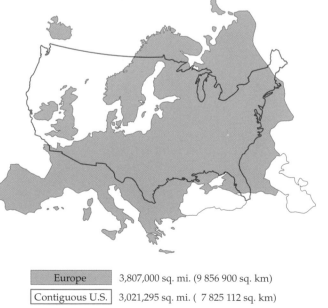

| Europe | 3,807,000 sq. mi. (9 856 900 sq. km) |
| Contiguous U.S. | 3,021,295 sq. mi. (7 825 112 sq. km) |

The Alps are an important region for farming and industry as well as a major tourist attraction. Railways crisscross the mountains that were a barrier to travel for centuries.

Vienna, Austria's capital, is the most prosperous city in Central Europe. Austria stands at the crossroads between former Communist states and democratically governed countries.

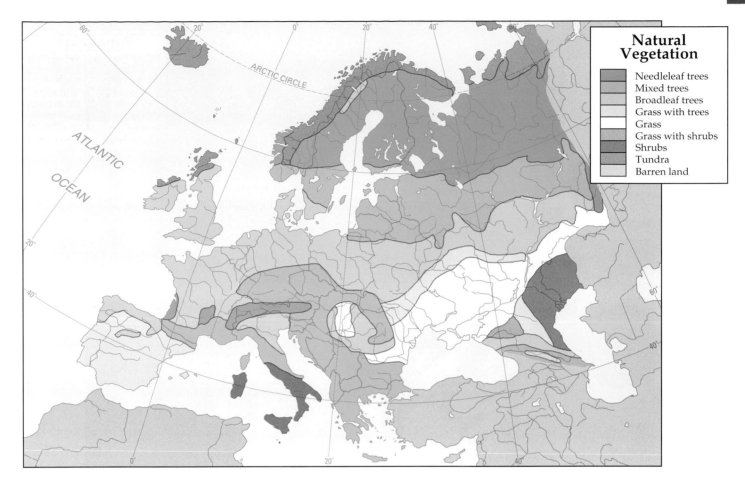

Natural Vegetation
- Needleleaf trees
- Mixed trees
- Broadleaf trees
- Grass with trees
- Grass
- Grass with shrubs
- Shrubs
- Tundra
- Barren land

ARCTIC CIRCLE

ATLANTIC OCEAN

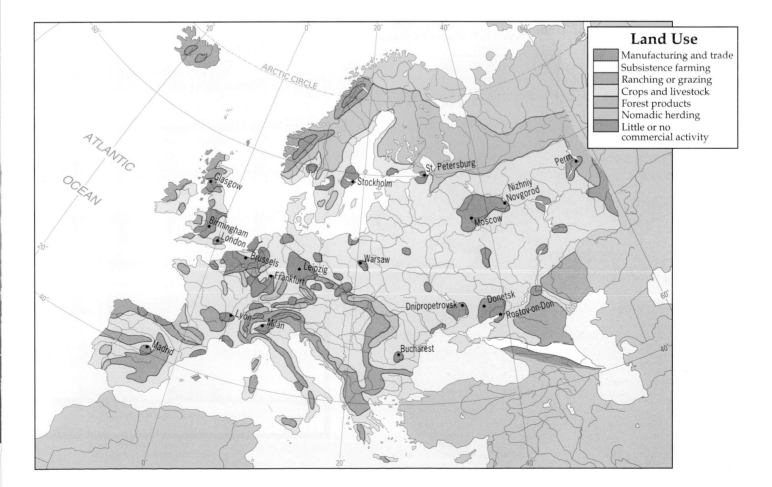

Land Use
- Manufacturing and trade
- Subsistence farming
- Ranching or grazing
- Crops and livestock
- Forest products
- Nomadic herding
- Little or no commercial activity

ARCTIC CIRCLE

ATLANTIC OCEAN

Glasgow
Birmingham
London
Brussels
Leipzig
Frankfurt
Lyon
Milan
Madrid
Stockholm
St. Petersburg
Perm
Nizhniy Novgorod
Moscow
Warsaw
Dnipropetrovsk
Donetsk
Rostov-on-Don
Bucharest

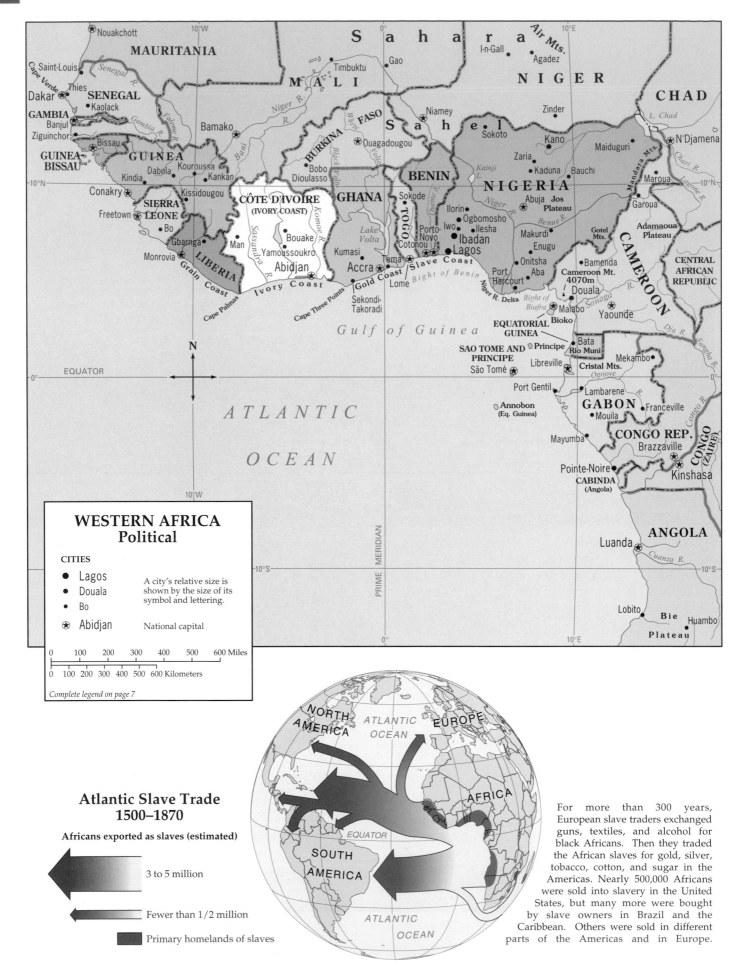

MAURITANIA

Nouakchott

S a h a r a

Air Mts.

I-n-Gall

Agadez

N I G E R

CHAD

L. Chad

Cape Verde
Saint-Louis
Senegal R.
Thies
Dakar
SENEGAL
Kaolack
GAMBIA
Banjul
Ziguinchor
GUINEA-
BISSAU
Bissau
GUINEA
Kindia
Conakry
Dabola
Kankan
Kissidougou
SIERRA
LEONE
Freetown
Bo
Gbarnga
Man
Monrovia
LIBERIA
Grain Coast
Cape Palmas
Ivory Coast
Cape Three Points

Timbuktu
Gao
M A L I
BURKINA FASO
Niger R.
Bani
Bamako
Kouroussa
Bobo Dioulasso
Ouagadougou

Niamey
White Volta
Black Volta
S a h e l
Sokoto
Zinder
Kano
Zaria
Kaduna
Maiduguri
N'Djamena
Chari R.
Mandara Mts.
Bauchi
Maroua

CÔTE D'IVOIRE
(IVORY COAST)
GHANA
Sokode
BENIN
TOGO
Sassandra R.
Bouake
Komoe R.
Yamoussoukro
Abidjan
Kumasi
Accra
Tema
Gold Coast
Sekondi-Takoradi

Lake Volta
Oueme R.
Porto-Novo
Cotonou
Lome
Slave Coast
Bight of Benin

Ilorin
Iwo
Ogbomosho
Ilesha
Ibadan
Lagos
Abuja
Jos Plateau
Kainji L.
Niger R.
NIGERIA
Benue R.
Makurdi
Enugu
Onitsha
Aba
Port Harcourt
Niger R. Delta
Bight of Biafra
Malabo
Bioko

Gotel Mts.
Adamaoua Plateau
CAMEROON
Cameroon Mt. 4070m
Douala
Sonaga
Yaounde
Dja R.
Sangha R.
CENTRAL
AFRICAN
REPUBLIC

Gulf of Guinea

EQUATORIAL
GUINEA
SAO TOME AND
PRINCIPE
São Tomé
Principe
Bata
Rio Muni
Libreville
Cristal Mts.
Mekambo
Ogooue R.

ATLANTIC

OCEAN

EQUATOR

Annobon
(Eq. Guinea)
Port Gentil
Lambarene
GABON
Mouila
Franceville
Mayumba
CONGO REP.
Brazzaville
Kinshasa
CONGO
(ZAIRE)
Pointe-Noire
CABINDA
(Angola)

ANGOLA
Luanda
Cuanza R.
Lobito
Bie
Plateau
Huambo

WESTERN AFRICA
Political

CITIES

● **Lagos**
● Douala   A city's relative size is shown by the size of its symbol and lettering.
• Bo
✪ Abidjan   National capital

0   100   200   300   400   500   600 Miles
0 100 200 300 400 500 600 Kilometers

Complete legend on page 7

Atlantic Slave Trade
1500–1870

Africans exported as slaves (estimated)

⬅ 3 to 5 million

⬅ Fewer than 1/2 million

⬛ Primary homelands of slaves

For more than 300 years, European slave traders exchanged guns, textiles, and alcohol for black Africans. Then they traded the African slaves for gold, silver, tobacco, cotton, and sugar in the Americas. Nearly 500,000 Africans were sold into slavery in the United States, but many more were bought by slave owners in Brazil and the Caribbean. Others were sold in different parts of the Americas and in Europe.

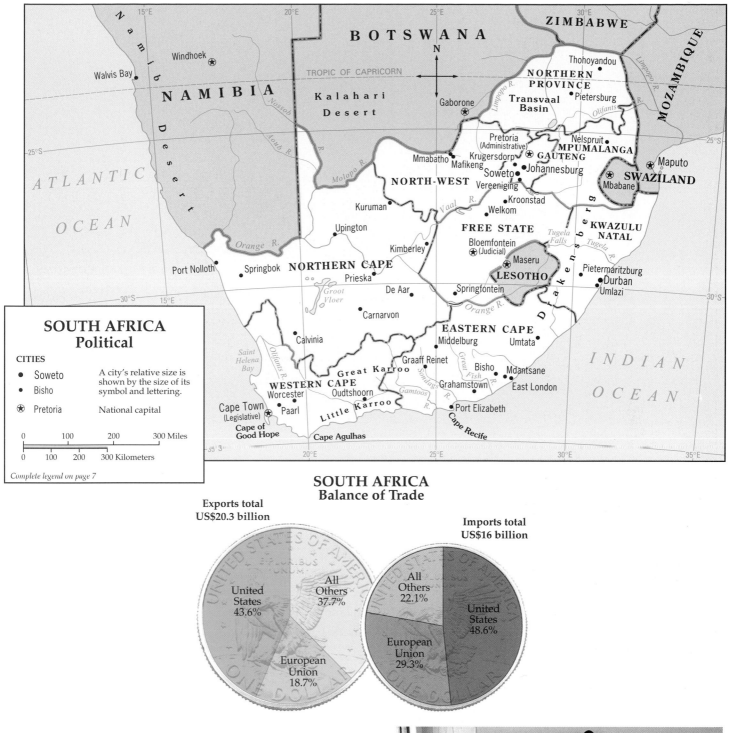

SOUTH AFRICA
Political

CITIES

- Soweto
- Bisho
- ✪ Pretoria

A city's relative size is shown by the size of its symbol and lettering.

National capital

0   100   200   300 Miles

0   100   200   300 Kilometers

Complete legend on page 7

SOUTH AFRICA
Balance of Trade

**Exports total
US$20.3 billion**

- United States 43.6%
- All Others 37.7%
- European Union 18.7%

**Imports total
US$16 billion**

- All Others 22.1%
- United States 48.6%
- European Union 29.3%

Ethnic Composition of South Africa

Other African ethnic groups include Setswana, Shangaan, Siswati, and others.

Europeans are primarily Dutch and British.

South Africa's total population: 39.1 million

- Sotho 15.4%
- Xhosa 18.1%
- African 76.4%
- Zulu 22%
- Asian 2.5%
- Mixed 8.5%
- European 12.6%
- Others 20.9%

With the end of legal apartheid in 1994, a new future lies ahead for the children of South Africa.

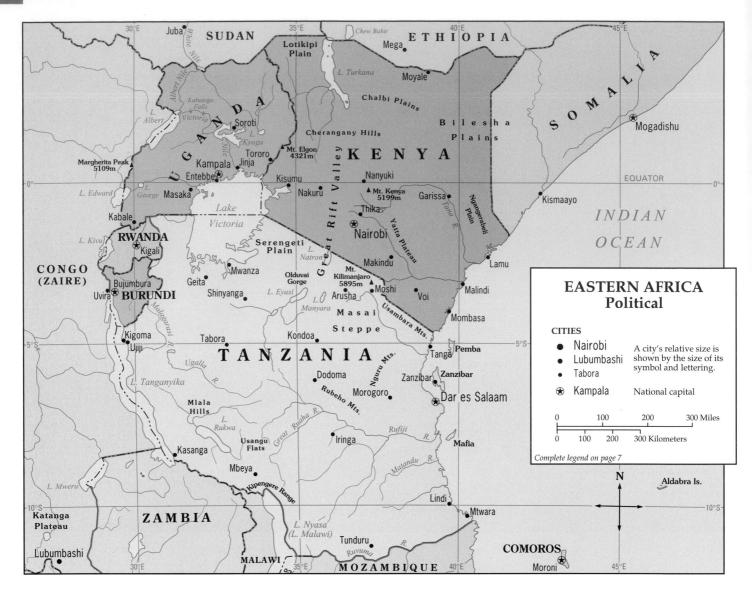

EASTERN AFRICA
Political

CITIES

● **Nairobi** — A city's relative size is shown by the size of its symbol and lettering.
● **Lubumbashi**
• **Tabora**

✪ **Kampala** — National capital

0 · · · 100 · · · 200 · · · 300 Miles
0 · 100 · 200 · 300 Kilometers

Complete legend on page 7

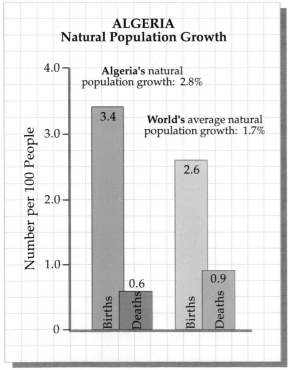

ALGERIA
Natural Population Growth

Algeria's natural population growth: 2.8%

World's average natural population growth: 1.7%

Number per 100 People

- 3.4 Births
- 0.6 Deaths
- 2.6 Births
- 0.9 Deaths

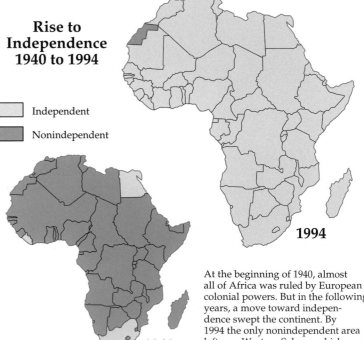

Rise to Independence
1940 to 1994

☐ Independent
■ Nonindependent

1994

1940

At the beginning of 1940, almost all of Africa was ruled by European colonial powers. But in the following years, a move toward independence swept the continent. By 1994 the only nonindependent area left was Western Sahara, which was controlled by Morocco.

Endangered Species

Present range of species

- Cheetah
- Black Rhinoceros
- Mountain Gorilla
- North African Ostrich

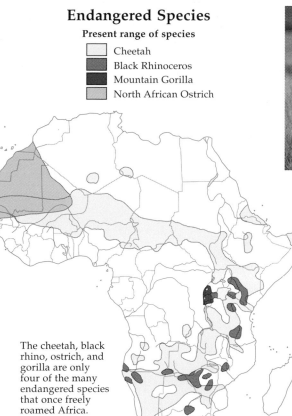

The cheetah, black rhino, ostrich, and gorilla are only four of the many endangered species that once freely roamed Africa.

The cheetah, a hunter of incredible speed, is losing both its habitat and prey to human encroachment into its territory.

The mountain gorilla leads a quiet life, living off forest vegetation. It has no real enemies except human beings.

The black rhinoceros lives on grassland and brush vegetation. Its distinctive horn makes it a target for poachers.

The flightless ostrich can roam the plains for long periods without water. Demand for its skin and plumes threaten its survival in the wild.

Ivory Trade

Annual exports

Kilograms		Pounds
More than 20 000		More than 44,000
10 000 to 20 000		22,000 to 44,000
Less than 10 000		Less than 22,000
None exported		
Not reported		

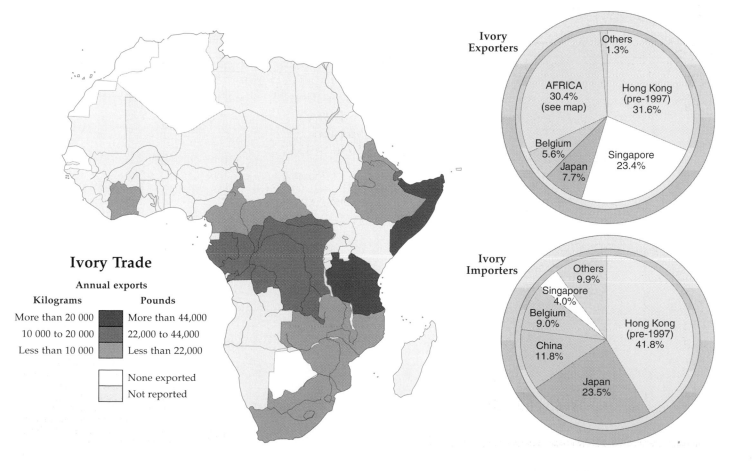

Ivory Exporters

- Others 1.3%
- Hong Kong (pre-1997) 31.6%
- AFRICA 30.4% (see map)
- Singapore 23.4%
- Belgium 5.6%
- Japan 7.7%

Ivory Importers

- Others 9.9%
- Singapore 4.0%
- Belgium 9.0%
- China 11.8%
- Hong Kong (pre-1997) 41.8%
- Japan 23.5%

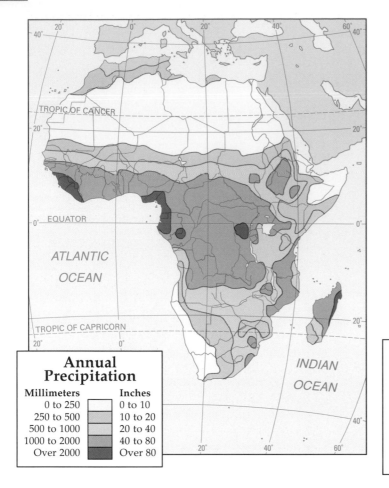

Annual Precipitation

Millimeters	Inches
0 to 250	0 to 10
250 to 500	10 to 20
500 to 1000	20 to 40
1000 to 2000	40 to 80
Over 2000	Over 80

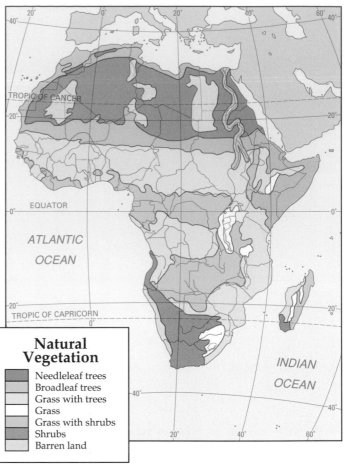

Natural Vegetation

Needleleaf trees
Broadleaf trees
Grass with trees
Grass
Grass with shrubs
Shrubs
Barren land

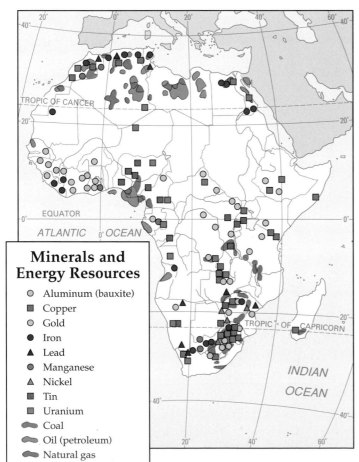

Minerals and Energy Resources

- Aluminum (bauxite)
- Copper
- Gold
- Iron
- Lead
- Manganese
- Nickel
- Tin
- Uranium
- Coal
- Oil (petroleum)
- Natural gas

A Moroccan market displays locally grown produce and handwoven carpets. Many Moroccans and other North Africans dress in traditional Islamic style.

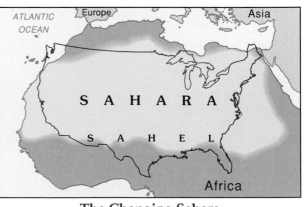

The Changing Sahara

The Sahara stretches across a greater area than the contiguous United States. During droughts it expands southward and in wet periods it shrinks back. Most recent years have been dry.

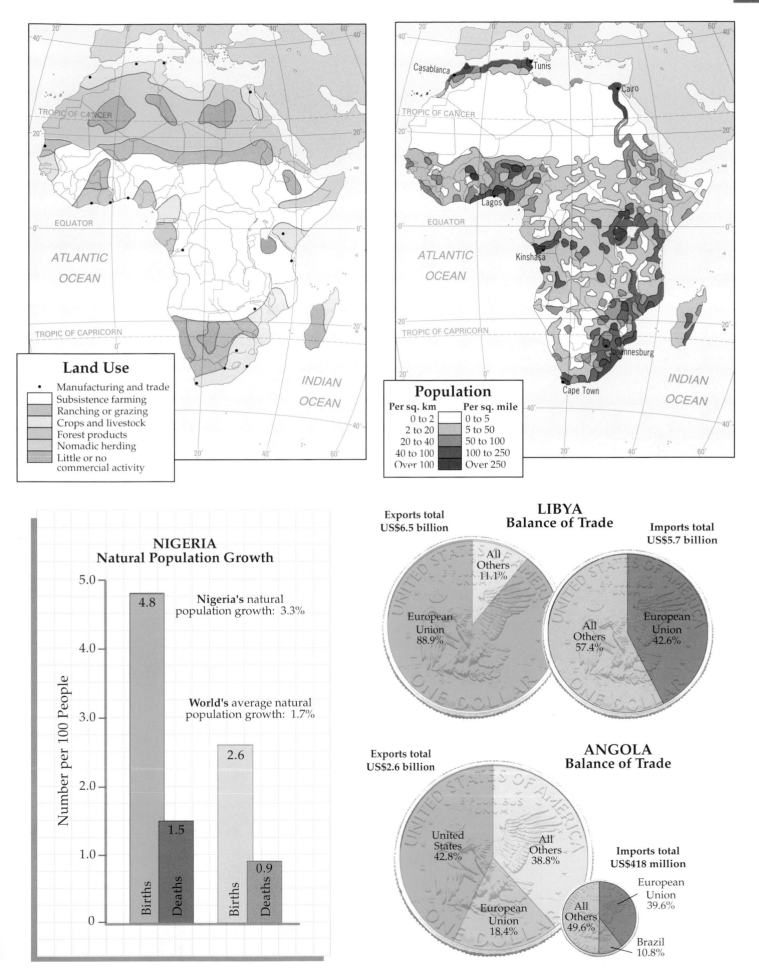

Land Use

- Manufacturing and trade
- Subsistence farming
- Ranching or grazing
- Crops and livestock
- Forest products
- Nomadic herding
- Little or no commercial activity

Population

Per sq. km	Per sq. mile
0 to 2	0 to 5
2 to 20	5 to 50
20 to 40	50 to 100
40 to 100	100 to 250
Over 100	Over 250

NIGERIA
Natural Population Growth

Nigeria's natural population growth: 3.3%

World's average natural population growth: 1.7%

Number per 100 People

5.0 — 4.8 Births — 1.5 Deaths
2.6 Births — 0.9 Deaths

LIBYA
Balance of Trade

Exports total US$6.5 billion
- European Union 88.9%
- All Others 11.1%

Imports total US$5.7 billion
- European Union 42.6%
- All Others 57.4%

ANGOLA
Balance of Trade

Exports total US$2.6 billion
- United States 42.8%
- All Others 38.8%
- European Union 18.4%

Imports total US$418 million
- European Union 39.6%
- All Others 49.6%
- Brazil 10.8%

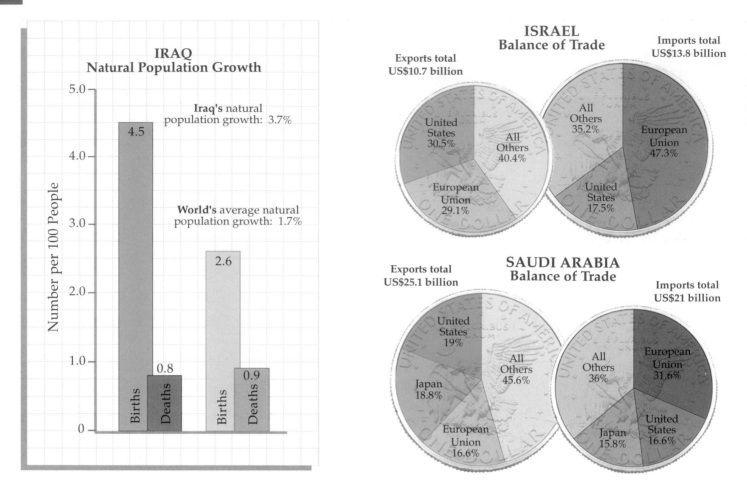

IRAQ
Natural Population Growth

Number per 100 People

Iraq's natural population growth: 3.7%

World's average natural population growth: 1.7%

4.5 — Births
0.8 — Deaths
2.6 — Births
0.9 — Deaths

ISRAEL
Balance of Trade

Exports total
US$10.7 billion

Imports total
US$13.8 billion

United States 30.5%
All Others 40.4%
European Union 29.1%

All Others 35.2%
European Union 47.3%
United States 17.5%

SAUDI ARABIA
Balance of Trade

Exports total
US$25.1 billion

Imports total
US$21 billion

United States 19%
All Others 45.6%
Japan 18.8%
European Union 16.6%

All Others 36%
European Union 31.6%
Japan 15.8%
United States 16.6%

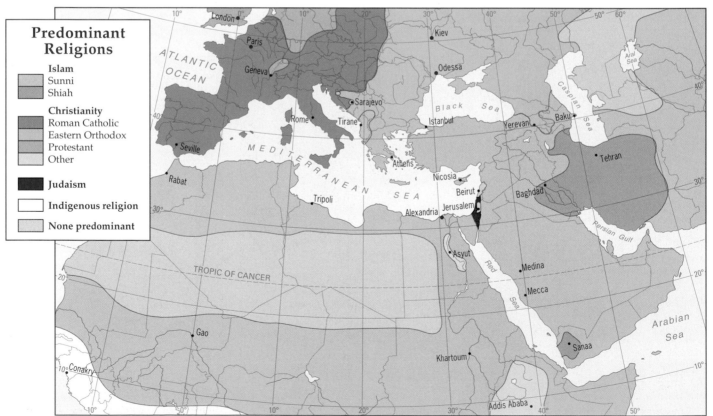

Predominant Religions

Islam
Sunni
Shiah

Christianity
Roman Catholic
Eastern Orthodox
Protestant
Other

Judaism

Indigenous religion

None predominant

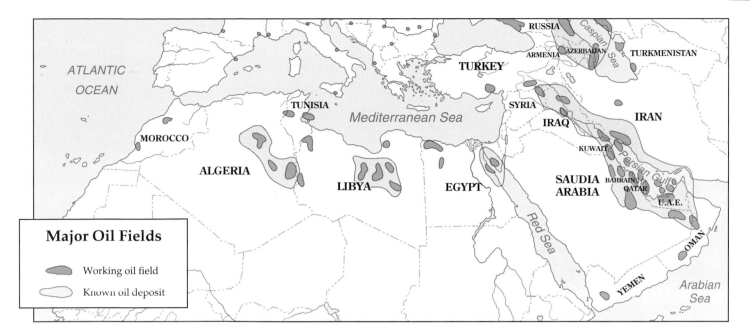

Major Oil Fields

Working oil field

Known oil deposit

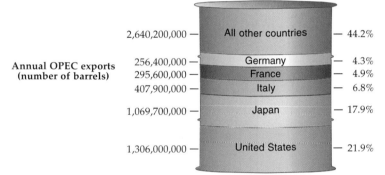

Annual OPEC exports (number of barrels)

2,640,200,000	All other countries	44.2%
256,400,000	Germany	4.3%
295,600,000	France	4.9%
407,900,000	Italy	6.8%
1,069,700,000	Japan	17.9%
1,306,000,000	United States	21.9%

Dependence on OPEC Oil

Japan and Italy import more than 80% of the oil they use from OPEC countries. The United States also relies on OPEC oil, but gets 73.5% of its oil from other sources.

Percentage of total OPEC exports

OPEC: Organization of Petroleum Exporting Countries

Changing Boundaries

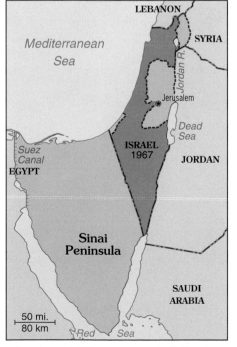

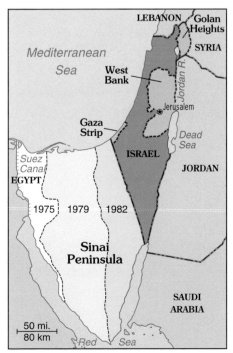

Israel occupied the area shown in dark orange until 1967. After the Six Day War of that year, it also controlled the parts of Egypt, Jordan, and Syria shown in light orange.

In stages during 1975, 1979, and 1982, Israel returned the Sinai Peninsula to Egypt. But Israel remained in control of the Gaza Strip, West Bank, and Golan Heights.

In 1993 Israeli and Palestinian leaders agreed on self-rule for Palestinians in Gaza and the city of Jericho. Jordan and Israel reached peace in 1994 and adjusted part of their boundary.

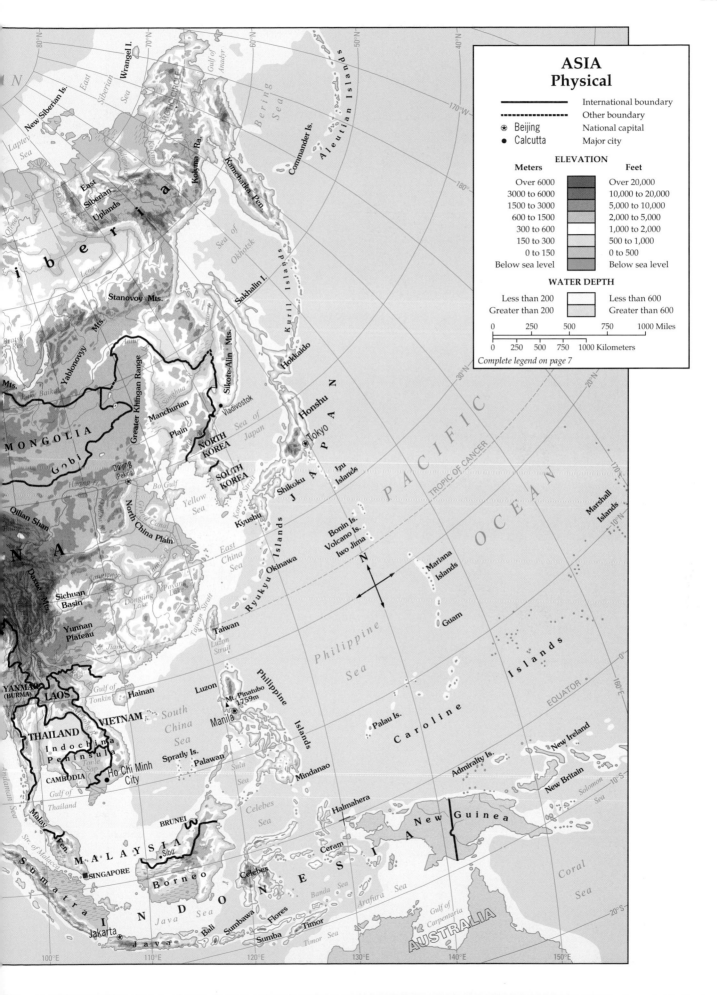

ASIA
Physical

International boundary
Other boundary
⊛ Beijing — National capital
● Calcutta — Major city

ELEVATION

Meters		Feet
Over 6000		Over 20,000
3000 to 6000		10,000 to 20,000
1500 to 3000		5,000 to 10,000
600 to 1500		2,000 to 5,000
300 to 600		1,000 to 2,000
150 to 300		500 to 1,000
0 to 150		0 to 500
Below sea level		Below sea level

WATER DEPTH

Less than 200		Less than 600
Greater than 200		Greater than 600

0   250   500   750   1000 Miles
0   250   500   750   1000 Kilometers

Complete legend on page 7

ARCTIC CIRCLE

New Siberian Is.
Wrangel I.
Laptev Sea
East Siberian Sea
Gulf of Anadyr
Olenek
East Siberian Uplands
S i b e r i a
Kolyma Ra.
Kamchatka Pen.
Bering Sea
Commander Is.
Aleutian Islands

Lena
Stanovoy Mts.
Bratsk Res.
Lake Baikal
Yablonovyy Mts.
Mts.
Amur
Greater Khingan Range
Sikote-Alin Mts.
Sakhalin I.
Sea of Okhotsk
Kuril Islands
Hokkaido

MONGOLIA
Gobi
Songhua
Manchurian Plain
Vladivostok
Sea of Japan
NORTH KOREA
SOUTH KOREA
Korea Strait
Honshu
Tokyo
J A P A N
Izu Islands

Beijing (Peking)
Huang He
Bo Gulf
Yellow Sea
Kyushu
Shikoku
Ryukyu Islands
Okinawa
Bonin Is.
Volcano Is.
Iwo Jima

Qilian Shan
North China Plain
Grand Canal
East China Sea
Yangtze
C H I N A
Sichuan Basin
Dongting Lake
Poyang Lake
Yunnan Plateau
Jiang
Taiwan
Luzon Strait
Taiwan Strait

P A C I F I C   O C E A N

TROPIC OF CANCER

Marshall Islands

Mariana Islands
Guam

N

Danu Mts.
MYANMAR (BURMA)
LAOS
VIETNAM
THAILAND
Gulf of Tonkin
Hainan
South China Sea
Luzon
Mt. Pinatubo 1759m
Manila
Philippine Islands
Philippine Sea

C a r o l i n e   I s l a n d s
Palau Is.

Indochina Peninsula
Tonle Sap
CAMBODIA
Ho Chi Minh City
Gulf of Thailand
Spratly Is.
Palawan
Sulu Sea
Mindanao

EQUATOR

Admiralty Is.
New Ireland
New Britain
Solomon Sea

Malay Pen.
Str. of Malacca
Andaman Sea
MALAYSIA
SINGAPORE
Sumatra
BRUNEI
Sibu
Borneo
Celebes Sea
Celebes
Ceram
Halmahera
New Guinea
I N D O N E S I A

Java Sea
Jakarta
Java
Bali
Sumbawa
Sumba
Flores
Timor
Banda Sea
Arafura Sea
Timor Sea
Gulf of Carpentaria
Coral Sea
AUSTRALIA

ASIA
Political

BOUNDARIES

———————————— International boundary

- - - - - - - - - - - Other boundary
(disputed or undefined)

CITIES

● Bombay

● Vladivostok   A city's relative size is
                     shown by the size of
∙ Mecca   its symbol and lettering.

⊛ Tokyo   National capital

```
0      250    500    750    1000 Miles
0   250  500  750  1000 Kilometers
```

Complete legend on page 7

New Siberian Is.

Wrangel I.

Laptev Sea

East Siberian Sea

Siberian Sea

ARCTIC CIRCLE

Gulf of Anadyr

ARCTIC CIRCLE

Aleutian Islands (U.S.)

Commander Is.

INTL. DATE LINE

Tiksi

Kolyma R.

Indigirka R.

Lena R.

Bering Sea

Petropavlovsk-Kamchatskiy

Magadan

Yakutsk

Lena R.

Sea of Okhotsk

Sakhalin I.

Kuril Islands (Russia)

Irkutsk   Chita

Lake Baikal

● Ulaanbaatar

MONGOLIA

Khabarovsk

Amur R.

Qiqihar

Harbin

Songhua R.

Changchun   Jilin

Fushun

Shenyang

Vladivostok

Sapporo

Sea of Japan

Sendai

Yokohama

J A P A N

⊛ Tokyo

Beijing (Peking)

NORTH KOREA

⊛ Pyongyang

Seoul ⊛

SOUTH KOREA

Kyoto Osaka

Dalian   Pusan

Hiroshima

Tianjin

Fukuoka

Taiyuan

Qingdao   Yellow Sea

C H I N A

Lanzhou

Qinghai Lake

Huang He

Yellow R.

Xian

Wuhan

Nanjing

Shanghai

Hangzhou

East China Sea

Ryukyu Islands (Japan)

Chengdu

Yangtze R.

Dongting Lake

Poyang Lake

Chongqing

Fuzhou

Taipei

TAIWAN

Taiwan Strait

Kunming

Guangzhou (Canton)

Hong Kong

Macao (Port.)

Luzon Strait

Mekong R.

Mandalay

Hanoi

Gulf of Tonkin

MYANMAR (BURMA)

LAOS

Vientiane

VIETNAM

Da Nang

Yangon (Rangoon)

THAILAND

Bangkok

Phnom Penh

CAMBODIA

Ho Chi Minh City

Gulf of Thailand

South China Sea

Spratly Is. (disputed)

Quezon City

Manila

PHILIPPINES

Cebu

Davao

Sulu Sea

Bonin Is. (Japan)

Volcano Is. (Japan)

TROPIC OF CANCER

P A C I F I C   O C E A N

Northern Mariana Islands (U.S.)

Guam (U.S.)

MARSHALL ISLANDS

Philippine Sea

PALAU

FEDERATED STATES OF MICRONESIA

EQUATOR

Songkhla

Medan

Kuala Lumpur

Str. of Malacca

SINGAPORE

Sibu

M A L A Y S I A

Bandar Seri Begawan

BRUNEI

Pontianak

Padang

Palembang

Banjarmasin

Celebes Sea

Manado

Ujung Pandang

Banda Sea

I N D O N E S I A

Jayapura

PAPUA NEW GUINEA

Solomon Sea

Jakarta

Bandung

Semarang

Surabaya

Java Sea

Kupang

Arafura Sea

Timor Sea

Gulf of Carpentaria

Coral Sea

AUSTRALIA

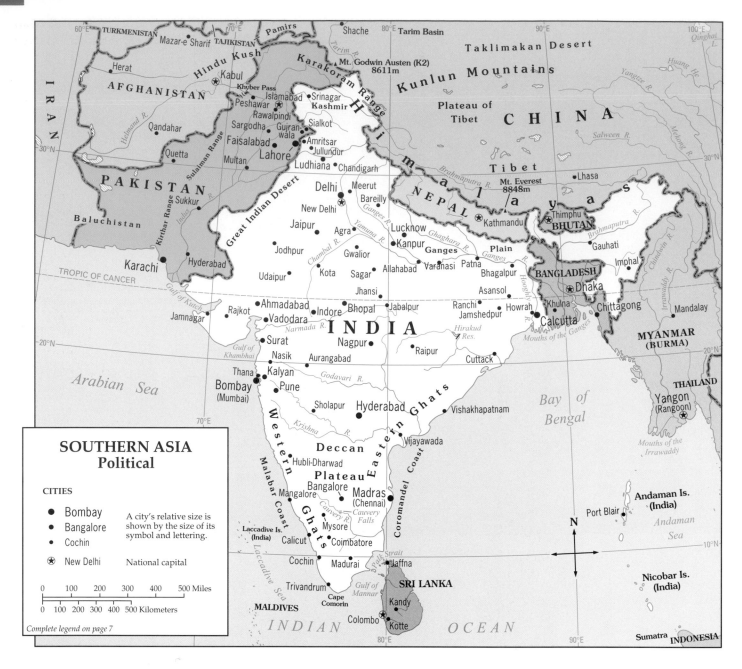

SOUTHERN ASIA
Political

CITIES

● Bombay   A city's relative size is
● Bangalore   shown by the size of its
• Cochin   symbol and lettering.

✪ New Delhi   National capital

0	100	200	300	400	500 Miles

0	100	200	300	400	500 Kilometers

Complete legend on page 7

India's Ganges River is considered sacred by Hindus, who bathe
in its waters to purify themselves.

Dry Monsoon
The climate of Southeastern Asia and India is
greatly influenced by large-scale seasonal wind
systems called **monsoons.** In winter, dry winds
generated over the cold surface of the land blow
toward the warmer oceans and keep clouds away.

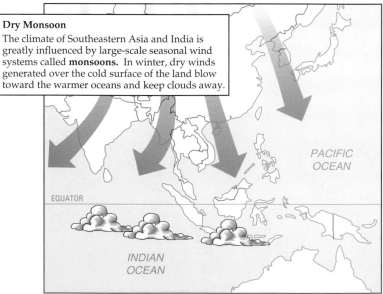

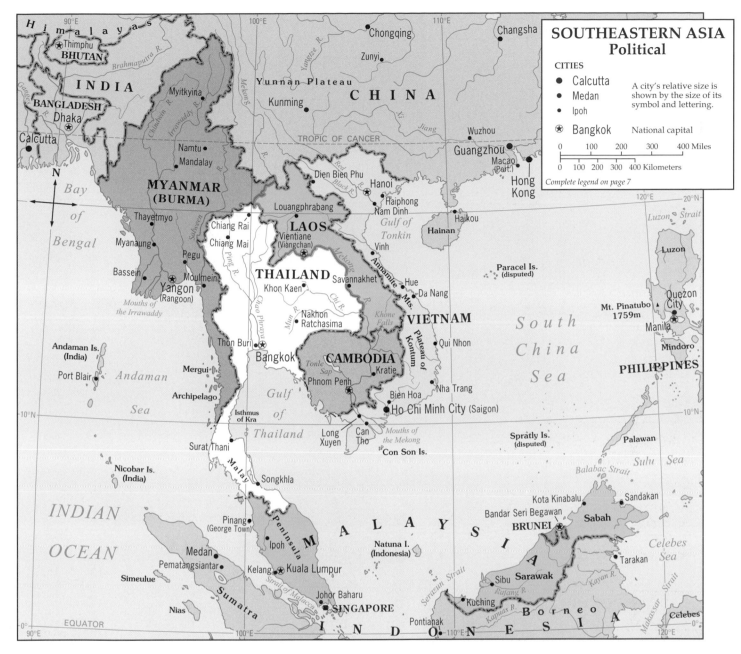

SOUTHEASTERN ASIA
Political

CITIES

● Calcutta

● Medan

• Ipoh

A city's relative size is shown by the size of its symbol and lettering.

✪ Bangkok · National capital

0   100   200   300   400 Miles

0   100   200   300   400 Kilometers

Complete legend on page 7

Map labels

Himalayas · BHUTAN · Thimphu · Brahmaputra R. · INDIA · BANGLADESH · Dhaka · Calcutta · Ganges · Chongqing · Changsha · Zunyi · Yunnan Plateau · CHINA · Kunming · Yangtze R. · Myitkyina · Chindwin R. · Irrawaddy R. · Mekong R. · Jiang · Wuzhou · Guangzhou · Macao (Port.) · Hong Kong · TROPIC OF CANCER · Namtu · Mandalay · MYANMAR (BURMA) · Dien Bien Phu · Black R. · Hanoi · Haiphong · Nam Dinh · Gulf of Tonkin · Haikou · Hainan · Thayetmyo · Bay · of · Bengal · Chiang Rai · Louangphrabang · LAOS · Vientiane (Viangchan) · Vinh · Luzon Strait · Myanaung · Chiang Mai · Salween R. · Ping R. · Luzon · Basset · Pegu · THAILAND · Mekong R. · Savannakhet · Annamite Mts. · Hue · Da Nang · Paracel Is. (disputed) · Moulmein · Khon Kaen · Chi R. · Mouths of the Irrawaddy · Yangon (Rangoon) · Chao Phraya · Mun R. · Nakhon Ratchasima · Khone Falls · VIETNAM · Plateau of Kontum · Qui Nhon · Mt. Pinatubo 1759m · Quezon City · Manila · Mindoro · South China Sea · Andaman Is. (India) · Thon Buri · Bangkok · CAMBODIA · Kratie · Port Blair · Andaman Sea · Mergui · Tonle Sap · Phnom Penh · Bien Hoa · Nha Trang · PHILIPPINES · Archipelago · Gulf · of · Thailand · Long Xuyen · Can Tho · Ho Chi Minh City (Saigon) · Mouths of the Mekong · Spratly Is. (disputed) · Palawan · Con Son Is. · Isthmus of Kra · Surat Thani · Nicobar Is. (India) · Songkhla · Sulu Sea · Balabac Strait · Kota Kinabalu · Sandakan · INDIAN · OCEAN · Malay · Peninsula · Pinang (George Town) · Bandar Seri Begawan · Sabah · BRUNEI · Celebes Sea · Ipoh · M A L A Y S I A · Natuna I. (Indonesia) · Tarakan · Medan · Pematangsiantar · Kelang · Kuala Lumpur · Sibu · Sarawak · Simeulue · Sumatra · Strait of Malacca · Johor Baharu · SINGAPORE · Nias · Kuching · Kapuas R. · Rejang R. · Borneo · Celebes · Pontianak · INDONESIA · Makassar Strait · EQUATOR

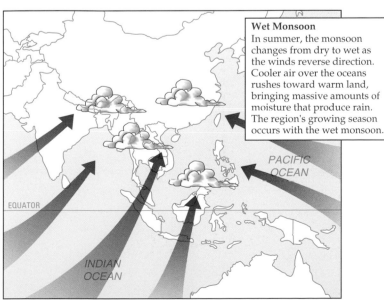

Wet Monsoon
In summer, the monsoon changes from dry to wet as the winds reverse direction. Cooler air over the oceans rushes toward warm land, bringing massive amounts of moisture that produce rain. The region's growing season occurs with the wet monsoon.

PACIFIC OCEAN · INDIAN OCEAN · EQUATOR

Terraces maximize the growing space for rice in hilly terrain. Rice is the most important food crop in southeastern Asia.

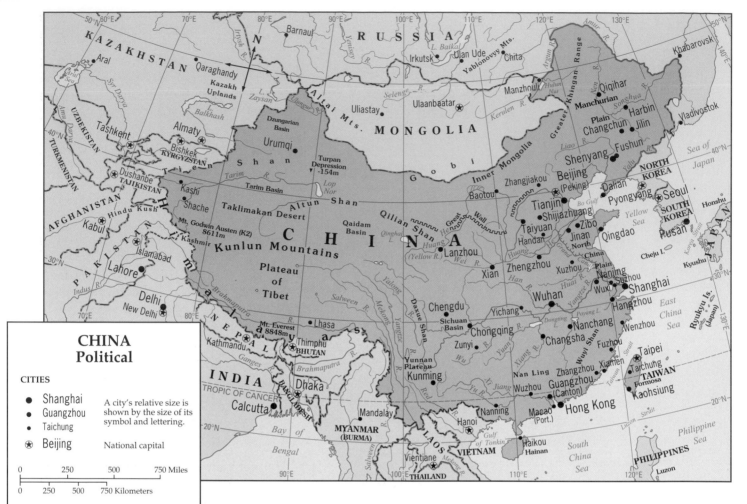

CHINA
Political

CITIES

● **Shanghai**

● Guangzhou   A city's relative size is
                     shown by the size of its
• Taichung   symbol and lettering.

⊛ **Beijing**   National capital

| 0 | 250 | 500 | 750 Miles |

| 0 | 250 | 500 | 750 Kilometers |

Complete legend on page 7

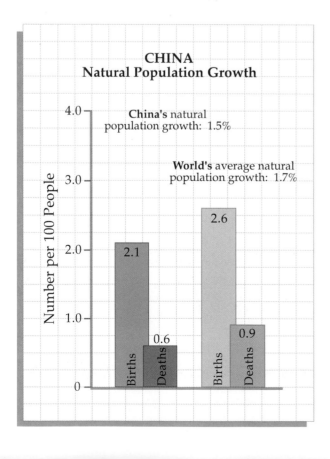

CHINA
Natural Population Growth

China's natural population growth: 1.5%

World's average natural population growth: 1.7%

Number per 100 People

- 4.0
- 3.0
- 2.0
- 1.0
- 0

2.1 Births
0.6 Deaths
2.6 Births
0.9 Deaths

Bicycles in China

Number of bicycles in use: 369.2 million

Number of automobiles in use: 1.4 million

Nearly half of the people who work in urban China commute by bicycle.

CHINA
Area Comparison

China, the third largest country in the world, is slightly larger than the United States. Only Russia and Canada are larger than China.

| China | 3,696,100 sq. mi. (9 572 900 sq. km) |
| Contiguous U.S. | 3,021,295 sq. mi. (7 825 112 sq. km) |

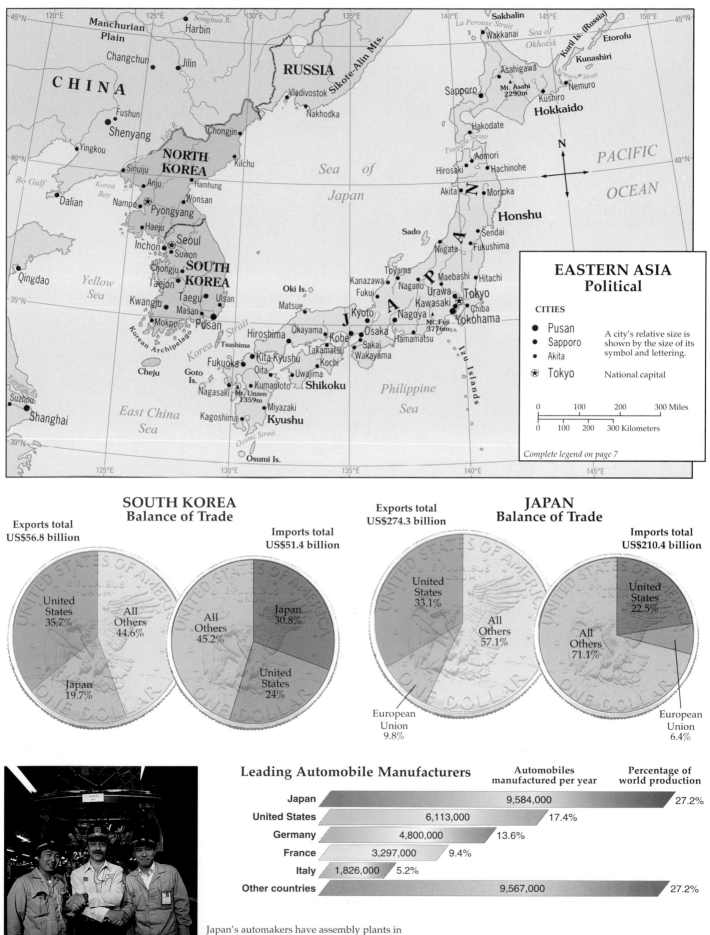

EASTERN ASIA
Political

CITIES

● Pusan

● Sapporo

• Akita

A city's relative size is shown by the size of its symbol and lettering.

✪ Tokyo National capital

| 0 | 100 | 200 | 300 Miles |

| 0 | 100 | 200 | 300 Kilometers |

Complete legend on page 7

SOUTH KOREA
Balance of Trade

Exports total
US$56.8 billion

United States 35.7%
All Others 44.6%
Japan 19.7%

Imports total
US$51.4 billion

Japan 30.8%
All Others 45.2%
United States 24%

JAPAN
Balance of Trade

Exports total
US$274.3 billion

United States 33.1%
All Others 57.1%
European Union 9.8%

Imports total
US$210.4 billion

United States 22.5%
All Others 71.1%
European Union 6.4%

Leading Automobile Manufacturers

	Automobiles manufactured per year	Percentage of world production
Japan	9,584,000	27.2%
United States	6,113,000	17.4%
Germany	4,800,000	13.6%
France	3,297,000	9.4%
Italy	1,826,000	5.2%
Other countries	9,567,000	27.2%

Japan's automakers have assembly plants in a number of locations in the United States.

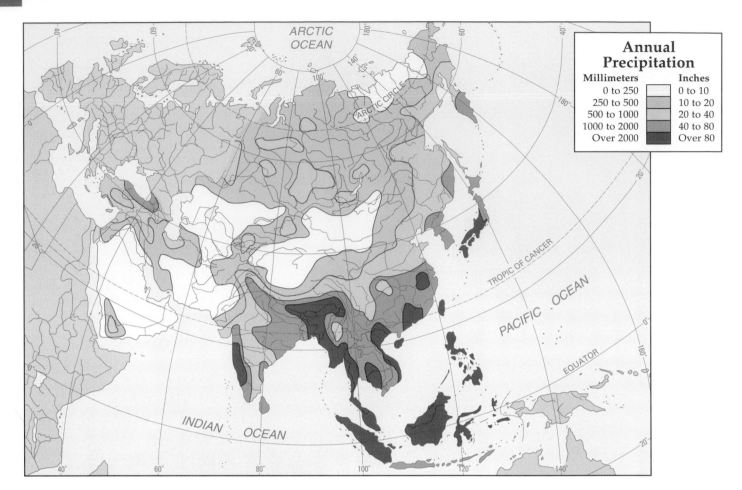

Annual Precipitation

Millimeters		Inches
0 to 250		0 to 10
250 to 500		10 to 20
500 to 1000		20 to 40
1000 to 2000		40 to 80
Over 2000		Over 80

The Himalayas, located in southern Asia, are the world's highest mountain system.

Cross Section of Asia

ELEVATION

Meters		Feet
Over 6000		Over 20,000
3000 to 6000		10,000 to 20,000
1500 to 3000		5,000 to 10,000
600 to 1500		2,000 to 5,000
300 to 600		1,000 to 2,000
150 to 300		500 to 1,000
0 to 150		0 to 500
Below sea level		Below sea level

INDONESIA
Area Comparison

The combined land area of Indonesia's 17,000 islands is about one-fourth the size of the contiguous United States. Three islands located partly or entirely in Indonesia—Sumatra, Borneo, and New Guinea—are each larger than all five Great Lakes combined.

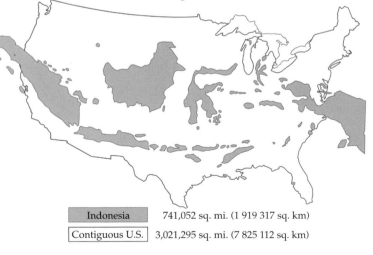

Indonesia	741,052 sq. mi. (1 919 317 sq. km)
Contiguous U.S.	3,021,295 sq. mi. (7 825 112 sq. km)

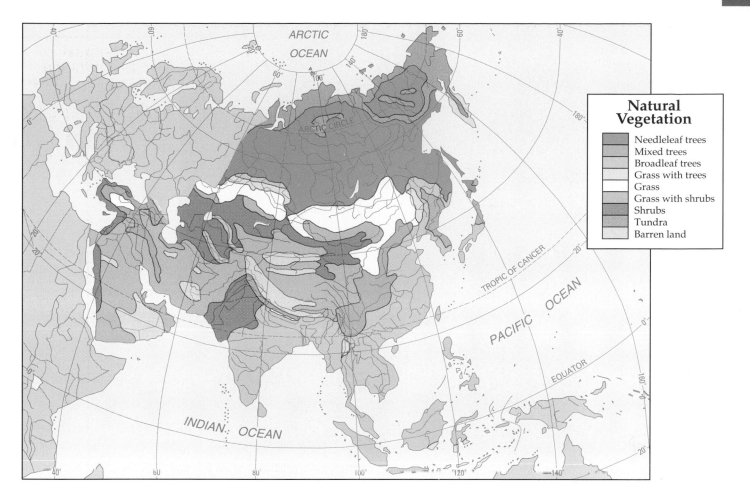

Natural Vegetation

- Needleleaf trees
- Mixed trees
- Broadleaf trees
- Grass with trees
- Grass
- Grass with shrubs
- Shrubs
- Tundra
- Barren land

INDIA
Balance of Trade

Exports total
US$14.3 billion

- European Union 20.9%
- United States 16.1%
- Russia 11.8%
- All Others 51.2%

Imports total
US$16.9 billion

- European Union 23.8%
- United States 12.3%
- All Others 63.9%

CHINA
Balance of Trade

Exports total
US$46.5 billion

- Hong Kong (pre-1997) 38.3%
- Japan 16.3%
- All Others 45.4%

Imports total
US$52.5 billion

- Hong Kong (pre-1997) 20.6%
- Japan 20.4%
- All Others 59%

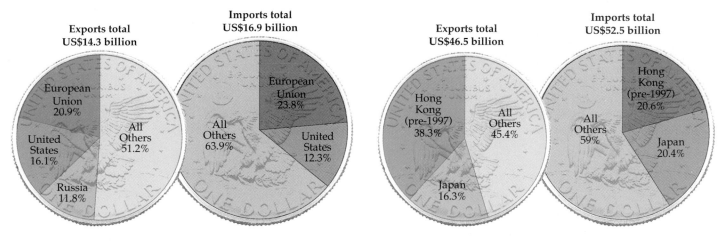

Tibet

CHINA

KOREA JAPAN

Yellow Sea

Pacific Ocean

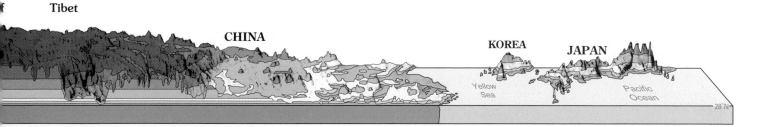

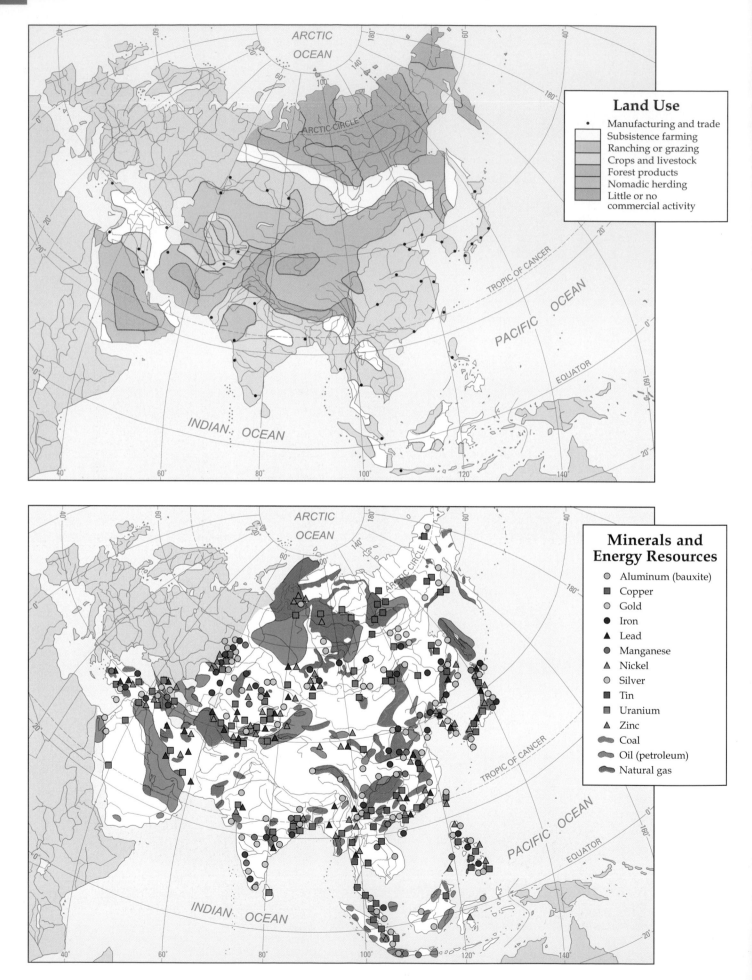

Land Use

- • Manufacturing and trade
- Subsistence farming
- Ranching or grazing
- Crops and livestock
- Forest products
- Nomadic herding
- Little or no commercial activity

Minerals and Energy Resources

- Aluminum (bauxite)
- Copper
- Gold
- Iron
- Lead
- Manganese
- Nickel
- Silver
- Tin
- Uranium
- Zinc
- Coal
- Oil (petroleum)
- Natural gas

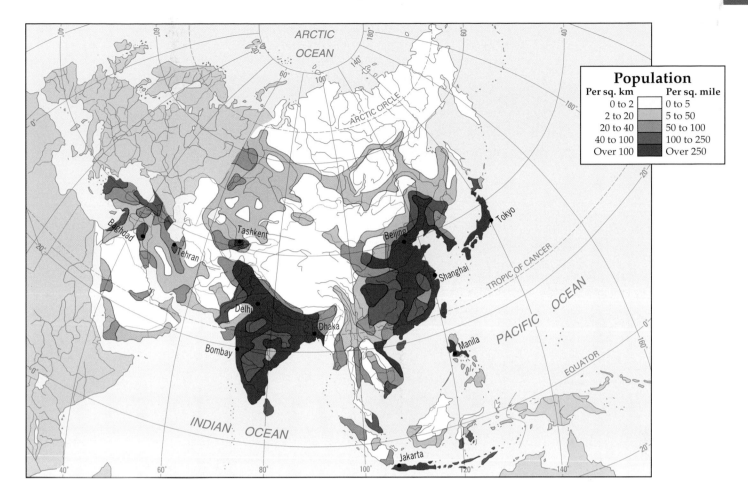

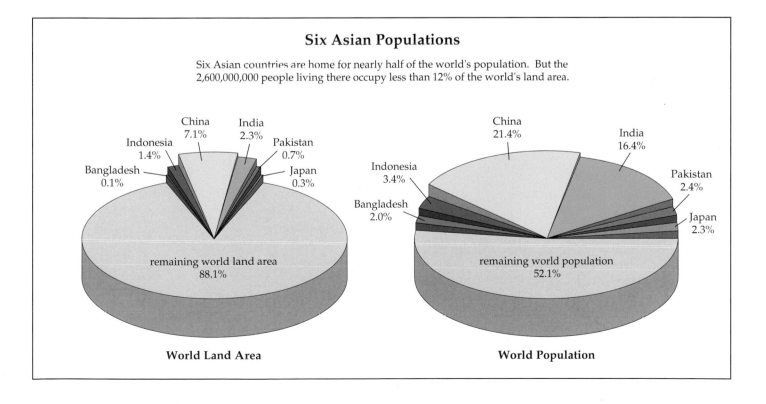

Six Asian Populations

Six Asian countries are home for nearly half of the world's population. But the 2,600,000,000 people living there occupy less than 12% of the world's land area.

World Land Area

China 7.1%
India 2.3%
Indonesia 1.4%
Pakistan 0.7%
Bangladesh 0.1%
Japan 0.3%
remaining world land area 88.1%

World Population

China 21.4%
India 16.4%
Indonesia 3.4%
Pakistan 2.4%
Bangladesh 2.0%
Japan 2.3%
remaining world population 52.1%

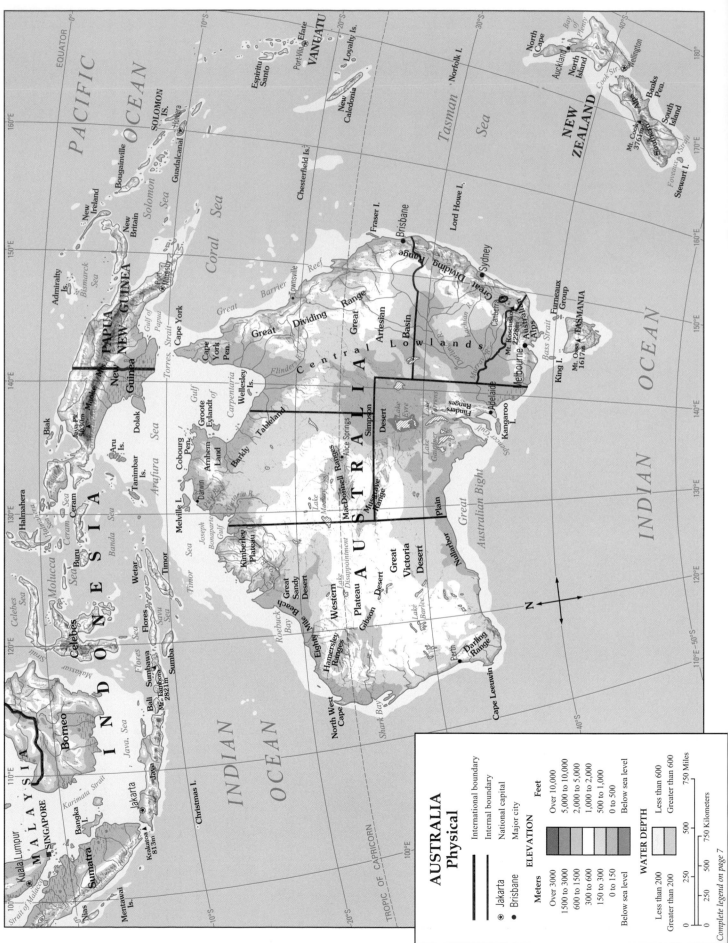

PACIFIC OCEAN

EQUATOR

INDONESIA

MALAYSIA

SINGAPORE

Kuala Lumpur

Sumatra

Borneo

Java

Jakarta

Celebes

Halmahera

Biak

Aru Is.

Tanimbar Is.

Timor

Wetar

Flores

Sumba

Sumbawa

Bali

Mt. Rinjani 3821m

Krakatoa 813m

Christmas I.

Nias

Mentawai Is.

Bangka I.

Java Pk. 4750m

PAPUA NEW GUINEA

New Guinea

Dolak

Admiralty Is.

New Ireland

Bougainville

New Britain

SOLOMON IS.

Guadalcanal

Honiara

Port Moresby

Bismarck Sea

Solomon Sea

Coral Sea

Gulf of Papua

Torres Strait

Cape York Pen.

Cape York

Great Barrier Reef

Townsville

Wellesley Is.

Groote Eylandt

Gulf of Carpentaria

Cobourg Pen.

Arnhem Land

Melville I.

Darwin

Bathurst I.

Joseph Bonaparte Gulf

Kimberley Plateau

Roebuck Bay

Eighty Mile Beach

North West Cape

Hamersley Ranges

Great Sandy Desert

Gibson Desert

Lake Disappointment

Western Plateau

Great Victoria Desert

Nullarbor Plain

Darling Range

Perth

Cape Leeuwin

Shark Bay

Lake Barlee

Lake Carnegie

Bardy

Tableland

Victoria R.

Flinders R.

Central Lowlands

AUSTRALIA

MacDonnell Ranges

Alice Springs

Musgrave Range

Simpson Desert

Lake Eyre

Lake Gairdner

Lake Torrens

Flinders Ranges

Adelaide

Spencer Gulf

Kangaroo I.

Gawler Ranges

Great Australian Bight

Great Dividing Range

Great Artesian Basin

Darling R.

Lachlan R.

Murrumbidgee

Murray R.

Brisbane

Fraser I.

Sydney

Canberra

Melbourne

Australian Alps

Mt. Kosciusko 2228m

King I.

Furneaux Group

Flinders I.

Bass Strait

TASMANIA

Mt. Ossa 1617m

INDIAN OCEAN

TROPIC OF CAPRICORN

NEW ZEALAND

North Cape

Auckland

North Island

Cook Str.

Mt. Cook 3764m

Southern Alps

South Island

Banks Pen.

Foveaux Strait

Stewart I.

Wellington

Bay of Plenty

VANUATU

Espiritu Santo

Port-Vila

Efate

New Caledonia

Loyalty Is.

Norfolk I.

Lord Howe I.

Chesterfield Is.

Tasman Sea

INDIAN OCEAN

N

AUSTRALIA
Physical

International boundary
Internal boundary

⊛ Jakarta   National capital
● Brisbane   Major city

ELEVATION
Meters   Feet
Over 3000   Over 10,000
1500 to 3000   5,000 to 10,000
600 to 1500   2,000 to 5,000
300 to 600   1,000 to 2,000
150 to 300   500 to 1,000
0 to 150   0 to 500
Below sea level Below sea level

WATER DEPTH
Less than 200   Less than 600
Greater than 200 Greater than 600

0   250   500   750 Miles
0   250   500   750 Kilometers

Complete legend on page 7

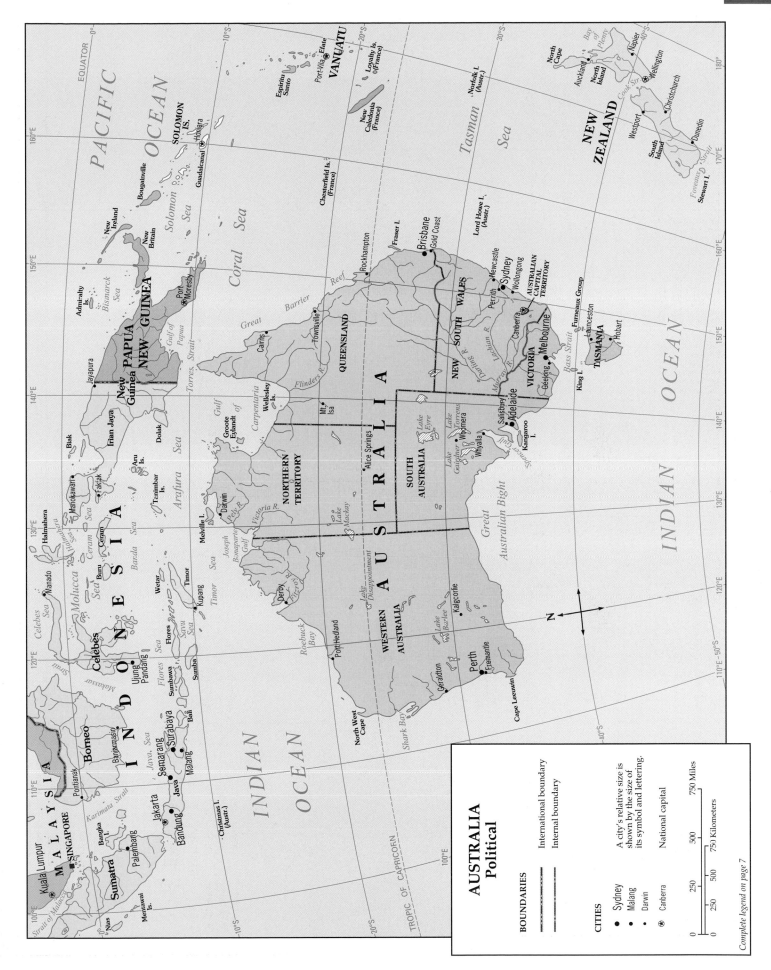

EQUATOR

PACIFIC OCEAN

SOLOMON IS.
Honiara
Guadalcanal
Bougainville
New Ireland
New Britain

VANUATU
Espiritu Santo
Port-Vila · Efate
Loyalty Is. (France)
New Caledonia (France)

Chesterfield Is. (France)

NEW ZEALAND
North Cape
Bay of Plenty
Napier
Wellington
Auckland
North Island
Cook Str.
Christchurch
Westport
South Island
Dunedin
Stewart I.
Foveaux Strait

Tasman Sea

Norfolk I. (Austr.)
Lord Howe I. (Austr.)

MALAYSIA
Kuala Lumpur
SINGAPORE
Borneo
Pontianak
Banjarmasin
Bangka I.
Sumatra
Palembang
Mentawai Is.
Nias

INDONESIA
Celebes
Celebes Sea
Manado
Halmahera
Molucca Sea
Ceram Sea
Buru
Ceram
Banda Sea
Wetar
Flores Sea
Flores
Savu Sea
Timor
Timor Sea
Kupang
Sumba
Sumbawa
Ujung Pandang
Makassar Strait
Bali
Java
Java Sea
Semarang
Surabaya
Malang
Bandung
Jakarta
Karimata Strait
Bangka I.
Christmas I. (Austr.)

Biak
Manokwari
Fakfak
Aru Is.
Tanimbar Is.
Irian Jaya
Jayapura
New Guinea

PAPUA NEW GUINEA
Admiralty Is.
Bismarck Sea
Port Moresby
Gulf of Papua
Torres Strait

Coral Sea
Solomon Sea

Arafura Sea
Dolak
Melville I.
Darwin
Bathurst I.

AUSTRALIA

NORTHERN TERRITORY
Alice Springs
Lake Mackay
Victoria R.
Daly R.

Gulf of Carpentaria
Wellesley Is.
Groote Eylandt
Great Barrier Reef

QUEENSLAND
Cairns
Townsville
Mt. Isa
Rockhampton
Flinders R.
Fraser I.
Brisbane
Gold Coast

SOUTH AUSTRALIA
Lake Eyre
Lake Torrens
Lake Gairdner
Woomera
Whyalla
Salisbury
Adelaide
Kangaroo I.
Spencer Gulf

NEW SOUTH WALES
Darling R.
Lachlan R.
Murray R.
Newcastle
Sydney
Wollongong
AUSTRALIAN CAPITAL TERRITORY
Canberra
Perth

VICTORIA
Melbourne
Geelong
Bass Strait
King I.
Furneaux Group
Launceston

TASMANIA
Hobart

WESTERN AUSTRALIA
Lake Disappointment
Kalgoorlie
Lake Barlee
Lake Carnegie
Derby
Roebuck Bay
Port Hedland
North West Cape
Shark Bay
Geraldton
Perth
Fremantle
Cape Leeuwin
Great Australian Bight

Joseph Bonaparte Gulf
Fitzroy R.

INDIAN OCEAN

N

TROPIC OF CAPRICORN

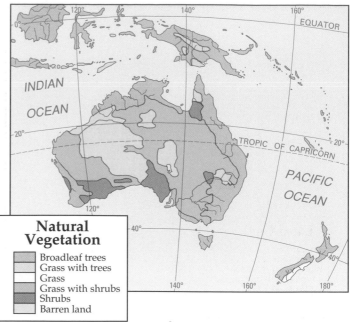

Annual Precipitation

Millimeters		Inches
0 to 250		0 to 10
250 to 500		10 to 20
500 to 1000		20 to 40
1000 to 2000		40 to 80
Over 2000		Over 80

Natural Vegetation

- Broadleaf trees
- Grass with trees
- Grass
- Grass with shrubs
- Shrubs
- Barren land

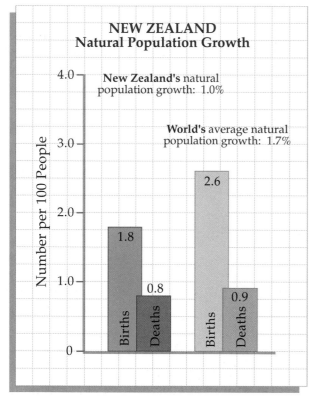

NEW ZEALAND
Natural Population Growth

New Zealand's natural population growth: 1.0%

World's average natural population growth: 1.7%

Number per 100 People

4.0

3.0

2.0 2.6

1.8

1.0 0.8 0.9

0

Births Deaths Births Deaths

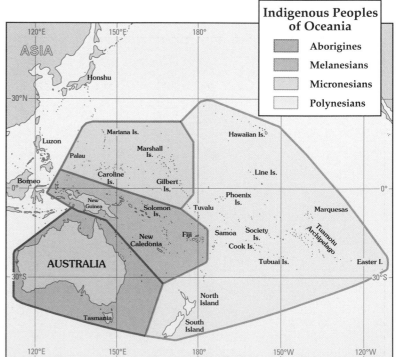

Sydney is Australia's largest city. Its Opera House and Harbour Bridge are internationally recognized landmarks.

Indigenous Peoples of Oceania

- Aborigines
- Melanesians
- Micronesians
- Polynesians

ASIA

Honshu

Luzon

Palau

Borneo

New Guinea

Mariana Is.

Marshall Is.

Caroline Is.

Gilbert Is.

Solomon Is.

New Caledonia

Fiji

Tuvalu

Hawaiian Is.

Line Is.

Phoenix Is.

Samoa

Society Is.

Cook Is.

Marquesas

Tuamotu Archipelago

Easter I.

Tubuai Is.

AUSTRALIA

Tasmania

North Island

South Island

Isolated Australia is home to many unique animals, including marsupials such as the kangaroo.

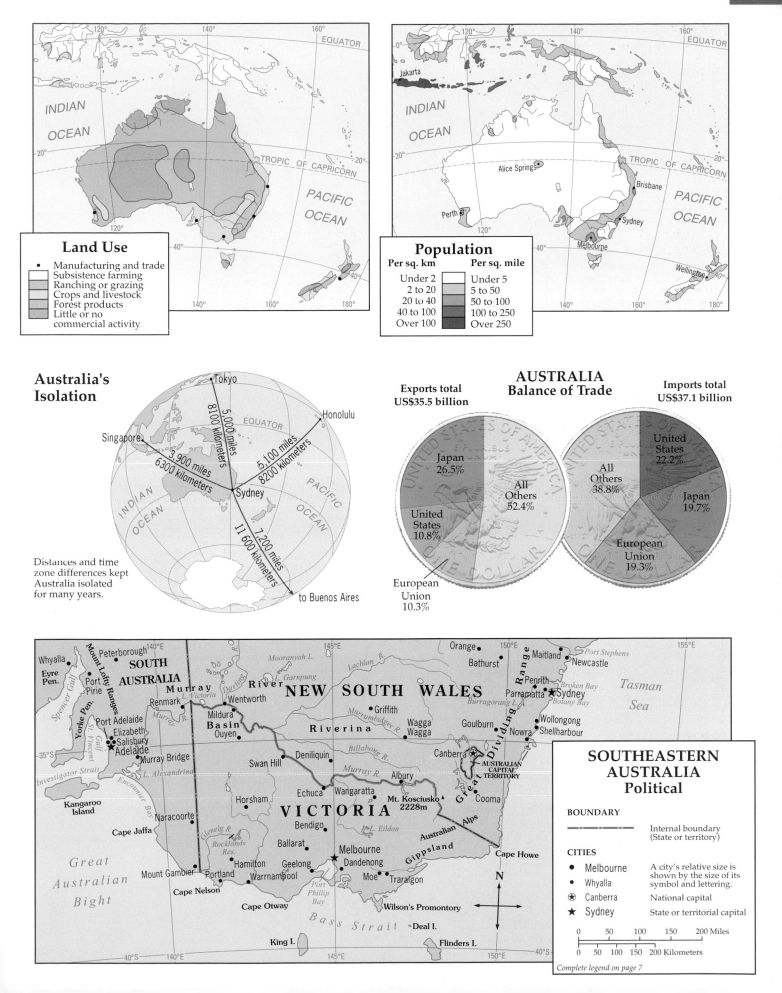

Land Use

- Manufacturing and trade
- Subsistence farming
- Ranching or grazing
- Crops and livestock
- Forest products
- Little or no commercial activity

Population

Per sq. km	Per sq. mile
Under 2	Under 5
2 to 20	5 to 50
20 to 40	50 to 100
40 to 100	100 to 250
Over 100	Over 250

Australia's Isolation

Tokyo
5,000 miles
8100 kilometers

Singapore
3,900 miles
6300 kilometers

Honolulu
5,100 miles
8200 kilometers

Sydney

7,200 miles
11 600 kilometers
to Buenos Aires

Distances and time zone differences kept Australia isolated for many years.

AUSTRALIA
Balance of Trade

Exports total US$35.5 billion

Japan 26.5%
United States 10.8%
All Others 52.4%
European Union 10.3%

Imports total US$37.1 billion

United States 22.2%
Japan 19.7%
European Union 19.3%
All Others 38.8%

SOUTHEASTERN AUSTRALIA
Political

BOUNDARY

—— Internal boundary (State or territory)

CITIES

- ● Melbourne — A city's relative size is shown by the size of its symbol and lettering.
- • Whyalla
- ✪ Canberra — National capital
- ★ Sydney — State or territorial capital

0 50 100 150 200 Miles

0 50 100 150 200 Kilometers

Complete legend on page 7

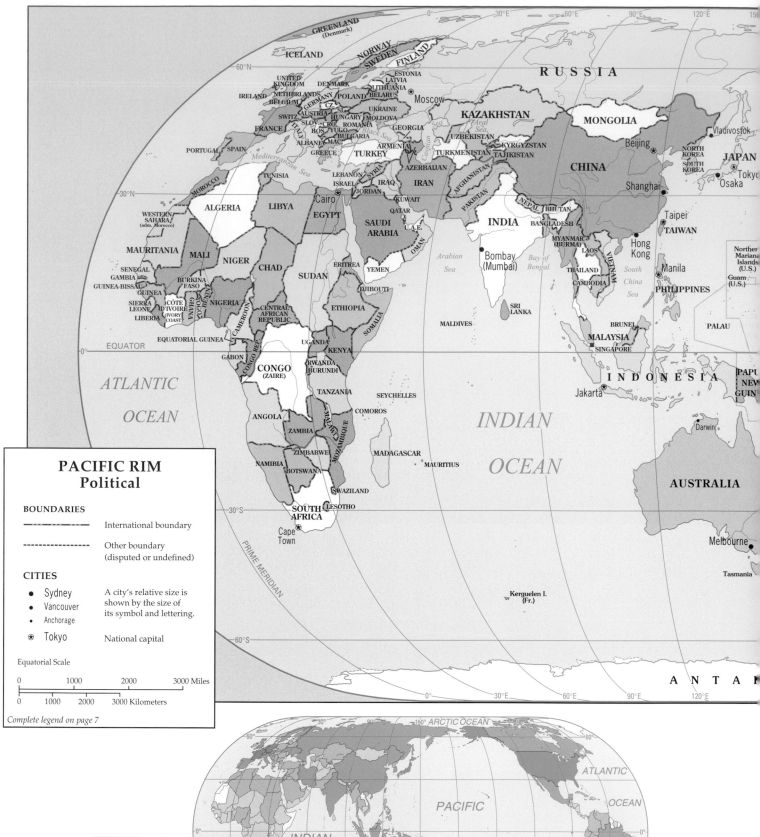

PACIFIC RIM
Political

BOUNDARIES

———————————— International boundary

- - - - - - - - - - - - - - Other boundary
(disputed or undefined)

CITIES

● Sydney

● Vancouver

• Anchorage

⊛ Tokyo   National capital

A city's relative size is
shown by the size of
its symbol and lettering.

Equatorial Scale

| 0 | 1000 | 2000 | 3000 Miles |

| 0 | 1000 | 2000 | 3000 Kilometers |

Complete legend on page 7

National Productivity
Total GNP, GDP

US$ million

	Under 1,000
	1,000 to 10,000
	10,000 to 100,000
	100,000 to 1,000,000
	Over 1,000,000

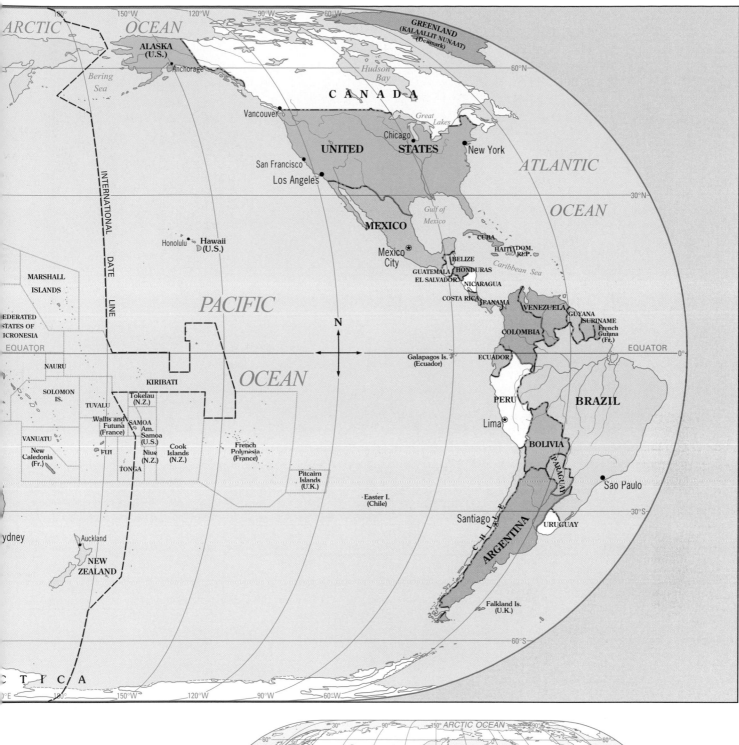

ARCTIC OCEAN

GREENLAND
(KALAALLIT NUNAAT)
(Denmark)

ALASKA
(U.S.)

Anchorage

Bering
Sea

60°N

C A N A D A

Hudson
Bay

Vancouver

Great
Lakes

Chicago

UNITED   STATES

New York

San Francisco

Los Angeles

ATLANTIC

30°N

OCEAN

MARSHALL
ISLANDS

Honolulu

Hawaii
(U.S.)

Gulf of
Mexico

MEXICO

CUBA

HAITI DOM.
REP.

FEDERATED
STATES OF
MICRONESIA

Mexico
City

Caribbean Sea

BELIZE

GUATEMALA HONDURAS
EL SALVADOR

NICARAGUA

PACIFIC

COSTA RICA PANAMA

VENEZUELA

GUYANA
SURINAME
French
Guiana
(Fr.)

N

COLOMBIA

EQUATOR

EQUATOR

0°

NAURU

Galapagos Is.
(Ecuador)

ECUADOR

OCEAN

SOLOMON
IS.

KIRIBATI

PERU

BRAZIL

TUVALU

Tokelau
(N.Z.)

Lima

Wallis and
Futuna
(France)

SAMOA
Am.
Samoa
(U.S.)

BOLIVIA

VANUATU

FIJI

Cook
Islands
(N.Z.)

French
Polynesia
(France)

PARAGUAY

Sao Paulo

New
Caledonia
(Fr.)

Niue
(N.Z.)

TONGA

Pitcairn
Islands
(U.K.)

Easter I.
(Chile)

30°S

Sydney

Auckland

Santiago

URUGUAY

NEW
ZEALAND

ARGENTINA

INTERNATIONAL DATE LINE

Falkland Is.
(U.K.)

60°S

ANTARCTICA

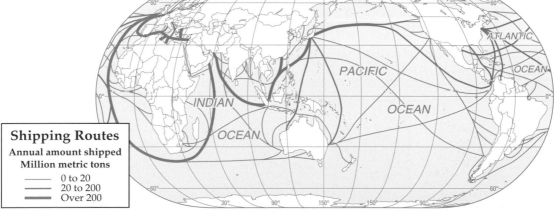

Shipping Routes
Annual amount shipped
Million metric tons
— 0 to 20
— 20 to 200
— Over 200

ARCTIC OCEAN

ATLANTIC
OCEAN

INDIAN
OCEAN

PACIFIC

OCEAN

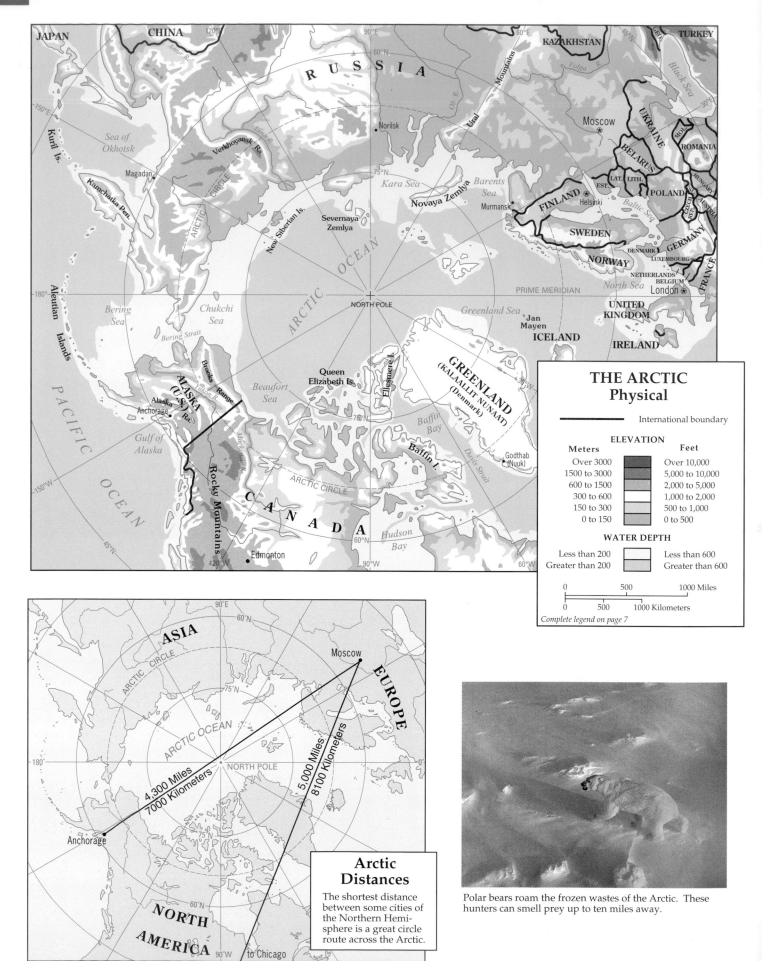

JAPAN
CHINA
120°E
90°E
60°E
KAZAKHSTAN
TURKEY

R U S S I A

Amur R.

Ural Mountains

Volga R.

MOSCOW

UKRAINE

MOL.

ROMANIA

150°E

Sea of
Okhotsk

Verkhoyansk Ra.

75°N

Norilsk

Kara Sea

Barents
Sea

Novaya Zemlya

Murmansk

Helsinki

FINLAND

BELARUS

EST.
LAT.
LITH.

POLAND

HUNGARY
AUSTRIA

CZECH REP.
SLOVAKIA

Magadan

ARCTIC

Kamchatka Pen.

CIRCLE

New Siberian Is.

Severnaya
Zemlya

ARCTIC OCEAN

SWEDEN

NORWAY

DENMARK

GERMANY

LUXEMBOURG

FRANCE

Baltic Sea

Kuril Is.

Aleutian

Islands

180°

Bering
Sea

Bering Strait

Chukchi
Sea

NORTH POLE

Greenland Sea

Jan
Mayen

ICELAND

PRIME MERIDIAN

NETHERLANDS

BELGIUM

London

North Sea

UNITED
KINGDOM

IRELAND

0°

PACIFIC

OCEAN

Beaufort
Sea

Brooks Range

ALASKA
(U.S.)

Anchorage

Alaska
Ra.

Yukon R.

Gulf of
Alaska

Rocky Mountains

Mackenzie R.

Queen
Elizabeth Is.

Ellesmere I.

GREENLAND
(KALAALLIT NUNAAT)
(Denmark)

30°W

Baffin
Bay

Baffin I.

Davis Strait

Godthab
(Nuuk)

75°N

150°W

C A N A D A

ARCTIC CIRCLE

60°N

Hudson
Bay

Edmonton

120°W

90°W

45°N

60°W

THE ARCTIC
Physical

———— International boundary

ELEVATION

Meters		Feet
Over 3000		Over 10,000
1500 to 3000		5,000 to 10,000
600 to 1500		2,000 to 5,000
300 to 600		1,000 to 2,000
150 to 300		500 to 1,000
0 to 150		0 to 500

WATER DEPTH

Less than 200		Less than 600
Greater than 200		Greater than 600

0   500   1000 Miles

0   500   1000 Kilometers

Complete legend on page 7

ASIA
90°E
60°E

ARCTIC CIRCLE

Moscow

EUROPE

75°N

180°

ARCTIC OCEAN

NORTH POLE

4,300 Miles
7000 Kilometers

5,000 Miles
8100 Kilometers

Anchorage

75°N

60°N

NORTH

AMERICA

90°W

to Chicago

Arctic
Distances

The shortest distance
between some cities of
the Northern Hemi-
sphere is a great circle
route across the Arctic.

Polar bears roam the frozen wastes of the Arctic. These
hunters can smell prey up to ten miles away.

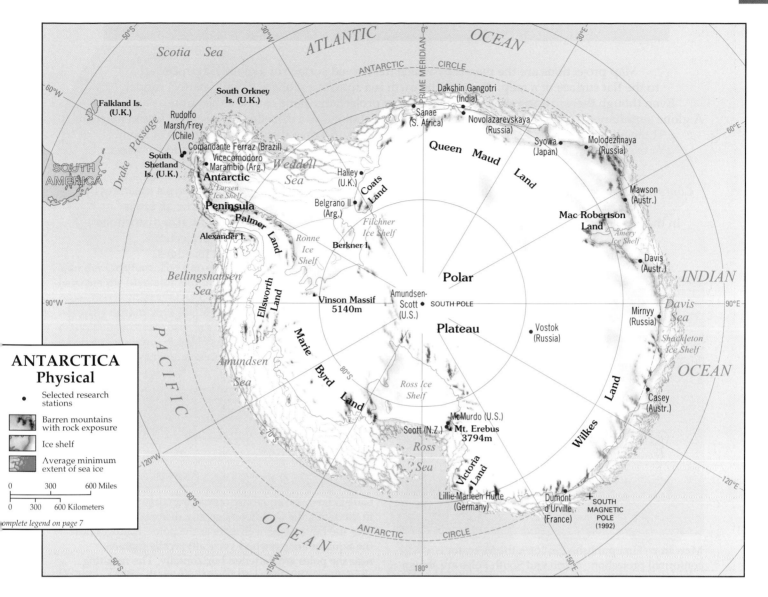

ANTARCTICA
Physical

- Selected research stations
- Barren mountains with rock exposure
- Ice shelf
- Average minimum extent of sea ice

| 0 | 300 | 600 Miles |
| 0 | 300 | 600 Kilometers |

complete legend on page 7

Antarctica's Ice Cap

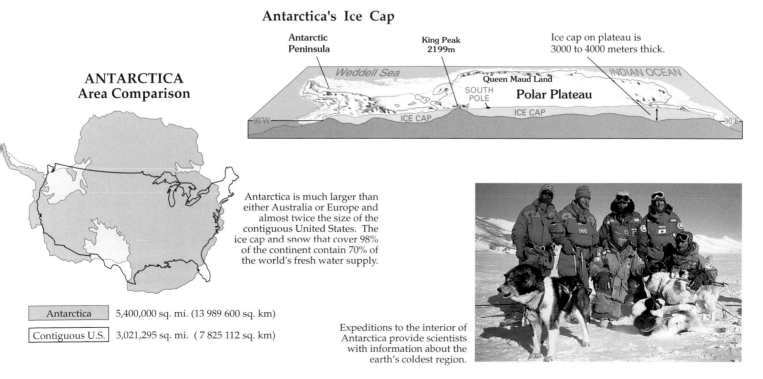

Antarctic Peninsula

King Peak 2199m

Ice cap on plateau is 3000 to 4000 meters thick.

Weddell Sea

Queen Maud Land

INDIAN OCEAN

SOUTH POLE

Polar Plateau

ICE CAP   ICE CAP

ANTARCTICA
Area Comparison

Antarctica is much larger than either Australia or Europe and almost twice the size of the contiguous United States. The ice cap and snow that cover 98% of the continent contain 70% of the world's fresh water supply.

| Antarctica | 5,400,000 sq. mi. (13 989 600 sq. km) |
| Contiguous U.S. | 3,021,295 sq. mi. (7 825 112 sq. km) |

Expeditions to the interior of Antarctica provide scientists with information about the earth's coldest region.

COUNTRY TABLES

COUNTRY	CAPITAL(S)	PRINCIPAL LANGUAGE(S)	POPULATION	AREA MI.² KM²	POP. DENSITY PER MI.² PER KM²	NATURAL POP. GROWTH PER 100 PEOPLE BIRTHS	– DEATHS	= % GAIN
Africa								
ALGERIA	Algiers	Arabic, French, Berber	26,401,000	919,595 2 381 741	28.7 11.1	3.4	0.6	2.8
ANGOLA	Luanda	Ovimbundu, Portuguese, Mbundu, Kongo	10,609,000	481,354 1 246 700	22.0 8.5	4.7	2.0	2.7
BENIN	Porto-Novo, Cotonou	Fon, French, Yoruba, Adja	4,928,000	43,450 112 600	113.4 43.8	4.9	1.8	3.1
BOTSWANA	Gaborone	Tswana, English, Shona	1,359,000	224,607 581 730	6.1 2.3	4.6	1.1	3.5
BURKINA FASO	Ouagadougou	Voltaic, Mande, Fulani, French	9,515,000	105,946 274 400	89.8 34.7	4.7	1.8	2.9
BURUNDI	Bujumbura	Rundi, French	5,657,000	10,740 27 816	526.7 203.4	4.7	1.5	3.2
CAMEROON	Yaounde	Fang, Bamileke, French, Duala, Fulani, Tikar, English	12,622,000	179,714 465 458	70.5 27.2	4.5	1.5	3.0
CAPE VERDE	Praia	Crioulo, Portuguese	346,000	1,557 4 033	222.2 85.8	3.2	0.8	2.4
CENTRAL AFRICAN REPUBLIC	Bangui	Banda, Baya, Sango, French, Ngbandi, Mbaka	2,930,000	240,324 622 436	12.2 4.7	4.5	1.8	2.7
CHAD	N'Djamena	Sara, Bagirmi, Kraish, Arabic, French	5,961,000	495,755 1 284 000	12.0 4.6	4.4	1.9	2.5
COMOROS	Moroni	Comorian, French, Arabic	497,000	719 1 862	691.2 266.9	4.7	1.3	3.4
CONGO (ZAIRE)	Kinshasa	Lingala, Swahili, Luba, Mongo, French	41,151,000	905,446 2 345 095	45.4 17.5	4.6	1.4	3.2
CONGO REPUBLIC	Brazzaville	Monokutuba, Kongo, French, Teke	2,692,000	132,047 342 000	20.4 7.9	4.5	1.5	3.0
CÔTE D'IVOIRE (IVORY COAST)	Abidjan	Akan, French, Kru, Gur Hindi	12,951,000	123,847 320 763	104.6 40.4	4.7	1.3	3.4
DJIBOUTI	Djibouti	Somali, Afar, French, Arabic	557,000	8,950 23 200	62.2 24.0	4.6	1.7	2.9
EGYPT	Cairo	Arabic	55,979,000	385,229 997 739	145.3 56.1	3.9	0.9	3.0
EQUATORIAL GUINEA	Malabo	Fana, Bubi, Spanish	367,000	10,831 28 051	33.9 13.1	4.3	1.8	2.5
ERITREA	Asmara	Amharic, Tigrinya	3,332,000	17,413 45 100	91.4 35.3	4.7	2.1	2.6
ETHIOPIA	Addis Ababa	Amharic, Oromo, Tigrinya, Gurage	50,745,000	483,123 1 251 282	111.9 43.2	4.7	2.1	2.6
GABON	Libreville	Fang, French, Puna/Sira/Nzebi	1,253,000	103,347 267 667	12.1 4.7	4.0	1.6	2.4
GAMBIA	Banjul	Malinke, Fulani, English	921,000	4,127 10 689	223.2 86.2	4.6	2.1	2.5
GHANA	Accra	Hausa, Akan, Mole-Dagbani, English	15,237,000	92,098 238 533	165.4 63.9	4.4	1.3	3.1
GUINEA	Conakry	Fulani, Malinke, Susu, French	7,232,000	94,926 245 857	76.2 29.4	4.8	2.2	2.6
GUINEA-BISSAU	Bissau	Crioulo, Fulani, Balante, Portuguese	1,015,000	13,948 36 125	72.8 28.1	4.2	2.0	2.2
KENYA	Nairobi	Swahili, Kikuyu, Luhya, Luo, Kamba, Kalenjin	26,985,000	224,961 582 646	120.0 46.3	4.9	1.1	3.8
LESOTHO	Maseru	Sotho, Zulu, English	1,854,000	11,720 30 355	158.2 61.1	4.1	1.2	2.9

Country: all independent countries, as well as selected dependencies. **Principal Language(s):** all official languages, as well as other primary languages spoken by a substantial proportion of the population. **Pop. Density:** population density, computed as population divided by area; given per square mile and per square kilometer. **Natural Pop. Growth:** annual population increase per 100 people; does not include population change due to immigration or emigration.

COUNTRY	CAPITAL(S)	PRINCIPAL LANGUAGE(S)	POPULATION	AREA MI.² KM²	POP. DENSITY PER MI.² PER KM²	NATURAL POP. GROWTH PER 100 PEOPLE BIRTHS – DEATHS = % GAIN		
LIBERIA	Monrovia	Krio, English, Kepelle, Bassa, Grebo	2,780,000	38,250 99 067	72.7 28.1	4.6	1.4	3.2
LIBYA	Tripoli	Arabic, Berber	4,447,000	678,400 1 757 000	6.6 2.5	4.5	0.8	3.7
MADAGASCAR	Antananarivo	Malagasy, French	12,803,000	226,658 587 041	56.5 21.8	4.6	1.4	3.2
MALAWI	Lilongwe, Zomba	Chewa, English, Lomwe, Yao, Ngoni	9,484,000	45,747 118 484	207.3 80.0	5.5	2.0	3.5
MALI	Bamako	Bambara, Fulani, Sehufo, Soninke, French	8,464,000	482,077 1 248 574	17.6 6.8	5.0	2.0	3.0
MAURITANIA	Nouakchott	Arabic, Wolof, French, Tukulor	2,108,000	398,000 1 030 700	5.3 2.0	4.7	1.9	2.8
MAURITIUS	Port-Louis	French Creole, Bhojpuri, Hindi, French, Tamil, Urdu, Telugu, English	1,081,000	788 2 040	1,371.8 529.9	2.0	0.6	1.4
MOROCCO	Rabat	Arabic, Berber	26,239,000	177,117 458 730	148.1 57.2	3.5	0.9	2.6
MOZAMBIQUE	Maputo	Makua, Tsonga, Senoc, Lomwe, Portuguese	14,842,000	313,661 812 379	47.3 18.3	4.5	1.8	2.7
NAMIBIA	Windhoek	Ovambo, Kavango, English	1,431,000	317,818 823 144	4.5 1.7	4.3	1.2	3.1
NIGER	Niamey	Hausa, Songhai/Zerma, French	8,281,000	458,075 1 186 408	18.1 7.0	5.1	2.0	3.1
NIGERIA	Abuja	English, Hausa, Yoruba, Igbo, Fulani	89,666,000	356,669 923 768	251.4 97.1	4.8	1.5	3.3
RWANDA	Kigali	Kwanda, French	7,347,000	10,169 26 338	722.5 279.0	5.1	1.7	3.4
SAO TOME AND PRINCIPE	Sao Tome	Crioulo, Portuguese	126,000	386 1 001	326.4 125.9	3.8	0.8	3.0
SENEGAL	Dakar	Wolof, Fulani, Serer Dyola, French, Malinke	7,691,000	75,951 196 712	101.3 39.1	4.5	1.8	2.7
SEYCHELLES	Victoria	Seselwa	71,000	175 453	405.7 156.7	2.4	0.8	1.6
SIERRA LEONE	Freetown	Mende, Temne, English, Krio	4,373,000	27,699 71 740	157.9 61.0	4.8	2.3	2.5
SOMALIA	Mogadishu	Somali, Arabic, English	7,872,000	246,000 637 000	32.0 12.4	4.9	1.9	3.0
SOUTH AFRICA	Cape Town, Pretoria, Bloemfontein	Zulu, Xhosa, Afrikaans, Sotho, English	39,085,000	473,290 1 225 815	82.1 31.7	3.3	0.9	2.4
SUDAN	Khartoum	Arabic, Dinka, Nubian, Beja, Nuer, Azande	29,971,000	966,757 2 503 890	31.0 12.0	4.5	1.5	3.0
SWAZILAND	Mbabane	Swazi, Zulu, English	826,000	6,704 17 364	123.2 47.6	4.7	1.2	3.5
TANZANIA	Dar es Salaam	Swahili, English, Nyamwezi	25,809,000	364,017 942 799	70.9 27.4	5.0	1.4	3.6
TOGO	Lome	Ewe-Adja, French, Tem-Kabre, Gurma	3,701,000	21,925 56 785	168.8 65.2	4.7	1.4	3.3
TUNISIA	Tunis	Arabic, French	8,413,000	59,664 154 530	141.0 54.4	2.6	0.5	2.1
UGANDA	Kampala	Swahili, Ganda, Teso, Soga, Nkole	17,194,000	93,070 241 040	184.7 71.3	5.1	1.5	3.6
WESTERN SAHARA (adm. Morocco)	El Aaiun	Arabic	209,000	97,344 252 120	2.1 0.8	4.8	2.3	2.5
ZAMBIA	Lusaka	Bemba, Tonga, Lozi, English, Chewa, Nyamja	8,303,000	290,586 752 614	28.6 11.0	5.1	1.3	3.8
ZIMBABWE	Harare	Shona, Ndebele, Nyanja, English	9,871,000	150,873 390 759	65.4 25.3	4.0	1.0	3.0

Country: all independent countries, as well as selected dependencies. **Principal Language(s):** all official languages, as well as other primary languages spoken by a substantial proportion of the population. **Pop. Density:** population density, computed as population divided by area; given per square mile and per square kilometer. **Natural Pop. Growth:** annual population increase per 100 people; does not include population change due to immigration or emigration.

COUNTRY	CAPITAL(S)	PRINCIPAL LANGUAGE(S)	POPULATION	AREA MI.² KM²	POP. DENSITY PER MI.² PER KM²	NATURAL POP. GROWTH PER 100 PEOPLE BIRTHS	DEATHS	% GAIN
Asia								
AFGHANISTAN	Kabul	Pashto, Dari, Uzbek, Turkmen	18,052,000	251,825 652 225	71.7 27.7	4.4	2.0	2.4
ARMENIA	Yerevan	Armenia	3,426,000	11,500 29 800	297.9 115.0	2.2	0.6	1.6
AZERBAIJAN	Baku	Azerbaijani, Russian, Armenian	7,237,000	33,400 86 600	216.7 83.6	2.6	0.6	2.0
BAHRAIN	Manama	Arabic	531,000	267 692	1,988.8 767.3	3.0	0.4	2.6
BANGLADESH	Dhaka	Bengali	110,602,000	55,598 143 998	1,989.3 768.1	3.6	1.2	2.4
BHUTAN	Thimphu, Paro	Dzongkha, Assamese	1,511,000	18,150 47 000	83.3 32.1	3.8	1.6	2.2
BRUNEI	Bandar Seri Begawan	Malay, Chinese, English	268,000	2,226 5 765	120.4 46.5	2.8	0.3	2.5
CAMBODIA	Phnom Penh	Khmer	8,974,000	70,238 181 916	127.8 49.3	4.2	1.7	2.5
CHINA	Beijing	Han: Mandarin; Han: other; Zhuang	1,172,054,000	3,696,522 9 573 993	317.1 122.4	2.1	0.6	1.5
CYPRUS	Nicosia	Greek, Turkish	756,000	3,572 9 251	211.6 81.7	1.9	0.9	1.0
GEORGIA	Tbilisi	Georgian, Russian, Armenian, Azerbaijani	5,482,000	26,900 69 700	203.8 78.7	1.7	0.8	0.9
INDIA	New Delhi	Hindi, Telugu, Bengali, Maratha, Tamil	889,700,000	1,222,243 3 165 596	727.9 281.1	3.1	1.0	2.1
INDONESIA	Jakarta	Sundanese, Bahasa Indonesia	184,796,000	741,052 1 919 317	249.4 96.3	2.9	1.1	1.8
IRAN	Tehran	Farsi, Azerbaijani, Kurdish, Gilaki	59,570,000	632,457 1 638 057	94.2 36.4	4.4	1.0	3.4
IRAQ	Baghdad	Arabic, Kurdish	18,838,000	167,975 435 052	112.1 43.3	4.5	0.8	3.7
ISRAEL	Jerusalem	Hebrew, Arabic, Yiddish, Russian	5,237,000	7,992 20 700	655.5 253.1	2.2	0.6	1.6
JAPAN	Tokyo	Japanese	124,330,000	145,883 377 835	852.3 329.1	1.0	0.7	0.3
JORDAN	Amman	Arabic	3,636,000	34,342 88 946	105.9 40.9	3.9	0.6	3.3
KAZAKHSTAN	Astana	Russian, Kazakh	17,008,000	1,049,200 2 717 300	16.2 6.3	2.2	0.8	1.4
KUWAIT	Kuwait	Arabic	1,190,000	6,880 17 818	173.0 66.8	2.7	0.2	2.5
KYRGYZSTAN	Bishkek	Kyrgyz, Russian, Uzbek	4,533,000	76,600 198 500	59.2 22.8	2.9	0.7	2.2
LAOS	Vientiane	Lao, Mon-Khmer, Miao and Munt	4,409,000	91,400 236 800	48.2 18.6	4.0	1.6	2.4
LEBANON	Beirut	Arabic, French, Armenian	2,803,000	3,950 10 230	709.6 274.0	2.9	0.7	2.2
MALAYSIA	Kuala Lumpur	Malay, English, Chinese, Tamil	18,630,000	127,584 330 442	146.0 56.4	2.9	0.5	2.4
MALDIVES	Male	Divehi	230,000	115 298	2,000.0 771.8	4.2	0.9	3.3
MONGOLIA	Ulaanbaatar	Khalkar, Kazak	2,182,000	604,800 1 566 500	3.6 1.4	3.7	0.9	2.8
MYANMAR (BURMA)	Yangon (Rangoon)	Burmese, Shan, Karen	43,446,000	261,228 676 577	166.4 64.2	3.2	1.2	2.0
NEPAL	Kathmandu	Nepali, Maithili, Bhojpuri	19,795,000	56,827 147 181	348.3 134.5	3.9	1.5	2.4

Country: all independent countries, as well as selected dependencies. **Principal Language(s):** all official languages, as well as other primary languages spoken by a substantial proportion of the population. **Pop. Density:** population density, computed as population divided by area; given per square mile and per square kilometer. **Natural Pop. Growth:** annual population increase per 100 people; does not include population change due to immigration or emigration.

COUNTRY	CAPITAL(S)	PRINCIPAL LANGUAGE(S)	POPULATION	AREA MI.^{2} KM^2	POP. DENSITY PER MI.^{2} PER KM^2	NATURAL POP. GROWTH PER 100 PEOPLE BIRTHS – DEATHS = % GAIN		
NORTH KOREA	Pyongyang	Korean	22,227,000	47,400 122 762	468.9 181.1	2.5	0.6	1.9
OMAN	Muscat	Arabic, Baluchi	1,640,000	118,150 306 000	13.9 5.4	4.4	0.9	3.5
PAKISTAN	Islamabad	Paunjabi, Pashto, Sindhi, Urdu	130,129,000	339,697 879 811	383.1 147.9	4.2	1.0	3.2
PHILIPPINES	Manila	Tagalog, English, Cebuanco	63,609,000	115,800 300 000	549.3 212.0	3.4	0.8	2.6
QATAR	Doha	Arabic	520,000	4,412 11 427	117.9 45.5	3.1	0.2	2.9
SAUDI ARABIA	Riyadh	Arabic	15,267,000	865,000 2 240 000	17.6 6.8	3.7	1.1	2.6
SINGAPORE	Singapore	Mandarin, English, Bahasa, Malaysian, Tamil	2,792,000	240 622	1,633.3 4 488.7	1.9	0.5	1.4
SOUTH KOREA	Seoul	Korean	43,663,000	38,326 99 263	1,139.3 439.9	1.7	0.6	1.1
SRI LANKA	Colombo, Kotte	Sinhalese, Tamil, English	17,464,000	25,332 65 610	689.4 266.2	2.2	0.6	1.6
SYRIA	Damascus	Arabic, Kurdish, Armenian	12,958,000	71,498 185 180	181.2 70.0	4.4	0.7	3.7
TAIWAN	Taipei	Min, Mandarin, Hakka	20,727,000	13,969 36 179	1,483.8 572.9	1.6	0.5	1.1
TAJIKISTAN	Dushanbe	Tajik, Uzbek, Russian	5,568,000	55,300 143 100	100.7 38.9	3.9	0.6	3.3
THAILAND	Bangkok	Thai, Lao, Chinese, Mon-Khmer	56,801,000	198,115 513 115	286.7 110.7	2.1	0.7	1.4
TURKEY	Ankara	Turkish, Kurdish, Arabic	58,584,000	300,948 779 452	194.7 75.2	2.8	0.7	2.1
TURKMENISTAN	Ashgabat	Turkmenian, Russian, Uzbek	3,859,000	188,500 488 100	20.5 7.9	3.4	0.7	2.7
UNITED ARAB EMIRATES	Abu Dhabi	Arabic	1,989,000	30,000 77 700	66.3 25.6	3.2	0.4	2.8
UZBEKISTAN	Tashkent	Uzbek, Russian, Tajik, Kazak	21,363,000	172,700 447 400	123.7 47.7	3.4	0.6	2.8
VIETNAM	Hanoi	Vietnamese, Tay, Tai	69,052,000	127,246 329 566	542.7 209.5	3.1	0.9	2.2
YEMEN	Sanaa	Arabic	12,147,000	205,356 531 869	59.2 22.8	5.1	1.9	3.2

Australia and Oceania

COUNTRY	CAPITAL(S)	PRINCIPAL LANGUAGE(S)	POPULATION	AREA MI.^{2} KM^2	POP. DENSITY PER MI.^{2} PER KM^2	BIRTHS	DEATHS	% GAIN
AUSTRALIA	Canberra	English	17,562,000	2,966,200 7 682 300	5.9 2.3	1.5	0.7	0.8
FIJI	Suva	Fijian, Hindi, English	748,000	7,056 18 274	106.0 40.9	2.7	0.5	2.2
FRENCH POLYNESIA (Fr.)	Papeete	Polynesian, French, Chinese	206,000	1,544 4 000	133.4 51.5	2.7	0.5	2.2
KIRIBATI	Tarawa (Bairiki)	Kiribati, English	75,000	313 811	238.7 92.1	3.2	0.9	2.3
MARSHALL ISLANDS	Majuro	Marshallese, English	50,000	70 181	714.3 276.2	4.2	0.6	3.6
MICRONESIA	Palikir	Chuukese, Pohnpeian, English	114,000	271 701	420.7 162.6	3.4	0.5	2.9
NAURU	Yaren	Nauruan, Kiribati	10,000	8.2 21.2	1,170.7 452.8	2.1	0.5	1.6

Country: all independent countries, as well as selected dependencies. **Principal Language(s):** all official languages, as well as other primary languages spoken by a substantial proportion of the population. **Pop. Density:** population density, computed as population divided by area; given per square mile and per square kilometer. **Natural Pop. Growth:** annual population increase per 100 people; does not include population change due to immigration or emigration.

COUNTRY	CAPITAL(S)	PRINCIPAL LANGUAGE(S)	POPULATION	AREA MI.² KM²	POP. DENSITY PER MI.² PER KM²	NATURAL POP. GROWTH PER 100 PEOPLE BIRTHS – DEATHS = % GAIN		
NEW CALEDONIA (Fr.)	Noumea	English, Maori, Malanesian, Polynesian	174,000	7,172 18 576	24.3 9.4	2.4	0.6	1.8
NEW ZEALAND	Wellington	English, Maori	3,481,000	104,454 270 534	33.3 12.9	2.1	0.6	1.0
PALAU	Koror	Palauan, English	16,000	188 488	83.5 32.2	2.5	0.6	1.9
PAPUA NEW GUINEA	Port Moresby	Papuan, English, Melanesian	3,834,000	178,704 462 840	21.5 8.3	3.5	1.2	2.3
SAMOA	Apia	Samoan, English	160,000	1,093 2 831	146.4 56.5	3.3	0.7	2.6
SOLOMON ISLANDS	Honiara	Melanesian, Papuan, English	339,000	10,954 28 370	30.9 11.9	4.4	1.0	3.4
TONGA	Nukualofa	Tongan, English	97,000	301 780	323.3 124.7	3.0	0.7	2.3
TUVALU	Funafuti	Tuvaluan, English, Kiribati	10,000	9.3 24.0	1,021.5 395.8	2.9	1.0	1.9
VANUATU	Port-Vila	Melanesian, English	154,000	4,707 12 190	32.7 12.6	4.1	0.8	3.3

Europe

COUNTRY	CAPITAL(S)	PRINCIPAL LANGUAGE(S)	POPULATION	AREA MI.² KM²	POP. DENSITY PER MI.² PER KM²	BIRTHS	DEATHS	% GAIN
ALBANIA	Tirana	Albanian	3,357,000	11,100 28 748	302.4 116.8	2.5	0.5	2.0
ANDORRA	Andorra la Vella	Spanish, Catalan, French, Portuguese	57,000	181 468	315.5 122.0	1.4	0.4	1.0
AUSTRIA	Vienna	German, Serbo-Croatian	7,857,000	32,378 83 859	242.7 93.7	1.2	1.1	0.1
BELARUS	Minsk	Belorussian, Russian	10,321,000	80,200 207 600	128.7 49.7	1.4	1.1	0.3
BELGIUM	Brussels	Dutch, French	10,021,000	11,787 30 528	850.2 328.3	1.2	1.1	0.1
BOSNIA AND HERZEGOVINA	Sarajevo	Serbo-Croatian	4,397,000	19,741 51 129	222.7 86.0	1.4	0.6	0.8
BULGARIA	Sofia	Bulgarian, Turkish	8,985,000	42,855 110 994	209.7 81.0	1.2	1.2	0.0
CROATIA	Zagreb	Serbo-Croatian	4,808,000	21,829 56 538	220.3 85.0	1.2	1.1	0.1
CZECH REPUBLIC	Prague	Czech, Moravian, Slovak, Hungarian	10,323,000	30,450 78 864	339.0 130.9	1.4	1.2	0.2
DENMARK	Copenhagen	Danish	5,167,000	16,638 43 093	310.6 119.9	1.2	1.2	0.0
ESTONIA	Tallinn	Estonian, Russian	1,592,000	17,413 45 100	91.4 35.3	1.4	1.2	0.2
FINLAND	Helsinki	Finnish, Swedish	5,033,000	130,559 338 145	38.5 14.9	1.3	1.0	0.3
FRANCE	Paris	French, Arabic	57,289,000	210,026 543 965	272.8 105.3	1.4	0.9	0.5
GERMANY	Berlin	German, Turkish	79,122,000	137,822 356 957	574.1 221.7	1.1	1.1	0.0
GREECE	Athens	Greek	10,288,000	50,949 131 957	201.9 78.0	1.0	0.9	0.1
HUNGARY	Budapest	Hungarian, Romany	10,318,000	35,920 93 033	287.2 110.9	1.2	1.4	−0.2
ICELAND	Reykjavik	Icelandic	261,000	39,699 102 819	6.6 2.5	1.9	0.7	1.2
IRELAND	Dublin	English, Irish	3,519,000	27,137 70 285	129.7 50.1	1.5	0.9	0.6
ITALY	Rome	Italian, Sardinian	57,158,000	116,324 301 277	491.4 189.7	1.0	0.9	0.1

Country: all independent countries, as well as selected dependencies. **Principal Language(s):** all official languages, as well as other primary languages spoken by a substantial proportion of the population. **Pop. Density:** population density, computed as population divided by area; given per square mile and per square kilometer. **Natural Pop. Growth:** annual population increase per 100 people; does not include population change due to immigration or emigration.

COUNTRY	CAPITAL(S)	PRINCIPAL LANGUAGE(S)	POPULATION	AREA MI.² KM²	POP. DENSITY PER MI.² PER KM²	NATURAL POP. GROWTH PER 100 PEOPLE BIRTHS – DEATHS = % GAIN		
LATVIA	Riga	Latvian, Russian	2,685,000	24,900 64 500	107.8 41.6	1.4	1.3	0.1
LIECHTENSTEIN	Vaduz	German	30,000	62 160	477.4 185.0	1.3	0.6	0.7
LITHUANIA	Vilnius	Lithuanian, Russian, Polish	3,801,000	25,213 65 301	150.8 58.2	1.5	1.1	0.4
LUXEMBOURG	Luxembourg	Luxemburgian, French, Portuguese, Italian, French, German	387,000	999 2 586	387.4 149.7	1.2	1.0	0.2
MACEDONIA	Skopje	Macedonian, Albanian, Serbo-Croatian, Turkish	2,050,000	9,928 25 713	206.5 79.7	1.7	0.7	1.0
MALTA	Valletta	Maltese, English	360,000	122 316	2,950.8 1 139.2	1.5	0.8	0.7
MOLDOVA	Chisinau	Moldovan, Russian, Ukrainian, Gagauz	4,394,000	13,000 33 700	338.0 130.4	1.8	1.0	0.8
MONACO	Monaco	French, Italian, Monegasque, English	30,000	0.75 1.95	40,400.0 15 538.5	2.2	1.8	0.4
NETHERLANDS	Amsterdam, The Hague	Dutch, Frisian, Turkish, Arabic	15,163,000	16,163 41 863	938.1 362.2	1.3	0.9	0.4
NORWAY	Oslo	Norwegian	4,283,000	125,050 323 878	34.3 13.2	1.4	1.1	0.3
POLAND	Warsaw	Polish	38,429,000	120,727 312 683	318.3 122.9	1.5	1.0	0.5
PORTUGAL	Lisbon	Portuguese	10,429,000	35,672 92 389	292.4 112.9	1.2	0.9	0.3
ROMANIA	Bucharest	Romanian, Hungarian	23,332,000	91,699 237 500	254.4 98.2	1.5	1.1	0.4
RUSSIA	Moscow	Russian	149,469,000	6,592,800 17 075 400	22.7 8.8	1.3	1.1	0.2
SAN MARINO	San Marino	Italian	24,000	24 61	983.3 386.9	1.0	0.7	0.3
SLOVAKIA	Bratislava	Slovak, Hungarian, Czech	5,282,000	18,932 49 035	279.0 107.7	1.4	1.2	0.2
SLOVENIA	Ljubljana	Slovene, Serbo-Croatian	1,985,000	7,821 20 256	353.8 98.0	1.2	1.0	0.2
SPAIN	Madrid	Castilian Spanish, Catalan, Galician, Basque	39,085,000	194,898 504 783	200.5 77.4	1.1	0.8	0.3
SWEDEN	Stockholm	Swedish	8,673,000	173,732 449 964	49.9 19.3	1.4	1.1	0.3
SWITZERLAND	Bern	German, French, Italian, Romansch	6,911,000	15,943 41 293	433.5 167.4	1.2	0.9	0.3
UKRAINE	Kiev	Ukrainian, Russian	52,135,000	233,100 603 700	223.7 86.4	1.3	1.2	0.1
UNITED KINGDOM	London	English, Welsh, Scots-Gaelic	57,730,000	94,251 244 110	612.5 236.5	1.4	1.1	0.3
VATICAN CITY	Vatican City	Italian, Latin	1,000	0.17 0.44	4,576.5 1 768.2	0.0	0.0	0.0
YUGOSLAVIA	Belgrade	Serbo-Croatian, Albanian, Hungarian	10,394,000	39,449 102 173	263.5 101.7	1.5	0.9	0.6

North America

COUNTRY	CAPITAL(S)	PRINCIPAL LANGUAGE(S)	POPULATION	AREA MI.² KM²	POP. DENSITY PER MI.² PER KM²	BIRTHS	DEATHS	% GAIN
ANTIGUA AND BARBUDA	St. John's	English	64,000	171 442	374.3 144.8	1.4	0.5	0.9
ARUBA (Neth.)	Oranjestad	Dutch, Papiamento	69,000	75 193	921.3 358.0	1.8	0.6	1.1
BAHAMAS	Nassau	English, French	264,000	5,382 13 939	49.1 18.9	1.9	0.5	1.4

Country: all independent countries, as well as selected dependencies. **Principal Language(s):** all official languages, as well as other primary languages spoken by a substantial proportion of the population. **Pop. Density:** population density, computed as population divided by area; given per square mile and per square kilometer. **Natural Pop. Growth:** annual population increase per 100 people; does not include population change due to immigration or emigration.

COUNTRY	CAPITAL(S)	PRINCIPAL LANGUAGE(S)	POPULATION	AREA MI.² KM²	POP. DENSITY PER MI.² PER KM²	NATURAL POP. GROWTH PER 100 PEOPLE BIRTHS	– DEATHS	= % GAIN
BARBADOS	Bridgetown	English	259,000	166 430	1,560.2 602.3	1.6	0.9	0.7
BELIZE	Belmopan	English, Spanish, Mayan, Garifuna	196,000	8,867 22 965	22.1 8.5	3.8	0.5	3.3
CANADA	Ottawa	English, French, Italian, German	27,737,000	3,849,674 9 970 610	7.2 2.8	1.4	0.7	0.7
COSTA RICA	San Jose	Spanish	3,161,000	19,730 51 100	160.2 61.9	2.8	0.4	2.4
CUBA	Havana	Spanish	10,848,000	42,804 110 861	253.4 97.9	1.8	0.6	1.2
DOMINICA	Roseau	English, French	72,000	290 750	248.3 96	2.2	0.7	1.5
DOMINICAN REPUBLIC	Santo Domingo	Spanish	7,471,000	18,704 48 443	399.4 154.2	2.7	0.7	2.0
EL SALVADOR	San Salvador	Spanish	5,460,000	8,124 21 041	672.1 259.5	3.4	0.8	2.6
GREENLAND (KALAALLIT NUNAAT) (Den.)	Godthab (Nuuk)	Greenlandic, Danish	57,000	840,000 2 175 600	0.1 0.0	2.2	0.8	1.4
GRENADA	St. George's	English	91,000	134 348	678.4 261.2	3.2	0.8	2.4
GUADELOUPE (Fr.)	Basse-Terre	French	400,000	687 1 780	582.2 224.7	2.0	0.6	1.4
GUATEMALA	Guatemala City	Spanish, Mayan, Black Carib	9,442,000	42,042 108 889	224.6 86.7	3.9	0.7	3.2
HAITI	Port-au-Prince	French	6,764,000	10,695 27 700	632.4 244.2	3.5	1.3	2.2
HONDURAS	Tegucigalpa	Spanish	4,996,000	43,277 112 088	115.4 44.6	3.8	0.7	3.1
JAMAICA	Kingston	English	2,445,000	4,244 10 991	576.1 222.5	2.5	0.6	1.9
MARTINIQUE (Fr.)	Fort-de-France	French	369,000	436 1 128	846.3 327.1	1.9	0.6	1.3
MEXICO	Mexico City	Spanish	84,439,000	756,066 1 958 201	111.7 43.1	3.3	0.5	2.8
NETHERLANDS ANTILLES (Neth.)	Willemstad	Dutch, Papiamento, English	191,000	308 800	620.1 238.8	2.4	0.6	1.5
NICARAGUA	Managua	Spanish, Miskito	4,131,000	50,464 130 700	81.9 31.6	3.9	0.7	3.2
PANAMA	Panama City	Spanish, English, Chibchan	2,515,000	29,157 75 517	86.3 33.3	2.5	0.5	2.0
PUERTO RICO (U.S.)	San Juan	Spanish, English	3,581,000	3,515 9 104	1,018.8 393.3	1.9	0.7	1.2
ST. KITTS AND NEVIS	Basseterre	English	43,000	104 269	414.4 160.2	2.2	1.1	1.1
ST. LUCIA	Castries	English, French	135,000	238 617	567.2 218.8	2.5	0.6	1.9
ST. VINCENT AND THE GRENADINES	Kingstown	English	109,000	150 389	726.7 280.2	2.6	0.6	2.0
TRINIDAD AND TOBAGO	Port-of-Spain	English	1,261,000	1,980 5 128	636.9 245.9	2.2	0.7	1.5
UNITED STATES OF AMERICA	Washington, D.C.	English, Spanish	255,414,000	3,679,192 9 529 063	69.4 26.8	1.6	0.9	0.7

Country: all independent countries, as well as selected dependencies. **Principal Language(s):** all official languages, as well as other primary languages spoken by a substantial proportion of the population. **Pop. Density:** population density, computed as population divided by area; given per square mile and per square kilometer. **Natural Pop. Growth:** annual population increase per 100 people; does not include population change due to immigration or emigration.

COUNTRY	CAPITAL(S)	PRINCIPAL LANGUAGE(S)	POPULATION	AREA MI.² KM²	POP. DENSITY PER MI.² PER KM²	NATURAL POP. GROWTH PER 100 PEOPLE BIRTHS – DEATHS = % GAIN		
South America								
ARGENTINA	Buenos Aires	Spanish	33,070,000	1,073,518 2 780 400	30.8 11.9	2.0	0.9	1.1
BOLIVIA	La Paz, Sucre	Spanish, Quechua, Aymara	7,739,000	424,164 1 098 581	18.2 7.0	4.3	1.4	2.9
BRAZIL	Brasilia	Portuguese	151,381,000	3,286,500 8 511 996	46.1 17.8	2.8	0.8	2.0
CHILE	Santiago, Valparaiso	Spanish, Mapuche	13,599,000	292,135 756 626	46.6 18.0	2.3	0.6	1.7
COLOMBIA	Bogota	Spanish	34,252,000	440,831 1 141 748	77.7 30.0	2.7	0.7	2.0
ECUADOR	Quito	Spanish, Quechua	10,607,000	104,505 270 667	101.5 39.2	3.5	0.8	2.7
FRENCH GUIANA (Fr.)	Cayenne	French	123,000	33,399 86 504	3.7 1.4	3.0	0.5	2.5
GUYANA	Georgetown	English, Hindi	748,000	83,044 215 083	9.0 3.5	2.4	0.6	1.8
PARAGUAY	Asuncion	Guarani, Spanish, Portuguese	4,519,000	157,048 406 752	28.8 11.1	3.4	0.7	2.7
PERU	Lima	Spanish, Quechua, Aymara	22,454,000	496,225 1 285 216	45.2 17.5	3.3	0.8	2.5
SURINAME	Paramaribo	Sranantonga, Dutch	404,000	63,251 163 820	6.4 2.5	2.6	0.6	2.0
URUGUAY	Montevideo	Spanish	3,130,000	68,037 176 215	46.0 17.8	1.8	1.0	0.8
VENEZUELA	Caracas	Spanish	20,184,000	352,144 912 050	57.3 22.1	2.8	0.4	2.4

Country: all independent countries, as well as selected dependencies. **Principal Language(s):** all official languages, as well as other primary languages spoken by a substantial proportion of the population. **Pop. Density:** population density, computed as population divided by area; given per square mile and per square kilometer. **Natural Pop. Growth:** annual population increase per 100 people; does not include population change due to immigration or emigration.

GLOSSARY

acid rain Rain or snow that carries acids formed from chemical pollutants in the atmosphere.

Antarctic Circle An imaginary line of latitude located at 66½°S, approximately 1,630 miles (2620 kilometers) from the South Pole.

Arctic Circle An imaginary line of latitude located at 66½°N, approximately 1,630 miles (2620 kilometers) from the North Pole.

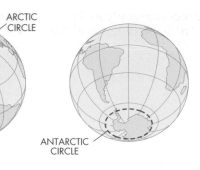

balance of trade The difference between how much a country exports and how much it imports, commonly measured in U.S. dollars. A country that exports more than it imports has a positive balance of trade, or *trade surplus*. A country that imports more than it exports has a negative balance of trade, or *trade deficit*.

center of population The location from which a country's population is equally distributed north, south, east, and west. The center of population changes as the population shifts from one region to another.

climate The usual weather conditions for a large area over a long period of time and through all seasons. Climate is affected by latitude, elevation, topography, ocean currents, and wind.

climograph Graph showing annual patterns of temperature and precipitation.

commodity One of the goods sold on the world market. Commodities may be agricultural products, manufactured items, or such natural resources as minerals.

deforestation Massive removal of trees from a forest.

elevation Height above sea level.

emigration Movement of people away from their native country or region to a new home elsewhere. The people moving away are called *emigrants*.

Equator An imaginary line that divides the earth into the Northern and Southern Hemispheres. All points along the Equator have a latitude of 0°.

European Union (EU) A group of European nations whose main goal is to establish themselves for trading purposes as a single market. The EU grew out of the European Economic Community.

export The sale of goods to a foreign country.

fossil fuels Natural fuels that were formed from the remains of plants and animals over millions of years. Principal fossil fuels are petroleum, natural gas, and coal.

gross domestic product (GDP) Annual value of all goods and services produced within a country's borders. GDP includes production by foreign-owned facilities.

gross national product (GNP) Annual value of all goods and services produced by companies that are owned by a country's citizens. GNP includes production in facilities operated by the nation's citizens in other countries.

immigration Movement of people into a new country of residence. The people moving in are called *immigrants*.

imperialism Action taken by one country to control or influence another country or territory in order to gain economic or political advantage.

import The purchase of goods produced in a foreign country.

indigenous Native to a particular region. Indigenous peoples are related to the earliest inhabitants of a region.

land use How people use the earth's surface and natural resources for economic purposes. Regions are identified by the dominant form of economy, such as farming, herding, or manufacturing.

latitude Distance from the Equator measured in degrees. Lines of latitude, or *parallels,* are numbered north and south from the Equator and appear on maps as east-west lines.

life expectancy The average number of years that a group of people may expect to live based on the prevailing death rates for that population. Life expectancy reflects the group's general health and welfare.

literacy The ability to both read and write. The percentage of literate people is a good indicator of a country's educational level, although literacy standards vary by country.

longitude Distance from the Prime Meridian measured in degrees. Lines of longitude, or *meridians,* are numbered east and west from the Prime Meridian and appear on maps as north-south lines.

map projection Any system for drawing lines of latitude and longitude onto a map. Projections are never completely accurate, distorting either sizes or shapes of the earth's land and water features.

natural population growth Annual population increase for a region or country. It is the difference between the number of births and the number of deaths and does not include change due to population movement.

natural vegetation The type of vegetation that can grow in a specific region's climate and soil without benefit of human intervention or cultivation.

Oceania Collective name for islands of the central and southern Pacific Ocean, usually including New Zealand and sometimes also including Australia.

Organization of Petroleum Exporting Countries (OPEC) Association of 11 nations that control most of the world's known oil reserves. OPEC members are Algeria, Indonesia, Iran, Iraq, Kuwait, Libya, Nigeria, Qatar, Saudi Arabia, United Arab Emirates, and Venezuela.

ozone A form of oxygen that occurs naturally in the atmosphere in small amounts. The layer of ozone in the upper atmosphere blocks most of the sun's harmful ultraviolet rays.

precipitation Water from the atmosphere that accumulates on the earth's surface as dew, rain, hail, sleet, or snow. For annual measures, ten inches of snow, sleet, or hail are counted as one inch of rain.

Prime Meridian The 0° meridian, which passes through Greenwich, England.

Sahel The drought-ridden area south of Africa's Sahara and extending east-west between Somalia and Senegal.

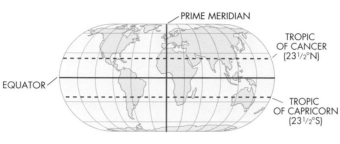

staple food A foodstuff that constitutes a major part of the diet for a region's population.

Tropic of Cancer An imaginary line of latitude located at 23½°N. It marks the northern boundary of the earth's tropical zone.

Tropic of Capricorn An imaginary line of latitude located at 23½°S. It marks the southern boundary of the earth's tropical zone.

wetlands A transition zone between land and water where the water level remains near or above the ground's surface for most of the year. Wetlands include swamps, marshes, and bogs.

Abbreviations

adm.	administered	km	kilometers	Oreg.	Oregon
Ala.	Alabama	Ky.	Kentucky	Pa.	Pennsylvania
Alb.	Albania	L., l.	Lake	Pen., pen.	Peninsula
Am. Samoa	American Samoa	La.	Louisiana	Pk., pk.	Peak
Ang.	Angola	Lat.	Latvia	Port.	Portugal
Arg.	Argentina	lat.	latitude	poss.	possession
Ariz.	Arizona	Liech.	Liechtenstein	Prov., prov.	Province
Ark.	Arkansas	Lith.	Lithuania	Pt.	Point
Aus.	Austria	long.	longitude	R., r.	River
Austr.	Australia	Lux.	Luxembourg	R.I.	Rhode Island
Azer.	Azerbaijan	m	meters	Ra.	Range
Bos.	Bosnia and Herzegovina	Mac.	Macedonia	Res., res.	Reservoir
		Mass.	Massachusetts	S. Afr.	South Africa
C.	Cape	Md.	Maryland	S. Dak.	South Dakota
C. Afr. Rep.	Central African Republic	Mex.	Mexico	S.C.	South Carolina
Calif.	California	mi.	miles	Sl., Slovak.	Slovakia
Colo.	Colorado	Mich.	Michigan	Slov.	Slovenia
Congo Rep.	Congo Republic	Minn.	Minnesota	Sp.	Spain
Conn.	Connecticut	Miss.	Mississippi	sq.	square
Cro.	Croatia	Mo.	Missouri	St., Ste.	Saint, Sainte
Cz., Cz. Rep.	Czech Republic	Mont.	Montana	Str.	Strait
D.C.	District of Columbia	Mt., Mts.	Mount, Mont, Mountain, Mountains	Switz.	Switzerland
Del.	Delaware			Tenn.	Tennessee
Den.	Denmark	N.C.	North Carolina	Terr., terr.	Territory
Dom. Rep.	Dominican Republic	N. Dak.	North Dakota	Tex.	Texas
Eq. Guinea	Equatorial Guinea	N.H.	New Hampshire	U.A.E.	United Arab Emirates
Est.	Estonia	N.J.	New Jersey	U.K.	United Kingdom
Fk.	Fork	N.Mex.	New Mexico	U.S.	United States
Fla.	Florida	N.P.	National Park	US$	United States dollars
Fr.	France, French	N.W.T.	Northwest Territories	U.S.S.R.	Union of Soviet Socialist Republics
ft.	feet	N.Y.	New York		
Ga.	Georgia	N.Z.	New Zealand	Va.	Virginia
I., Is.	Island, Islands	Nebr.	Nebraska	Vt.	Vermont
Ill.	Illinois	Neth.	Netherlands	W. Va.	West Virginia
Ind.	Indiana	Nev.	Nevada	Wash.	Washington
Intl.	International	Nor.	Norway	Wis.	Wisconsin
It.	Italy	O.	Ocean	Wyo.	Wyoming
Kans.	Kansas	Okla.	Oklahoma	Yugo.	Yugoslavia

INDEX

The index lists all the place names that appear in the book. Each entry includes a brief description of what or where it is, its latitude and longitude, and its main page reference. Many of the entries also include phonetic pronunciations. The key to the system of phonetic respelling is given on the inside back cover, so it can be turned to easily.

The entry for a physical feature is alphabetized by the proper part of its name, not by the descriptive part. For example, Lake Superior is listed as *Superior, L.*, and Mount Etna is listed as *Etna, Mt.* The entry for a city, however, is alphabetized by the first word in its name, no matter what it is, so that the city of Lake Charles, Louisiana, is listed as *Lake Charles*. Similarly, foreign names such as Rio Grande are alphabetized by the first word in the name.

Names beginning with *St.* are spelled *Saint* in the index. Abbreviations that are used in the index and in other parts of the book are listed on page 149.

Name (Pronunciation), *Description* (Lat., Long.)	Page

A

Aachen (AH kuhn), *Germany* (51 °N, 6 °E) — 99
Aba (ah BAH), *Nigeria* (5 °N, 7 °E) — 108
Abadan, *Iran* (30 °N, 49 °E) — 115
Abeche, *Chad* (14 °N, 21 °E) — 114
Abeokuta (AB ee OH kuht uh), *Nigeria* (7 °N, 3 °E) — 108
Aberdeen, *Scotland* (57 °N, 2 °W) — 98
Aberdeen, *S. Dak.* (46 °N, 99 °W) — 62
Aberdeen, *Wash.* (47 °N, 124 °W) — 60
Aberystwyth (AB uh RIS twith), *Wales* (52 °N, 4 °W) — 98
Abidjan (AB ih JAHN), *Côte d'Ivoire* (5 °N, 4 °W) — 108
Abilene (AB uh LEEN), *Kans.* (39 °N, 97 °W) — 64
Abilene, *Tex.* (32 °N, 100 °W) — 66
Abitibi, L.(AB uh TIHB ee), *Ontario* (49 °N, 80 °W) — 46
Abitibi R. , *Ontario* (51 °N, 81 °W) — 46
Absaroka Range (ab SAHR uh kuh), *Wyo.* (44 °N, 110 °W) — 61
Abu Dhabi (AHB oo DAHB ee), *United Arab Emirates* (24 °N, 55 °E) — 115
Abuja (ah BOO juh), *Nigeria* (9 °N, 8 °E) — 108
Abuna R. (ah boo NAH), *South America* (10 °S, 67 °W) — 90
Acadia N.P. (uh KAY dee uh), *Maine* (44 °N, 68 °W) — 73
Acapulco (AH kah POOL koh), *Mexico* (17 °N, 100 °W) — 84
Accra, *Ghana* (6 °N, 0 °) — 108
Aconcagua (AH kawng KAH gwah), *mt. in South America* (33 °S, 70 °W) — 88
Ad Dammam, *Saudi Arabia* (27 °N, 50 °E) — 115
Adamaoua Plateau (AH duh MAH wuh), *Africa* (8 °N, 15 °E) — 108
Adams, Mt., *Wash.* (46 °N, 121 °W) — 60
Adana, *Turkey* (37 °N, 35 °E) — 115
Addis Ababa (AD ihs AB uh buh), *Ethiopia* (9 °N, 39 °E) — 107
Adelaide (AD uh LAYD), *Australia* (35 °S, 138 °E) — 133
Aden (AHD uhn), *Yemen* (13 °N, 45 °E) — 115
Aden, Gulf of, *Arabian Sea* (13 °N, 48 °E) — 115
Adige R. (AHD uh JAY), *Italy* (46 °N, 11 °E) — 99
Adirondack Mts., *N.Y.* (44 °N, 74 °W) — 72
Admiralty I., *Papua New Guinea* (2 °S, 147 °E) — 130
Adriatic Sea, *Europe* (44 °N, 13 °E) — 99
Aegean Sea, *Mediterranean Sea* (38 °N, 25 °E) — 99
Afghanistan, *country in Asia* (34 °N, 65 °E) — 120
Africa, *continent* — 7
Agadez, *Niger* (17 °N, 8 °E) — 107
Agalega Is., *Indian Ocean* (10 °S, 57 °E) — 106
Agra, *India* (27 °N, 78 °E) — 122
Agrinion (ah GREEN yawn), *Greece* (39 °N, 21 °E) — 99
Aguanus R. (ah GWAHN uhs), *Quebec* (50 °N, 62 °W) — 47
Aguasabon R., *Ontario* (49 °N, 87 °W) — 46
Aguascalientes (AH wuh SKAHL YEN tuhs), *Mexico* (22 °N, 102 °W) — 84
Aguja, Point (ah GOO hah), *Peru* (6 °S, 81 °W) — 90
Agulhas, Cape (uh GUHL uhs), *South Africa* (35 °S, 20 °E) — 109

Agulhas Negras, *mt. in Brazil* (22 °S, 46 °W) — 88
Ahaggar Mts., *Africa* (24 °N, 6 °E) — 114
Ahmadabad, *India* (23 °N, 73 °E) — 122
Ahvaz, *Iran* (31 °N, 49 °E) — 115
Air Mts., *Niger* (18 °N, 8 °E) — 106
Aix-en-Provence (AYK SAHN pruh VAHNS), *France* (44 °N, 5 °E) — 98
Ajaccio (ah YAHCH OH), *Corsica* (42 °N, 9 °E) — 98
Akimiski I., *James Bay* (53 °N, 80 °W) — 46
Akita (ah KEET uh), *Japan* (40 °N, 140 °E) — 125
Akron, *Ohio* (41 °N, 81 °W) — 71
Al Aziziyah (al AZ ee ZEE yuh), *Libya* (33 °N, 13 °E) — 114
Al Fashir (AL FAH shuhr), *Sudan* (14 °N, 25 °E) — 115
Al Fayyum (AL fay YOOM), *Egypt* (29 °N, 31 °E) — 115
Al Jawf, *Libya* (24 °N, 23 °E) — 115
Al Minya, *Egypt* (28 °N, 31 °E) — 115
Alabama, *state in U.S.* (33 °N, 87 °W) — 68
Alabama R., *Ala.* (32 °N, 88 °W) — 68
Alamogordo (AL uh muh GAWRD oh), *N. Mex.* (33 °N, 106 °W) — 59
Aland Is., *Finland* (60 °N, 21 °E) — 95
Alaska, *state of U.S.* (65 °N, 155 °W) — 57
Alaska, Gulf of, *Pacific O.* (59 °N, 145 °W) — 57
Alaska Pen., *Alaska* (55 °N, 164 °W) — 57
Alaska Range, *Alaska* (63 °N, 150 °W) — 57
Albania, *country in Europe* (41 °N, 20 °E) — 99
Albany, *Ga.* (32 °N, 84 °W) — 69
Albany, *N.Y.* (43 °N, 74 °W) — 72
Albany, *Oreg.* (45 °N, 123 °W) — 60
Albany R., *Ontario* (51 °N, 82 °W) — 46
Albemarle Sound, *N.C.* (36 °N, 76 °W) — 71
Albert, L., *Africa* (2 °N, 31 °E) — 110
Albert Nile, *r. in Uganda* (3 °N, 31 °E) — 110
Alberta, *prov. in Canada* (57 °N, 115 °W) — 44-45
Alborg (AWL bawrg), *Denmark* (57 °N, 10 °E) — 98
Albuquerque (AL buh kur kee), *N. Mex.* (35 °N, 107 °W) — 59
Albury, *Australia* (36 °S, 147 °E) — 133
Aldabra Is., *Indian O.* (9 °S, 46 °E) — 106
Aldan R., *Russia* (63 °N, 133 °E) — 101
Alenquer (ah leng KEHR), *Brazil* (2 °S, 55 °W) — 90
Alenuihaha Channel (AHL uh NOO ee HAH HAH), *Hawaii* (20 °N, 156 °W) — 57
Aleppo, *Syria* (36 °N, 37 °E) — 115
Aleutian Is. (uh LOO shuhn), *Bering Sea* (52 °N, 180 °) — 57
Alexander Archipelago, *Alaska* (57 °N, 135 °W) — 57
Alexander I., *Antarctica* (70 °S, 70 °W) — 137
Alexandria, *Egypt* (31 °N, 30 °E) — 115
Alexandria, *La.* (32 °N, 93 °W) — 67
Alexandria, *Minn.* (46 °N, 95 °W) — 62
Alexandria, *Va.* (39 °N, 77 °W) — 71
Alexandrina, L., *Australia* (36 °S, 139 °E) — 133
Algeria, *country in Africa* (28 °N, 3 °E) — 114
Algiers (al JEERS), *Algeria* (37 °N, 3 °E) — 114
Alice Springs, *Australia* (24 °S, 134 °E) — 131
Allahabad (AL uh huh BAD), *India* (26 °N, 82 °E) — 122
Allatoona L., *Ga.* (34 °N, 85 °W) — 68

Allegheny Mts. (AL uh GAY nee), *U.S.* (38 °N, 80 °W) — 71
Allegheny Plateau, *U.S.* (39 °N, 80 °W) — 71
Allegheny Res., *U.S.* (42 °N, 79 °W) — 72
Allegheny R., *Pa.* (41 °N, 80 °W) — 72
Allentown, *Pa.* (41 °N, 75 °W) — 72
Alliance, *Nebr.* (42 °N, 103 °W) — 64
Alliance, *Ohio* (41 °N, 81 °W) — 71
Allier R. (al YAY), *France* (46 °N, 3 °E) — 98
Alma, *Quebec* (48 °N, 72 °W) — 47
Almaty, *Kazakhstan* (43 °N, 77 °E) — 100
Alpena, *Mich.* (45 °N, 83 °W) — 63
Alpine, *Tex.* (30 °N, 104 °W) — 66
Alps, *mt. range in Europe* (46 °N, 10 °E) — 99
Alsace (al SAS), *region of France* (48 °N, 8 °E) — 98
Altai Mts. (AL ty), *Asia* (49 °N, 90 °E) — 118
Altamaha R., *Ga.* (32 °N, 82 °W) — 69
Altamira, *Brazil* (3 °S, 52 °W) — 90
Altamonte Springs (AL tuh MAHNT), *Fla.* (29 °N, 81 °W) — 69
Alton, *Ill.* (39 °N, 90 °W) — 65
Altona, *Manitoba* (49 °N, 98 °W) — 45
Altoona, *Pa.* (40 °N, 78 °W) — 72
Altun Shan (ahl toon shahn), *mts. in China* (40 °N, 90 °E) — 124
Alvaro Abregon Res., *Mexico* (28 °N, 110 °W) — 82
Am Timan, *Chad* (11 °N, 20 °E) — 107
Amarillo, *Tex.* (35 °N, 102 °W) — 66
Amazon Basin, *South America* (4 °S, 65 °W) — 88
Amazon, Mouths of the, *Brazil* (0 °, 50 °W) — 88
Amazon R., *South America* (3 °S, 59 °W) — 90
American Falls Res., *Idaho* (43 °N, 113 °W) — 61
American Samoa, *poss. of U.S.* (14 °S, 170 °W) — 135
Americus, *Ga.* (32 ° 84 °W) — 69
Amery Ice Shelf, *Antarctica* (70 °S, 70 °E) — 137
Ames, *Iowa* (42 °N, 94 °W) — 65
Amherst, *Nova Scotia* (46 °N, 64 °W) — 47
Amiens (AM ee uhnz), *France* (50 °N, 2 °E) — 98
Amirante Is. (AM uh RANT), *Indian O.* (5 °S, 53 °E) — 106
Amistad L., *Saskatchewan* (55 °N, 102 °W) — 45
Amistad Res., *Mexico and U.S.* (30 °N, 101 °W) — 66
Amman, *Jordan* (32 °N, 36 °E) — 115
Amritsar (uhm RIHT suhr), *India* (32 °N, 75 °E) — 122
Amsterdam, *Netherlands* (53 °N, 5 °E) — 98
Amsterdam I., *Indian O.* (38 °S, 78 °E) — 11
Amu Darya (AHM oo DAHR yuh), *r. in Asia* (40 °N, 63 °E) — 100
Amundsen Gulf, *Beaufort Sea* (71 °N, 125 °W) — 40
Amundsen Sea, *Antarctica* (70 °S, 110 °W) — 137
Amur R. (ah MOOR), *Asia* (53 °N, 123 °E) — 119
An Nafud (AN nuh FOOD), *desert in Saudi Arabia* (28 °N, 40 °E) — 115
Anadyr (an uh DIR), *Russia* (65 °N, 178 °E) — 101
Anadyr, Gulf of, *Bering Sea* (65 °N, 178 °W) — 101
Anaheim (AN uh HYM), *Calif.* (34 °N, 118 °W) — 58
Anatolia (AN uh TOH lee uh), *region of Turkey* (38 °N, 30 °E) — 115
Anchorage, *Alaska* (61 °N, 150 °W) — 57
Ancona (ang KOH nuh), *Italy* (44 °N, 14 °E) — 99
Andaman Is., *Bay of Bengal* (12 °N, 93 °E) — 122

Name (Pronunciation), *Description* (Lat, Long)	Page
Andaman Sea, *Indian O.* (12°N, 96°E)	122
Anderson, *Ind.* (40°N, 86°W)	70
Anderson, *S.C.* (35°N, 83°W)	69
Andes, *mt. range in South America* (10°S, 77°W)	88
Andorra, *country in Europe* (43°N, 2°E)	98
Andorra la Vella (an DAWR uh lah VEL ah), *Andorra* (43°N, 2°E)	98
Andros I., *Atlantic O.* (24°N, 78°W)	83
Androscoggin R., *Maine* (44°N, 71°W)	73
Anegada Passage, *Caribbean Sea* (18°N, 64°W)	83
Angel de la Guarda I., *Mexico* (29°N, 113°W)	82
Angel Falls, *waterfall in Venezuela* (6°N, 63°W)	90
Angelina, *Tex.* (30°N, 94°W)	67
Angers (ahn ZHAY), *France* (47°N, 1°W)	98
Angikuni L., *Nunavut* (62°N, 100°W)	45
Angola, *country in Africa* (12°S, 17°E)	107
Angostura Res., *Mexico* (16°N, 92°W)	82
Anguilla (ang GWIL uh), *island in Caribbean Sea* (18°N, 63°W)	83
Anju (AHN joo), *N. Korea* (40°N, 126°E)	125
Ankara, *Turkey* (40°N, 33°E)	115
Ann, Cape, *Mass.* (43°N, 71°W)	73
Ann Arbor, *Mich.* (42°N, 84°W)	63
Annaba (an NAHB uh), *Algeria* (37°N, 8°E)	114
Annamite Mts., *Asia* (17°N, 106°E)	123
Annapolis, *Md.* (39°N, 76°W)	71
Anniston, *Ala.* (34°N, 86°W)	68
Annobon, *island in Atlantic O.* (2°S, 6°E)	108
Antalya (ANT uhl YAH), *Turkey* (37°N, 31°E)	115
Antananarivo (AHN tuh NAH nuh REE voh), *Madagascar* (19°S, 47°E)	107
Antarctic Pen., *Antarctica* (66°S, 60°W)	137
Antarctica, *continent*	7
Anticosti I., *Quebec* (49°N, 62°W)	47
Antigua and Barbuda, *country in Caribbean Sea* (18°N, 62°W)	85
Antioch, *Turkey* (36°N, 36°E)	115
Antofagasta (AN toh fuh GAS tuh), *Chile* (24°S, 70°W)	89
Antwerp, *Belgium* (51°N, 4°E)	98
Aomori (OW muh ree), *Japan* (41°N, 141°E)	125
Apalachee Bay, *Fla.* (30°N, 85°W)	69
Apalachicola (AP uh LACH uh KOHL uh), *Fla.* (30°N, 85°W)	68
Apalachicola R., *Fla.* (30°N, 85°W)	68
Apaporis R. (AHP uh POHR ees), *Colombia* (1°S, 70°W)	90
Apennines, *mt. range in Italy* (43°N, 13°E)	99
Apostle Is. (uh PAHS uhl), *L. Superior* (47°N, 91°W)	63
Appalachian Mts., *U.S.* (37°N, 82°W)	53
Appleton, *Wis.* (44°N, 88°W)	63
Apure R. (uh POOR uh), *Venezuela* (8°N, 68°W)	90
Aquitaine Basin, *France* (44°N, 1°W)	98
Arabian Desert, *Egypt* (26°N, 34°E)	115
Arabian Pen., *Asia* (20°N, 45°E)	115
Arabian Sea, *Indian O.* (15°N, 65°E)	118
Aracaju (AR uh kuh ZHOO), *Brazil* (11°S, 37°W)	89
Arafura Sea (ar uh FOOR uh), *Indian O.* (9°S, 135°E)	130
Aral, *Kazakhstan* (47°N, 62°E)	100
Aral Sea (AR uhl), *Asia* (45°N, 60°E)	118
Ararat, Mt., *Turkey* (40°N, 44°E)	115
Arbuckle Mts., *Okla.* (34°N, 97°W)	67
Arcadia, *Fla.* (27°N, 84°W)	69
Arches N. P., *Utah* (39°N, 110°W)	59
Arctic Ocean	7
Ardennes (ahr DEN), *mts. in Belgium* (50°N, 5°E)	98
Ardmore, *Okla.* (34°N, 97°W)	67
Arena, Point, *Calif.* (39°N, 124°W)	58
Arequipa (AR uh KEE pah), *Peru* (16°S, 72°W)	89
Argentina, *country in South America* (35°S, 65°W)	89
Arhus (AWR hoos), *Denmark* (56°N, 10°E)	96
Arica (uh REE kuh), *Chile* (19°S, 70°W)	89
Aripuana R. (AR uhp wuh NA), *Brazil* (5°S, 60°W)	90
Arizona, *state in U.S.* (34°N, 114°W)	58-59
Arkabutla L. (ahr kuh BUHT lay), *Miss.* (35°N, 90°W)	68
Arkansas, *state in U.S.* (35°N, 94°W)	67
Arkansas R., *U.S.* (37°N, 93°W)	52-53
Arkhangelsk (ur KAHN gihlsk), *Russia* (65°N, 41°E)	100
Arlington, *Tex.* (33°N, 97°W)	67
Arlington, *Va.* (39°N, 77°W)	71
Arlington Heights, *Ill.* (42°N, 88°W)	65
Armenia, *country in Asia* (40°N, 45°E)	100
Armstrong, *Ontario* (50°N, 89°W)	46
Arnhem (AHRN hem), *Netherlands* (52°N, 6°W)	98
Arnhem Land, *Australia* (13°S, 134°E)	130
Aroostook R. (uh ROOS tuhk), *Maine* (47°N, 68°W)	73
Aru Is., *Arafura Sea* (6°S, 134°E)	130
Aruba, *overseas part of Neth.* (12°N, 70°W)	83
Arusha (uh ROOSH uh), *Tanzania* (3°S, 37°E)	110
Arvada, *Colo.* (40°N, 105°W)	59
Arviat, *Nunavut* (62°N, 94°W)	45
Asahi, Mt. (ah SAH hee), *Japan* (44°N, 143°E)	125
Asahikawa (ah SAH hee KAY wuh), *Japan* (44°N, 142°E)	125
Asansol (AHS uhn SOHL), *India* (24°N, 87°E)	122
Asbury Park, *N.J.* (40°N, 74°W)	72
Ascension I. (uh SEHN shuhn), *island in Atlantic O.* (8°S, 14°W)	106
Asheboro, *N.C.* (36°N, 80°W)	71
Asheville, *N.C.* (36°N, 83°W)	70-71
Asheweig R., *Ontario* (54°N, 87°W)	46
Ashgabat, *Turkmenistan* (38°N, 58°E)	100
Ashland, *Ky.* (38°N, 83°W)	70
Ashland, *Wis.* (47°N, 91°W)	63
Ashtabula (ASH tuh BYOO luh), *Ohio* (42°N, 81°W)	71
Ashuanipi, L. (ASH wuh NIHP ee), *Newfoundland* (52°N, 67°W)	47
Ashuapmushuan R. (uh SHAH muhsh WAHN), *Quebec* (49°N, 73°W)	47
Asia, *continent*	7
Asir, *region of Saudi Arabia* (18°N, 42°E)	115
Asmara, *Ethiopia* (15°N, 39°E)	107
Aspen, *Colo.* (39°N, 107°W)	59
Assab, *Eritrea* (13°N, 44°E)	115
Assateague I. (AS uh TEEG), *Atlantic O.* (38°N, 75°W)	71
Assiniboine, Mt. (uh SIHN uh BOYN), *British Columbia* (51°N, 116°W)	44
Assiniboine R., *Canada* (52°N, 102°W)	45
Astana, *Kazakhstan* (51°N, 71°E)	100
Astoria, *Oreg.* (46°N, 124°W)	60
Astrakhan, *Russia* (46°N, 48°E)	100
Asuncion (AH SOON see awn), *Paraguay* (25°S, 57°W)	89
Aswan, *Egypt* (24°N, 33°E)	115
Aswan High Dam, *Egypt* (24°N, 33°E)	115
Asyut (AS ee YOOT), *Egypt* (27°N, 31°E)	115
At Taif (at TAY if), *Saudi Arabia* (21°N, 41°E)	115
Atacama Desert, *South America* (23°S, 69°W)	88
Atbara R., *Africa* (17°N, 35°E)	106
Atchafalaya Bay (uh CHAF uh LY uh), *La.* (30°N, 92°W)	67
Atchafalaya R. , *La.* (31°N, 92°W)	67
Atchison, *Kans.* (40°N, 95°W)	65
Athabasca, L., *Canada* (60°N, 109°W)	45
Athabasca R., *Canada* (58°N, 111°W)	45
Athens, *Ga.* (34°N, 83°W)	69
Athens, *Greece* (38°N, 24°E)	99
Athens, *Ohio* (39°N, 82°W)	71
Atikokan, *Ontario* (49°N, 92°W)	46
Atikonak, L., *Newfoundland* (52°N, 64°W)	47
Atlanta, *Ga.* (34°N, 84°W)	68-69
Atlantic City, *N.J.* (39°N, 75°W)	72
Atlantic Coastal Plain, *U.S.* (32°N, 81°W)	53
Atlantic Ocean	7
Atlas Mts., *Africa* (32°N, 6°W)	114
Attawapiskat (AT uh wuh PIHS kuht), *Ontario* (53°N, 82°W)	46
Attawapiskat R., *Ontario* (53°N, 86°W)	46
Attikamagen L., *Newfoundland* (55°N, 67°W)	47
Attleboro, *Mass.* (42°N, 71°W)	73
Atyrau, *Kazakhstan* (47°N, 52°E)	100
Au Sable R. (oh SAY buhl), *Mich.* (45°N, 84°W)	63
Au Sable R. , *N.Y.* (44°N, 74°W)	72
Auburn (AW buhrn), *Ala.* (33°N, 85°W)	68
Auburn, *Maine* (44°N, 70°W)	73
Auburn, *Nebr.* (40°N, 96°W)	65
Auburn, *N.Y.* (43°N, 77°W)	72
Auburn, *Wash.* (47°N, 122°W)	60
Auckland (AWK luhnd), *New Zealand* (37°S, 175°E)	131
Auglaize R. (oh GLAYZ), *Ohio* (41°N, 84°W)	70
Augsburg (AWGZ buhrg), *Germany* (48°N, 11°E)	99
Augusta, *Ga.* (33°N, 82°W)	69
Augusta, *Maine* (44°N, 70°W)	73
Aurangabad (ow RUNG uh BAHD), *India* (20°N, 76°E)	122
Aurora, *Colo.* (40°N, 105°W)	59
Aurora, *Ill.* (42°N, 88°W)	65
Austin, *Minn.* (44°N, 93°W)	63
Austin, *Tex.* (30°N, 98°W)	67
Australia, *country and continent*	7
Australian Alps, *Australia* (37°S, 148°E)	133
Australian Capital Terr., *Australia* (36°S, 149°E)	133
Austria, *country in Europe* (47°N, 14°E)	99
Avignon (ah vee NYAWN), *France* (44°N, 5°E)	98
Axel Heiberg I., *Arctic O.* (80°N, 92°W)	43
Ayr, *Scotland* (55°N, 5°W)	98
Azerbaijan, *country in Europe and Asia* (41°N, 48°E)	100
Azores, *islands in Atlantic O.* (38°N, 25°W)	106
Azov, Sea of, *Europe* (46°N, 37°E)	95

B

Name (Pronunciation), *Description* (Lat, Long)	Page
B. Everett Jordan L., *N.C.* (36°N, 79°W)	71
Babine L. (BAH been), *British Columbia* (55°N, 126°W)	44
Babol (bah BOHL), *Iran* (37°N, 53°E)	115
Bad R., *S. Dak.* (44°N, 101°W)	62
Badlands, *S. Dak.* (44°N, 103°W)	62
Badlands N.P., *S. Dak.* (44°N, 102°W)	62
Baffin Bay, *Arctic O.* (74°N, 65°W)	41
Baffin I., *Baffin Bay* (70°N, 72°W)	41
Baghdad, *Iraq* (33°N, 44°E)	115
Bahama Is., *Atlantic O.* (24°N, 76°W)	83
Bahamas, *country in Atlantic O.* (24°N, 76°W)	85
Bahia Blanca (bu HEE uh BLANG kuh), *Argentina* (39°S, 62°W)	89
Bahrain, *country in Asia* (27°N, 51°E)	115
Baie-Comeau (bay KOH moh), *Quebec* (49°N, 68°W)	47
Baikal, L., *Russia* (52°N, 105°E)	100
Baja California (BAH hah), *region of Mexico* (30°N, 115°W)	82
Baker, *Oreg.* (45°N, 118°W)	60
Baker Lake, *Northwest Terr.* (65°N, 96°W)	42
Bakersfield, *Calif.* (35°N, 119°W)	58
Bakhtaran, *Iran* (34°N, 47°E)	115
Baku, *Azerbaijan* (40°N, 50°E)	100
Balabac Strait (buh LAHB AHK), *Borneo and Palawan* (8°N, 117°E)	123
Balaton (BAL uh TAHN), *lake in Hungary* (47°N, 18°E)	99
Baldy Peak, *Ariz.* (34°N, 110°W)	59

Name (Pronunciation), *Description* (Lat., Long.)	Page
Balearic Is., *Mediterranean Sea* (39°N, 3°E)	114
Balearic Sea, *Europe* (40°N, 2°E)	114
Baleine, River de la, *Quebec* (55°N, 77°W)	46-47
Bali, *island in Flores Sea* (8°S, 105°E)	130
Balkan Mts., *Europe* (43°N, 24°E)	99
Balkan Pen., *Europe* (42°N, 25°E)	95
Balkhash, L., *Kazakhstan* (47°N, 75°E)	100
Ballarat, *Australia* (38°S, 144°E)	133
Balmertown, *Ontario* (51°N, 94°W)	46
Balqash, *Kazakhstan* (47°N, 75°E)	100
Balsas R., *Mexico* (18°N, 100°W)	82
Baltic Sea, *Europe* (55°N, 18°E)	94-95
Baltimore, *Md.* (39°N, 77°W)	71
Baluchistan (buh LOO chih STAN), *region of Pakistan* (27°N, 66°E)	122
Bamako, *Mali* (13°N, 8°W)	107
Bamenda, *Cameroon* (6°N, 10°E)	108
Bancroft, *Ontario* (45°N, 78°W)	46
Banda Sea, *Indian O.* (5°S, 128°E)	130
Bandar Seri Begawan, *Brunei* (5°N, 115°E)	123
Bandar-e Abbas, *Iran* (27°N, 56°E)	115
Bandung, *Indonesia* (7°S, 108°E)	31
Banff, *Alberta* (51°N, 115°W)	44
Banff N. P. (BAMF), *Alberta* (51°N, 116°W)	44
Bangalore, *India* (13°N, 78°E)	122
Bangka, *island in Karimata Strait* (2°S, 106°E)	130
Bangkok, *Thailand* (14°N, 100°E)	123
Bangladesh, *country in Asia* (24°N, 90°E)	122
Bangor, *Maine* (45°N, 69°W)	73
Bangui (bahng GEE), *Central African Republic* (4°N, 19°E)	107
Bangweulu, L. (BANG wee OO loo), *Zambia* (11°S, 30°E)	106
Banja Luka (BAHN yuh LOO kuh), *Bosnia and Herzegovina* (45°N, 17°E)	99
Banjarmasin (bahn jur MAH sihn), *Indonesia* (3°S, 114°E)	131
Banjul (BAHN jool), *Gambia* (13°N, 17°W)	108
Banks I., *Arctic O.* (73°N, 120°W)	42
Banks I., *Hecate Strait* (53°N, 130°W)	44
Banks Pen., *New Zealand* (44°S, 173°E)	130
Baotou (bow toh), *China* (40°N, 110°E)	124
Bar Harbor, *Maine* (44°N, 68°W)	73
Baranof I., *Gulf of Alaska* (57°N, 135°W)	57
Barbados (bahr BAY dohz), *country in Caribbean Sea* (14°N, 59°W)	85
Barberton, *Ohio* (41°N, 82°W)	71
Barcelona (bahr suh LOH nuh), *Spain* (41°N, 2°E)	114
Bardai (bahr DY), *Chad* (22°N, 17°E)	107
Bareeda, *Somalia* (12°N, 51°E)	107
Bareilly (buh RAY lee), *India* (28°N, 79°E)	122
Barents Sea (BAR uhnts), *Arctic O.* (69°N, 40°E)	95
Bari, *Italy* (41°N, 17°E)	99
Barkley, L., *U.S.* (37°N, 88°W)	71
Barkly Tableland, *plateau in Australia* (16°S, 134°E)	130
Barlee, L., *Australia* (31°S, 121°E)	130
Barnaul (bahr nuh OOL), *Russia* (53°N, 83°E)	100
Barnstable, *Mass.* (42°N, 70°W)	73
Barquisimeto (BAHR kee see MAY toh), *Venezuela* (10°N, 69°W)	90
Barranquilla (BAHR uhn KEE uh), *Colombia* (11°N, 75°W)	90
Barrie, *Ontario* (44°N, 80°W)	46
Barrow, Point, *Alaska* (71°N, 156°W)	57
Barrow R., *Ireland* (52°N, 7°W)	98
Barstow (BAHR stoh), *Calif.* (35°N, 117°W)	58
Bartholomew Bayou, *r. in U.S.* (33°N, 92°W)	67
Bartlesville, *Okla.* (37°N, 96°W)	67
Bartlett, *Tenn.* (37°N, 90°W)	70
Basel (BAHZ uhl), *Switzerland* (48°N, 8°E)	99
Basin and Range, *U.S.* (40°N, 118°W)	58
Baskatong Res., *Quebec* (47°N, 76°W)	47
Basra, *Iraq* (31°N, 48°E)	115
Bass Strait, *Australia and Tasmania* (40°S, 145°E)	133
Bassein (buh SAYN), *Myanmar* (17°N, 95°E)	123
Bastia, *Corsica* (43°N, 9°E)	98
Bastrop, *La.* (33°N, 92°W)	67

Name (Pronunciation), *Description* (Lat., Long.)	Page
Bata, *Equatorial Guinea* (2°N, 10°E)	108
Batabano Gulf (baht uh buh NOH), *Caribbean Sea* (22°N, 83°W)	83
Bath, *England* (51°N, 2°W)	98
Bathurst (BATH urst), *Australia* (34°S, 150°E)	133
Bathurst, *New Brunswick* (48°N, 66°W)	47
Bathurst I., *Arctic O.* (76°N, 100°W)	40
Batna, *Algeria* (36°N, 6°E)	114
Baton Rouge (BAT uhn ROOZH), *La.* (31°N, 91°W)	67
Battle Creek, *Mich.* (42°N, 85°W)	63
Battle R., *Alberta* (52°N, 112°W)	44-45
Batumi, *Georgia* (41°N, 42°E)	100
Bauchi (BOW chee), *Nigeria* (10°N, 10°E)	108
Bay City, *Mich.* (44°N, 84°W)	63
Bayou d'Arbonne L. (BY yoo DAHR BON), *La.* (33°N, 92°W)	67
Bayreuth (by ROYT), *Germany* (50°N, 12°E)	99
Baytown, *Tex.* (30°N, 95°W)	67
Beals Creek, *r. in Tex.* (32°N, 103°W)	66
Bear I., *James Bay* (54°N, 81°W)	46
Bear L., *U.S.* (42°N, 111°W)	59
Bear Lodge Mts., *Wyo.* (45°N, 104°W)	61
Bear R., *Idaho* (43°N, 112°W)	61
Beatrice (bee AH trus), *Nebr.* (40°N, 97°W)	64
Beaufort Sea, *Arctic O.* (72°N, 135°W)	57
Beaumont (BOH mont), *Tex.* (30°N, 94°W)	67
Beauport (bo PAWR), *Quebec* (47°N, 71°W)	47
Beaver I., *L. Michigan* (46°N, 86°W)	63
Beaver L., *Ark.* (36°N, 94°W)	67
Beaver R., *Canada* (54°N, 111°W)	45
Beaverhead Mts., *Idaho* (44°N, 113°W)	61
Beaverton, *Oreg.* (45°N, 123°W)	60
Bechar (bay SHAHR), *Algeria* (32°N, 2°W)	114
Beckley, *W. Va.* (38°N, 81°W)	71
Bedford, *Ind.* (39°N, 87°W)	70
Beijing (bay JIHNG), *China* (40°N, 116°E)	124
Beira (BAY ruh), *Mozambique* (20°S, 35°E)	107
Beirut (bay ROOT), *Lebanon* (33°N, 36°E)	115
Belarus (BEHL ah ruhs), *country in Europe* (52°N, 27°E)	97
Belcher Is., *Hudson Bay* (56°N, 79°W)	43
Belem (buh LEM), *Brazil* (1°S, 48°W)	89
Belfast, *Northern Ireland* (55°N, 6°W)	98
Belgium (BEL jum), *country in Europe* (51°N, 5°E)	98
Belgrade, *Yugoslavia* (45°N, 21°E)	99
Belize (buh LEEZ), *country in Central America* (17°N, 89°W)	84
Bell R., *Quebec* (50°N, 78°W)	47
Bella Coola, *British Columbia* (52°N, 127°W)	44
Belle Glade, *Fla.* (27°N, 81°W)	69
Belle Isle, Strait of, *Canada* (52°N, 57°W)	41
Bellefontaine (behl FOWNT uhn), *Ohio* (40°N, 84°W)	70
Belleville, *Ill.* (39°N, 90°W)	65
Belleville, *Ontario* (44°N, 77°W)	46
Bellevue (BEHL vyoo), *Nebr.* (41°N, 96°W)	64
Bellevue, *Wash.* (48°N, 122°W)	60
Bellingham, *Wash.* (49°N, 123°W)	60
Bellingshausen Sea (BEH lingz HOWZ ehn), *Antarctica* (68°S, 85°W)	137
Belmopan (BEL moh PAN), *Belize* (17°N, 89°W)	84
Belo Horizonte (BAY loh HAWR uh ZAHN tee), *Brazil* (20°S, 44°W)	89
Beloit (buh LOYT), *Wis.* (43°N, 89°W)	63
Bemidji (buh MIJ ee), *Minn.* (47°N, 95°W)	62
Ben Nevis, *mt. in Scotland* (57°N, 5°W)	98
Bend, *Oreg.* (44°N, 121°W)	60
Bendigo, *Australia* (37°S, 146°E)	133
Bengal, Bay of (ben GAWL), *Indian O.* (17°N, 90°E)	122
Benghazi (ben GAH zee), *Libya* (32°N, 20°E)	114
Benin, *country in Africa* (8°N, 2°E)	108
Benin, Bight of, *gulf in Africa* (6°N, 3°E)	108
Bennington, *Vt.* (43°N, 73°W)	73
Benton Harbor, *Mich.* (42°N, 87°W)	63
Benue R. (BAYN WAY), *Africa* (8°N, 9°E)	108
Berea (buh REE uh), *Ky.* (38°N, 84°W)	70
Berens R., *Canada* (52°N, 97°W)	45
Bergen, *Norway* (60°N, 5°E)	96

Name (Pronunciation), *Description* (Lat., Long.)	Page
Bering Sea (BAYR ing), *Pacific O.* (57°N, 175°W)	136
Bering Strait, *U.S. and Russia* (65°N, 168°W)	57
Berkeley, *Calif.* (38°N, 122°W)	58
Berkner I., *Antarctica* (80°S, 45°W)	137
Berkshire Hills, *Mass.* (42°N, 73°W)	73
Berlin, *Germany* (52°N, 13°E)	99
Berlin, *N.H.* (44°N, 71°W)	73
Bermuda Is. (buhr MYOO duh), *Atlantic O.* (32°N, 65°W)	36
Bern, *Switzerland* (47°N, 7°E)	99
Besancon (buh ZAN suhn), *France* (47°N, 6°E)	98
Bessemer, *Ala.* (33°N, 87°W)	68
Bethany, *Mo.* (40°N, 94°W)	65
Bethel, *Alaska* (61°N, 162°W)	57
Bethel Park, *Pa.* (40°N, 80°W)	72
Bethesda (buh THES duh), *Md.* (39°N, 77°W)	71
Bethlehem, *Pa.* (41°N, 75°W)	72
Bettendorf, *Iowa* (42°N, 91°W)	65
Bhagalpur (BAHG uhl POOR), *India* (25°N, 87°E)	122
Bhopal (boh PAHL), *India* (23°N, 77°E)	122
Bhutan (boo TAHN), *country in Asia* (28°N, 91°E)	122
Biafra, Bight of (bee AHF ruh), *gulf in Africa* (4°N, 8°E)	108
Biak (bee YAK), *island in Pacific O.* (1°S, 136°E)	130
Bialystok (bee AHL uh STAWK), *Poland* (53°N, 23°E)	99
Biddeford, *Maine* (43°N, 69°W)	73
Bie Plateau, *Angola* (13°S, 17°E)	106
Bielefeld (BEE luh FELT), *Germany* (52°N, 9°E)	99
Bien Hoa (bee EHN WAH), *Vietnam* (11°N, 107°E)	123
Bienville, L. (bee EHN VIHL), *Quebec* (55°N, 73°W)	47
Big Belt Mts., *Mont.* (46°N, 111°W)	61
Big Bend Dam, *S. Dak.*, (44°N, 100°W)	62
Big Bend N. P., *Tex.* (29°N, 103°W)	66
Big Black R., *Miss.* (33°N, 90°W)	68
Big Blue R., *U.S.* (41°N, 97°W)	64
Big Cypress Swamp, *Fla.* (26°N, 81°W)	69
Big L., *Maine* (45°N, 68°W)	73
Big Lost R., *Idaho* (44°N, 114°W)	61
Big Muddy R., *Ill.* (38°N, 89°W)	65
Big Sandy R., *U.S.* (38°N, 83°W)	70
Big Sioux R. (SOO), *S. Dak.* (44°N, 97°W)	62
Big Spring, *Tex.* (32°N, 102°W)	66
Big Stone L., *Minn.* (45°N, 97°W)	62
Big Trout L., *Ontario* (54°N, 90°W)	46
Bighorn L., *U.S.* (45°N, 108°W)	61
Bighorn Mts., *U.S.* (45°N, 108°W)	61
Bighorn R., *U.S.* (44°N, 108°W)	61
Bilbao (bil BAH oh), *Spain* (43°N, 3°W)	114
Billabong R., *Australia* (35°S, 145°E)	133
Billings, *Mont.* (46°N, 109°W)	61
Biloxi, *Miss.* (30°N, 89°W)	68
Bimini Is. (BIHM uh nee), *Straits of Florida*, (26°N, 79°W)	69
Binghamton, *N.Y.* (42°N, 76°W)	72
Bioko (bee OH koh), *island in Gulf of Guinea* (4°N, 9°E)	108
Birau, *Central African Rep.* (10°N, 23°E)	115
Birch Mts., *Alberta* (58°N, 113°W)	44
Birmingham, *Ala.* (34°N, 87°W)	68
Birmingham, *England* (53°N, 2°W)	98
Biscay, Bay of (BIS kay), *Europe* (45°N, 5°W)	98
Biscayne N.P. (bis KAYN), *Fla.* (25°N, 80°W)	69
Biscotasi L., *Ontario* (47°N, 82°W)	46
Bishkek, *Kyrgyzstan* (43°N, 75°E)	100
Bisho (BEE SHOH), *South Africa* (33°S, 27°E)	109
Bishop, *Calif.* (37°N, 118°W)	58
Biskra, *Algeria* (35°N, 6°E)	114
Bismarck, *N. Dak.* (47°N, 101°W)	62
Bismarck Sea, *Pacific O.* (4°S, 147°E)	130
Bissau (bih SAW), *Guinea-Bissau* (12°N, 16°W)	108
Bitola (BEET uhl YAH), *Macedonia* (41°N, 21°E)	99
Bitterroot Range, *U.S.* (47°N, 115°W)	60-61
Bitterroot R., *Mont.* (46°N, 114°W)	61
Black Forest, *region of Germany* (48°N, 8°E)	99
Black Hills, *S. Dak.* (44°N, 104°W)	62
Black L., *Saskatchewan* (59°N, 105°W)	45

Name (Pronunciation), *Description* (Lat., Long.)	**Page**

Black Mesa (MAY suh), *Ariz.* (37°N, 110°W) — 59
Black R., *Ark.* (36°N, 91°W) — 67
Black R., *N.Y.* (44°N, 77°W) — 72
Black R., *Vietnam* (22°N, 104°E) — 123
Black Sea, *Europe and Asia* (43°N, 35°E) — 95
Black Sea Lowland, *Ukraine* (46°N, 30°E) — 95
Black Volta R., *Africa* (12°N, 3°W) — 108
Black Warrior R., *Ala.* (34°N, 87°W) — 68
Blackfoot R., *Mont.* (47°N, 113°W) — 61
Blacksburg, *Va.* (37°N, 81°W) — 71
Blair, *Nebr.* (42°N, 96°W) — 64
Blanc, Cape (blangk), *Africa* (21°N, 18°W) — 106
Blanc, Mont (blahn, mawn), *France and Italy* (45°N, 7°E) — 98
Blanca Bay (BLAHNG kuh), *Argentina* (39°S, 62°W) — 88
Blanchard R., *Ohio* (41°N, 84°W) — 70
Blanco, Cape (BLANG koh), *Oreg.* (43°N, 125°W) — 60
Blind River, *Ontario* (46°N, 83°W) — 46
Bloemfontein (BLOOM fahn TAYN), *South Africa* (29°S, 26°E) — 109
Bloodvein R., *Canada* (52°N, 96°W) — 45
Bloomington, *Ill.* (41°N, 89°W) — 65
Bloomington, *Ind.* (39°N, 87°W) — 70
Bloomington, *Minn.* (44°N, 96°W) — 62-63
Blue Mt., *Pa.* (41°N, 76°W) — 72
Blue Mts., *U.S.* (45°N, 119°W) — 60
Blue Nile, *r. in Africa* (14°N, 34°E) — 106
Blue Ridge, *U.S.* (36°N, 82°W) — 71
Bluefield, *W. Va.* (37°N, 81°W) — 71
Bluefields, *Nicaragua* (12°N, 84°W) — 85
Blytheville, *Ark.* (36°N, 90°W) — 67
Bo, *Sierra Leone* (8°N, 11°W) — 108
Bo Gulf, *Yellow Sea* (38°N, 120°E) — 124
Boa Vista (boh uh VEESH tuh), *Brazil* (3°N, 61°W) — 90
Bobo Dioulasso (BOH BOH doo LAS oh), *Burkina Faso* (11°N, 4°W) — 108
Boca Raton (BOH kuh ruh TOHN), *Fla.* (26°N, 80°W) — 69
Bogalusa (BOH guh LOO suh), *La.* (31°N, 90°W) — 67
Bogota (boh guh TAH), *Colombia* (4°N, 74°W) — 90
Bohemia (boh HEE mee uh), *region of Czech Rep.* (50°N, 14°E) — 99
Boise (BOY zee), *Idaho* (44°N, 116°W) — 60
Boise R., *Idaho* (44°N, 116°W) — 60
Bokna Fiord, *Norway* (59°N, 6°E) — 94
Bolivia (boh LIHV ee uh), *country in South America* (17°S, 65°W) — 89
Bologna (buh LOHN yuh), *Italy* (44°N, 11°E) — 99
Bolzano (bohlt SAI IN oh), *Italy* (47°N, 11°E) — 99
Bombay, *India* (19°N, 73°E) — 122
Bonaire, *island of Netherlands Antilles* (12°N, 68°W) — 83
Bonifacio, Strait of (BAHN uh FAHCH oh), *Mediterranean Sea* (41°N, 9°E) — 99
Bonin Is., *Philippine Sea* (27°N, 141°E) — 119
Bonn, *Germany* (51°N, 7°E) — 99
Bonneville Dam, *Wash.* (46°N, 122°W) — 60
Boothia, Gulf of (BOO thee uh), *Nunavut* (72°N, 91°W) — 41
Boothia Pen., *Nunavut* (71°N, 94°W) — 41
Borah Pk., *Idaho* (44°N, 114°W) — 61
Bordeaux (bawr DOH), *France* (45°N, 1°W) — 98
Borgne L. (BAWRN), *La.* (30°N, 90°W) — 67
Borneo, *island in South China Sea* (0°, 113°E) — 119
Bornholm, *island in Baltic Sea* (55°N, 15°E) — 96
Bosnia and Herzegovina (HERT suh goh VEE nuh), *country in Europe* (44°N, 18°E) — 99
Bosporus (BAHS puhr uhs), *strait in Turkey* (41°N, 29°E) — 95
Bossier City (BOH zhur), *La.* (33°, 94°W) — 67
Boston, *Mass.* (42°N, 71°W) — 73
Boston Mts., *Ark.* (36°N, 93°W) — 67
Botany Bay, *Australia* (34°S, 151°E) — 133
Bothnia, Gulf of, *Baltic Sea* (62°N, 20°E) — 94-95
Botswana, *country in Africa* (22°S, 24°E) — 107
Bouake (BWAH KAY), *Côte d'Ivoire* (7°N, 5°W) — 108
Bougainville (BOO guhn VIHL), *island in Solomon Sea* (6°S, 155°E) — 130

Boulder (BOHL duhr), *Colo.* (40°N, 105°W) — 59
Boulder City, *Nev.* (36°N, 115°W) — 58
Bountiful, *Utah* (41°N, 112°W) — 59
Bow R. (BOH), *Alberta* (51°N, 113°W) — 44-45
Bowling Green, *Ky.* (37°N, 86°W) — 70
Bowling Green, *Ohio* (41°N, 84°W) — 70
Boysen Res., *Wyo.* (43°N, 108°W) — 61
Bozeman (BOHZ muhn), *Mont.* (46°N, 110°W) — 61
Bradenton, *Fla.* (27°N, 83°W) — 69
Bradford, *England* (54°N, 2°W) — 98
Brahmaputra R., (brah muh POO truh), *Asia* (27°N, 92°E) — 122
Braila (bruh EE luh), *Romania* (45°N, 28°E) — 99
Brainerd, *Minn.* (46°N, 94°W) — 62
Brampton, *Ontario* (44°N, 80°W) — 46
Branco R. (brang koh), *South America* (0°N, 62°W) — 90
Brandenburg, *Germany* (52°N, 13°E) — 99
Brandon, *Manitoba* (50°N, 100°W) — 45
Branford, *Fla.* (30°N, 83°W) — 69
Branson, *Mo.* (37°N, 93°W) — 65
Brantford, *Ontario* (43°N, 80°W) — 46
Bras d'Or L. (brad AWR), *Nova Scotia* (46°N, 61°W) — 47
Brasilia (brah SEEL yuh), *Brazil* (16°S, 48°W) — 89
Brasov (brah SHAWV), *Romania* (46°N, 26°E) — 99
Bratislava (BRAH tuh SLAH vuh), *Slovakia* (48°N, 17°E) — 99
Bratsk Res., *Russia* (55°N, 102°E) — 119
Brattleboro, *Vt.* (43°N, 73°W) — 73
Braunschweig (BROWN shvyg), *Germany* (52°N, 10°E) — 99
Brawley, *Calif.* (33°N, 115°W) — 58
Brazil, *country in South America* (10°S, 55°W) — 89
Brazilian Highlands, *Brazil* (17°S, 48°W) — 88
Brazos R. (BRAZ uhs), *Tex.* (32°N, 97°W) — 66-67
Brazzaville, *Congo Rep.* (4°S, 15°E) — 107
Bremen (BREHM uhn), *Germany* (53°N, 9°E) — 99
Bremerhaven (brem uhr HAHV uhn), *Germany* (54°N, 9°E) — 99
Bremerton, *Wash.* (48°N, 123°W) — 60
Brescia (BRESH uh), *Italy* (46°N, 10°E) — 99
Brest, *France* (48°N, 5°W) — 98
Breton Sound (BREHT uhn), *Gulf of Mexico* (29°N, 89°W) — 67
Brewton, *Ala.* (31°N, 87°W) — 68
Bridgeport, *Conn.* (41°N, 73°W) — 73
Brindisi (BRIN duh zee), *Italy* (41°N, 18°E) — 99
Brisbane (BRIHS bayn), *Australia* (27°S, 153°E) — 131
Bristol, *England* (51°N, 3°W) — 98
Bristol, *Va. and Tenn.* (37°N, 80°W) — 71
Bristol Bay, *Alaska* (58°N, 159°W) — 57
Bristol Channel, *United Kingdom* (51°N, 3°W) — 98
British Columbia, *prov. in Canada* (55°N, 125°W) — 44
British Isles, *Europe* (52°N, 7°W) — 94
Brittany, *region of France* (48°N, 4°W) — 98
Brno (BUHR noh), *Czech Republic* (49°N, 17°E) — 99
Broadback R., *Quebec* (51°N, 79°W) — 46
Brockton, *Mass.* (42°N, 71°W) — 73
Brockville, *Ontario* (45°N, 76°W) — 47
Broken Arrow, *Okla.* (36°N, 96°W) — 67
Broken Bay, *Australia* (34°S, 151°E) — 133
Broken Bow L., *Okla.* (34°N, 95°W) — 67
Broken Bow Res., *Okla.* (34°N, 95°W) — 67
Brookings, *S. Dak.* (44°N, 97°W) — 62
Brooks Range, *Alaska* (67°N, 155°W) — 57
Brownsville, *Tex.* (26°N, 97°W) — 67
Brownwood, *Tex.* (32°N, 99°W) — 66
Bruce Peninsula N. P., *Ontario* (45°N, 81°W) — 46
Brunei (broon EYE), *country in Asia* (4°N, 114°E) — 123
Brunswick, *Ga.* (31°N, 81°W) — 69
Brunswick, *Maine* (44°N, 70°W) — 73
Brussels, *capital of Belgium* (51°N, 4°E) — 98
Bryan, *Tex.* (31°N, 96°W) — 67
Bryansk (bree ANSK), *Russia* (53°N, 34°E) — 97
Bryce Canyon N. P. (BRYS), *Utah* (38°N, 112°W) — 59
Bucaramanga (boo kuh ruh MAHNG guh), *Colombia* (7°N, 73°W) — 90
Buchanan, L., *Tex.* (31°N, 98°W) — 66

Bucharest (BYOO kuh REST), *Romania* (44°N, 26°E) — 99
Budapest (BOO duh PEST), *Hungary* (47°N, 19°E) — 99
Buenaventura (BWAY nuh vehn TOOR uh), *Colombia* (4°N, 77°W) — 90
Buenos Aires (BWAY nohs EYE rays), *Argentina* (35°S, 58°W) — 89
Buffalo, *N.Y.* (43°N, 79°W) — 72
Buffalo, *S. Dak.* (46°N, 104°W) — 62
Buffalo, *Wyo.* (44°N, 107°W) — 61
Buffalo Narrows, *Saskatchewan* (57°N, 109°W) — 45
Bug River (boog), *Europe* (53°N, 22°E) — 99
Bujumbura (boo juhm BOOR uh), *Burundi* (3°S, 29°E) — 110
Bukhoro (boo KOH roh), *Uzbekistan* (40°N, 64°E) — 115
Bulawayo (boo luh WAH yo), *Zimbabwe* (20°S, 29°E) — 107
Bulgaria, *country in Europe* (43°N, 25°E) — 99
Bull Shoals L., *U.S.* (36°N, 93°W) — 67
Bun Plains, *Kenya* (1°N, 41°E) — 110
Bureinskiy Mts., *Russia* (50°N, 135°E) — 101
Burgas (boor GAHS), *Bulgaria* (42°N, 27°E) — 99
Burgundy, *region of France* (47°N, 4°E) — 98
Burkina Faso (bur KEE nuh FAH soh), *country in Africa* (12°N, 4°W) — 108
Burlington, *Iowa* (41°N, 91°W) — 65
Burlington, *N.C.* (36°N, 80°W) — 71
Burlington, *Vt.* (45°N, 73°W) — 73
Burma, *alternate name for Myanmar* (22°N, 95°E) — 123
Burnaby, *British Columbia* (49°N, 123°W) — 44
Burntwood R., *Manitoba* (56°N, 98°W) — 45
Burragorang L., *Australia* (36°S, 150°E) — 133
Bursa, *Turkey* (40°N, 29°E) — 115
Buru (BOO roo), *island in Molucca Sea* (3°S, 127°E) — 130
Burundi (buh RUHN dee), *country in Africa* (3°S, 30°E) — 110
Bushehr (boo SHEHR), *Iran* (29°N, 51°E) — 115
Butte (byoot), *Mont.* (46°N, 113°W) — 61
Bydgoszcz (BID GAWSH), *Poland* (53°N, 18°E) — 99

C

Caballo Res. (kuh BAH yoh), *N. Mex.* (33°N, 107°W) — 59
Cabinda (kuh BEEN duh), *terr. of Angola* (5°S, 12°E) — 107
Cabonga Res., *Quebec* (47°N, 77°W) — 47
Cacak (CHAH chawk), *Yugoslavia* (44°N, 20°E) — 99
Caddo L. (KAD oh), *U.S.* (33°N, 94°W) — 67
Cadillac, *Mich.* (44°N, 85°W) — 63
Caen (kahn), *France* (49°N, 0°) — 98
Cagliari (KAHL yuh ree), *Sardinia* (39°N, 9°E) — 99
Cairns (kayrns), *Australia* (17°S, 146°E) — 131
Cairo (KY roh), *Egypt* (30°N, 31°E) — 115
Cairo (KAY roh), *Ill.* (37°N, 89°W) — 65
Calais (KAL ay), *France* (51°N, 2°E) — 98
Calcanhar, Point, *Brazil* (5°S, 35°W) — 88
Calcasieu L. (KAL kuh SHOO), *La.* (30°N, 94°W) — 67
Calcasieu R., *La.* (31°N, 93°W) — 67
Calcutta (kal KUT uh), *India* (23°N, 88°E) — 122
Caldwell, *Idaho* (44°N, 117°W) — 60
Calexico, *Calif.* (33°N, 116°W) — 58
Calgary (KAL guh ree), *Alberta* (51°N, 114°W) — 44
Cali (KAH lee), *Colombia* (3°N, 77°W) — 90
Calicut, *India* (11°N, 76°E) — 122
California, *state in U.S.* (38°N, 121°W) — 58
California, Gulf of, *Pacific O.* (30°N, 114°W) — 82
California Aqueduct, *Calif.* (36°N, 120°W) — 58
Callao (kah YAH oh), *Peru* (12°S, 77°W) — 90
Caloosahatchee R. (kuh LOO suh HACH ee), *Fla.* (27°N, 82°W) — 69
Calumet City (KAL yuh MEHT), *Ill.* (42°N, 88°W) — 65
Calvinia (kal VIHN ee uh), *South Africa* (31°S, 20°E) — 109
Cambodia, *country in Asia*, (13°N, 105°E) — 123
Cambrian Mts. (KAM bree uhn), *Wales* (52°N, 4°W) — 98
Cambridge (KAYM brihj), *England* (52°N, 0°) — 98
Cambridge, *Mass.* (42°N, 71°W) — 73

Name (Pronunciation), *Description* (Lat., Long.)	Page
Cambridge, *Ohio* (40°N, 82°W)	71
Cambridge Bay, *Nunavut* (69°N, 105°W)	42
Camden, *N.J.* (40°N, 75°W)	72
Cameroon (kam uh ROON), *country in Africa* (6°N, 12°E)	108
Cameroon Mt., *Cameroon* (5°N, 9°E)	108
Campbell River, *British Columbia* (50°N, 125°W)	44
Campbellton, *New Brunswick* (48°N, 67°W)	47
Campeche (kam PAY chay), *Mexico* (20°N, 91°W)	84
Campeche, Bay of, *Gulf of Mexico* (18°N, 94°W)	84
Campinas (kam PEE nuhs), *Brazil* (23°S, 47°W)	89
Campo Grande (KAHM poo GRAN dee), *Brazil* (20°S, 55°W)	89
Campos (KAM puhs), *Brazil* (22°S, 41°W)	89
Campos, *plain in South America* (22°S, 50°W)	88
Can Tho (kuhn TOH), *Vietnam* (10°N, 105°E)	123
Canada, *country in North America* (60°N, 100°W)	42-43
Canadian R., *U.S.* (36°N, 102°W)	52-53
Canadian Shield, *region of Canada* (60°N, 101°W)	40-41
Canandaigua L. (KAN uhn DAY gwuh), *N.Y.* (43°N, 77°W)	72
Canary Is., *Atlantic O.* (28°N, 16°W)	114
Canaveral, Cape, *Fla.* (29°N, 80°W)	69
Canberra (KAN behr uh), *Australia* (35°S, 149°E)	131
Candlewood, L., *Conn.* (41°N, 74°W)	72-73
Caniapiscau Res. (KAN ee uh PIHS koh), *Quebec* (54°N, 70°W)	47
Caniapiscau R., *Quebec* (55°N, 70°W)	47
Cannonball R., *N. Dak.* (46°N, 102°W)	62
Canso, *Nova Scotia* (45°N, 61°W)	47
Cantabrian Mts. (kan TAH bree uhn), *Spain* (43°N, 6°W)	114
Canterbury, *England* (51°N, 1°E)	98
Canton (KAN tuhn), *Ohio* (41°N, 81°W)	71
Canyon Ferry L., *Mont.* (46°N, 112°W)	61
Canyonlands N. P., *Utah* (38°N, 110°W)	59
Cape Breton Highlands N.P., *Nova Scotia* (47°N, 63°W)	47
Cape Breton I., *Nova Scotia* (47°N, 61°W)	47
Cape Coral, *city in Fla.* (27°N, 82°W)	69
Cape Fear R., *N.C.* (35°N, 79°W)	71
Cape Girardeau (juh RAHR doh), *Mo.* (37°N, 90°W)	65
Cape Town, *South Africa* (34°S, 18°E)	109
Cape Verde, *country in Atlantic O.* (16°N, 25°W)	10
Cape York Pen., *Australia* (13°S, 143°E)	130
Capitol Reef N. P., *Utah* (38°N, 111°W)	59
Caqueta R. (KAH kuh TAH), *Colombia* (0°, 73°W)	90
Caracas (kuh RAH kuhs), *Venezuela* (11°N, 67°W)	90
Caratasca Lagoon (KAHR uh TAHS kuh), *Honduras* (15°N, 83°W)	83
Carbondale, *Ill.* (38°N, 89°W)	65
Cardiff (KAHR dif), *Wales* (52°N, 3°W)	98
Cardston, *Alberta* (49°N, 113°W)	44
Caribbean Sea (KAR uh BEE uhn), *Atlantic O.* (16°N, 80°W)	83
Caribou (KAR uh BOO), *Maine* (47°N, 68°W)	73
Caribou Mts., *Alberta* (59°N, 115°W)	44
Carlsbad, *N. Mex.* (32°N, 104°W)	59
Carlsbad Caverns N. P., *N. Mex.* (32°N, 105°W)	59
Carlyle L. (kahr LYL), *Ill.* (39°N, 89°W)	65
Carnarvon (kahr NAHR vuhn), *South Africa* (31°S, 22°E)	109
Caroline Is., *Pacific O.* (8°N, 140°E)	9
Carpathian Mts. (kahr PAY thee un), *Europe* (49°N, 19°E)	99
Carpentaria, Gulf of, *Australia* (14°S, 140°E)	130
Carrara, *Italy* (44°N, 10°E)	99
Carson City, *Nev.* (39°N, 120°W)	58
Carson R., *U.S.* (39°N, 120°W)	58
Carson Sink, *seasonal lake of Nev.* (40°N, 118°W)	58
Cartagena, *Colombia* (10°N, 75°W)	90
Carthage, *Tunisia* (37°N, 10°E)	114
Cary, *N.C.* (36°N, 79°W)	71
Casa Grande (KAS uh GRAN dee), *Ariz.* (33°N, 112°W)	59
Casablanca (KAS uh BLANG kuh), *Morocco* (34°N, 8°W)	114

Name (Pronunciation), *Description* (Lat., Long.)	Page
Cascade Range (kas KAYD), *U.S.* (42°N, 122°W)	60
Cascade Res., *Idaho* (45°N, 116°W)	60
Casco Bay (KAS koh), *Maine* (44°N, 70°W)	73
Casper, *Wyo.* (43°N, 106°W)	61
Caspian Depression, *Russia* (47°N, 47°E)	95
Caspian Sea, *Europe and Asia* (42°N, 50°E)	95
Cassiar Mts., *Canada* (59°N, 130°W)	44
Cat I., *Bahamas* (24°N, 75°W)	69
Catania, *Sicily* (38°N, 15°E)	99
Catanzaro, *Italy* (39°N, 17°E)	99
Catoche, Cape (kuh TOH chee), *Mexico* (22°N, 87°W)	82
Catskill Mts., *N.Y.* (42°N, 75°W)	72
Cauca R., *Colombia* (7°N, 76°W)	90
Caucasus Mts. (KAW kuh suhs), *Europe and Asia* (44°N, 41°E)	95
Cauvery Falls (KOH vuh ree), *India* (12°N, 77°E)	122
Cauvery R., *India* (11°N, 79°E)	122
Cayenne (ky EHN), *Fr. Guiana* (5°N, 52°W)	90
Cayman Is. (KAY muhn), *Caribbean Sea* (19°N, 81°W)	83
Cayos Miskitos, *islands in Caribbean Sea* (15°N, 83°W)	83
Cayuga L. (kuh OO guh), *N.Y.* (42°N, 77°W)	72
Cebu (seh BOO), *Philippines* (10°N, 124°E)	121
Cedar City (SEED uhr), *Utah* (38°N, 113°W)	58
Cedar Creek L., *Tex.* (32°N, 96°W)	67
Cedar Falls, *Iowa* (42°N, 92°W)	65
Cedar L., *Manitoba* (53°N, 100°W)	45
Cedar Rapids, *Iowa* (42°N, 92°W)	65
Cedar R., *Iowa* (42°N, 92°W)	65
Cedros I. (SAY druhs), *Mexico* (28°N, 115°W)	82
Celebes (SEL uh BEEZ), *island in Molucca Sea* (2°S, 120°E)	84
Celebes Sea, *Asia* (3°N, 122°E)	119
Celtic Sea (KEL tik), *Europe* (50°N, 8°W)	98
Center Hill L., *Tenn.* (36°N, 86°W)	70
Central African Republic, *country in Africa* (7°N, 20°E)	107
Central America, *region in North America* (15°N, 90°W)	8
Central Lowland, *U.S.* (41°N, 90°W)	53
Central Lowlands, *Australia* (22°S, 142°E)	130
Central Patricia, *Ontario* (51°N, 90°W)	46
Central Russian Upland, *Russia* (55°N, 34°E)	95
Central Siberian Plateau, *Russia* (68°N, 98°E)	100
Ceram (SAY rahm), *island in Banda Sea* (3°S, 129°E)	130
Ceram Sea, *Indian O.* (2°S, 130°E)	130
Cerf I., *Indian O.* (9°S, 51°E)	106
Ceuta (SAY oo tuh), *terr. of Spain* (36°N, 5°W)	114
Chaco Canyon (CHAHK oh), *N. Mex.* (36°N, 108°W)	59
Chad, *country in Africa* (15°N, 18°E)	107
Chad, L., *Africa* (13°N, 14°E)	108
Chadron (SHAD ruhn), *Nebr.* (43°N, 103°W)	64
Chagos Archipelago, *island group in Indian O.* (6°S, 73°E)	120
Chalbi Plains, *Kenya* (3°N, 37°E)	110
Chaleur Bay (shuh LOOR), *Canada* (48°N, 65°W)	47
Chambal R., *India* (25°N, 76°E)	122
Chamberlain L., *Maine* (46°N, 71°W)	73
Champagne (sham PAYN), *region of France* (49°N, 4°E)	98
Champaign (sham PAYN), *Ill.* (40°N, 88°W)	65
Champlain, L. (sham PLAYN), *North America* (45°N, 73°W)	73
Chandeleur Is. (SHAN duh LOOR), *Gulf of Mexico* (30°N, 89°W)	67
Chandeleur Sound, *Gulf of Mexico* (30°N, 89°W)	67
Chandigarh, *India* (31°N, 77°E)	122
Chandler, *Ariz.* (33°N, 112°W)	59
Chandler, *Quebec* (48°N, 65°W)	47
Changchun, *China* (44°N, 125°E)	124
Changsha (chahng shah), *China* (28°N, 113°E)	124
Channel Is., *English Channel* (49°N, 3°W)	98
Channel Is., *Pacific O.* (34°N, 120°W)	58
Channel Is. N.P., *Calif.* (34°N, 120°W)	58
Chao Phraya (chow PRY uh), *r. in Thailand* (15°N, 100°E)	123

Name (Pronunciation), *Description* (Lat., Long.)	Page
Chapala, L., *Mexico* (20°N, 103°W)	82
Chapel Hill, *N.C.* (36°N, 79°W)	71
Chapleau (chap LOH), *Ontario* (48°N, 83°W)	46
Chari River (SHAHR ee), *Africa* (11°N, 16°E)	106
Chariton R. (SHAR uht uhn), *U.S.* (40°N, 93°W)	65
Charles, Cape, *Va.* (37°N, 76°W)	71
Charlesbourg (sharl BOOR), *Quebec* (47°N, 71°W)	47
Charleston, *Ill.* (40°N, 88°W)	65
Charleston, *S.C.* (33°N, 80°W)	69
Charleston, *W. Va.* (38°N, 82°W)	71
Charlestown, *Ind.* (38°N, 86°W)	70
Charlevoix (SHAHR luh voy), *Mich.* (45°N, 85°W)	63
Charlotte, *N.C.* (35°N, 81°W)	71
Charlottesville, *Va.* (38°N, 78°W)	71
Charlottetown, *Prince Edward I.* (47°N, 62°W)	47
Charlton I., *James Bay* (52°N, 79°W)	46
Chartres (SHAHR truh), *France* (48°N, 2°E)	98
Chatham (CHAT uhm), *Ontario* (42°N, 82°W)	46
Chattahoochee R., *U.S.* (32°N, 85°W)	68-69
Chattanooga, *Tenn.* (35°N, 85°W)	70
Chaudiere R. (shoh DYER), *Quebec* (46°N, 71°W)	47
Chautauqua L. (shuh TAW kwuh), *N.Y.* (42°N, 79°W)	72
Cheat R., *W. Va.* (40°N, 80°W)	71
Chehalis R. (chih HAY luhs), *Wash.* (47°N, 123°W)	60
Cheju (CHAY joo), *island in East China Sea* (34°N, 126°E)	125
Chelan, L., *Wash.* (48°N, 120°W)	60
Chelyabinsk, *Russia* (55°N, 61°E)	100
Chemnitz, *Germany* (51°N, 13°E)	99
Chemung R. (shi MUHNG), *N.Y.* (42°N, 77°W)	72
Cheney Res. (CHEE nee), *Kans.* (38°N, 98°W)	64
Chengdu, *China* (31°N, 104°E)	124
Cher R. (SHEHR), *France* (47°N, 2°E)	98
Cherangany Hills, *Kenya* (2°N, 37°E)	110
Cherbourg (SHEHR boorg), *France* (50°N, 2°W)	98
Chernivtsi, *Ukraine* (48°N, 26°E)	99
Chernobyl (chuhr NOH buhl), *Ukraine* (51°N, 30°E)	100
Cherokee L., *Tenn.* (36°N, 84°W)	70
Cherokees, Lake O' the, *Okla.* (37°N, 95°W)	67
Cherskiy Range, *Russia* (70°N, 145°E)	101
Chesapeake (CHES uh peek), *Va.* (37°N, 76°W)	71
Chesapeake Bay, *U.S.* (37°N, 76°W)	71
Chester, *Pa.* (40°N, 75°W)	72
Chesterfield Inlet, *Hudson Bay* (63°N, 91°W)	41
Chesterfield I., *Pacific O.* (19°S, 160°E)	131
Chesuncook L. (chuh SUHN kook), *Maine* (46°N, 71°W)	73
Chetumal Bay (CHAY tyoo MAHL), *Caribbean Sea* (18°N, 88°W)	82-83
Chew Bakir, *l. in Africa* (5°N, 38°E)	110
Cheyenne (shy AN), *Wyo.* (41°N, 105°W)	61
Cheyenne R., *U.S.* (43°N, 105°W)	61
Chi R. (CHEE), *Thailand* (16°N, 104°E)	123
Chiang Mai (chee AHNG MY), *Thailand* (19°N, 99°E)	123
Chiang Rai (chee AHNG RY), *Thailand* (20°N, 100°E)	123
Chiba (CHEE buh), *Japan* (36°N, 140°E)	125
Chibougamau (shuh BOO guh moh), *Quebec* (50°N, 74°W)	47
Chic-Choc Mts., *Quebec* (49°N, 67°W)	47
Chicago, *Ill.* (42°N, 88°W)	65
Chickamauga L. (CHIK uh MAW guh), *Tenn.* (35°N, 85°W)	70
Chickasawhay R. (CHIK uh SAW way), *Miss.* (31°N, 89°W)	68
Chiclayo (chuh KLY OH), *Peru* (7°S, 80°W)	90
Chico (CHEE koh), *Calif.* (40°N, 122°W)	58
Chicoutimi (shuh KOOT uh mee), *Quebec* (48°N, 71°W)	47
Chidley, Cape (CHID lee), *Canada* (61°N, 64°W)	41
Chihuahua (chih WAH wah), *Mexico* (29°N, 106°W)	84
Chile, *country in South America* (35°S, 71°W)	89
Chillicothe (CHIHL uh KAHTH ee), *Mo.* (40°N, 94°W)	65

Name (Pronunciation), *Description* (Lat., Long.)	**Page**
Chillicothe , *Ohio* (39°N, 83°W)	70
Chilliwhack (CHIL uh WAK), *British Columbia* (49°N, 122°W)	44
Chiloe I. (CHEE luh WAY), *Chile* (43°S, 74°W)	88
Chimborazo, Mt., *Ecuador* (2°S, 79°W)	90
Chimbote (chim BOH tee), *Peru* (9°S, 79°W)	90
China, *country in Asia* (35°N, 105°E)	124
Chinchaga R., *Canada* (58°N, 119°W)	44
Chincoteague Bay (SHING kuh TEEG), *Atlantic O.* (38°N, 75°W)	71
Chindwin R., *Myanmar* (24°N, 95°E)	123
Chinle Wash, *U.S.* (37°N, 110°W)	59
Chios (KEE aws), *island in Aegean Sea* (38°N, 26°E)	99
Chippewa R., *Minn.* (45°N, 96°W)	62
Chippewa R., *Wis.* (45°N, 91°W)	63
Chiputneticook Lakes (SHIP uht NET ih KOOK), *North America* (46°N, 68°W)	73
Chisasibi, *Quebec*, (54°N, 79°W)	47
Chisinau (KOY muh, 29°E)	100
Chita, *Russia* (52°N, 114°E)	100
Chittagong, *Bangladesh* (22°N, 91°E)	122
Choctawhatchee R. (CHAHK tuh HACH ee), *U.S.* (31°N, 86°W)	68
Chongjin (CHUNG JEEN), *North Korea* (42°N, 130°E)	125
Chongju, *South Korea* (37°N, 127°E)	125
Chongqing (chuhng chihng), *China* (29°N, 106°E)	124
Chonos Archipelago, *island group in Chile* (45°S, 74°W)	88
Chowan R. (chuh WAHN), *U.S.* (36°N, 77°W)	71
Christchurch, *New Zealand* (43°S, 173°E)	131
Christmas I., *Indian O.* (11°S, 106°E)	130
Chukchi Peninsula (CHUHK chee), *Russia* (66°N, 175°E)	101
Chukchi Sea, *Arctic O.* (70°N, 170°W)	57
Chula Vista (CHOO luh VIS tuh), *Calif.* (33°N, 117°W)	58
Churchill, *Manitoba* (59°N, 93°W)	45
Churchill Falls, *city in Newfoundland* (53°N, 64°W)	47
Churchill Falls, *waterfall in Newfoundland* (54°N, 64°W)	47
Churchill L., *Saskatchewan* (56°N, 108°W)	45
Churchill R., *Manitoba* (59°N, 94°W)	45
Churchill R., *Newfoundland* (53°N, 63°W)	47
Cimarron R. (SIM uh ROHN), *U.S.* (37°N, 99°W)	66-67
Cincinnati, *Ohio* (39°N, 85°W)	70
Ciudad Bolivar (syoo DAHD boh LEE vahr), *Venezuela* (8°N, 64°W)	90
Ciudad Guayana, *Venezuela* (9°N, 63°W)	90
Claire, L., *Alberta* (59°N, 112°W)	45
Clarion, *Pa.* (41°N, 79°W)	72
Clark Fork, *r. in U.S.* (48°N, 116°W)	60-61
Clark Hill L., *U.S.* (34°N, 82°W)	69
Clarke City, *Quebec* (50°N, 67°W)	47
Clarks Fork, *r. in U.S.* (45°N, 109°W)	61
Clarksburg, *W. Va.* (39°N, 80°W)	71
Clarksdale, *Miss.* (34°N, 91°W)	68
Clarksville, *Tenn.* (37°N, 87°W)	70
Clarksville, *Va.* (37°N, 79°W)	71
Clear L., *Calif.* (39°N, 123°W)	58
Clearwater, *Fla.* (28°N, 83°W)	69
Clearwater Mts., *Idaho* (46°N, 116°W)	60
Clearwater R., *Canada* (57°N, 111°W)	45
Clearwater R., *Idaho* (46°N, 116°W)	60
Clermont-Ferrand (klehr MOHN fuh RAN), *France* (46°N, 3°E)	98
Cleveland, *Ohio* (42°N, 82°W)	71
Cleveland, *Tenn.* (35°N, 85°W)	70
Cleveland Heights, *Ohio* (41°N, 82°W)	71
Clinch R., *U.S.* (37°N, 83°W)	70-71
Clinton, *Iowa* (42°N, 90°W)	65
Clovis, *N. Mex.* (34°N, 105°W)	59
Cluj-Napoca, *Romania* (47°N, 24°E)	99
Clyde River, *Nunavut* (71°N, 69°W)	43
Coachella Canal (KOH CHEHL uh), *Calif.* (33°N, 115°W)	58

Name (Pronunciation), *Description* (Lat., Long.)	**Page**
Coast Mts., *British Columbia* (53°N, 127°W)	44
Coast Ranges, *U.S.* (37°N, 122°W)	52
Coats I., *Hudson Bay* (62°N, 82°W)	41
Coats Land, *region of Antarctica* (78°S, 25°W)	137
Cobalt, *Ontario* (47°N, 80°W)	46
Cobh (KOHV), *Ireland* (52°N, 8°W)	98
Cobourg Pen., *Australia* (12°S, 135°E)	130
Cochin (koh CHIHN), *India* (10°N, 76°E)	122
Cochrane (KAWK ruhn), *Ontario* (49°N, 81°W)	46
Cockburn I. (KOH buhrn), *L. Huron* (46°N, 83°W)	46
Coco R., *North America* (14°N, 84°W)	83
Cocos I., *Pacific O.* (5°N, 87°W)	90
Cod, Cape, *Mass.* (42°N, 70°W)	73
Cody, *Wyo.* (44°N, 109°W)	61
Coeur d'Alene (KAWR duh LAYN), *Idaho* (48°N, 117°W)	60
Coeur d'Alene L., *Idaho* (47°N, 117°W)	60
Coffeyville, *Kans.* (37°N, 96°W)	65
Coiba I., *Panama* (7°N, 82°W)	83
Coimbatore (KOYM buh TOHR), *India* (11°N, 77°E)	122
Cold L., *Canada* (55°N, 110°W)	45
College, *Alaska* (65°N, 148°W)	57
College Station, *Tex.* (31°N, 96°W)	67
Cologne (koh LOHN), *Germany* (51°N, 7°E)	99
Colombia, *country in South America* (3°N, 73°W)	90
Colombo, *Sri Lanka* (7°N, 80°E)	122
Colon (koh LOHN), *Panama* (9°N, 80°W)	85
Colorado, *state in U.S.* (39°N, 107°W)	59
Colorado Plateau, *U.S.* (37°N, 112°W)	59
Colorado R., *Argentina* (38°S, 68°W)	88
Colorado R., *Tex.* (30°N, 97°W)	66-67
Colorado R., *U.S.* (34°N, 114°W)	52
Colorado River Aqueduct, *Calif.* (34°N, 115°W)	58
Colorado Springs, *Col.* (39°N, 105°W)	59
Columbia, *Md.* (39°N, 77°W)	71
Columbia, *Mo.* (39°N, 92°W)	65
Columbia, *S.C.* (34°N, 81°W)	69
Columbia, *Tenn.* (36°N, 87°W)	70
Columbia Mts., *British Columbia* (52°N, 119°W)	44
Columbia Plateau, *U.S.* (44°N, 118°W)	60
Columbia R., *North America* (47°N, 120°W)	60
Columbus, *Ga.* (32°N, 85°W)	68
Columbus, *Ind.* (39°N, 86°W)	70
Columbus, *Miss.* (33°N, 88°W)	68
Columbus, *Nebr.* (41°N, 97°W)	64
Columbus, *Ohio* (40°N, 83°W)	70
Colville R., *Alaska* (69°N, 156°W)	57
Colwyn Bay (KAWL wuhn), *Wales* (53°N, 4°W)	98
Commander Is., *Bering Sea* (55°N, 167°E)	121
Como, L. (KOH moh), *Italy* (46°N, 9°E)	99
Comodoro Rivadavia, *Arg.* (46°S, 68°W)	89
Comorin, Cape, *India* (8°N, 78°E)	122
Comoros, *country in Indian O.* (13°S, 43°E)	107
Con Son Is. (KOHN SOHN), *South China Sea* (9°N, 106°E)	123
Conakry, *Guinea* (10°N, 14°W)	108
Concepcion (kuhn SEP see OHN), *Chile* (37°S, 73°W)	89
Conception, Point, *Calif.* (35°N, 121°W)	58
Conchas Res. (KAHN chus), *N. Mex.* (35°N, 104°W)	59
Conchita Res. (KAHN CHEE tuh), *N. Mex.* (36°N, 106°W)	59
Conchos R., *Mexico* (29°N, 105°W)	82
Concord, *N.H.* (43°N, 71°W)	73
Concord, *N.C.* (35°N, 81°W)	71
Concordia (kuhn KAWRD ee uh), *Kans.* (40°N, 98°W)	64
Conecuh R. (kuh NAY kuh), *Ala.* (31°N, 87°W)	68
Conemaugh R. (KAHN uh MOH), *Pa.* (41°N, 79°W)	72
Congo, *country in Africa* (3°S, 24°E)	107
Congo Basin, *Africa* (0°, 20°E)	106
Congo Rep., *country in Africa* (3°S, 15°E)	107
Congo R., *Africa* (2°N, 20°E)	106
Connecticut, *state in U.S.* (42°N, 73°W)	72-73
Connecticut R., *U.S.* (43°N, 73°W)	73
Conroe (KAHN ROH), *Tex.* (30°N, 95°W)	67
Constance L. (KAHN stuhns), *Europe* (48°N, 9°E)	99

Name (Pronunciation), *Description* (Lat., Long.)	**Page**
Constanta, *Romania* (44°N, 29°E)	99
Constantine, *Algeria* (36°N, 7°E)	114
Conway, *Ark.* (35°N, 92°W)	67
Cook Inlet, *Alaska* (60°N, 153°W)	57
Cook Is., *poss. of N.Z.* (20°S, 158°W)	135
Cook, Mt., *New Zealand* (44°S, 170°E)	130
Cook Strait, *New Zealand* (40°S, 173°E)	130
Cooma, *Australia* (36°S, 149°E)	133
Cooper R., *S.C.* (33°N, 80°W)	69
Cooperstown, *N.Y.* (43°N, 75°W)	72
Coos Bay, *Oreg.* (43°N, 124°W)	60
Coosa R. (KOO suh), *Ala.* (34°N, 86°W)	68
Copenhagen, *Denmark* (56°N, 13°E)	96
Coral Gables, *Fla.* (26°N, 80°W)	69
Coral Sea, *Pacific O.* (13°S, 150°E)	130
Coral Springs, *Fla.* (26°N, 80°W)	69
Coralville Res., *Iowa* (42°N, 92°W)	65
Cordillera Oriental, *range of Andes* (3°N, 77°W)	90
Cordoba (KAWRD uh buh), *Argentina* (31°S, 64°W)	89
Cordoba, *Spain* (38°N, 5°W)	114
Cordova (kawr DOH vuh), *Alaska* (61°N, 146°W)	57
Corfu (kawr FOO), *island in Ionian Sea* (40°N, 20°E)	99
Corinth, *Miss.* (35°N, 88°W)	68
Cork, *Ireland* (52°N, 9°W)	98
Corner Brook, *Newfoundland* (49°N, 58°W)	43
Cornwall, *Ontario* (45°N, 75°W)	47
Coromandel Coast, *India* (15°N, 81°E)	122
Coronada Bay, *Costa Rica* (9°N, 85°W)	83
Coronation Gulf, *Nunavut* (68°N, 112°W)	40
Corowa, *Australia* (36°S, 146°E)	133
Corpus Christi (KAWR puhs KRIHS tee), *Tex.* (28°N, 97°W)	67
Corpus Christi Bay, *Gulf of Mexico* (28°N, 97°W)	67
Corpus Christi, L., *Tex.* (28°N, 98°W)	67
Corrientes, Cape, *Mexico* (20°N, 105°W)	82
Corsica, *island in Mediterranean Sea* (42°N, 9°E)	98
Corsicana (KAWR sih KAHN uh), *Tex.* (32°N, 96°W)	67
Cortland, *N.Y.* (43°N, 76°W)	72
Corvallis, *Oreg.* (45°N, 123°W)	60
Cosenza (koh ZEN suh), *Italy* (39°N, 16°E)	99
Costa Rica, *country in Central America* (10°N, 84°W)	85
Côte d'Ivoire (koht deev WAHR), *country in Africa* (8°N, 5°W)	108
Cotonou (KOHT uh NOO), *Benin* (6°N, 2°E)	108
Cotopaxi, Mt., *Ecuador* (1°S, 78°W)	90
Cottonwood R., *Kans.* (38°N, 97°W)	64
Council Bluffs, *Iowa* (41°N, 96°W)	64-65
Coventry, *England* (52°N, 1°W)	98
Covington, *Ky.* (39°N, 85°W)	70
Cowlitz R., *Wash.* (46°N, 123°W)	60
Cozumel I., *Mexico* (20°N, 87°W)	83
Craiova (kruh YOH vuh), *Romania* (44°N, 24°E)	99
Cranbrook, *British Columbia* (50°N, 116°W)	44
Crater Lake N.P., *Oreg.* (43°N, 122°W)	60
Crawford, *Nebr.* (43°N, 103°W)	64
Crawfordsville, *Ind.* (40°N, 87°W)	70
Cree L., *Saskatchewan* (57°N, 106°W)	45
Crete (kreet), *island in Mediterranean Sea* (34°N, 25°E)	99
Crete, Sea of, *Europe and Asia* (36°N, 25°E)	99
Crimean Pen. (kry MEE uhn), *Ukraine* (45°N, 34°E)	95
Cristobal Colon, Mt., *Colombia* (11°N, 74°W)	90
Croatia (kro AY shuh), *country in Europe* (46°N, 16°E)	99
Crooked R., *British Columbia* (55°N, 123°W)	44
Cross City, *Fla.* (30°N, 83°W)	69
Cross L., *Manitoba* (55°N, 97°W)	45
Crossville, *Tenn.* (36°N, 85°W)	70
Crow Agency, *Mont.* (46°N, 107°W)	61
Crozet Is. (kro ZAY), *Indian O.* (46°S, 50°E)	107
Crystal Mts., *Gabon* (1°N, 11°E)	108
Cuanza R. (KWAN zuh), *Angola* (9°S, 13°E)	106
Cuba (KYOO buh), *country in Caribbean Sea* (23°N, 80°W)	85
Cucuta (KOO kuht uh), *Colombia* (8°N, 73°W)	90

Name (Pronunciation), *Description* (Lat., Long.)	Page
Cuenca (KWENG kuh), *Ecuador* (3°S, 79°W)	90
Cuiaba (KYOO yuh BAH), *Brazil* (16°S, 56°W)	89
Cumana, *Venezuela* (10°N, 64°W)	90
Cumberland, *Md.* (40°N, 79°W)	71
Cumberland Gap, *mt. pass in Ky. and Va.* (37°N, 84°W)	70
Cumberland, L., *Ky.* (37°N, 85°W)	70
Cumberland Plateau, *U.S.* (36°N, 84°W)	70-71
Cumberland R., *U.S.* (36°N, 86°W)	70
Cumberland Sound, *Labrador Sea* (66°N, 67°W)	41
Cunene R. (kyoo NAY nuh), *Angola* (17°S, 14°E)	106
Curacao, *island of Netherlands Antilles* (12°N, 69°W)	83
Curitiba (KOOR ih TEE buh), *Brazil* (25°S, 49°W)	89
Current R., *U.S.* (37°N, 91°W)	65
Cuzco (KOOS koh), *Peru* (14°S, 72°W)	89
Cut Bank Creek, *Mont.* (49°N, 113°W)	61
Cuttack (KUHT uhk), *India* (21°N, 86°E)	122
Cyclades (SIK luh DEEZ), *islands in Aegean Sea* (37°N, 24°E)	99
Cyprus (SY pruhs), *country in Mediterranean Sea* (35°N, 33°E)	115
Cyrenaica (SIH ruh NAY ih cuh), *region of Libya* (32°N, 22°E)	114
Czech Republic, *country in Europe* (49°N, 15°E)	99
Czestochowa (CHEN stuh KOH vuh), *Poland* (51°N, 19°E)	99

D

Name (Pronunciation), *Description* (Lat., Long.)	Page
Da Nang, *Vietnam* (16°N, 108°E)	123
Dabola, *Guinea* (11°N, 11°W)	108
Dahlak Archipelago, *island group in Red Sea* (16°N, 90°E)	115
Dakar, *Senegal* (15°N, 17°W)	108
Dakhilah Oasis (DAHK luh), *Egypt* (25°N, 29°E)	115
Dale Hollow L., *Tenn.* (37°N, 85°W)	70
Dalhart, *Tex.* (36°N, 102°W)	66
Dalian (dah lehn), *China* (39°N, 122°E)	124
Dallas, *Tex.* (33°N, 97°W)	67
Dalles, The (DALZ), *Oreg.* (46°N, 121°W)	60
Dalmatia, *region of Europe* (43°N, 17°E)	99
Dalton, *Ga.* (35°N, 85°W)	68
Daly City, *Calif.* (38°N, 122°W)	58
Damascus, *Syria* (34°N, 36°E)	115
Damavand, Mt., *Iran* (36°N, 52°E)	115
Dan R., *U.S.* (37°N, 79°W)	71
Danbury, *Conn.* (41°N, 73°W)	73
Dandenong, *Australia* (38°S, 145°E)	133
Dansville, *N.Y.* (43°N, 78°W)	72
Danube R., *Europe* (44°N, 27°E)	99
Danville, *Ill.* (40°N, 88°W)	65
Danville, *Va.* (37°N, 79°W)	71
Dar es Salaam, *Tanzania* (7°S, 39°E)	110
Dardanelle L., *Ark.* (35°N, 93°W)	67
Dardanelles, *strait of Europe and Asia* (40°N, 25°E)	99
Darien, Gulf of, *Caribbean Sea* (9°N, 77°W)	83
Darling Range, *Australia* (33°S, 117°E)	130
Darling R., *Australia* (32°S, 143°E)	133
Darnah, *Libya* (33°N, 23°E)	114
Darwin, *Australia* (12°S, 131°E)	131
Dauphin (DAW fuhn), *Manitoba* (51°N, 100°W)	45
Davao, *Philippines* (7°N, 126°E)	121
Davenport, *Iowa* (42°N, 91°W)	65
Davie, *Fla.* (26°N, 80°W)	69
Davis, *Calif.* (39°N, 122°W)	58
Davis Mts., *Tex.* (31°N, 104°W)	66
Davis Sea, *Antarctica* (65°S, 90°E)	137
Davis Strait, *Canada and Greenland* (67°N, 59°W)	41
Dawson, *Yukon Terr.* (64°N, 140°W)	42
Dawson Creek, *British Columbia* (56°N, 120°W)	44
Daxue Shan (dah shyoo shahn), *mts. in China* (30°N, 102°E)	124
Dayton, *Ohio* (40°N, 84°W)	70
Daytona Beach, *Fla.* (29°N, 81°W)	69
De Aar (dee AHR), *South Africa* (31°S, 24°E)	109
Dead Sea, *Asia* (31°N, 35°E)	115
Deal I., *Bass Strait* (39°S, 148°E)	133
Dearborn, *Mich.* (42°N, 83°W)	63

Name (Pronunciation), *Description* (Lat., Long.)	Page
Dease Lake (DEES), *British Columbia* (58°N, 130°W)	44
Death Valley, *Calif.* (36°N, 117°W)	58
Death Valley N.P., *Calif.* (36°N, 117°W)	58
Debrecen (DEB ruht SEHN), *Hungary* (47°N, 22°E)	99
Decatur (deh KAY tuhr), *Ala.* (35°N, 87°W)	68
Decatur, *Ga.* (34°N, 84°W)	69
Decatur, *Ill.* (40°N, 89°W)	65
Deccan Plateau, *India* (18°N, 77°E)	122
Decelles, Res., *Quebec* (48°N, 78°W)	46
Decorah (deh KOHR uh), *Iowa* (43°N, 92°W)	65
Defiance, *Ohio* (41°N, 84°W)	70
DeKalb, *Ill.* (42°N, 89°W)	65
Del Norte (del NOHRT), *Colo.* (38°N, 106°W)	59
Del Rio, *Tex.* (29°N, 101°W)	66
Delaware, *state in U.S.* (39°N, 76°W)	71
Delaware Bay, *U.S.* (39°N, 75°W)	71
Delaware R., *U.S.* (40°N, 75°W)	72
Delhi (DEL ee), *India* (29°N, 77°E)	122
Delmarva Pen., *U.S.* (38°N, 76°W)	71
Denakil Depression, *lowland in Ethiopia* (14°N, 40°E)	115
Denali N. P., *Alaska* (63°N, 150°W)	57
Deniliquin (duh NIHL uh kwihn), *Australia* (36°S, 145°E)	133
Denison, *Iowa* (42°N, 95°W)	65
Denmark, *country in Europe* (56°N, 9°E)	96
Denmark Strait, *Greenland and Iceland* (67°N, 27°W)	41
Dennison, *Ohio* (40°N, 81°W)	71
Denton, *Tex.* (33°N, 97°W)	67
Denver, *Colo.* (40°N, 105°W)	59
Derby, *Australia* (17°S, 124°E)	131
Derry, *N.H.* (43°N, 71°W)	73
Des Moines (di MOYN), *Iowa* (42°N, 94°W)	65
Des Moines R., *Iowa* (43°N, 94°W)	65
Deschutes R. (dih SHOOTS), *Oreg.* (45°N, 121°W)	60
Detroit, *Mich.* (42°N, 83°W)	63
Devils Tower, *mt. in Wyo.* (45°N, 105°W)	61
Devils L., *N. Dak.* (48°N, 99°W)	62
Devils R., *Tex.* (30°N, 101°W)	66
Devon I., *Baffin Bay* (75°N, 85°W)	41
Dhaka, *Bangladesh* (24°N, 90°E)	122
Dickinson, *N. Dak.* (47°N, 103°W)	62
Diefenbaker (DEE fuhn BAY kuhr), L., *Saskatchewan* (51°N, 107°W)	45
Dien Bien Phu (DYEN byen FOO), *Vietnam* (21°N, 103°E)	123
Digby, *Nova Scotia* (45°N, 66°W)	47
Dijon (dee ZHOHN), *France* (47°N, 5°E)	98
Dillingham, *Alaska* (59°N, 159°W)	57
Dillon L., *Ohio* (40°N, 82°W)	71
Dinaric Alps, *mt. range in Europe* (44°N, 17°E)	99
Disappointment, L., *Australia* (24°S, 123°E)	130
District of Columbia, *U.S.* (39°N, 77°W)	71
Dixon Entrance, *strait between Alaska and British Columbia* (54°N, 133°W)	57
Diyarbakir, *Turkey* (38°N, 40°E)	115
Dja R. (JAH), *Africa* (3°N, 13°E)	108
Djibouti (jih BOO tee), *country in Africa* (12°N, 43°E)	107
Djibouti, *Djibouti* (12°N, 43°E)	107
Dnepr Lowland (NEE puhr), *Ukraine* (53°N, 29°E)	95
Dnepr R., *Ukraine* (49°N, 34°E)	95
Dnestr R., (NEE stuhr), *Ukraine* (48°N, 28°E)	95
Dnipropetrovsk (NEHP roh pih TRAWFSK), *Ukraine* (48°N, 35°E)	97
Dodecanese (doh DEK uh NEEZ), *islands in Aegean Sea* (37°N, 26°E)	99
Dodge City, *Kans.* (38°N, 100°W)	64
Dodoma, *Tanzania* (6°S, 36°E)	110
Doha, *Qatar* (25°N, 52°E)	115
Dolak, *island in Arafura Sea* (8°S, 139°E)	130
Dolores R. (duh LOHR uhs), *Colo.* (39°N, 109°W)	59
Dominica, *country in Caribbean Sea* (16°N, 61°W)	85
Dominican Republic, *country in Caribbean Sea* (19°N, 71°W)	85
Don R., *Russia* (47°N, 40°E)	95

Name (Pronunciation), *Description* (Lat., Long.)	Page
Donegal Bay (DAHN ih GAWL), *Ireland* (55°N, 8°W)	98
Donets R., *Ukraine* (49°N, 38°E)	95
Donetsk, *Ukraine* (48°N, 38°E)	97
Dongting L., *China* (29°N, 112°E)	124
Door Pen., *Wis.* (45°N, 87°W)	63
Dordogne R. (dawr DOHN), *France* (45°N, 1°E)	98
Dore L., *Saskatchewan* (55°N, 108°W)	45
Dortmund (DAWRT MOONT), *Germany* (52°N, 7°E)	99
Dothan, *Ala.* (31°N, 85°W)	68
Douala, *Cameroon* (4°N, 10°E)	108
Double Mountain Fork, *r. in Tex.* (34°N, 102°W)	66
Doubs R. (DOO), *France* (47°N, 5°E)	98
Douglas, *Ariz.* (31°N, 110°W)	59
Douglas, *Wyo.* (43°N, 105°W)	61
Douro R., (DOHR yoo), *Portugal* (41°N, 8°W)	94
Dover (DOH vuhr), *Del.* (39°N, 75°W)	71
Dover, *England* (51°N, 1°E)	98
Dover, *N.H.* (43°N, 71°W)	73
Dover, Strait of, *England and France* (51°N, 1°E)	98
Drake Passage, *South America* (57°S, 65°W)	88
Drakensberg, *mt. range in South Africa* (31°S, 27°E)	109
Drava R., *Europe* (46°N, 17°E)	99
Dresden (DREZ dehn), *Germany* (51°N, 14°E)	99
Driftless Area, *U.S.* (43°N, 91°W)	63
Drumheller, *Alberta* (51°N, 113°W)	44-45
Drummond I., *L. Huron* (48°N, 84°W)	63
Drummondsville, *Quebec* (46°N, 73°W)	47
Dry Tortugas, *islands in Gulf of Mexico* (25°N, 83°W)	69
Dryden, *Ontario* (50°N, 93°W)	46
Dubawnt L., *Northwest Terr. and Nunavut* (63°N, 101°W)	45
Dubayy, *United Arab Emirates* (25°N, 55°E)	115
Dublin, *Ga.* (33°N, 83°W)	69
Dublin, *Ireland* (53°N, 6°W)	98
Dubrovnik (DOO BRAWV nik), *Croatia* (43°N, 18°E)	99
Dubuque (duh BYOOK), *Iowa* (43°N, 91°W)	65
Duck Mt. N. P., *Manitoba* (52°N, 101°W)	45
Duero R. (DWER oh), *Europe* (42°N, 3°W)	98
Duluth (duh LOOTH), *Minn.* (47°N, 92°W)	63
Dundalk (DUHN dawk), *Ireland* (54°N, 6°W)	98
Dundee (duhn DEE), *Scotland* (56°N, 3°W)	98
Dunedin, *New Zealand* (46°S, 171°E)	131
Durance R. (doo RAHNS), *France* (44°N, 5°E)	98
Durango, *Colo.* (37°N, 108°W)	59
Durant (doo RANT), *Okla.* (34°N, 96°W)	67
Durban, *South Africa* (30°S, 31°E)	109
Durham, *N.C.* (36°N, 79°W)	71
Dushanbe (du SHAM buh), *Tajikistan* (38°N, 69°E)	100
Dusseldorf (DOO suhl DAWRF), *Germany* (51°N, 7°E)	99
Dutch Harbor, *Alaska* (54°N, 167°W)	57
Dyersburg, *Tenn.* (36°N, 89°W)	70
Dzhugdzhur Range, *Russia* (58°N, 140°E)	101
Dzungarian Basin (ZUNG GAR ee uhn), *Asia* (45°N, 86°E)	124

E

Name (Pronunciation), *Description* (Lat., Long.)	Page
Eagle L., *Maine* (46°N, 71°W)	73
Eagle Mountain L., *Tex.* (33°N, 98°W)	67
Eagle Pass, *Tex.* (29°N, 100°W)	66
Eagle R., *Newfoundland* (54°N, 57°W)	47
East Chicago, *Ind.* (42°N, 87°W)	70
East China Sea, *Asia* (30°N, 125°E)	125
East Fork White R., *Ind.* (39°N, 86°W)	70
East Frisian Is. (FRIZH uhn), *North Sea* (54°N, 7°E)	99
East Lansing, *Mich.* (43°N, 84°W)	63
East Liverpool, *Ohio* (41°N, 81°W)	71
East London, *South Africa* (33°S, 27°E)	109
East Nishnabotna R. (NISH nuh BAHT nuh), *Iowa* (41°N, 96°W)	64-65
East Point, *Ga.* (34°N, 84°W)	69
East Saint Louis, *Ill.* (39°N, 90°W)	65

Name (Pronunciation), *Description* (Lat., Long.)	Page
East Siberian Sea, *Arctic O.* (73°N, 165°E)	119
East Siberian Uplands, *Siberia* (66°N, 135°E)	119
Easter I., *poss. of Chile* (27°S, 110°W)	135
Eastern Cape, *prov. of South Africa* (33°S, 26°E)	109
Eastern Ghats, *mt. range in India* (13°N, 78°E)	122
Eastern Transvaal, *prov. of South Africa* (26°S, 30°E)	109
Eastmain, *Quebec* (52°N, 79°W)	46
Eastmain R., *Quebec* (52°N, 76°W)	46-47
Easton, *Pa.* (41°N, 75°W)	72
Eastport, *Maine* (45°N, 69°W)	73
Eau Claire (oh KLAYR), *Wis.* (45°N, 92°W)	63
Ebro R., *Spain* (42°N, 2°W)	114
Echuca (ee CHOO kah), *Australia* (36°S, 145°E)	133
Ecuador (EHK wuh dohr), *country in South America* (1°S, 78°W)	90
Edinburg, *Tex.* (26°N, 98°W)	66
Edinburgh (ED ihn BUH ruh), *Scotland* (56°N, 3°W)	98
Edirne (ay DIHR nuh), *Turkey* (42°N, 27°E)	115
Edmond, *Okla.* (36°N, 97°W)	67
Edmonds, *Wash.* (48°N, 122°W)	60
Edmonton, *Alberta* (54°N, 113°W)	44
Edmundston, *New Brunswick* (47°N, 68°W)	47
Edward, L., *Africa* (0°, 30°E)	110
Edwards Plateau, *Tex.* (31°N, 101°W)	66
Eel R., *Calif.* (41°N, 124°W)	58
Efate (ay FAHT ee), *island in Pacific O.* (18°S, 169°E)	130
Effingham, *Ill.* (39°N, 88°W)	65
Egypt, *country in Africa* (25°N, 30°E)	114
Eighty Mile Beach, *Australia* (21°S, 119°E)	130
Eildon, L. (EEL duhn), *Australia* (37°S, 146°E)	133
Ekwan R., *Ontario* (53°N, 82°W)	46
El Aaiun (EHL ah YOON), *Western Sahara* (27°N, 13°W)	112
El Chicon (chee KOHN), *mt. in Mexico* (17°N, 93°W)	82
El Dorado (EHL duh RAH doh), *Ark.* (33°N, 93°W)	67
El Obeid, *Sudan* (13°N, 30°E)	115
El Paso, *Tex.* (32°N, 106°W)	66
El Salvador, *country in Central America* (13°N, 89°W)	84
Elazig (EHL uh ZUH), *Turkey* (39°N, 39°E)	115
Elba, *island in Tyrrhenian Sea* (43°N, 10°E)	99
Elbe R., *Europe* (54°N, 10°E)	99
Elbert, Mt., *Colo.* (39°N, 106°W)	59
Elblag (EL BLAWNG), *Poland* (54°N, 19°E)	99
Elbrus, Mt., *Russia* (43°N, 42°E)	95
Elburz Mts., *Iran* (36°N, 52°E)	114
Elephant Butte Res., *N. Mex.* (33°N, 107°W)	59
Eleuthera I., *Bahamas* (25°N, 76°W)	69
Elgin (EL jhn), *Ill.* (42°N, 88°W)	65
Elgon, Mt., *Africa* (1°N, 34°E)	110
Elizabeth, *Australia* (35°S, 138°E)	133
Elizabeth, *N.J.* (41°N, 74°W)	72
Elizabeth City, *N.C.* (36°N, 76°W)	71
Elizabethton, *Tenn.* (36°N, 82°E)	71
Elizabethtown, *N.C.* (35°N, 79°W)	71
Elk City, *Okla.* (35°N, 99°W)	66
Elk City Res., *Kans.* (37°N, 96°W)	64
Elk Is. N. P., *Alberta* (54°N, 113°W)	44-45
Elkhart, *Ind.* (42°N, 86°W)	70
Elkhorn R., *Nebr.* (42°N, 98°W)	64
Elkins, *W. Va.* (39°N, 80°W)	71
Elko, *Nev.* (41°N, 116°W)	62
Ellef Ringnes I. (EL uhf RING nays), *Arctic O.* (79°N, 102°W)	40
Ellensburg, *Wash.* (47°N, 121°W)	60
Ellesmere I., *Arctic O.* (80°N, 77°W)	41
Ellsworth, *Maine* (45°N, 68°W)	73
Ellsworth Land, *region of Antarctica* (85°S, 90°W)	137
Elmhurst, *Ill.* (42°N, 88°W)	65
Elmira (el MY ruh), *N.Y.* (42°N, 77°W)	72
Elwell, L., *Mont.* (48°N, 111°W)	61
Ely (EE lee), *Minn.* (48°N, 92°W)	63
Ely, *Nev.* (39°N, 115°W)	58
Elyria (ih LIHR ee uh), *Ohio* (41°N, 82°W)	71

Name (Pronunciation), *Description* (Lat., Long.)	Page
Emamshahr (eh MAHM SHAHR), *Iran* (36°N, 55°E)	115
Embarrass R. (AHM braw), *Ill.* (39°N, 88°W)	65
Emi Koussi (AY mee KYOO suh), *mt. in Chad* (20°N, 19°E)	106
Emporia (em POHR ee uh), *Kans.* (38°N, 96°W)	64
Encounter Bay, *Australia* (36°S, 138°E)	133
Enfield, *Conn.* (42°N, 73°W)	73
England, *part of United Kingdom* (53°N, 1°W)	98
English Channel, *England and France* (50°N, 2°W)	98
Enid (EE nid), *Okla.* (36°N, 98°W)	67
Ennadai L., *Nunavut* (61°N, 101°W)	45
Ennedi Plateau (EN uh DEE), *Africa* (18°N, 23°E)	115
Ensenada (EN suh NAHD uh), *Mexico* (32°N, 117°W)	58
Entebbe (ehn TEHB ih), *Uganda* (0°, 32°E)	110
Enugu (ah NOO goo), *Nigeria* (6°N, 7°E)	108
Equatorial Guinea, *country in Africa* (2°N, 9°E)	108
Erebus, Mt. (EHR uh buhs), *Antarctica* (78°S, 167°E)	137
Erfurt, *Germany* (51°N, 11°E)	99
Erg Chech, *desert in Africa* (25°N, 2°W)	114
Erg Iguidi, *desert in Africa* (26°N, 7°W)	114
Erie, *Pa.* (42°N, 80°W)	72
Erie, L., *North America* (42°N, 82°W)	46
Erie Canal (EER ee), *N.Y.* (43°N, 77°W)	72
Eritrea (EH rih TREE yuh), *country in Africa* (15°N, 39°E)	107
Erzurum (ERZ ROOM), *Turkey* (40°N, 41°E)	115
Esbjerg (EHS byerhg), *Denmark* (55°N, 30°E)	99
Escambia R., *Fla.* (31°N, 87°W)	68
Escanaba (ES kuh NAHB uh), *Mich.* (46°N, 87°W)	63
Escondido (EHS kun DEED oh), *Calif.* (33°N, 117°W)	58
Eskisehir (EHS kih shuh HIHR), *Turkey* (40°N, 30°E)	115
Espiritu Santo, *island in Pacific O.* (15°S, 167°E)	130
Essen, *Germany* (51°N, 7°E)	99
Essequibo R. (ES uh KWEE boh), *Guyana* (4°N, 58°W)	90
Essex, Mt., *Vt.* (45°N, 73°W)	73
Estevan (EHS tuh VAN), *Saskatchewan* (49°N, 103°W)	45
Estonia, *country in Europe* (59°N, 26°E)	97
Ethiopia, *country in Africa* (10°N, 40°E)	107
Ethiopian Highlands, *Africa* (10°N, 37°E)	106
Etna, Mt., *Sicily* (38°N, 15°E)	99
Etobicoke, *Ontario* (44°N, 80°W)	46
Etorofu (EHT uh ROH foo), *island in Sea of Okhotsk* (45°N, 147°E)	125
Etosha Pan, *dry lake in Namibia* (19°S, 16°E)	106
Euboea (EV yuh), *island in the Aegean Sea* (39°N, 24°E)	99
Euclid (YOO klid), *Ohio* (41°N, 82°W)	71
Eufaula L. (yoo FAW luh), *Okla.* (35°N, 96°W)	67
Eugene, *Oreg.* (44°N, 123°W)	60
Eugenia, Cape, *Mexico* (28°N, 115°W)	82
Euphrates R., *Asia* (35°N, 41°E)	115
Eureka, *Calif.* (41°N, 124°W)	62
Europe, *continent*	7
Eutsuk L. (OOT SUHK), *British Columbia* (53°N, 126°W)	44
Evans L., *Quebec* (51°N, 77°W)	46-47
Evanston, *Ill.* (42°N, 88°W)	65
Evanston, *Wyo.* (41°N, 111°W)	61
Evansville, *Ind.* (38°N, 88°W)	70
Everest, Mt., *China and Nepal* (28°N, 87°E)	122
Everett, *Wash.* (48°N, 122°W)	60
Everglades, The, *swamp in Fla.* (26°N, 81°W)	69
Everglades N.P., *Fla.* (25°N, 81°W)	69
Exeter (EHK suht uhr), *England* (51°N, 4°W)	98
Eyasi, L. (ay YAH say), *Tanzania* (3°S, 35°E)	110
Eyre, L. (AYR), *Australia* (29°S, 138°E)	130
Eyre Pen., *Australia* (33°S, 136°E)	133

F

Name (Pronunciation), *Description* (Lat., Long.)	Page
Faeroe Is. (FAYR oh), *overseas part of Denmark* (62°N, 7°W)	94
Faffak, *Indonesia* (3°S, 132°E)	131
Fairbanks, *Alaska* (65°N, 148°W)	57

Name (Pronunciation), *Description* (Lat., Long.)	Page
Fairmont, *Minn.* (44°N, 94°W)	62
Fairmont, *W. Va.* (39°N, 80°W)	71
Fairweather, Mt., *British Columbia* (59°N, 138°W)	40
Faisalabad (FY SAHL uh BAHD), *Pakistan* (31°N, 73°E)	122
Falcon Res., *Tex.* (27°N, 99°W)	66
Faleme R. (fal uh MAY), *Africa* (13°N, 11°W)	108
Falfurrias (fal FYOOR ee uhs), *Tex.* (27°N, 98°W)	66
Falkland Is., *Atlantic O.* (52°S, 60°W)	89
Fall River, *Mass.* (42°N, 71°W)	73
Farafirah Oasis (fuh RAHF uh ruh), *Egypt* (27°N, 28°E)	115
Farasan Is., *Red Sea* (17°N, 42°E)	115
Farewell, Cape, *Greenland* (59°N, 43°W)	41
Fargo, *N. Dak.* (47°N, 97°W)	62
Farmington, *Maine* (45°N, 70°W)	73
Farmington, *N. Mex.* (37°N, 108°W)	59
Fawn R., *Ontario* (55°N, 88°W)	46
Fayette (fay EHT), *Iowa* (43°N, 92°W)	65
Fayetteville, *Ark.* (36°N, 94°W)	67
Fayetteville, *N.C.* (35°N, 79°W)	71
Fderik, *Mauritania* (23°N, 13°W)	107
Fear, Cape, *N.C.* (34°N, 78°W)	71
Federated States of Micronesia, *country in Pacific O.* (10°N, 150°W)	135
Feira de Santana (FAY uhr uh duh san TAN uh), *Brazil* (12°S, 39°W)	89
Fergus Falls, *Minn.* (46°N, 96°W)	62
Fernando de Noronha, *island in Atlantic O.* (4°S, 32°W)	89
Fernie, *British Columbia* (50°N, 115°W)	44
Ferrara, *Italy* (45°N, 12°E)	99
Feuilles R. (FOO uh YUH), *Quebec* (59°N, 71°W)	41
Fez, *Morocco* (34°N, 5°W)	114
Fifth Cataract, *waterfall in Sudan* (18°N, 34°E)	115
Figuig (fih GIHG), *Morocco* (32°N, 2°W)	114
Fiji, *country in Pacific O.* (20°S, 178°E)	135
Filchner Ice Shelf, *Antarctica* (82°S, 30°W)	137
Findlay, *Ohio* (41°N, 84°W)	70
Finisterre, Cape (FIN uh STEHR), *Spain* (43°N, 9°W)	114
Finland, *country in Europe* (62°N, 24°E)	97
Finland, Gulf of, *Baltic Sea* (60°N, 25°E)	95
Finlay R., *British Columbia* (58°N, 126°W)	44
Firebag Hills, *Canada* (57°N, 110°W)	45
First Cataract, *waterfall in Egypt* (24°N, 33°E)	115
Firth of Forth, *bay in Scotland* (56°N, 3°W)	108
Fitchburg, *Mass.* (43°N, 72°W)	73
Flagstaff, *Ariz.* (35°N, 112°W)	59
Flagstaff L., *Maine* (45°N, 70°W)	73
Flambeau R. (FLAM boh), *Wis.* (45°N, 91°W)	63
Flaming Gorge Res., *Wyo.* (41°N, 110°W)	61
Flanders, *region of Europe* (51°N, 2°E)	98
Flathead L., *Mont.* (48°N, 114°W)	61
Flathead R., *North America* (49°N, 114°W)	61
Flattery, Cape, *Washington* (48°N, 125°W)	60
Flin Flon, *Manitoba* (55°N, 102°W)	45
Flinders I., *Bass Strait* (40°S, 148°E)	133
Flinders Ranges, *Australia* (33°S, 138°E)	130
Flinders R., *Australia* (18°S, 141°E)	130
Flint, *Mich.* (43°N, 84°W)	63
Flint Hills, *Kans.* (38°N, 97°W)	64
Flint R., *Ga.* (32°N, 84°W)	69
Florence, *Ala.* (35°N, 88°W)	68
Florence, *Italy* (44°N, 11°E)	99
Florence, *S.C.* (34°N, 80°W)	69
Flores, *island in Sava Sea* (9°S, 121°E)	130
Flores Sea, *Indian O.* (7°S, 120°E)	130
Florianopolis, *Brazil* (28°S, 49°W)	89
Florida, *state in U.S.* (30°N, 83°W)	68-69
Florida, Straits of, *U.S. and Cuba* (24°N, 81°W)	69
Florida Bay, *Fla.* (25°N, 81°W)	69
Florida Keys, *islands in Caribbean Sea* (25°N, 81°W)	69
Florida Pen., *Fla.* (28°N, 81°W)	69
Florina (FLAWR uh nuh), *Greece* (41°N, 21°E)	99
Florissant, *Mo.* (39°N, 90°W)	65
Floyd R., *Iowa* (43°N, 96°W)	64
Foggia (FAW juh), *Italy* (42°N, 16°E)	99
Folsom L., *Calif.* (39°N, 121°W)	58

Name (Pronunciation), Description (Lat., Long.)	Page
Fond-du-Lac (FAHN duh LAK), *Saskatchewan* (59°N, 107°W)	45
Fond du Lac, *Wis.* (44°N, 89°W)	63
Fond-du-Lac R., *Saskatchewan* (59°N, 104°W)	45
Fonseca, Gulf of, *Pacific O.* (13°N, 88°W)	82-83
Forest City, *Iowa* (43°N, 94°W)	65
Forestville, *Quebec* (49°N, 69°W)	47
Forillon N. P. (FOH ree YOHN), *Quebec* (49°N, 64°W)	47
Fort Albany, *Ontario* (52°N, 82°W)	46
Fort Chipewyan, *Alberta* (59°N, 111°W)	45
Fort Collins, *Colo.* (41°N, 105°W)	59
Fort Dodge, *Iowa* (43°N, 94°W)	65
Fort Frances, *Ontario* (49°N, 93°W)	46
Fort Knox, *Ky.* (38°N, 86°W)	70
Fort Lauderdale, *Fla.* (26°N, 80°W)	69
Fort Liard (LEE AHRD), *Northwest Terr.* (60°N, 123°W)	44
Fort Loudoun L. (LOWD uhn), *Tenn.* (36°N, 84°W)	70
Fort McMurray, *Alberta* (57°N, 111°W)	45
Fort Myers, *Fla.* (27°N, 82°W)	69
Fort Nelson, *British Columbia* (59°N, 123°W)	44
Fort Nelson R., *British Columbia* (59°N, 123°W)	44
Fort Peck Dam, *Mont.* (48°N, 106°W)	61
Fort Peck L., *Mont.* (48°N, 107°W)	61
Fort Pierce, *Fla.* (27°N, 80°W)	69
Fort Randall Dam, *S. Dak.* (43°N, 99°W)	62
Fort Resolution, *Northwest Terr.* (61°N, 114°W)	44
Fort Saint John, *British Columbia* (56°N, 121°W)	44
Fort Scott, *Kans.* (38°N, 95°W)	65
Fort Severn, *Ontario* (57°N, 88°W)	43
Fort Simpson, *Northwest Terr.* (62°N, 121°W)	44
Fort Smith, *Ark.* (35°N, 94°W)	67
Fort Smith, *Northwest Terr.* (60°N, 112°W)	45
Fort Stockton, *Tex.* (31°N, 103°W)	66
Fort Vermillion, *Alberta* (58°N, 116°W)	44
Fort Walton Beach, *Fla.* (30°N, 87°W)	68
Fort Wayne, *Ind.* (41°N, 85°W)	70
Fort Worth, *Tex.* (33°N, 97°W)	67
Fort Yukon (YOO kahn), *Alaska* (67°N, 145°W)	57
Fortaleza, *Brazil* (4°S, 39°W)	89
Fourth Cataract, *waterfall in Sudan* (19°N, 32°E)	115
Foveaux Strait (FOH VOH), *New Zealand* (47°S, 168°E)	130
Fox R., *U.S.* (42°N, 88°W)	65
Fox R., *Wis.* (44°N, 89°W)	63
Foxe Basin, *Nunavut* (67°N, 80°W)	41
Foxe Channel, *Nunavut* (65°N, 80°W)	41
Foxe Pen., *Baffin I.* (65°N, 76°W)	41
Framingham (FRAY ming HAM), *Mass.* (42°N, 72°W)	73
France, *country in Europe* (47°N, 0°)	98
Franceville (frahns VEEL), *Gabon* (2°S, 14°E)	108
Francis Case, L., *S. Dak.* (43°N, 99°W)	62
Francois L. (FRANG SWUH), *British Columbia* (54°N, 126°W)	44
Frankfort, *Ky.* (38°N, 85°W)	70
Frankfurt, *Germany* (50°N, 9°E)	99
Franklin, *N.C.* (35°N, 83°W)	70
Franklin D. Roosevelt L., *Wash.* (48°N, 118°W)	60
Franz Josef Land, *island group in Arctic O.* (82°N, 55°E)	100
Fraser I., *Australia* (25°S, 153°E)	130
Fraser Plateau, *British Columbia* (53°N, 125°W)	44
Fraser R., *Canada* (51°N, 122°W)	44
Frederick, *Md.* (39°N, 77°W)	71
Fredericksburg, *Va.* (38°N, 77°W)	71
Fredericton, *New Brunswick* (46°N, 67°W)	47
Fredonia, *N.Y.* (42°N, 79°W)	72
Freemantle, *Australia* (32°S, 116°E)	131
Freeport, *Ill.* (42°N, 90°W)	65
Freetown, *Sierra Leone* (8°N, 13°W)	108
Fremont (FREE MAHNT), *Calif.* (38°N, 122°W)	58
Fremont, *Nebr.* (41°N, 96°W)	64
Fremont, *Ohio* (41°N, 83°W)	70
French Guiana (gee AH nuh), *overseas state of France* (4°N, 53°W)	90
French Lick, *Ind.* (39°N, 87°W)	70
French Polynesia, *poss. of France* (20°S, 140°W)	135

Name (Pronunciation), Description (Lat., Long.)	Page
Frenchman R., *North America* (49°N, 108°W)	45
Fresno, *Calif.* (37°N, 120°W)	58
Fria, Cape, *Africa* (18°S, 12°E)	106
Frio, Cape, *Brazil* (23°S, 42°W)	88
Frisian Is., *Europe* (53°N, 5°E)	94
Frobisher Bay, *Canada* (63°N, 67°W)	41
Frobisher L., *Saskatchewan* (56°N, 108°W)	45
Front Range, *Colo.* (40°N, 106°W)	59
Fuerte R., *Mexico* (27°N, 109°W)	82
Fuji, Mt. (FOO jee), *Japan* (35°N, 139°E)	125
Fukui (foo KOO ee), *Japan* (36°N, 136°E)	125
Fukuoka, *Japan* (34°N, 130°E)	125
Fukushima (FOO kuh SHEE muh), *Japan* (37°N, 140°E)	125
Fulton, *Ky.* (37°N, 89°W)	70
Fundy, Bay of, *North America* (45°N, 65°W)	47
Fundy N.P., *New Brunswick* (46°N, 65°W)	47
Furnas Res., *Brazil* (21°S, 46°W)	88
Furneaux Group (FUHR noh), *islands in Bass Strait* (40°S, 148°E)	130
Fushun (fyu shoon), *China* (42°N, 124°E)	124
Fuzhou (FYU zhoo), *China* (26°N, 119°E)	124
Fyn (FIN), *island in Katlegat* (55°N, 10°E)	99

G

Name (Pronunciation), Description (Lat., Long.)	Page
Gabes, Gulf of (GAHB uhs), *Tunisia* (34°N, 10°E)	114
Gabon, *country in Africa* (1°S, 12°E)	108
Gaborone (GAHB uh ROHN ee), *Botswana* (24°S, 26°E)	107
Gadsden, *Ala.* (34°N, 86°W)	68
Gagnon (gah NYON), *Quebec* (52°N, 68°W)	47
Gainesville, *Fla.* (30°N, 82°W)	69
Gairdner, L., *Australia* (32°S, 136°E)	130
Galapagos Is. (guh LAH puh GOHS), *Pacific O.* (0°, 91°W)	90
Galati (guh LATS ee), *Romania* (45°N, 28°E)	99
Galena (guh LEEN uh), *Ill.* (42°N, 90°W)	65
Galesburg (GAYLZ buhrg), *Ill.* (41°N, 90°W)	65
Gallatin R., *Mont.* (45°N, 111°W)	61
Gallinas, Point, *Colombia* (12°N, 72°W)	90
Gallup, *N. Mex.* (36°N, 109°W)	59
Galveston, *Tex.* (29°N, 95°W)	67
Galveston Bay, *Tex.* (30°N, 94°W)	67
Galway, *Ireland* (53°N, 9°W)	98
Galway Bay, *Ireland* (53°N, 9°W)	98
Gambia (GAM bee uh), *country in Africa* (13°N, 15°W)	108
Gambia R., *Africa* (13°N, 14°W)	108
Gamtoos R., *South Africa* (34°S, 25°E)	109
Ganges, Mouths of the (GAN jeez), *delta in Asia* (22°N, 89°E)	122
Ganges Plain, *India* (26°N, 84°E)	122
Ganges R., *India* (25°N, 86°E)	122
Gao, *Mali* (17°N, 0°)	107
Garabogazkol Aylagy, *gulf in Caspian Sea* (41°N, 53°E)	115
Garden City, *Kans.* (38°N, 101°W)	64
Garibaldi, Mt. (GAR uh BAWL dee), *British Columbia* (50°N, 123°W)	44
Garissa, *Kenya* (1°S, 40°E)	110
Garland, *Tex.* (33°N, 97°W)	67
Garnpung, L., *Australia* (34°S, 143°E)	133
Garonne R. (guh RAHN), *France* (44°N, 1°E)	98
Garoua (guh ROO uh), *Cameroon* (9°N, 13°E)	108
Garrison Dam, *N. Dak.* (48°N, 101°W)	62
Gary, *Ind.* (42°N, 87°W)	70
Gasconade R. (GAS kuh NAYD), *Mo.* (38°N, 92°W)	65
Gaspe (gah SPAY), *Quebec* (49°N, 65°W)	47
Gaspe Pen., *Quebec* (48°N, 67°W)	47
Gaston, L., *U.S.* (37°N, 78°W)	71
Gastonia, *N.C.* (35°N, 81°W)	71
Gates of the Arctic N. P., *Alaska* (68°N, 154°W)	57
Gatineau R. (GAT uhn OH), *Quebec* (45°N, 76°W)	47
Gauhati, *India* (26°N, 92°E)	122
Gauteng, *prov. of South Africa* (25°S, 29°E)	109
Gavin's Point Dam, *S. Dak.* (43°N, 97°W)	62
Gaza Strip, *terr. in Asia* (32°N, 34°E)	115

Name (Pronunciation), Description (Lat., Long.)	Page
Gaziantep, *Turkey* (37°N, 37°E)	115
Gbarnga, *Liberia* (7°N, 9°W)	108
Gdansk (guh DAHNSK), *Poland* (54°N, 19°E)	99
Gdansk, Gulf of, *Poland* (55°N, 19°E)	99
Gdynia (guh DIN ee uh), *Poland* (54°N, 18°E)	99
Geelong (juh LAWNG), *Australia* (38°S, 144°E)	133
Geita, *Tanzania* (3°S, 32°E)	110
Genesee R. (JEN uh SEE), *N.Y.* (42°N, 78°W)	72
Geneseo (JEN uh SEE oh), *N.Y.* (43°N, 78°W)	72
Geneva, *Switzerland* (46°N, 6°E)	99
Geneva, L., *Switzerland* (46°N, 7°E)	99
Genoa (JEHN oh uh), *Italy* (44°N, 9°E)	99
George, L., *Fla.* (29°N, 82°W)	69
George, L., *N.Y.* (44°N, 73°W)	72
George, L., *Uganda* (0°, 30°E)	110
George Res., *U.S.* (32°N, 85°W)	68
George R., *Quebec* (58°N, 66°W)	41
George West, *Tex.* (28°N, 98°W)	66
Georgetown, *Guyana* (7°N, 58°W)	90
Georgetown, *Ky.* (38°N, 85°W)	70
Georgetown, *Md.* (39°N, 76°W)	71
Georgia, *country in Asia* (42°N, 43°E)	100
Georgia, *state in U.S.* (33°N, 83°W)	68-69
Georgia, Strait of, *British Columbia* (49°N, 125°W)	44
Georgian Bay, *Canada* (45°N, 81°W)	46
Georgian Bay Is. N.P., *L. Huron* (45°N, 80°W)	46
Geraldton, *Australia* (29°S, 115°E)	131
Germantown, *Tenn.* (37°N, 90°W)	70
Germany, *country in Europe* (52°N, 12°E)	99
Germiston (JEHR muh stuhn), *South Africa* (26°S, 28°E)	109
Gettysburg, *Pa.* (40°N, 77°W)	72
Ghadamis, *Libya* (30°N, 10°E)	114
Ghaghara R. (GAHG uh ruh), *Asia* (27°N, 83°E)	122
Ghana, *Africa* (8°N, 2°W)	108
Ghat, *Libya* (25°N, 10°E)	114
Ghent (gehnt), *Belgium* (51°N, 4°E)	98
Gibraltar (jih BRAWL tuhr), *terr. of United Kingdom* (36°N, 5°W)	114
Gibraltar, Strait of, *Europe and Africa* (36°N, 6°W)	114
Gibson Desert, *Australia* (24°S, 120°E)	130
Gila R. (HEE luh), *U.S.* (33°N, 114°W)	58-59
Gillam, *Manitoba* (56°N, 95°W)	45
Gillette (juh LEHT), *Wyo.* (44°N, 106°W)	61
Gimli, *Manitoba* (51°N, 97°W)	45
Gippsland, *Australia* (37°S, 148°E)	133
Gironde R. (juh RAHND), *France* (45°N, 1°W)	98
Giza (GEE zuh), *Egypt* (30°N, 31°E)	115
Glacier Bay N.P. (GLAY shuhr), *Alaska* (59°N, 137°W)	57
Glacier N.P., *British Columbia* (51°N, 118°W)	44
Glacier N.P., *Mont.* (49°N, 114°W)	61
Glasgow (GLAS GOH), *Ky.* (37°N, 86°W)	70
Glasgow (GLAHZ goh), *Scotland* (56°N, 4°W)	98
Glen Canyon Dam, *Ariz.* (37°N, 111°W)	59
Glendale, *Ariz.* (34°N, 112°W)	59
Glendale, *Calif.* (34°N, 118°W)	58
Glendive (GLEHN DYV), *Mont.* (47°N, 105°W)	61
Glenelg R., *Australia* (37°S, 143°E)	133
Gobi (GOH bee), *desert in Asia* (44°N, 109°E)	119
Godavari R. (guh DAHV uh ree), *India* (19°N, 77°E)	122
Goderich (GAHD RICH), *Ontario* (44°N, 82°W)	46
Gods L., *Manitoba* (55°N, 94°W)	45
Gods R., *Manitoba* (55°N, 93°W)	45
Godthab (GAWT hob), *Greenland* (64°N, 51°W)	35
Godwin Austen, Mt., *China and Pakistan* (36°N, 77°E)	122
Gogebic Range (goh GEE bik), *Mich.* (47°N, 90°W)	63
Goiania (goy AN ee uh), *Brazil* (17°S, 49°W)	89
Golan Heights, *terr. in Asia* (33°N, 36°E)	115
Gold Coast, *Australia* (28°S, 153°E)	131
Gold Coast, *region in Africa* (5°N, 0°)	108
Goldsboro, *N.C.* (35°N, 78°W)	71
Good Hope, Cape of, *South Africa* (34°S, 18°E)	109
Goodland, *Kans.* (39°N, 102°W)	64
Goose L., *U.S.* (42°N, 121°W)	58

Name (Pronunciation), *Description* (Lat., Long.)	Page
Gorgan (gohr GAHN), *Iran* (37°N, 54°E)	115
Gorki Res., *Russia* (57°N, 43°E)	95
Gotaland, *region of Sweden* (57°N, 13°E)	94
Goteborg (YUH tuh BAWR yuh), *Sweden* (58°N, 12°E)	99
Gotel Mts., *Africa* (7°N, 11°E)	108
Gotland, *island in Baltic Sea* (57°N, 19°E)	94
Goto Is. (GOHT oh), *island in East China Sea* (33°N, 129°E)	125
Gott Peak, *British Columbia* (50°N, 122°W)	44
Gouin, Res. (GWAN), *Quebec* (48°N, 74°W)	47
Goulburn (GOHL buhrn), *Australia* (35°S, 150°E)	133
Graaff Reinet (GRAHF RY nut), *South Africa* (32°S, 25°E)	109
Grafton, *N. Dak.* (48°N, 97°W)	62
Graham, *Tex.* (33°N, 99°W)	66
Grahamstown, *South Africa* (33°S, 27°E)	109
Grain Coast, *region of Africa* (5°N, 10°W)	108
Grampian Mts., *Scotland* (57°N, 4°W)	98
Gran Chaco, *plains in central South America* (24°S, 63°W)	88
Granada, *Spain* (37°N, 4°W)	114
Granby, *Quebec* (45°N, 73°W)	47
Grand Bahama I., *Atlantic O.* (27°N, 78°W)	83
Grand Canal, *China* (36°N, 116°E)	124
Grand Canyon, *Ariz.* (36°N, 113°W)	58-59
Grand Canyon N.P., *Ariz.* (36°N, 112°W)	59
Grand Coulee Dam, *Wash.* (48°N, 119°W)	60
Grand Erg de Bilma, *desert in Africa* (19°N, 14°E)	114
Grand Erg Occidental, *desert in Algeria* (30°N, 1°E)	114
Grand Erg Oriental, *desert in Algeria* (31°N, 7°E)	114
Grand Falls, *New Brunswick* (47°N, 68°W)	47
Grand Forks, *N. Dak.* (48°N, 97°W)	62
Grand Haven, *Mich.* (43°N, 86°W)	63
Grand I., *L. Superior* (47°N, 87°W)	63
Grand Island, *Nebr.* (41°N, 98°W)	64
Grand Junction, *Colo.* (39°N, 108°W)	59
Grand L., *La.* (30°N, 93°W)	67
Grand L., *New Brunswick* (46°N, 67°W)	47
Grand L., *Ohio* (41°N, 84°W)	70
Grand Manan I., *Bay of Fundy* (45°N, 67°W)	47
Grand Rapids, *Manitoba* (53°N, 99°W)	45
Grand Rapids, *Mich.* (43°N, 86°W)	63
Grand R., *Mich.* (43°N, 86°W)	63
Grand R., *S. Dak.* (46°N, 102°W)	62
Grand R., *U.S.* (40°N, 94°W)	65
Grand Teton N.P., *Wyo.* (44°N, 110°W)	61
Grand Traverse Bay, *Mich.* (45°N, 86°W)	63
Grande 4, Res. de la, *Quebec* (54°N, 73°W)	47
Grande Prairie, *Alberta* (55°N, 119°W)	44
Grande R., *Nicaragua* (14°N, 84°W)	83
Grande 3, Res. de la, *Quebec* (54°N, 75°W)	47
Grande 2, Res. de la, *Quebec* (54°N, 77°W)	46-47
Granville L., *Manitoba* (56°N, 100°W)	45
Grasslands N.P., *Saskatchewan* (48°N, 107°W)	45
Grays Harbor, *Wash.* (47°N, 124°W)	60
Graz, *Austria* (47°N, 15°E)	99
Great Abaco I., *Atlantic O.* (27°N, 77°W)	83
Great Artesian Basin, *Australia* (24°S, 145°E)	130
Great Australian Bight, *gulf in Indian O.* (34°S, 130°E)	130
Great Barrier Reef, *Australia* (15°S, 146°E)	130
Great Basin, *U.S.* (39°N, 117°W)	58
Great Basin N.P., *Nev.* (39°N, 114°W)	58
Great Bear L., *Northwest Terr.* (66°N, 121°W)	40
Great Bend, *Kans.* (38°N, 99°W)	64
Great Britain, *island in North Sea* (52°N, 2°W)	98
Great Dismal Swamp, *U.S.* (37°N, 76°W)	71
Great Divide Basin, *Wyo.* (42°N, 108°W)	61
Great Dividing Range, *Australia* (34°S, 149°E)	133
Great Escarpment, *natural feature of Brazil* (27°S, 49°W)	88
Great Falls, *Mont.* (47°N, 111°W)	61
Great Fish R., *South Africa* (33°S, 27°E)	109
Great Hungarian Plain, *Europe* (46°N, 18°E)	99
Great Inagua I., *Atlantic O.* (21°N, 74°W)	83
Great Indian Desert, *India* (25°N, 71°E)	122
Great Karroo, *plateau in South Africa* (33°S, 23°E)	109
Great Lakes, *North America* (49°N, 86°W)	46-47
Great Miami R., *Ohio* (39°N, 85°W)	70
Great Plains, *North America* (50°N, 108°W)	36
Great Rift Valley, *Africa* (2°S, 35°E)	110
Great Ruaha R. (roo AH hah), *Tanzania* (8°S, 35°E)	110
Great Russian Plains, *Russia* (55°N, 45°E)	100
Great Salt L., *Utah* (41°N, 112°W)	59
Great Salt L. Desert, *U.S.* (41°N, 113°W)	58
Great Sandy Desert, *Australia* (19°S, 124°E)	130
Great Sandy Desert, *Oreg.* (44°N, 121°W)	60
Great Slave L., *Northwest Terr.* (62°N, 114°W)	44-45
Great Smoky Mts., *U.S.* (36°N, 85°W)	70-71
Great Smoky Mts. N.P., *U.S.* (36°N, 84°W)	70
Great Valley, *Appalachian Mts.* (38°N, 79°W)	70-71
Great Victoria Desert, *Australia* (28°S, 126°E)	130
Great Wall, *China* (38°N, 105°E)	124
Greater Antilles, *island group in Caribbean Sea* (20°N, 77°W)	83
Greater Khingan Range, *China* (44°N, 119°E)	124
Greece, *country in Europe* (38°N, 22°E)	99
Greeley, *Colo.* (40°N, 105°W)	59
Green Bay, *L. Michigan* (45°N, 88°W)	63
Green Bay, *city in Wis.* (44°N, 88°W)	63
Green Mts., *Vt.* (44°N, 73°W)	73
Green R., *Ky.* (37°N, 87°W)	70
Green R., *U.S.* (42°N, 110°W)	61
Greenland, *overseas part of Denmark* (75°N, 40°W)	37
Greensboro, *N.C.* (36°N, 80°W)	71
Greensburg, *Ind.* (39°N, 86°W)	70
Greenville, *Miss.* (33°N, 91°W)	69
Greenville, *N.C.* (36°N, 77°W)	71
Greenville, *S.C.* (35°N, 82°W)	69
Greenwood, *Miss.* (33°N, 90°W)	68
Greenwood, *S.C.* (32°N, 84°W)	69
Grenada, *country in Caribbean Sea* (12°N, 62°W)	85
Grenoble (gruh NOH buhl), *France* (45°N, 6°E)	98
Gresham, *Oreg.* (45°N, 122°W)	60
Griffith, *Australia* (34°S, 146°E)	133
Grinnell (gruh NEHL), *Iowa* (42°N, 93°W)	65
Groningen (GROH ning guhn), *Netherlands* (53°N, 7°E)	98
Groot Vloer (GROHT VLAWR), *l. in South Africa* (30°S, 21°E)	109
Groote Eylandt (gryoot EYE lund), *island in Gulf of Carpentaria* (14°S, 137°E)	130
Groton (GRAHT uhn), *Conn.* (41°N, 72°W)	73
Groundhog R., *Ontario* (48°N, 82°W)	46
Groznyy (GRAWZ nee), *Russia* (43°N, 46°E)	97
Guadalajara (GWAH duh luh HAHR uh), *Mexico* (21°N, 103°W)	84
Guadalcanal, *island in Solomon Sea* (9°S, 160°E)	130
Guadalquivir R., *Europe* (38°N, 6°W)	114
Guadalupe I. (GWAH duh LOOP), *Mexico* (29°N, 118°W)	82
Guadalupe Mts., *U.S.* (32°N, 105°W)	66
Guadalupe Mts. N.P., *U.S.* (32°N, 105°W)	66
Guadalupe Pk., *Tex.* (32°N, 105°W)	66
Guadalupe R., *Tex.* (29°N, 97°W)	67
Guadeloupe (GWAH duh LOOP), *overseas state of France* (17°N, 62°W)	85
Guadiana R., *Spain* (39°N, 7°W)	114
Guam, *poss. of U.S.* (14°N, 143°E)	134
Guangzhou (gwahng joh), *China* (23°N, 113°E)	124
Guantanamo (gwahn TAH nuh MOH), *Cuba* (20°N, 75°W)	85
Guapore R. (GWAHP uh RAY), *South America* (12°S, 65°W)	90
Guardafui, Cape (GAHRD uf WEE), *Somalia* (12°N, 51°E)	106
Guatemala, *country in Central America* (15°N, 90°W)	84
Guatemala City, *Guatemala* (15°N, 91°W)	84
Guaviare R. (gwav YAHR ee), *South America* (3°N, 73°W)	90
Guayaquil (GWAH yah KEEL), *Ecuador* (2°S, 80°W)	90
Guayaquil, Gulf of, *Pacific O.* (3°S, 80°W)	90
Guiana Highlands (gee AH nuh), *South America* (4°N, 65°W)	90
Guinea (GIHN ee), *country in Africa* (10°N, 10°W)	108
Guinea-Bissau (GIHN ee bih SOW), *country in Africa* (12°N, 15°W)	108
Guinea, Gulf of, *Atlantic O.* (0°, 0°)	108
Gujranwala (GOOJ ruhn WAHL uh), *Pakistan* (32°N, 74°E)	122
Gulf Coastal Plain, *U.S.* (31°N, 94°W)	53
Gulf St. Vincent, *Australia* (35°S, 138°E)	133
Gulfport, *Miss.* (30°N, 89°W)	68
Gunisao R. (guhn ih SAY oh), *Manitoba* (54°N, 97°W)	45
Gunnison R., *Colo.* (39°N, 108°W)	59
Guntersville L., *Ala.* (34°N, 86°W)	68
Guyana, *country in South America* (5°N, 59°W)	90
Guymon (GY muhn), *Okla.* (37°N, 101°W)	66
Gwaii Haanas N.P., *British Columbia* (52°N, 132°W)	44
Gwalior, *India* (26°N, 78°E)	122
Gydan Pen., *Russia* (70°N, 80°E)	118

H

Name (Pronunciation), *Description* (Lat., Long.)	Page
Habuna, *Brazil* (15°S, 39°W)	89
Hachinohe (HAHCH ih noh hay), *Japan* (40°N, 142°E)	125
Haeju (HY JOO), *North Korea* (38°N, 126°E)	125
Hafun, Cape (ha FOON), *Somalia* (10°N, 51°E)	115
Hagerstown, *Md.* (40°N, 78°W)	71
Hague, The, *Netherlands* (52°N, 4°E)	98
Hai Phong (HY FONG), *Vietnam* (21°N, 107°E)	123
Haikou (hy koh), *China* (20°N, 110°E)	124
Hainan, *island in South China Sea* (20°N, 110°E)	124
Haiti (HAY tee), *country in Caribbean Sea* (19°N, 72°W)	85
Hakodate (HAHK uh DAHT ee), *Japan* (42°N, 141°E)	125
Haleakala N. P. (HAHL ee AHK uh LAH), *Hawaii* (21°N, 156°W)	57
Halifax, *Nova Scotia* (44°N, 63°W)	47
Halle (HAHL uh), *Germany* (52°N, 12°E)	99
Halmahera, *island in Philippine Sea* (1°N, 128°E)	130
Halmahera Sea, *Indian O.* (0°, 129°E)	130
Hamadan, *Iran* (35°N, 48°E)	115
Hamah, *Syria* (35°N, 37°E)	115
Hamamatsu (HAHM uh MAHT soo), *Japan* (35°N, 138°E)	125
Hamburg, *Germany* (54°N, 10°E)	99
Hamden, *Conn.* (41°N, 73°W)	73
Hamhung (HAHM HOONG), *North Korea* (40°N, 128°E)	125
Hamilton, *Ala.* (34°N, 88°W)	68
Hamilton, *Australia* (38°S, 142°E)	133
Hamilton, *Ohio* (39°N, 85°W)	70
Hamilton, *Ontario* (43°N, 80°W)	46
Hammerfest, *Norway* (71°N, 24°E)	97
Hammersley Ranges, *Australia* (22°S, 118°E)	130
Hammond, *Ind.* (42°N, 87°W)	70
Hampton, *Va.* (37°N, 76°W)	71
Han R. (hahn), *China* (33°N, 111°E)	124
Handan, *China* (37°N, 114°E)	124
Hangzhou, *China* (31°N, 120°E)	124
Hannibal, *Mo.* (40°N, 91°W)	65
Hannover, *Germany* (52°N, 10°E)	99
Hanoi, *Vietnam* (21°N, 106°E)	123
Happy Valley–Goose Bay, *Newfoundland* (53°N, 60°W)	47
Harare, *Zimbabwe* (18°S, 31°E)	107
Harbin, *China* (46°N, 127°E)	124
Hardanger Fiord (hahr DANG guhr), *Norway* (60°N, 6°E)	94
Harer, *Ethiopia* (9°N, 42°E)	107
Hargeysa, *Somalia* (9°N, 44°E)	107
Harlan, *Ky.* (37°N, 83°W)	70
Harlingen (HAHR ling uhn), *Tex.* (26°N, 98°W)	67
Harney Basin, *Oreg.* (43°N, 120°W)	60
Harney Pk., *S. Dak.* (44°N, 104°W)	62
Harper, *Liberia* (4°N, 8°W)	107
Harpers Ferry, *W. Va.* (39°N, 78°W)	71

Name (Pronunciation), *Description* (Lat., Long.)	**Page**
Harricana R. (HAR ih KAN aw), *Quebec* (51 °N, 79 °W)	46
Harrisburg, *Pa.* (40 °N, 77 °W)	72
Harrisonburg, *Va.* (39 °N, 79 °W)	71
Hartford, *Conn.* (42 °N, 73 °W)	73
Hartwell L., *U.S.* (34 °N, 83 °W)	69
Hasa, *region of Saudi Arabia* (27 °N, 48 °E)	115
Hastings, *Nebr.* (41 °N, 98 °W)	64
Hatchie R., *U.S.* (36 °N, 90 °W)	70
Hatteras, Cape, *N.C.* (35 °N, 76 °W)	71
Hatteras I., *Pamlico Sound* (36 °N, 76 °W)	71
Hattiesburg, *Miss.* (31 °N, 89 °W)	68
Havana, *Cuba* (23 °N, 82 °W)	85
Havasu, L. (HAV uh SOO), *Ariz.* (34 °N, 114 °W)	58
Haverhill, *Mass.* (43 °N, 71 °W)	73
Havre (HAV uhr), *Mont.* (48 °N, 110 °W)	61
Havre-Saint-Pierre (HAV ruh SAN PYAIR), *Quebec* (50 °N, 64 °W)	47
Hawaii (huh WY ee), *state in U.S.* (21 °N, 157 °W)	57
Hawaii, *island in Pacific O.* (20 °N, 156 °W)	57
Hawaii Volcanoes N.P., *Hawaii* (20 °N, 156 °W)	57
Hay R., *Canada* (59 °N, 119 °W)	44
Hay River, *city in Northwest Terr.* (61 °N, 116 °W)	44
Hayes R., *Manitoba* (56 °N, 93 °W)	45
Hays, *Kans.* (39 °N, 99 °W)	64
Hayward, *Wis.* (46 °N, 92 °W)	63
Hazelton, *British Columbia* (55 °N, 128 °W)	44
Hearst, *Ontario* (50 °N, 84 °W)	46
Heart R., *N. Dak.* (47 °N, 102 °W)	62
Hebgen L., *Mont.* (45 °N, 111 °W)	61
Hebrides (HEHB rih DEEZ), *island group in Atlantic O.* (57 °N, 7 °W)	94
Hecate Strait (HEK uht), *British Columbia* (53 °N, 131 °W)	44
Hejaz, *region of Saudi Arabia* (24 °N, 38 °E)	115
Hekla, *mt. in Iceland* (64 °N, 20 °W)	94
Helena, *Mont.* (47 °N, 112 °W)	61
Hell's Canyon, *Snake R.* (45 °N, 117 °W)	60
Helsingborg (HEHL sing BAWR), *Sweden* (56 °N, 13 °E)	99
Helsinki, *Finland* (60 °N, 25 °E)	97
Hempstead, *N.Y.* (41 °N, 74 °W)	72-73
Henderson, *Ky.* (38 °N, 88 °W)	70
Henderson, *Nev.* (36 °N, 115 °W)	58
Henderson, *N.C.* (36 °N, 78 °W)	71
Hendersonville, *Tenn.* (36 °N, 87 °W)	70
Henrietta Maria, Cape, *Ontario* (55 °N, 82 °W)	46
Henry Mts., *Utah* (38 °N, 111 °W)	59
Herat (heh RAHT), *Afghanistan* (34 °N, 62 °E)	120
Hereford (HUHR furd), *Tex.* (35 °N, 102 °W)	66
Hermosillo (EHR muh SEE yoh), *Mexico* (29 °N, 111 °W)	84
Hetch Hetchy Aqueduct, *Calif.* (38 °N, 121 °W)	58
Hialeah (HY uh LEE uh), *Fla.* (26 °N, 80 °W)	69
Hibbing, *Minn.* (47 °N, 93 °W)	63
Hickory, *N.C.* (36 °N, 81 °W)	71
Hickory, L., *N.C.* (36 °N, 81 °W)	71
High Point, *N.C.* (36 °N, 80 °W)	71
High Rock L., *N.C.* (36 °N, 80 °W)	71
Highlands, *region of Scotland* (57 °N, 4 °W)	98
Hillsboro, *Ohio* (39 °N, 84 °W)	70
Hilo, *Hawaii* (20 °N, 155 °W)	57
Himalayas, *mt. range in Asia* (28 °N, 85 °E)	122
Hindu Kush, *mt. range in Asia* (37 °N, 72 °E)	122
Hinton, *Alberta* (53 °N, 118 °W)	44
Hirakud Res., *India* (22 °N, 84 °E)	122
Hirosaki, *Japan* (41 °N, 140 °E)	125
Hiroshima (HEER oh SHEE muh), *Japan* (34 °N, 132 °E)	125
Hispaniola, *island in Caribbean Sea* (19 °N, 72 °W)	83
Hitachi, *Japan* (37 °N, 141 °E)	125
Hjalmar L. (YEHL muhr), *Northwest Terr.* (62 °N, 115 °W)	45
Ho Chi Minh City (ho chee mihn), *Vietnam* (11 °N, 107 °E)	123
Hobart, *Australia* (43 °S, 147 °E)	131
Hobbs, *N. Mex.* (33 °N, 103 °W)	59
Hoh R., *Wash.* (48 °N, 124 °W)	60

Name (Pronunciation), *Description* (Lat., Long.)	**Page**
Hokkaido, *island in Sea of Japan* (43 °N, 143 °E)	125
Holguin (awl GEEN), *Cuba* (21 °N, 76 °W)	85
Holland, *Mich.* (43 °N, 86 °W)	63
Hollywood, *Fla.* (26 °N, 80 °W)	69
Holt, *Mo.* (39 °N, 94 °W)	65
Holyoke (HOHL YOHK), *Mass.* (42 °N, 73 °W)	73
Homestead, *Fla.* (25 °N, 80 °W)	69
Homs, *Syria* (35 °N, 37 °E)	115
Hondo R., *North America* (18 °N, 89 °W)	82
Honduras, *country in Central America* (15 °N, 87 °W)	84
Honduras, Gulf of, *Caribbean Sea* (16 °N, 88 °W)	82
Hong Kong, *China* (22 °N, 114 °E)	124
Honiara (HOHN ee AHR ah), *Solomon Islands* (9 °S, 160 °E)	131
Honolulu, *Hawaii* (21 °N, 158 °W)	57
Honshu, *island in Sea of Japan* (38 °N, 140 °E)	125
Hood, Mt., *Oreg.* (45 °N, 122 °W)	60
Hooghly R. (HOO glee), *India* (23 °N, 88 °E)	122
Hoover, *Ala.* (33 °N, 87 °W)	68
Hoover Dam, *U.S.* (36 °N, 115 °W)	58
Hope, *Ark.* (34 °N, 94 °W)	67
Hopkinsville, *Ky.* (37 °N, 87 °W)	70
Hormuz, Strait of, *Persian Gulf and Gulf of Oman* (27 °N, 57 °E)	115
Horn, Cape, *South America* (56 °S, 68 °W)	88
Horn Plateau, *Northwest Terr.* (62 °N, 120 °W)	44
Horsham, *Australia* (37 °S, 143 °E)	133
Hot Springs, *Ark.* (34 °N, 93 °W)	67
Hot Springs, *S. Dak.* (43 °N, 103 °W)	62
Hot Springs N.P., *Ark.* (34 °N, 93 °W)	67
Houghton (HOH tuhn), *Mich.* (47 °N, 89 °W)	63
Houma (HOH muh), *La.* (30 °N, 91 °W)	67
Houston, *Miss.* (34 °N, 89 °W)	68
Houston, *Tex.* (30 °N, 95 °W)	67
Howe, Cape, *Australia* (37 °S, 150 °E)	133
Howrah, *India* (23 °N, 88 °E)	122
Hrodna, *Ukraine* (54 °N, 24 °E)	99
Huai R. (hwy), *China* (33 °N, 115 °E)	124
Huallaga R. (wa YAG uh), *Peru* (8 °S, 76 °W)	90
Huambo, *Angola* (13 °S, 16 °E)	107
Huancayo, *Peru* (12 °S, 75 °W)	90
Huang He (WANG hee), *r. in China* (41 °N, 110 °E)	124
Huascaran, Mt. (WAHS kuh RAHN), *Peru* (9 °S, 78 °W)	90
Huber Heights, *Ohio* (40 °N, 84 °W)	70
Hubli-Dharward (HOOB lee dahr WAHRD), *India* (15 °N, 75 °E)	122
Hudson Bay, *Canada* (60 °N, 85 °W)	41
Hudson Bay Lowlands, *Canada* (57 °N, 93 °W)	45
Hudson R., *N.Y.* (42 °N, 74 °W)	72
Hudson Strait, *Hudson Bay and Labrador Sea* (62 °N, 70 °W)	40
Hue (hoo AY), *Vietnam* (16 °N, 107 °E)	123
Hull, *England* (54 °N, 0 °)	98
Hull, *Quebec* (46 °N, 76 °W)	47
Humboldt R., *Nev.* (41 °N, 117 °W)	58
Humphreys Peak (HUHM freez), *Ariz.* (35 °N, 112 °W)	59
Hungary, *country in Europe* (47 °N, 18 °E)	99
Huntington, *W. Va.* (38 °N, 82 °W)	71
Huntington Beach, *Calif.* (34 °N, 118 °W)	58
Huntsville, *Ala.* (35 °N, 87 °W)	68
Huntsville, *Ontario* (45 °N, 79 °W)	46
Huntsville, *Tex.* (31 °N, 96 °W)	67
Huron (HYOO ruhn), *S. Dak.* (44 °N, 98 °W)	62
Huron, L., *North America* (45 °N, 82 °W)	46
Hutchinson, *Kans.* (38 °N, 98 °W)	64
Huttonsville, *W. Va.* (39 °N, 80 °W)	71
Hyco L., *N.C.* (36 °N, 79 °W)	71
Hyderabad, *India* (17 °N, 78 °E)	122
Hyderabad, *Pakistan* (25 °N, 68 °E)	122

I

Name (Pronunciation), *Description* (Lat., Long.)	**Page**
I-n-Gall, *Niger* (17 °N, 6 °E)	107
I-n-Salah, *Algeria* (28 °N, 4 °E)	107
Iasi (YASH ee), *Romania* (47 °N, 28 °E)	99

Name (Pronunciation), *Description* (Lat., Long.)	**Page**
Ibadan, *Nigeria* (8 °N, 4 °E)	108
Ibague (EE buh GAY), *Colombia* (4 °N, 75 °W)	90
Iberian Pen., *Europe* (39 °N, 5 °W)	114
Iceland, *country in Atlantic O.* (65 °N, 20 °W)	96
Idaho, *state in U.S.* (44 °N, 115 °W)	60-61
Idaho Falls, *Idaho* (44 °N, 112 °W)	61
Iguacu Falls (ih GWAH syu), *waterfall in South America* (26 °S, 54 °W)	88
Iguidi Desert, *Africa* (28 °N, 7 °W)	106
IJsselmeer (EYE suhl MER), *l. in Netherlands* (53 °N, 5 °E)	98
Ilesha, *Nigeria* (8 °N, 5 °E)	108
Iliamna L. (IHL ee AM nuh), *Alaska* (59 °N, 155 °W)	57
Illinois, *state in U.S.* (40 °N, 90 °W)	65
Illinois R., *Ill.* (39 °N, 91 °W)	65
Ilorin (EE luh REEN), *Nigeria* (9 °N, 5 °E)	108
Imperial, *Nebr.* (41 °N, 102 °W)	64
Imperial Valley, *Calif.* (33 °N, 116 °W)	58
Imphal (IMP huhl), *India* (25 °N, 94 °E)	122
Inari, L., *Finland* (69 °N, 28 °E)	95
Inchon (IHN CHAHN), *South Korea* (37 °N, 127 °E)	125
Independence, *Mo.* (39 °N, 94 °W)	65
India, *country in Asia* (25 °N, 80 °E)	122
Indian L., *Ontario* (47 °N, 82 °W)	46
Indian Ocean	7
Indiana, *Pa.* (41 °N, 79 °W)	72
Indiana, *state in U.S.* (40 °N, 86 °W)	70
Indianapolis, *Ind.* (40 °N, 86 °W)	70
Indigirka R., *Russia* (68 °N, 148 °E)	119
Indio (IN dee OH), *Calif.* (34 °N, 116 °W)	58
Indochina Pen., *Asia* (15 °N, 105 °E)	119
Indonesia, *country in Asia* (3 °S, 115 °E)	121
Indore (ihn DOHR), *India* (23 °N, 76 °E)	122
Indus R., *Asia* (25 °N, 68 °E)	122
Infiernillo Res., *Mexico* (19 °N, 102 °W)	82
Inner Hebrides, *island group in Atlantic O.* (57 °N, 6 °W)	98
Inner Mongolia, *region of China* (42 °N, 110 °E)	124
Innsbruck (IHNZ bruk), *Austria* (47 °N, 11 °E)	99
Interior Plains, *Canada* (50 °N, 105 °W)	45
International Falls, *Minn.* (49 °N, 93 °W)	62-63
Intracoastal Waterway, *canal in La.* (30 °N, 93 °W)	67
Inuvik (ih NOO vihk), *Northwest Terr.* (68 °N, 134 °W)	42
Inverness (IHN vuhr NEHS), *Scotland* (57 °N, 4 °W)	98
Investigator Strait, *Australia* (36 °S, 137 °E)	133
Ionian Is., *Greece* (38 °N, 20 °E)	99
Ionian Sea, *Europe* (38 °N, 18 °E)	99
Iowa, *state in U.S.* (42 °N, 94 °W)	64-65
Iowa City, *Iowa* (42 °N, 92 °W)	65
Iowa R., *Iowa* (42 °N, 92 °W)	65
Ipoh (EE poh), *Malaysia* (5 °N, 101 °E)	123
Ipswich, *England* (52 °N, 1 °E)	98
Iqaluit, *Nunavut* (64 °N, 68 °W)	43
Iquique (ih KEE keh), *Chile* (20 °S, 70 °W)	89
Iquitos (ih KEET ohs), *Peru* (4 °S, 73 °W)	90
Iraklion, *Crete* (35 °N, 25 °E)	99
Iran, *country in Asia* (31 °N, 54 °E)	115
Iran, Plateau of, *Iran* (33 °N, 59 °E)	115
Iraq, *country in Asia* (32 °N, 44 °E)	115
Irazu, *mt. in Costa Rica* (10 °N, 84 °W)	83
Irbil, *Iraq* (36 °N, 44 °E)	115
Ireland, *country in Europe* (54 °N, 8 °W)	98
Irian Jaya, *region of Indonesia* (4 °S, 138 °E)	131
Iringa (ih RING guh), *Tanzania* (8 °S, 36 °E)	110
Iriri R. (IHR uh REE), *Brazil* (4 °S, 53 °W)	90
Irish Sea, *Europe* (54 °N, 5 °W)	98
Irkutsk, *Russia* (52 °N, 104 °E)	100
Iron River, *Mich.* (46 °N, 89 °W)	63
Ironton, *Ohio* (39 °N, 83 °W)	70
Ironwood, *Mich.* (46 °N, 90 °W)	62
Irrawaddy, Mouths of the, *delta in Burma* (16 °N, 95 °E)	123
Irrawaddy R., *Asia* (20 °N, 94 °E)	123
Irtysh R. (ir TISH), *Russia* (58 °N, 70 °E)	100
Irving, *Tex.* (33 °N, 97 °W)	67
Isfahan, *Iran* (33 °N, 52 °E)	115
Iskut R., *North America* (57 °N, 132 °W)	44

Name (Pronunciation), *Description* (Lat., Long.)	Page
Isla de Providencia, *island in Caribbean Sea* (14°N, 82°W)	83
Islamabad, *Pakistan* (34°N, 73°E)	122
Island L., *Manitoba* (54°N, 94°W)	45
Isle of Youth, *Cuba* (22°N, 83°W)	83
Isle Royale, *Mich.* (48°N, 89°W)	63
Isle Royale N.P., *Mich.* (48°N, 89°W)	63
Isles de la Bahia (EEZ LAHS DAY lah buh HEE uh), *Honduras* (16°N, 87°W)	83
Isparta (is pahr TAH), *Turkey* (38°N, 31°E)	115
Israel, *country in Asia* (31°N, 35°E)	115
Istanbul, *Turkey* (41°N, 29°E)	115
Istokpoga, L. (IHS tahk POH guh), *Fla.* (27°N, 81°W)	69
Itacoatiara (ee ta kwa TYAH ra), *Brazil* (3°S, 58°W)	90
Italy, *country in Europe* (42°N, 13°E)	99
Itasca, L. (eye TAS kuh), *Minn.* (47°N, 95°W)	62
Ithaca, *N.Y.* (42°N, 76°W)	72
Ivory Coast, *region of Africa* (5°N, 5°W)	108
Iwo (EE WOH), *Nigeria* (8°N, 4°E)	108
Iwo Jima, *Pacific O.* (25°N, 142°E)	119
Izabal, L., *Guatemala* (15°N, 89°W)	82
Izhevsk, *Russia* (57°N, 53°E)	100
Izmir, *Turkey* (38°N, 27°E)	115
Izu Is. (EE zoo), *Philippine Sea* (34°N, 140°E)	125

J

Name (Pronunciation), *Description* (Lat., Long.)	Page
J. Percy Priest L., *Tenn.* (36°N, 87°W)	70
Jabalpur (JUHB uhl POOR), *India* (23°N, 80°E)	122
Jackson, *Ala.* (32°N, 88°W)	68
Jackson, *Mich.* (42°N, 84°W)	63
Jackson, *Miss.* (32°N, 90°W)	68
Jackson, *Ohio* (39°N, 83°W)	70
Jackson, *Tenn.* (36°N, 89°W)	70
Jackson, *Wyo.* (44°N, 110°W)	61
Jacksonville, *Fla.* (30°N, 82°W)	69
Jacksonville, *Ill.* (40°N, 90°W)	65
Jacksonville, *N.C.* (35°N, 77°W)	71
Jaffa, Cape, *Australia* (37°S, 140°E)	133
Jaffna, *Sri Lanka* (10°N, 80°E)	122
Jahrom (yah ROHM), *Iran* (28°N, 54°E)	115
Jaipur (JY POOR), *India* (27°N, 76°E)	122
Jakarta, *Indonesia* (6°S, 107°E)	131
Jamaica, *country in Caribbean Sea* (18°N, 78°W)	85
Jamaica Channel, *Caribbean Sea* (19°N, 76°W)	83
James Bay, *Canada* (54°N, 81°W)	46
James R., *Mo.* (37°N, 93°W)	65
James R., *U.S.* (46°N, 98°W)	62
James R., *Va.* (38°N, 78°W)	71
Jamestown, *N.Y.* (42°N, 79°W)	72
Jamestown, *N. Dak.* (47°N, 99°W)	62
Jamestown, *Va.* (37°N, 77°W)	71
Jamnagar, *India* (22°N, 70°E)	122
Jamshedpur (JAHM shed POOR), *India* (23°N, 86°E)	122
Jan Mayen (yahn MY uhn), *island in Greenland Sea* (71°N, 8°W)	136
Janesville, *Wis.* (43°N, 89°W)	63
Japan, *country in Asia* (36°N, 138°E)	125
Japan, Sea of, *Asia* (40°N, 135°E)	125
Japura R., *South America* (0°, 74°W)	90
Jasper, *Alberta* (53°N, 118°W)	44
Jasper N.P., *Alberta* (52°N, 117°W)	44
Java, *island in Java Sea* (8°S, 110°E)	130
Java Sea, *Indian O.* (6°S, 113°E)	130
Jaya Peak, *Indonesia* (4°S, 137°E)	130
Jayapura, *Indonesia* (2°S, 141°E)	131
Jefferson City, *Mo.* (39°N, 92°W)	65
Jefferson, Mt., *Oreg.* (45°N, 122°W)	60
Jefferson R., *Mont.* (46°N, 112°W)	61
Jeffersonville, *Ind.* (38°N, 86°W)	70
Jericho (JEHR uh koh), *West Bank* (32°N, 35°E)	117
Jerusalem, *Israel* (32°N, 35°E)	115
Jhansi, *India* (25°N, 79°E)	122
Jidda, *Saudi Arabia* (21°N, 39°E)	115
Jilin, *China* (44°N, 127°E)	124
Jinan (jyee nahn), *China* (37°N, 117°E)	124
Jinja, *Uganda* (0°, 33°E)	110

Name (Pronunciation), *Description* (Lat., Long.)	Page
Joao Pessoa (ZHWOW puh SOH uh), *Brazil* (7°S, 35°W)	89
Jodhpur (JAHD puhr), *India* (26°N, 73°E)	122
Johannesburg, *South Africa* (26°S, 28°E)	109
John Day, *Oreg.* (44°N, 119°W)	60
John Day Dam, *Columbia R.* (46°N, 121°W)	60
John Day R., *Oreg.* (45°N, 120°W)	60
John H. Kerr Res., *U.S.* (37°N, 78°W)	71
John Redmond Res., *Kans.* (38°N, 96°W)	64
Johnson City, *Tenn.* (36°N, 82°W)	71
Johnstown, *Pa.* (40°N, 79°W)	72
Johor Baharu (juh HOHR BAHR oo), *Malaysia* (2°N, 104°E)	123
Joliet, *Ill.* (42°N, 88°W)	65
Joliette, *Quebec* (46°N, 73°W)	47
Jonesboro, *Ark.* (36°N, 91°W)	67
Jonkoping (YUHN chuh pihng), *Sweden* (58°N, 14°E)	99
Jonquiere (ZHOHN kee EHR), *Quebec* (48°N, 71°W)	47
Joplin, *Mo.* (37°N, 95°W)	65
Jordan, *country in Asia* (31°N, 37°E)	115
Jordan R., *Asia* (32°N, 36°E)	117
Jos Plateau, *Nigeria* (10°N, 9°E)	108
Joseph Bonaparte Gulf, *Indian O.* (14°S, 128°E)	130
Joshua Tree N.P., *Calif.* (33°N, 116°W)	58
Juan de Fuca, Strait of (hwahn duh FYOO kuh), *U.S. and Canada* (48°N, 125°W)	44
Juan Fernandez Is., *Pacific O.* (33°S, 80°W)	88
Juarez (HWAHR ehz), *Mexico* (32°N, 106°W)	84
Juazeiro (zhwu ZEE roo), *Brazil* (9°S, 41°W)	89
Juba, *Sudan* (5°N, 31°E)	107
Judith R., *Mont.* (48°N, 110°W)	61
Jullundur, *India* (31°N, 76°E)	122
Juneau (JOO noh), *Alaska* (58°N, 134°W)	57
Juniata R., *Pa.* (40°N, 78°W)	72
Jurua R. (zhoor WAH), *Brazil* (7°S, 70°W)	90
Juruena R. (ZHOOR WAY nuh), *Brazil* (7°S, 58°W)	90
Jutland, *pen. of Denmark* (56°N, 9°E)	99

K

Name (Pronunciation), *Description* (Lat., Long.)	Page
Kabale, *Uganda* (1°S, 30°E)	110
Kabalega Falls (kuh BAHL ih guh), *Uganda* (2°S, 32°E)	110
Kabinakagami R., *Ontario* (49°N, 84°W)	46
Kabul (KAH bool), *Afghanistan* (34°N, 69°E)	120
Kaduna (kuh DOO nuh), *Nigeria* (11°N, 7°E)	108
Kagoshima, *Japan* (32°N, 131°E)	125
Kahoolawe (kah HOH uh LAH wee), *island in Pacific O.* (21°N, 157°W)	57
Kailua (ky LOO uh), *Hawaii* (21°N, 158°W)	57
Kailua Kona (ky LOO uh KOH nuh), *Hawaii* (20°N, 156°W)	57
Kainji L., *Nigeria* (10°N, 5°E)	108
Kaiwi Channel (KY wee), *Hawaii* (21°N, 158°W)	57
Kalahari Desert, *Africa* (23°S, 22°E)	106
Kalamazoo, *Mich.* (42°N, 86°W)	63
Kalemie, *Congo* (6°S, 29°E)	107
Kalgoorlie, *Australia* (31°S, 121°E)	131
Kaliningrad (kuh LEE nihn GRAD), *Russia* (55°N, 21°E)	100
Kalispell, *Mont.* (48°N, 114°W)	61
Kalisz (KAHL eesh), *Poland* (52°N, 18°E)	99
Kalyan (kuhl YAHN), *India* (19°N, 73°E)	122
Kama R., *Russia* (56°N, 53°E)	95
Kama Upland, *Russia* (58°N, 53°E)	95
Kamchatka Pen., *Russia* (55°N, 160°E)	119
Kamilukuak L., *Northwest Terr.* (62°N, 100°W)	45
Kamloops, *British Columbia* (51°N, 120°W)	44
Kampala, *Uganda* (0°, 33°E)	110
Kamskoye Res., *Russia* (59°N, 57°E)	95
Kamuela, *Hawaii* (20°N, 156°W)	57
Kanaaupscow R., *Quebec* (55°N, 73°W)	47
Kananga, *Congo* (6°S, 22°E)	107
Kanawha R., *W. Va.* (38°N, 82°W)	71
Kanazawa (kuh NAHZ uh wuh), *Japan* (37°N, 137°E)	125
Kandy, *Sri Lanka* (7°N, 81°E)	122
Kane Basin, *North America* (79°N, 70°W)	41

Name (Pronunciation), *Description* (Lat., Long.)	Page
Kaneohe (KAHN ee OH ee), *Hawaii* (21°N, 158°W)	57
Kangaroo I., *Bass Strait* (36°S, 137°E)	133
Kanin Pen., *Russia* (68°N, 45°E)	95
Kankakee (KANG kuh KEE), *Ill.* (41°N, 88°W)	65
Kankakee R., *U.S.* (41°N, 88°W)	65
Kankan, *Guinea* (10°N, 9°W)	108
Kannapolis, *N.C.* (35°N, 81°W)	71
Kano, *Nigeria* (12°N, 8°E)	108
Kanpur, *India* (26°N, 80°E)	122
Kansas, *state in U.S.* (38°N, 100°W)	64-65
Kansas City, *Kans.* (39°N, 95°W)	65
Kansas City, *Mo.* (39°N, 95°W)	65
Kansas R., *U.S.* (39°N, 97°W)	64-65
Kaohsiung (kah oh SYOONG), *Taiwan* (23°N, 120°E)	124
Kaolack (KOW LAK), *Senegal* (14°N, 16°W)	108
Kapiskau R., *Ontario* (53°N, 82°W)	46
Kapuas R. (KAHP uh WAHS), *Indonesia* (1°N, 112°E)	123
Kapuskasing (KAP uh SKAY sing), *Ontario* (49°N, 82°W)	46
Kara Kum Desert, *Turkmenistan* (40°N, 57°E)	100
Kara Sea, *Arctic O.* (72°N, 62°E)	100
Karachi, *Pakistan* (25°N, 67°E)	122
Karakoram Range (KAR uh KOHR uhm), *Asia* (36°N, 76°E)	122
Kariba L., *Africa* (17°S, 28°E)	106
Karimata Strait, *Sumatra and Borneo* (1°S, 108°E)	130
Kasai R. (kuh SY), *Africa* (3°S, 17°E)	106
Kasanga (kuh SAHNG guh), *Tanzania* (8°S, 31°E)	110
Kasba L., *Nunavut* (60°N, 102°W)	45
Kashechewan, *Ontario* (52°N, 82°W)	46
Kashi (kah shee), *China* (40°N, 76°E)	124
Kashmir, *region of Asia* (34°N, 75°E)	122
Kaskaskia R. (kas KAS kee uh), *Ill.* (39°N, 89°W)	65
Kassel, *Germany* (51°N, 9°E)	99
Kastamonu (KAHS tuh moh NOO), *Turkey* (41°N, 34°E)	115
Katahdin, Mt. (kuh TAHD uhn), *Maine* (46°N, 71°W)	73
Katanga Plateau, *Congo* (10°S, 26°E)	106
Kathmandu (kaht mahn DOO), *Nepal* (28°N, 85°E)	122
Katmai N. P. (KAT MY), *Alaska* (59°N, 155°W)	57
Katowice (KAHT uh VEET suh), *Poland* (50°N, 19°E)	99
Kattegal, *strait between Sweden and Denmark* (57°N, 11°E)	94
Kauai (KOW eye), *island in Pacific O.* (22°N, 159°W)	57
Kauai Channel, *Hawaii* (22°N, 159°W)	57
Kaulakahai Channel (KOW luh KAH HEE), *Hawaii* (22°N, 160°W)	57
Kaunakakai (KOW nuh KAH KEE), *Hawaii* (21°N, 157°W)	57
Kaunas, *Lithuania* (55°N, 24°E)	99
Kawartha Lakes (kuh WAWR thuh), *Ontario* (45°N, 78°W)	46
Kawasaki, *Japan* (36°N, 140°E)	125
Kayseri (KY zuh REE), *Turkey* (39°N, 35°E)	115
Kazakh Uplands, *Kazakhstan* (48°N, 75°E)	118
Kazakhstan, *country in Asia and Europe* (48°N, 65°E)	100
Kazan, *Russia* (56°N, 49°E)	97
Kearney (KAHR nee), *Nebr.* (41°N, 99°W)	64
Kechika R., *British Columbia* (59°N, 127°W)	44
Keene (KEEN), *N.H.* (43°N, 72°W)	73
Kejimkujik N. P. (KEHJ uh muh KOO jee), *Nova Scotia* (44°N, 65°W)	47
Kekaha (kay KAH HAH), *Hawaii* (22°N, 160°W)	57
Kelang, *Malaysia* (3°N, 102°E)	123
Kelowna (kih LOHN uh), *British Columbia* (50°N, 120°W)	44
Kemp, L., *Tex.* (34°N, 99°W)	66
Kempt, L., *Quebec* (47°N, 74°W)	47
Kenai Fjords N. P. (KEE NY), *Alaska* (60°N, 150°W)	57
Kenai Pen., *Alaska* (60°N, 150°W)	57
Kenitra (kuh NEE truh), *Morocco* (34°N, 7°W)	114

Name (Pronunciation), *Description* (Lat., Long.)	Page
Kennebec R., *Maine* (45°N, 70°W)	73
Kenner, *La.* (30°N, 90°W)	67
Kennewick, *Wash.* (46°N, 119°W)	60
Kenogami R. (kuh NAHG uh mee), *Ontario* (50°N, 85°W)	46
Kenora, *Ontario* (50°N, 94°W)	46
Kenosha (kuh NOH shuh), *Wis.* (43°N, 88°W)	63
Kent, *Ohio* (41°N, 81°W)	71
Kent, *Wash.* (47°N, 122°W)	60
Kentucky, *state in U.S.* (37°N, 87°W)	70-71
Kentucky L., *U.S.* (37°N, 88°W)	71
Kentucky R., *Ky.* (38°N, 85°W)	70
Kenya, *country in Africa* (1°N, 37°E)	110
Kenya, Mt., *Kenya* (0°, 37°E)	110
Keokuk (KEE uh KUHK), *Iowa* (40°N, 91°W)	65
Kerch, *Ukraine* (45°N, 36°E)	97
Kerguelen I., *Indian O.* (56°S, 69°E)	9
Kerman, *Iran* (30°N, 57°E)	115
Kern R., *Calif.* (35°N, 119°W)	58
Kerulen R. (KEHR uh LEHN), *Asia* (48°N, 114°E)	124
Kesagami L. (kuh SAHG uh mee), *Ontario* (50°N, 80°W)	46
Ketchikan, *Alaska* (55°N, 132°W)	57
Kettering, *Ohio* (40°N, 84°W)	70
Keuka L. (KYOO kuh), *N.Y.* (42°N, 77°W)	72
Keweenaw Bay (KEE wih NAW), *L. Superior* (47°N, 88°W)	63
Keweenaw Pen., *Mich.* (47°N, 88°W)	63
Key West, *Fla.* (25°N, 82°W)	69
Khabarovsk, *Russia* (49°N, 135°E)	101
Khambai, Gulf of, *Arabian Sea* (21°N, 72°E)	122
Khania, *Crete* (35°N, 24°E)	99
Kharkiv, *Ukraine* (50°N, 36°E)	97
Khartoum (kahr TOOM), *Sudan* (16°N, 33°E)	107
Khon Kaen (KAWN KAN), *Thailand* (17°N, 103°E)	123
Khone Falls, *Mekong R.* (14°N, 106°E)	123
Khulna (KOOL nuh), *Bangladesh* (23°N, 90°E)	122
Khyber Pass (KY buhr), *Asia* (34°N, 71°E)	122
Kiel (KEEL), *Germany* (54°N, 10°E)	99
Kiel Canal, *Germany* (54°N, 9°E)	99
Kiev, *Ukraine* (50°N, 31°E)	100
Kigali, *Rwanda* (2°S, 30°E)	110
Kigoma (kih GOH muh), *Tanzania* (5°S, 30°E)	110
Kilauea (KEE low AY ah), *volcano in Hawaii* (19°N, 155°W)	57
Kilbuck Mts., *Alaska* (60°N, 160°W)	57
Kilchu (KIL choh), *N. Korea* (41°N, 129°E)	125
Kilimanjaro, Mt., *Africa* (3°S, 37°E)	110
Killeen (kil LEEN), *Tex.* (31°N, 98°W)	67
Kim R., *Cameroon* (7°N, 11°E)	108
Kimberley, *British Columbia* (50°N, 116°W)	44
Kimberley, *South Africa* (28°S, 25°E)	109
Kimberly Plateau, *Australia* (16°S, 127°E)	130
Kinabasket, L., *British Columbia* (52°N, 118°W)	44
Kindersley, *Saskatchewan* (51°N, 109°W)	45
Kindia (KIHN dee uh), *Guinea* (10°N, 13°W)	108
King I., *Bass Strait* (40°S, 144°E)	133
King William I., *Arctic O.* (69°N, 98°W)	42
Kingman, *Ariz.* (35°N, 114°W)	58
Kings Canyon N. P., *Calif.* (37°N, 119°W)	58
Kingsport, *Tenn.* (37°N, 83°W)	71
Kingston, *Jamaica* (18°N, 77°W)	85
Kingston, *Ontario* (44°N, 76°W)	47
Kinshasa, *Congo* (4°S, 15°E)	107
Kinston, *N.C.* (35°N, 78°W)	71
Kipawa, L., *Quebec* (47°N, 79°W)	46
Kipengere Range (kip uhn GAY ruh), *Tanzania* (10°S, 35°E)	110
Kiribati, *country in Pacific O.* (1°S, 173°W)	135
Kirkland Lake, *Ontario* (48°N, 80°W)	46
Kirksville, *Mo.* (40°N, 93°W)	65
Kirkuk (kihr KOOK), *Iraq* (35°N, 45°E)	113
Kirkwood, *Mo.* (39°N, 90°W)	65
Kirov, *Russia* (59°N, 50°E)	100
Kirthar Range (kir TAHR), *Pakistan* (27°N, 67°E)	122
Kiruna, *Sweden* (68°N, 20°E)	97
Kirwin Res., *Kans.* (40°N, 99°W)	64
Kisangani (KEE suhn GAYN ee), *Congo* (1°N, 25°E)	107

Name (Pronunciation), *Description* (Lat., Long.)	Page
Kismaayo (kis MY yoo), *Somalia* (0°, 42°E)	107
Kissidougou (KEE see DOO goo), *Guinea* (9°N, 10°W)	108
Kissimmee (kihs IHM ee), *Fla.* (28°N, 82°W)	69
Kissimmee, L., *Fla.* (28°N, 81°W)	69
Kissimmee R., *Fla.* (27°N, 81°W)	69
Kisumu (kih SOO moo), *Kenya* (0°, 35°E)	110
Kita-Kyushu (kee TAH KYOO shu), *Japan* (34°N, 131°E)	125
Kitchener, *Ontario* (43°N, 81°W)	46
Kitimat, *British Columbia* (54°N, 129°W)	44
Kittatinny Mts., *N.J.* (41°N, 75°W)	72
Kitty Hawk, *N.C.* (36°N, 76°W)	71
Kitwe (KEE TWAY), *Zambia* (13°S, 28°E)	107
Kivu, L. (KEE VOO), *Africa* (2°S, 29°E)	110
Klagenfurt (KLAHG uhn FOORT), *Austria* (47°N, 14°E)	99
Klamath Falls (KLAM uth), *Oreg.* (42°N, 122°W)	60
Klamath Mts., *U.S.* (42°N, 123°W)	58
Kluane N.P. (kloo AWN ee), *Yukon Terr.* (60°N, 138°W)	44
Knife R., *N. Dak.* (47°N, 102°W)	62
Knoxville, *Tenn.* (36°N, 84°W)	70
Kobe (KOH bee), *Japan* (35°N, 135°E)	125
Kobuk Valley N.P. (koh BOOK), *Alaska* (67°N, 160°W)	57
Kochi (KOH chee), *Japan* (34°N, 134°E)	125
Kodiak, *Alaska* (58°N, 153°W)	57
Kodiak I., *Alaska* (57°N, 154°W)	57
Kokomo (KOH kuh MOH), *Ind.* (41°N, 86°W)	70
Kola Pen., *Russia* (67°N, 38°E)	95
Kolguyev I., *Russia* (69°N, 49°E)	95
Kolwezi (kohl WAY zee), *Congo* (11°S, 25°E)	106
Kolyma Range (kuh LEE muh), *Russia* (63°N, 160°E)	101
Kolyma R., *Russia* (67°N, 155°E)	101
Komoe R., *Africa* (10°N, 4°W)	108
Kondoa (kahn DOH uh), *Tanzania* (5°S, 36°E)	110
Kontum, Plateau of, *Vietnam* (13°N, 108°E)	123
Konya, *Turkey* (38°N, 33°E)	115
Kootenay N.P. (KOOT uh nay), *British Columbia* (51°N, 116°W)	44
Kootenay R., *North America* (50°N, 115°W)	44
Korce (KAWR chuh), *Albania* (41°N, 21°E)	99
Korea Bay, *Asia* (39°N, 124°E)	125
Korea Strait, *South Korea and Japan* (34°N, 128°E)	125
Korean Archipelago, *is. in Korea Strait* (34°N, 127°E)	125
Koryak Mts., *Russia* (62°N, 170°E)	101
Kosciusko, Mt. (KAHZ ee UHS koh), *Australia* (37°S, 148°E)	133
Kosice (KAW shuht SAY), *Slovakia* (49°N, 21°E)	99
Kosovo, *prov. of Serbia* (43°N, 21°E)	99
Kota, *India* (25°N, 76°E)	122
Kota Kinabalu (KOHT uh KIHN uh buh LOO), *Malaysia* (6°N, 116°E)	123
Kotte (KOH tay), *Sri Lanka* (7°N, 80°E)	122
Kotzebue (KAHT suh BYOO), *Alaska* (67°N, 163°W)	57
Kotzebue Sound, *Alaska* (67°N, 164°W)	57
Kouchibouguac N. P. (koo SHEE boo GWAK), *New Brunswick* (47°N, 65°W)	47
Kouroussa (koo ROO suh), *Guinea* (11°N, 10°W)	108
Kra, Isthmus of, *Asia* (10°N, 99°E)	123
Krakatoa, *mt. in Indonesia* (6°S, 1°E)	130
Krakow (KRAK ow), *Poland* (50°N, 20°E)	99
Krasnodar, *Russia* (45°N, 39°E)	95
Krasnowodsk, *Turkmenistan* (40°N, 53°E)	100
Krasnoyarsk, *Russia* (56°N, 93°E)	100
Kratie (krah TYAH), *Cambodia* (12°N, 106°E)	123
Krishna R., *India* (16°N, 75°E)	122
Kristiansand, *Norway* (58°N, 8°E)	98
Kroonstad (KROHN STAT), *South Africa* (28°S, 27°E)	109
Krugersdorp, *South Africa* (26°S, 28°E)	109
Krusevac (KROO shuh VAHTS), *Yugoslavia* (44°N, 21°E)	99
Kuala Lumpur, *Malaysia* (3°N, 102°E)	123

Name (Pronunciation), *Description* (Lat., Long.)	Page
Kuching, *Malaysia* (2°N, 110°E)	123
Kumamoto (KOOM uh MOH toh), *Japan* (33°N, 131°E)	125
Kumasi (koo MAHS ee), *Ghana* (7°N, 2°W)	108
Kunashiri, *island in Sea of Okhotsk* (45°N, 146°E)	125
Kunlun Mts., *China* (37°N, 80°E)	124
Kunming, *China* (25°N, 103°E)	124
Kupang (KOO PANG), *Indonesia* (10°S, 124°E)	131
Kurdistan (KOORD uh STAN), *region of Asia* (37°N, 44°E)	115
Kurgan, *Russia* (55°N, 65°E)	100
Kuria Muria I. (KOOR ee uh MOOR ee uh), *island in Arabian Sea* (17°N, 56°E)	115
Kuril Is. (KOO rihl), *Sea of Okhotsk* (46°N, 152°E)	119
Kursk (KOORSK), *Russia* (52°N, 36°E)	100
Kuruman (KOOR uh MAHN), *South Africa* (27°S, 23°E)	109
Kushiro (KOOSH ee ROH), *Japan* (43°N, 144°E)	125
Kuskokwim Mts., *Alaska* (63°N, 156°W)	57
Kuskokwim R., *Alaska* (63°N, 155°W)	57
Kutch, Gulf of (KUCH), *India* (23°N, 70°E)	122
Kuujjuaq, *Quebec* (58°N, 69°W)	43
Kuujjuarapik, *Quebec* (56°N, 78°W)	46
Kuwait (koo WAYT), *country in Asia* (29°N, 48°E)	115
Kuwait, *Kuwait* (30°N, 48°E)	115
Kuybyshev Res. (KWEE buh shehf), *Russia* (55°N, 50°E)	93
Kwangju (GWAWNG JOO), *South Korea* (35°N, 126°E)	125
KwaZulu/Natal, *prov. of South Africa* (28°S, 31°E)	109
Kyoga, L. (kee OH guh), *Uganda* (2°N, 33°E)	110
Kyoto, *Japan* (35°N, 136°E)	125
Kyrgyzstan, *country in Asia* (42°N, 75°E)	100
Kyushu (kee YOO shoo), *island in East China Sea* (33°N, 131°E)	125
Kyzyl Kum Desert (kuh ZIHL KOOM), *Kazakhstan* (47°N, 62°E)	100

L

Name (Pronunciation), *Description* (Lat., Long.)	Page
La Coruna (LAHK uh ROON yuh), *Spain* (43°N, 8°W)	114
La Crosse, *Wis.* (44°N, 91°W)	63
La Grande R., *Quebec* (54°N, 78°W)	46
La Grange, *Ga.* (33°N, 85°W)	68
La Malbaie (lah mal BAY), *Quebec* (48°N, 70°W)	47
La Mauricie N. P. (luh MAWR ee SEE), *Quebec* (47°N, 73°W)	47
La Paz, *Bolivia* (16°S, 68°W)	89
La Paz, *Mexico* (24°N, 110°W)	84
La Perouse Strait (LAHP uh ROOZ), *Asia* (46°N, 142°E)	125
La Plata, *Argentina* (35°S, 58°W)	89
La Rochelle (lah roh SHEHL), *France* (46°N, 1°W)	98
La Ronge (luh ROHNZH), *Saskatchewan* (55°N, 105°W)	45
La Salle, *Ill.* (41°N, 89°W)	65
La Sarre, *Quebec* (49°N, 79°W)	46
La Serena, *Chile* (30°S, 71°W)	89
La Tuque (luh TYOOK), *Quebec* (47°N, 73°W)	47
Labrador, *region of North America* (54°N, 60°W)	47
Labrador City, *Newfoundland* (53°N, 67°W)	47
Labrador Sea, *Atlantic O.* (57°N, 50°W)	41
Lac La Ronge (LAK la RONZH), *Saskatchewan* (55°N, 105°W)	45
Lac Seul (lak SOHL), *Ontario* (50°N, 93°W)	45
Laccadive Is., *Laccadive Sea* (11°N, 73°E)	122
Laccadive Sea, *Indian O.* (10°N, 75°E)	122
Lachlan R. (LAHK luhn), *Australia* (33°S, 146°E)	133
Laconia (luh KOH nee uh), *N.H.* (43°N, 72°W)	73
Ladoga, L., *Russia* (61°N, 31°E)	95
Lafayette (LAHF ee ET), *Ind.* (40°N, 87°W)	70
Lafayette, *La.* (30°N, 92°W)	67
Lafourche Bayou (luh FOOSH), *r. in La.* (30°N, 91°W)	67
Lagos (LAH gohs), *Nigeria* (6°N, 3°E)	108
Lahore, *Pakistan* (32°N, 74°E)	122
Lake Charles, *La.* (30°N, 93°W)	67

Name (Pronunciation), *Description* (Lat., Long.)	**Page**
Lake City, *Minn.* (42°N, 92°W)	63
Lake Clark N.P., *Alaska* (61°N, 153°W)	57
Lake Havasu City (HAV uh SOO), *Ariz.* (34°N, 114°W)	58
Lake Region, *Finland* (63°N, 27°E)	95
Lakeland, *Fla.* (28°N, 82°W)	69
Lakewood, *Colo.* (40°N, 105°W)	59
Lakewood, *Ohio* (41°N, 82°W)	71
Lamar (luh MAHR), *Colo.* (38°N, 103°W)	59
Lambarene (LAHM buh RAY nee), *Gabon* (1°S, 10°E)	108
Lamia (luh MEE uh), *Greece* (39°N, 22°E)	99
Lampedusa (LAM puh DOO suh), *island in Mediterranean Sea*, (36°N, 13°E)	99
Lamu (LAHM oo), *Kenya* (2°S, 41°E)	110
Lanai, *island in Pacific O.* (21°N, 157°W)	57
Lanai City (luh NY), *Hawaii* (21°N, 157°W)	57
Lancaster, *Calif.* (35°N, 118°W)	58
Lancaster, *Ohio* (40°N, 83°W)	70
Lancaster, *Pa.* (40°N, 76°W)	72
Lancaster Sound, *Nunavut* (74°N, 85°W)	41
Lander, *Wyo.* (43°N, 109°W)	61
Land's End, *cape in England* (50°N, 6°W)	98
Lanier, L. (luh NIHR), *Ga.* (34°N, 84°W)	69
Lansing, *Mich.* (43°N, 85°W)	63
Lanzhou (lahn joh), *China* (36°N, 103°E)	124
Laos (LAH ohs), *country in Asia* (20°N, 102°E)	123
Lapland, *region of Europe* (68°N, 20°E)	94-95
Laptev Sea, *Arctic O.* (75°N, 125°E)	119
Laramie, *Wyo.* (41°N, 105°W)	61
Laramie Mts., *Wyo.* (42°N, 105°W)	61
Laredo, *Tex.* (28°N, 99°W)	66
Larisa, *Greece* (40°N, 22°E)	99
Larsen Ice Shelf, *Antarctica* (68°S, 60°W)	137
Las Cruces (lahs KROO sihs), *N. Mex.* (32°N, 107°W)	59
Las Palmas, *Canary Islands* (28°N, 15°W)	114
Las Vegas, *Nev.* (36°N, 115°W)	58
Lassen Volcanic N. P., *Calif.* (41°N, 121°W)	58
Latakia (LAT uh KEE uh), *Syria* (36°N, 36°E)	115
Latvia, *country in Europe* (57°N, 23°E)	97
Launceston, *Australia* (41°S, 147°E)	131
Laurel, *Miss.* (32°N, 89°W)	68
Laurentian Highlands (law REHN shuhn), *Quebec* (47°N, 74°W)	47
Laval (luh VAL), *Quebec* (46°N, 74°W)	47
Lawrence, *Kans.* (39°N, 95°W)	65
Lawrence, *Mass.* (43°N, 71°W)	73
Lawrenceburg, *Tenn.* (35°N, 87°W)	70
Lawton, *Okla.* (35°N, 98°W)	66
Layton, *Utah* (41°N, 112°W)	59
Le Havre (luh HAHV ruh), *France* (49°N, 0°)	98
Le Mans (luh MAHN), *France* (48°N, 0°)	98
Leaf R., *Miss.* (31°N, 89°W)	68
Leavenworth (LEHV uhn WUHRTH), *Kans.* (39°N, 95°W)	65
Lebanon, *country in Asia* (34°N, 37°E)	115
Lebanon, *N.H.* (44°N, 72°W)	73
Lee's Summit, *Mo.* (39°N, 94°W)	65
Leech L., *Minn.* (47°N, 94°W)	62
Leeds, *England* (54°N, 2°W)	98
Leeuwin, Cape (LYOO ihn), *Australia* (33°S, 115°E)	130
Leeward Is., *Caribbean Sea* (17°N, 62°W)	83
Leghorn, *Italy* (44°N, 10°E)	99
Leicester (LEHS tuhr), *England* (53°N, 1°W)	98
Leipzig, *Germany* (51°N, 12°E)	99
Lemhi Range (LEHM hy), *Idaho* (45°N, 114°W)	61
Lena R., *Russia* (69°N, 124°E)	119
Leon, *Mexico* (21°N, 102°W)	84
Lerma R., *Mexico* (20°N, 100°W)	82
Lesbos, *island in Aegean Sea* (39°N, 26°E)	99
Lesotho, *country in Africa* (30°S, 28°E)	107
Lesser Antilles, *island group in Caribbean Sea* (15°N, 62°W)	83
Lesser Slave L., *Alberta* (55°N, 115°W)	44
Lethbridge, *Alberta* (50°N, 112°W)	45
Levisa Fork (luh VY suh), *r. in Ky.* (38°N, 83°W)	70
Lewis and Clark L., *U.S.* (43°N, 98°W)	62
Lewis Range, *Mont.* (48°N, 113°W)	61
Lewis Smith L., *Ala.* (34°N, 87°W)	68
Lewiston, *Idaho* (46°N, 117°W)	60
Lewiston, *Maine* (44°N, 70°W)	73
Lewistown, *Mont.* (47°N, 109°W)	61
Lewisville, *Tex.* (33°N, 97°W)	67
Lewisville, L., *Tex.* (33°N, 97°W)	67
Lexington, *Ky.* (38°N, 85°W)	70
Lexington, *Va.* (38°N, 79°W)	71
Lhasa (LAH suh), *China* (30°N, 91°E)	124
Liao R. (lee OW), *China* (44°N, 120°E)	124
Liard R., *Canada* (59°N, 126°W)	44
Liberal, *Kans.* (37°N, 101°W)	64
Liberia, *country in Africa* (7°N, 10°W)	108
Libreville, *Gabon* (0°, 9°E)	108
Libya, *country in Africa* (26°N, 16°E)	**114-115**
Libyan Desert, *Africa* (25°N, 26°E)	115
Licking R., *Ky.* (39°N, 84°W)	70
Liechtenstein (LIHK tuhn STYN), *country in Europe* (47°N, 10°E)	99
Liege (lee AYZH), *Belgium* (51°N, 6°E)	98
Ligurian Sea (lih GYOO rih uhn), *Europe* (44°N, 9°E)	99
Lihue (lih HYOO ee), *Hawaii* (22°N, 159°W)	57
Lille (leel), *France* (51°N, 3°E)	98
Lillehammer (LIHL uh HAHM uhr), *Norway* (61°N, 10°E)	96
Lilongwe (lih LAWNG way), *Malawi* (14°S, 34°E)	107
Lima (LEE muh), *Peru* (12°S, 77°W)	90
Lima (LY muh), *Ohio* (41°N, 84°W)	70
Limerick, *Ireland* (53°N, 9°W)	98
Limnos, *island in Aegean Sea* (40°N, 25°E)	99
Limoges (lee MOHZH), *France* (46°N, 1°E)	98
Limon (LY muhn), *Colo.* (40°N, 105°W)	59
Limon (lih MAWN), *Costa Rica* (10°N, 83°W)	85
Limpopo R. (lihm POH POH), *Africa* (23°S, 32°E)	109
Lincoln, *Maine* (45°N, 68°W)	73
Lincoln, *Nebr.* (41°N, 97°W)	64
Lindenhurst, *N.Y.* (41°N, 73°W)	73
Lindesnes, Cape, *Norway* (58°N, 7°E)	98
Lindi (LIHN dee), *Tanzania* (10°S, 40°E)	110
Linz, *Austria* (48°N, 14°E)	99
Lions, Gulf of, *Mediterranean Sea* (43°N, 4°E)	98
Lipari Is., *Tyrrhenian Sea* (39°N, 15°E)	99
Lisbon, *Portugal* (39°N, 9°W)	114
Lithuania, *country in Europe* (55°N, 23°E)	97
Little Bighorn R., *Mont.* (45°N, 108°W)	61
Little Colorado R., *U.S.* (36°N, 111°W)	59
Little Current R., *Ontario* (51°N, 85°W)	46
Little Kanawha R. (kuh NAW wuh), *W. Va.* (39°N, 81°W)	71
Little Karroo, *plateau in South Africa* (34°S, 22°E)	109
Little Mecatina R., *Canada* (52°N, 61°W)	47
Little Missouri Badlands, *N. Dak.* (47°N, 103°W)	62
Little Rock, *Ark.* (35°N, 92°W)	67
Little Sioux R. (SOO), *Iowa* (43°N, 95°W)	64-65
Little Tennessee R., *U.S.* (36°N, 84°W)	70
Little Wabash R., *Ill.* (38°N, 88°W)	65
Liverpool, *England* (53°N, 3°W)	98
Livingston, L., *Tex.* (31°N, 95°W)	67
Ljiji, *Tanzania* (5°S, 30°E)	110
Ljubljana (LYOO BLYAH nah), *Slovenia* (46°N, 14°E)	99
Llano Estacado (LAHN oh es tuh KAHD oh), *plain in U.S.* (33°N, 103°W)	66
Llano R., *Tex.* (30°N, 99°W)	66
Llanos (LAH nohz), *plain in South America* (7°N, 71°W)	90
Lloyd George, Mt., *British Columbia* (58°N, 125°W)	44
Lloydminster, *Alberta* (53°N, 110°W)	45
Lobito, *Angola* (12°S, 14°E)	107
Loch Ness (lawk nehs), *lake in Scotland* (57°N, 4°W)	98
Lodi (LAWD ee), *Calif.* (38°N, 121°W)	58
Lodz (LOOJ), *Poland* (52°N, 19°E)	99
Lofoten Is., *Norway* (69°N, 15°E)	96
Logan, *Utah* (42°N, 112°W)	59
Logan, *W. Va.* (38°N, 82°W)	71
Logan, Mt., *Yukon Terr.* (61°N, 140°W)	44
Logan Mts., *Yukon Terr.* (62°N, 128°W)	44
Logansport, *Ind.* (41°N, 86°W)	70
Loire R. (lwahr), *France* (48°N, 1°W)	98
Lome (loh MAY), *Togo* (6°N, 1°E)	108
Lompoc (LAHM PAHK), *Calif.* (35°N, 120°W)	58
London, *England* (52°N, 0°)	98
London, *Ontario* (43°N, 81°W)	46
Londonderry, *Northern Ireland* (55°N, 7°W)	98
Long Bay, *S.C.* (34°N, 79°W)	69
Long Beach, *Calif.* (34°N, 118°W)	58
Long Branch, *N.J.* (40°N, 74°W)	72
Long I., *Hudson Bay* (55°N, 80°W)	46
Long I., *N.Y.* (41°N, 73°W)	72-73
Long I. Sound, *U.S.* (41°N, 73°W)	73
Long Xuyen (lowng SWEE uhn), *Vietnam* (10°N, 105°E)	123
Longfellow Mts., *Maine* (45°N, 70°W)	73
Longlac (LAWNG lak), *Ontario* (50°N, 87°W)	46
Longmont, *Colo.* (40°N, 105°W)	59
Longs Pk., *Colo.* (40°N, 106°W)	59
Longueuil (lawng GAYL), *Quebec* (46°N, 74°W)	47
Longview, *Tex.* (32°N, 95°W)	67
Longview, *Wash.* (46°N, 123°W)	60
Lookout, Cape, *N.C.* (35°N, 76°W)	71
Lop Nor (lawp nawr), *l. in China* (40°N, 90°E)	124
Lorain, *Ohio* (41°N, 82°W)	71
Lord Howe I., *Tasman Sea* (31°S, 159°E)	130
Los Alamos (law SAL uh MOHS), *N. Mex.* (36°N, 106°W)	59
Los Angeles, *Calif.* (34°N, 118°W)	58
Los Angeles Aqueduct, *Calif.* (35°N, 118°W)	58
Lot R. (LAHT), *France* (44°N, 1°E)	98
Lotikipi Plains, *Africa* (4°N, 35°E)	110
Louangphrabang (LWAHNG prah BAHNG), *Laos* (20°N, 102°E)	123
Louisiana, *state in U.S.* (32°N, 93°W)	67
Louisville, *Ky.* (38°N, 86°W)	70
Lowell (LOH uhl), *Mass.* (43°N, 71°W)	73
Lower Arrow L., *British Columbia* (50°N, 118°W)	44
Lower Pen., *Mich.* (44°N, 85°W)	63
Lower Red Lake, *Minn.* (48°N, 95°W)	62
Lower Tunguska R., *Russia* (65°N, 92°E)	**118-119**
Loyalty Is., *Pacific O.* (21°S, 168°E)	130
Luanda, *Angola* (9°S, 13°E)	107
Lubango, *Angola* (15°S, 13°E)	107
Lubbock, *Tex.* (34°N, 102°W)	66
Lubeck, *Germany* (54°N, 11°E)	99
Lublin, *Poland* (51°N, 23°E)	99
Lubumbashi, *Congo* (12°S, 27°E)	107
Lucknow (LUHK NOW), *India* (27°N, 81°E)	122
Ludhiana (LOOD ee AHN ah), *India* (31°N, 76°E)	122
Ludington, *Mich.* (44°N, 86°W)	63
Lufkin, *Tex.* (31°N, 95°W)	67
Lule R. (LOO luh), *Sweden* (66°N, 21°E)	95
Lunenburg (LOO nuhn BURG), *Nova Scotia* (44°N, 64°W)	47
Lusaka, *Zambia* (15°S, 28°E)	107
Luxembourg (LUHK sum BURG), *country in Europe* (50°N, 6°E)	98
Luxembourg, *Luxembourg* (49°N, 6°E)	98
Luxor, *Egypt* (26°N, 33°E)	115
Luzon, *island in Philippine Sea* (17°N, 121°E)	119
Luzon Strait, *Philippines and Taiwan* (21°N, 121°E)	119
Lviv (luh VAWF), *Ukraine* (50°N, 24°E)	97
Lyall, Mt., *Canada* (50°N, 115°W)	44
Lynchburg, *Va.* (37°N, 79°W)	71
Lyndon B. Johnson, L., *Tex.* (31°N, 98°W)	66
Lynn (LIN), *Mass.* (42°N, 71°W)	73
Lynn Lake, *Manitoba* (57°N, 101°W)	45
Lyon (lyawn), *France* (46°N, 5°E)	98

M

Name (Pronunciation), *Description* (Lat., Long.)	**Page**
Macao, (muh KOW), *poss. of Portugal* (22°N, 113°E)	124
Macapa (MAHK uh PAH), *Brazil* (0°, 52°W)	90
MacDonnell Ranges, *Australia* (24°S, 130°E)	130
Macedonia, *country in Europe* (42°N, 22°E)	99
Maceio (MAS ay OH), *Brazil* (10°S, 36°W)	89
MacFarlane R., *Saskatchewan* (59°N, 108°W)	45
Machala, *Ecuador* (3°S, 80°W)	90

Name (Pronunciation), *Description* (Lat., Long.)	**Page**
Mackay, L., *Australia* (22°S, 129°E)	130
Mackenzie Bay, *Canada* (70°N, 138°W)	40
Mackenzie Mts., *Canada* (64°N, 130°W)	44
Mackenzie R., *Northwest Terr.* (65°N, 125°W)	40
Mackinac, Straits of, *Mich.* (46°N, 85°W)	63
Macomb (muh KOHM), *Ill.* (40°N, 91°W)	65
Macon (MAY kuhn), *Ga.* (33°N, 84°W)	69
MacRobertson Land, *region of Antarctica* (70°S, 60°E)	137
Madagascar, *country in Africa* (20°S, 45°E)	107
Madawaska R., *Ontario* (45°N, 76°W)	46-47
Madeira Falls (muh DEER uh), *waterfall in Brazil* (10°S, 65°W)	90
Madeira Is., *Atlantic O.* (33°N, 17°W)	114
Madeira R., *Brazil* (8°S, 64°W)	90
Madeleine Is. (MAD uh LAYN), *Gulf of Saint Lawrence* (47°N, 62°W)	47
Madison, *Ind.* (39°N, 86°W)	70
Madison, *Wis.* (43°N, 89°W)	63
Madison R., *Mont.* (45°N, 112°W)	61
Madisonville, *Ky.* (37°N, 88°W)	70
Madras, *India* (13°N, 80°E)	122
Madre Lagoon, *Mexico* (25°N, 98°W)	82
Madrid, *Spain* (40°N, 4°W)	96
Madurai (MAHD uh RY), *India* (10°N, 78°E)	122
Maebashi (MAH yuh BAHSH ee), *Japan* (36°N, 139°E)	125
Mafeking (MAF uh king), *South Africa* (26°S, 26°E)	109
Mafia (MAHF ee uh), *island in Indian O.* (8°S, 40°E)	110
Magadan, *Russia* (60°N, 151°E)	101
Magdalena R., *Colombia* (7°N, 75°W)	90
Magdeburg, *Germany* (52°N, 12°E)	99
Magellan, Strait of, *South America* (53°S, 70°W)	88
Magpie R., *Quebec* (50°N, 65°W)	47
Maiduguri (my DOO guh ree), *Nigeria* (12°N, 13°E)	108
Main R. (MYN), *Germany* (50°N, 5°E)	99
Maine, *state in U.S.* (45°N, 70°W)	73
Maitland, *Australia* (33°S, 152°E)	133
Maji, *Ethiopia* (6°N, 36°E)	107
Makassar Strait, *Borneo and Celebes* (3°S, 117°E)	130
Makgadikgadi Pans, *dry lakes in Botswana* (21°S, 25°E)	106
Makindu, *Kenya* (2°S, 38°E)	110
Makran, *region of Asia* (26°N, 62°E)	115
Makurdi (mah KOOR dee), *Nigeria* (8°N, 9°E)	108
Malabar Coast, *India* (14°N, 74°E)	122
Malabo, *Eq. Guinea* (4°N, 9°E)	108
Malacca, Strait of, *Sumatra and Malay Pen.* (4°N, 100°E)	119
Malaga, *Spain* (37°N, 4°W)	114
Malakal, *Sudan* (10°N, 32°E)	107
Malang (muh LAHNG), *Indonesia* (8°S, 113°E)	131
Malaren, L., *Sweden* (59°N, 17°E)	107
Malawi, *country in Africa* (13°S, 34°E)	107
Malay Pen., *Asia* (5°N, 101°E)	123
Malaysia, *country of Asia* (3°N, 102°E)	123
Maldives, *country in Indian O.* (3°N, 74°E)	122
Male (MAH lay), *Maldives* (4°N, 74°E)	120
Malheur L. (mal HOOR), *Oreg.* (43°N, 119°W)	60
Mali (MAH lee), *country in Africa* (16°N, 2°W)	107
Malindi (muh LIHN dee), *Kenya* (3°S, 40°E)	110
Malmo, *Sweden* (56°N, 13°E)	96
Malpelo I., *Pacific O.* (4°N, 81°W)	90
Malta, *country in Europe* (36°N, 15°E)	99
Malta, *Mont.* (48°N, 108°W)	61
Maltese Is., *Mediterranean Sea* (36°N, 15°E)	99
Malugarasi R., *Tanzania* (5°S, 30°E)	110
Mammoth Cave N. P., *Ky.* (37°N, 86°W)	70
Mamore R. (MAHM uh RAY), *South America* (14°S, 65°W)	88
Man, *Côte d'Ivoire* (7°N, 8°W)	108
Man, Isle of, *poss. of United Kingdom* (54°N, 5°W)	98
Manado, *Indonesia* (1°N, 125°E)	131
Managua, *Nicaragua* (12°N, 86°W)	85
Managua, L., *Nicaragua* (12°N, 86°W)	83
Manama, *Bahrain* (26°N, 51°E)	115
Manassas (muh NAS uhs), *Va.* (39°N, 77°W)	71
Manaus, *Brazil* (3°S, 60°W)	90
Manchester, *Conn.* (42°N, 72°W)	73
Manchester, *England* (53°N, 2°W)	98
Manchester, *Ky.* (37°N, 84°W)	70
Manchester, *N.H.* (43°N, 71°W)	73
Manchurian Plain, *China* (45°N, 125°E)	124
Mandalay, *Myanmar* (22°N, 96°E)	123
Mandan, *N. Dak.* (47°N, 101°W)	62
Mandara Mts. (mahn DAH ruh), *Nigeria* (10°N, 14°E)	108
Mangalore (MANG guh LAWR), *India* (13°N, 75°E)	122
Manhattan, *Kans.* (39°N, 97°W)	64
Manicouagan L. (MAN uh KWAHG uhn), *Quebec* (52°N, 68°W)	47
Manicouagan R., *Quebec* (51°N, 68°W)	47
Manila, *Philippines* (14°N, 121°E)	121
Manistee R. (MAN uh STEE), *Mich.* (44°N, 86°W)	63
Manitoba, *prov. in Canada* (57°N, 95°W)	45
Manitoba, L., *Canada* (51°N, 98°W)	45
Manitou Is. (MAN uh TOO), *L. Michigan* (45°N, 86°W)	63
Manitoulin I. (MAN uh TOO luhn), *L. Huron* (46°N, 83°W)	46
Manitowoc (MAN uht uh WAHK), *Wis.* (44°N, 88°W)	63
Maniwaki (MAN uh WAW kee), *Quebec* (46°N, 76°W)	47
Manizales (MAN uh ZAHL uhs), *Colombia* (5°N, 76°W)	90
Mankato (man KAY toh), *Minn.* (44°N, 94°W)	62
Mannar, Gulf of (muh NAHR), *Asia* (8°N, 79°E)	122
Mannheim, *Germany* (49°N, 9°E)	99
Manokawari, *Indonesia* (1°S, 134°E)	131
Manouane, L. (mah NOO uhn), *Quebec* (51°N, 71°W)	47
Mansel I., *Hudson Bay* (62°N, 80°W)	41
Mansfield, *Ohio* (41°N, 83°W)	71
Mansfield, *Pa.* (42°N, 77°W)	72
Mansfield, Mt., *Vt.* (45°N, 73°W)	73
Manyara, L. (muhn YAHR uh), *Tanzania* (3°S, 36°E)	110
Maoke Mts. (MOW kay), *New Guinea* (4°S, 139°E)	130
Maple Creek, *Saskatchewan* (50°N, 109°W)	45
Maputo, *Mozambique* (26°S, 33°E)	107
Mar del Plata, *Argentina* (38°S, 58°W)	89
Maracaibo, (MAR uh KY boh), *Venezuela* (11°N, 72°W)	90
Maracaibo, L., *Venezuela* (10°N, 72°W)	90
Marajo I., *Brazil* (1°S, 49°W)	88
Maranon R., *Peru* (5°S, 75°W)	90
Marathon, *Ontario* (49°N, 86°W)	46
Marcy, Mt., *N.Y.* (44°N, 74°W)	72
Margarita, *island in Caribbean Sea* (11°N, 64°W)	90
Margherita, *mt. in Congo* (0°, 30°E)	110
Mariana Is., *Pacific O.* (17°N, 145°E)	9
Marias R. (muh RY uhs), *Mont.* (48°N, 111°W)	61
Maribor, *Slovenia* (47°N, 16°E)	99
Marie Byrd Land, *region of Antarctica* (78°S, 120°W)	137
Marietta, *Ga.* (34°N, 85°W)	68
Marietta, *Ohio* (39°N, 82°W)	71
Marion, *Ind.* (41°N, 86°W)	70
Marion, *Ohio* (41°N, 83°W)	70
Marion, *Va.* (37°N, 82°W)	71
Marion, L., *S.C.* (33°N, 80°W)	69
Maritsa R., *Europe* (42°N, 26°E)	99
Markham, *Ontario* (44°N, 79°W)	46
Mark Twain L., *Mo.* (40°N, 92°W)	65
Marmara, Sea of (MAHR muhr uh), *Black and Mediterranean Seas* (41°N, 28°E)	95
Marne R. (MAHRN), *France* (48°N, 4°E)	98
Maroa (mah ROH ah), *Venezuela* (3°N, 68°W)	90
Maroua (muh ROO uh), *Cameroon* (11°N, 14°E)	108
Marquette, *Mich.* (47°N, 87°W)	65
Marrakech, *Morocco* (32°N, 8°W)	114
Marseille (mahr SAY), *France* (43°N, 5°E)	98
Marshall, *Minn.* (44°N, 96°W)	62
Marshall, *Tex.* (33°N, 94°W)	67
Marshall Islands, *country in Pacific O.* (10°N, 165°E)	135
Marshalltown, *Iowa* (42°N, 93°W)	65
Marshfield, *Wis.* (45°N, 90°W)	63
Martha's Vineyard, *Mass.* (41°N, 71°W)	73
Martin, L., *Ala.* (34°N, 86°W)	68
Martinique (mahr tuh NEEK), *overseas state of France* (15°N, 61°W)	85
Martinsburg, *W. Va.* (39°N, 78°W)	71
Martinsville, *Va.* (37°N, 80°W)	71
Maryland, *state in U.S.* (39°N, 77°W)	71
Marysville, *Kans.* (40°N, 97°W)	64
Maryville, *Tenn.* (36°N, 84°W)	70
Masai Steppe (mah SY), *Tanzania* (5°S, 37°E)	110
Masaka, *Uganda* (0°, 32°E)	110
Masan, *South Korea* (35°N, 129°E)	125
Mascarene Is. (MAS kuh REEN), *Indian O.* (21°S, 57°E)	106
Maseru (MAZ uh ROO), *Lesotho* (29°S, 27°E)	107
Masirah (muh SIHR uh), *island in Arabian Sea* (21°N, 59°E)	115
Mason City, *Iowa* (43°N, 93°W)	65
Massachusetts, *state in U.S.* (42°N, 72°W)	73
Massachusetts Bay, *Mass.* (42°N, 71°W)	73
Masset, *British Columbia* (54°N, 132°W)	44
Massif Central, *mt. region in France* (45°N, 3°E)	98
Massillon, *Ohio* (41°N, 82°W)	71
Matagami, *Quebec* (50°N, 78°W)	46
Matagorda Bay (MAT uh GAWRD uh), *Gulf of Mexico* (29°N, 96°W)	67
Matamoros, *Mexico* (26°N, 97°W)	84
Matandu R., *Tanzania* (9°S, 39°E)	110
Matane (muh TAN), *Quebec* (49°N, 68°W)	47
Mato Grosso Plateau, *Brazil* (13°S, 58°W)	88
Matsu (MAHT soo), *Japan* (35°N, 133°E)	125
Mattagami R. (muh TAG uh mee), *Ontario* (48°N, 81°W)	46
Mattoon, *Ill.* (39°N, 88°W)	65
Maturin (MAHT uh REEN), *Venezuela* (10°N, 63°W)	90
Maui (MOW ee), *island in Pacific O.* (21°N, 156°W)	57
Maumee R. (maw MEE), *U.S.* (41°N, 84°W)	70
Mauna Kea (MOW nuh KEE uh), *mt. in Hawaii* (20°N, 156°W)	57
Mauna Loa, *mt. in Hawaii* (19°N, 155°W)	57
Mauritania, *country in Africa* (20°N, 10°W)	107
Mauritius, *country in Indian O.* (20°S, 57°E)	107
May, Cape, *N.J.* (39°N, 75°W)	72
Mayfield, *Ky.* (37°N, 89°W)	70
Mayotte, *island in Indian O.* (13°S, 45°E)	106
Maysville, *Ky.* (39°N, 84°W)	70
Mayumba (muh YOOM buh), *Gabon* (3°S, 11°E)	108
Mazar-e Sharif (muh ZAHR ee shuh REEF), *Afghanistan* (37°N, 67°E)	122
Mazatlan, *Mexico* (23°N, 106°W)	84
Mbabane (EM buh BAHN), *Swaziland* (26°S, 31°E)	107
Mbandaka (EM bahn DAHK uh), *Congo* (0°, 18°E)	107
Mbeya (EM BAY uh), *Tanzania* (9°S, 33°E)	110
Mbuji-Mayi (em BOO jee MY ee), *Congo* (6°S, 24°E)	106
McAllen, *Tex.* (26°N, 98°W)	66
McComb, *Miss.* (31°N, 90°W)	68
McConaughy, L., *Nebr.* (41°N, 102°W)	64
McCook, *Nebr.* (40°N, 101°W)	64
McGrath, *Alaska* (63°N, 155°W)	57
McKenzie, *Tenn.* (36°N, 89°W)	70
McKenzie R., *Oreg.* (44°N, 122°W)	60
McKinley, Mt., *Alaska* (63°N, 151°W)	57
M'Clintock Channel, *Nunavut* (72°N, 103°W)	40
M'Clure Strait, *Arctic O.* (75°N, 120°W)	40
McMillan, L., *N. Mex.* (33°N, 104°W)	59
McMinnville, *Tenn.* (36°N, 86°W)	70
Mdantsane, *South Africa* (33°S, 27°E)	109
Mead, L., *U.S.* (36°N, 114°W)	58
Meadow Lake, *Saskatchewan* (54°N, 108°W)	45
Mealy Mts., *Newfoundland* (53°N, 59°W)	47
Mecca, *Saudi Arabia* (21°N, 40°E)	115
Medan, *Indonesia* (4°N, 98°E)	121
Medellin, *Colombia* (6°N, 76°W)	90
Medford, *Oreg.* (42°N, 123°W)	60
Medicine Bow Mts., *Wyo.* (41°N, 106°W)	61
Medicine Hat, *Alberta* (50°N, 111°W)	45

Name (Pronunciation), *Description* (Lat., Long.)	Page
Medina, *Saudi Arabia* (24˚N, 40˚E)	115
Mediterranean Sea, *Europe, Africa, and Asia* (38˚N, 5˚E)	114-115
Medora (mih DOHR uh), *N. Dak.* (47˚N, 104˚W)	62
Meerut (MAY ruht), *India* (29˚N, 78˚E)	122
Mega, *Ethiopia* (4˚N, 38˚E)	107
Mekambo, *Gabon* (1˚N, 14˚E)	108
Meknes, *Morocco* (34˚N, 6˚W)	114
Mekong, Mouths of the (MAY KAWNG), *delta in Vietnam* (10˚N, 106˚E)	123
Mekong R., *Asia* (17˚N, 105˚E)	118-119
Mekrou R. (MEHK roo), *Africa* (12˚N, 2˚E)	108
Melbourne (MEHL buhrn), *Australia* (38˚S, 145˚E)	133
Melbourne, *Fla.* (28˚N, 81˚W)	69
Melfort, *Saskatchewan* (53˚N, 105˚W)	45
Melilla (muh LEE uh), *terr. of Spain* (35˚N, 3˚W)	114
Melville I., *Arctic O.* (75˚N, 110˚W)	40
Melville I., *Australia* (11˚S, 131˚E)	130
Melville, L., *Newfoundland* (54˚N, 59˚W)	47
Melville Pen., *Nunavut* (68˚N, 84˚W)	41
Memphis, *Tenn.* (35˚N, 90˚W)	70
Menasha, *Wis.* (44˚N, 88˚W)	63
Mendocino, Cape, *Calif.* (40˚N, 124˚W)	58
Mendoza, *Argentina* (33˚S, 69˚W)	89
Menihek Lakes, *Newfoundland* (54˚N, 67˚W)	47
Menominee Range (muh NAHM uh nee), *U.S.* (46˚N, 89˚W)	63
Mentawai Is., *Indonesia* (2˚S, 100˚E)	130
Mentor, *Ohio* (42˚N, 81˚W)	71
Meramec R. (MEHR uh MAK), *Mo.* (38˚N, 91˚W)	65
Merced (muhr SED), *Calif.* (37˚N, 121˚W)	58
Meredith, L., *Tex.* (36˚N, 102˚W)	66
Mergui Archipelago (MUHR GWEE), *Myanmar* (12˚N, 97˚E)	123
Merida (MER uh duh), *Mexico* (21˚N, 90˚W)	84
Meridian, *Miss.* (32˚N, 89˚W)	68
Merrillville, *Ind.* (42˚N, 87˚W)	70
Merrimack R., *N.H.* (43˚N, 72˚W)	73
Mesa (MAY suh), *Ariz.* (33˚N, 112˚W)	59
Mesa Verde N.P. (MAY suh VUR dee), *Colo.* (37˚N, 108˚W)	59
Mesabi Range (muh SAHB ee), *Minn.* (47˚N, 93˚W)	63
Meshed, *Iran* (36˚N, 60˚E)	115
Mesopotamia (MEHS uh puh TAY mee uh), *region of Iraq* (32˚N, 45˚E)	115
Messina (muh SEE nuh), *Sicily* (38˚N, 15˚E)	99
Messina, Strait of, *Mediterranean Sea* (38˚N, 16˚E)	99
Methow R. (MET HOW), *Wash.* (48˚N, 120˚W)	60
Metz, *France* (49˚N, 5˚E)	98
Meuse R. (myooz), *France* (49˚N, 5˚E)	98
Mexicali, *Mexico* (33˚N, 115˚W)	84
Mexico, *country in North America* (24˚N, 103˚W)	84-85
Mexico, Gulf of, *Atlantic O.* (27˚N, 90˚W)	36
Mexico, Plateau of, *Mexico* (24˚N, 103˚W)	82
Mexico City, *Mexico* (19˚N, 99˚W)	84
Miami, *Fla.* (26˚N, 80˚W)	69
Miami Beach, *Fla.* (26˚N, 80˚W)	69
Michigan, *state in U.S.* (45˚N, 85˚W)	63
Michigan, L., *U.S.* (42˚N, 87˚W)	53
Michigan City, *Ind.* (42˚N, 87˚W)	70
Michipicoten I. (MIHSH uh puh KOHT uhn), *L. Superior* (48˚N, 86˚W)	46
Middleburg, *South Africa* (31˚S, 25˚E)	109
Middle Loup R. (LOOP), *Nebr.* (42˚N, 100˚W)	64
Middlesboro, *Ky.* (37˚N, 84˚W)	70
Middletown, *Ohio* (40˚N, 84˚W)	70
Midland, *Mich.* (44˚N, 84˚W)	63
Midland, *Tex.* (32˚N, 102˚W)	66
Miguel Aleman Res., *Mexico* (18˚N, 97˚W)	82
Milan, *Italy* (45˚N, 9˚E)	99
Mildura (mihl DOOR uh), *Australia* (34˚S, 142˚E)	133
Miles City, *Mont.* (46˚N, 106˚W)	61
Milford, *Del.* (39˚N, 75˚W)	71
Milford Res., *Kans.* (39˚N, 97˚W)	64
Milk R., *North America* (48˚N, 109˚W)	61

Name (Pronunciation), *Description* (Lat., Long.)	Page
Mille Lacs L. (mil LAKS), *Minn.* (46˚N, 94˚W)	62
Millville, *N.J.* (39˚N, 75˚W)	72
Millwood L., *Ark.* (34˚N, 94˚W)	67
Milwaukee, *Wis.* (43˚N, 88˚W)	63
Minas Basin (MY nuhs), *bay in Nova Scotia* (45˚N, 64˚W)	47
Minch, The, *strait in Hebrides Is.* (58˚N, 6˚W)	98
Mindanao (MIHN duh NAH oh), *island in Philippine Sea* (8˚N, 126˚E)	119
Mindoro (mihn DOHR OH), *island in South China Sea* (13˚N, 121˚E)	123
Mingan (MING guhn), *Quebec* (50˚N, 64˚W)	47
Mingan Archipelago Reserve, *Quebec* (50˚N, 64˚W)	47
Minneapolis, *Minn.* (45˚N, 93˚W)	62-63
Minnesota, *state in U.S.* (46˚N, 95˚W)	62-63
Minnesota R., *Minn.* (45˚N, 95˚W)	62
Minot (MY naht), *N. Dak.* (48˚N, 101˚W)	62
Minsk, *Belarus* (54˚N, 28˚E)	97
Miquelon (MIK uh LAHN), *island in Atlantic O.* (47˚N, 56˚W)	41
Miramichi R. (MIHR uh muh SHEE), *New Brunswick* (47˚N, 66˚W)	47
Mirim L., *South America* (33˚S, 53˚W)	88
Mishawaka, *Ind.* (42˚N, 86˚W)	70
Miskigum R., *Ohio* (40˚N, 82˚W)	71
Miskolc (MISH KOHLTS), *Hungary* (48˚N, 21˚E)	99
Missinaibi R. (MIS uh NY bee), *Ontario* (50˚N, 83˚W)	46
Mississagi R. (MIHS uh SAHG ee), *Ontario* (46˚N, 83˚W)	46
Mississauga, *Ontario* (44˚N, 80˚W)	46
Mississinewa L., *Ind.* (41˚N, 86˚W)	70
Mississippi, *state in U.S.* (32˚N, 90˚W)	68
Mississippi R., *U.S.* (32˚N, 92˚W)	53
Mississippi R. Delta, *La.* (29˚N, 89˚W)	67
Missoula, *Mont.* (47˚N, 114˚W)	61
Missouri, *state in U.S.* (38˚N, 94˚W)	65
Missouri City, *Tex.* (29˚N, 96˚W)	67
Missouri R., *U.S.* (42˚N, 96˚W)	52-53
Mistassibi R., *Quebec* (51˚N, 72˚W)	47
Mistassini, L., *Quebec* (51˚N, 73˚W)	47
Misurata (MIS uh RAHT uh), *Libya* (32˚N, 15˚E)	114
Mitchell, *S. Dak.* (44˚N, 98˚W)	62
Mitchell, Mt., *N.C.* (36˚N, 82˚W)	71
Mittelland Canal, *Germany* (54˚N, 11˚E)	99
Miyazaki (mee AHZ AHK ee), *Japan* (32˚N, 131˚E)	125
Mlala Hills, *Tanzania* (7˚S, 32˚E)	110
Mmabatho (mah BAH toh), *South Africa* (26˚S, 26˚E)	109
Moab, *Utah* (39˚N, 110˚W)	59
Mobile, *Ala.* (31˚N, 88˚W)	68
Mobile Bay, *Ala.* (31˚N, 87˚W)	68
Mobridge, *S. Dak.* (46˚N, 100˚W)	62
Mocha (MOH kuh), *Yemen* (13˚N, 43˚E)	115
Modena (MAWD ee nuh), *Italy* (45˚N, 11˚E)	99
Modesto, *Calif.* (38˚N, 121˚W)	58
Moe (MOH ee), *Australia* (38˚S, 146˚E)	133
Mogadishu, *Somalia* (2˚N, 45˚E)	107
Mogollon Rim (MUHG ee OHN), *Ariz.* (34˚N, 111˚W)	59
Mohave, L. (muh HAHV ee), *U.S.* (33˚N, 115˚W)	58
Moisie R. (mwa ZEE), *Quebec* (52˚N, 67˚W)	47
Mojave Desert (muh HAH vee), *Calif.* (35˚N, 117˚W)	58
Mokpo (MAHK POH), *S. Korea* (35˚N, 126˚E)	125
Moldova, *country in Europe* (47˚N, 28˚E)	97
Moline, *Ill.* (42˚N, 90˚W)	65
Molokai, *island in Pacific O.* (21˚N, 157˚W)	57
Molopo R. (muh LOH POH), *Africa* (27˚S, 21˚E)	109
Molucca Sea, *Indian O.* (1˚S, 125˚E)	130
Mombasa, *Kenya* (4˚S, 40˚E)	110
Mona Passage, *Caribbean Sea* (18˚N, 68˚W)	83
Monaco, *country in Europe* (44˚N, 7˚E)	98
Moncton (MUHNG tun), *New Brunswick* (46˚N, 65˚W)	47
Mongolia, *country in Asia* (46˚N, 101˚E)	120-121
Mono L. (MOH noh), *Calif.* (38˚N, 119˚W)	58

Name (Pronunciation), *Description* (Lat., Long.)	Page
Monongahela R. (muh NAHN guh HEE luh), *U.S.* (40˚N, 80˚W)	72
Monroe, *La.* (32˚N, 92˚W)	67
Monroe, *N.C.* (35˚N, 81˚W)	71
Monroe L., *Ind.* (30˚N, 86˚W)	70
Monroeville, *Pa.* (40˚N, 80˚W)	72
Monrovia, *Liberia* (6˚N, 11˚W)	108
Montana, *state in U.S.* (47˚N, 113˚W)	60-61
Montauk Point (MAHN TAWK), *N.Y.* (41˚N, 72˚W)	73
Montego Bay, *Jamaica* (18˚N, 78˚W)	85
Montenegro (mahn tuh NEE groh), *republic of Yugoslavia* (43˚N, 19˚E)	99
Monterey, *Calif.* (37˚N, 122˚W)	58
Monterey Bay, *Calif.* (37˚N, 122˚W)	58
Monterrey, *Mexico* (26˚N, 100˚W)	84
Montes Claros, *Brazil* (17˚S, 44˚W)	89
Montevideo (MAHN tuh vih DAY oh), *Uruguay* (35˚S, 56˚W)	89
Montgomery, *Ala.* (32˚N, 86˚W)	68
Montmagny (MO mah NYEE), *Quebec* (47˚N, 71˚W)	47
Montpelier (mahnt PEEL yuhr), *Vt.* (44˚N, 73˚W)	73
Montpellier (MOHN pehl YUH), *France* (46˚N, 4˚E)	98
Montreal, *Quebec* (46˚N, 73˚W)	47
Montreal R., *Ontario* (47˚N, 80˚W)	46
Montserrat, *island in Caribbean Sea* (17˚N, 62˚W)	83
Mooranyah L., *Australia* (33˚S, 144˚E)	133
Moorhead (MOHR hed), *Minn.* (47˚N, 97˚W)	62
Moose Factory, *Ontario* (51˚N, 81˚W)	46
Moose Jaw, *Saskatchewan* (51˚N, 106˚W)	45
Moose L., *Manitoba* (54˚N, 100˚W)	45
Moose R., *Ontario* (51˚N, 82˚W)	46
Moosehead L., *Maine* (46˚N, 70˚W)	73
Moosonee, *Ontario* (51˚N, 81˚W)	46
Morava R., *Europe* (49˚N, 18˚E)	98
Moravia (muh RAY vee uh), *region of Czech Rep.* (49˚N, 17˚E)	99
Moray Firth, *bay in Scotland* (58˚N, 4˚W)	98
Moreau R. (MOHR OH), *S. Dak.* (45˚N, 102˚W)	62
Morehead, *Ky.* (38˚N, 83˚W)	70
Morehead City, *N.C.* (35˚N, 77˚W)	71
Morelia, *Mexico* (20˚N, 101˚W)	84
Morgantown, *W. Va.* (40˚N, 80˚W)	71
Morioka (MOHR ee OH kuh), *Japan* (40˚N, 141˚E)	125
Morocco, *country in Africa* (32˚N, 7˚W)	114
Morogoro (MOH roh GOH roh), *Tanzania* (7˚S, 38˚E)	110
Moroni, *Comoros* (11˚S, 43˚W)	107
Moscow (MAHS koh), *Idaho* (47˚N, 117˚W)	60
Moscow (MAHS kow), *Russia* (56˚N, 38˚E)	97
Moses L., *Wash.* (47˚N, 119˚W)	60
Moshi, *Tanzania* (3˚S, 37˚E)	110
Mosquito Coast, *Nicaragua* (13˚N, 84˚W)	83
Mosquito Gulf, *Caribbean Sea* (9˚N, 81˚W)	83
Mostar (MOH STAHR), *Bosnia and Herzegovina* (43˚N, 18˚E)	99
Mosul (moh SYOOL), *Iraq* (36˚N, 43˚E)	115
Mouila, *Gabon* (2˚S, 11˚E)	108
Moulmein (mool MAHN), *Myanmar* (16˚N, 98˚E)	123
Moultrie, L. (MOHL tree), *S.C.* (33˚N, 80˚W)	69
Moundou (MOON DOO), *Chad* (7˚N, 16˚E)	106
Mount Desert I., *Atlantic O.* (44˚N, 68˚W)	73
Mount Gambier, *Australia* (38˚S, 141˚E)	133
Mount Isa, *Australia* (20˚S, 139˚E)	131
Mount Lofty Ranges, *Australia* (33˚S, 139˚E)	133
Mount Pleasant, *S.C.* (33˚N, 80˚W)	69
Mount Rainier N.P. (ruh NEER), *Wash.* (47˚N, 122˚W)	60
Mount Revelstoke N. P., *British Columbia* (51˚N, 118˚W)	44
Mount Vernon, *Ill.* (38˚N, 89˚W)	65
Moyale (moh YAHL ee), *Kenya* (3˚N, 39˚E)	110
Mozambique (MOH zuhm BEEK), *country in Africa* (18˚S, 34˚E)	107
Mozambique Channel, *Indian O.* (20˚S, 40˚E)	106
Mtwara (ehm TWAHR uh), *Tanzania* (10˚S, 40˚E)	110
Mulhouse (muh LOOZ), *France* (48˚N, 7˚E)	98

Name (Pronunciation), *Description* (Lat., Long.)	Page

Multan (mool TAHN), *Pakistan* (30°N, 71°E) 122
Mumbai (muhm BY), *alternative name for Bombay* (19°N, 73°E) 122
Mun R. (MOON), *Thailand* (15°N, 102°E) 123
Muncho Lake, *British Columbia* (59°N, 126°W) 44
Muncie, *Ind.* (40°N, 86°W) 70
Munich, *Germany* (48°N, 12°E) 99
Munising (MYOO nuh SING), *Mich.* (46°N, 87°W) 63
Munster (MOON stuhr), *Germany* (52°N, 8°E) 99
Murcia (MUHR shuh), *Spain* (38°N, 1°W) 114
Murdo (MUHR doh), *S. Dak.* (44°N, 101°W) 62
Mures R. (MYOOR esh), *Europe* (46°N, 24°E) 99
Murfreesboro, *Tenn.* (36°N, 86°W) 70
Murmansk, *Russia* (69°N, 33°E) 97
Murray, L., *S.C.* (34°N, 81°W) 69
Murray Bridge, *Australia* (35°S, 139°E) 133
Murray R., *Australia* (34°S, 142°E) 133
Murray River Basin, *Australia* (34°S, 142°E) 133
Murrumbidgee R. (MUHR uhm BIJ ee), *Australia* (35°S, 145°E) 133
Murzuq, *Libya* (26°N, 14°E) 106
Muscat (muhs KAT), *Oman* (24°N, 59°E) 115
Musgrave Range, *Australia* (25°S, 130°E) 130
Muskegon (muhs KEE guhn), *Mich.* (43°N, 86°W) 63
Muskegon R., *Mich.* (43°N, 86°W) 63
Muskogee (muh SKOH gee), *Okla.* (36°N, 95°W) 67
Muskwa R., *British Columbia* (59°N, 123°W) 44
Musquaro, L., *Quebec* (51°N, 61°W) 47
Musselshell R., *Mont.* (46°N, 108°W) 61
Mutton Bay, *Quebec* (51°N, 59°W) 47
Mwanza, *Tanzania* (3°S, 33°E) 110
Mweru, L., *Africa* (9°S, 29°E) 106
Myanaung (MYAN AWNG), *Myanmar* (18°N, 95°E) 123
Myanmar (myahn MAHR), *country in Asia* (22°N, 95°E) 123
Myitkyina (MEE chee NOH), *Myanmar* (25°N, 97°E) 123
Myrtle Beach, *S.C.* (34°N, 79°W) 69
Mysore, *India* (12°N, 77°E) 122

N

Naches R., *Tex.* (30°N, 94°W) 67
Nacogdoches (nak uh DOH chuz), *Tex.* (32°N, 95°W) 67
Nagano (nah GAHN oh), *Japan* (37°N, 138°E) 125
Nagasaki (NAHG uh SAHK ee), *Japan* (33°N, 130°E) 125
Nagoya (nuh GOY uh), *Japan* (35°N, 137°E) 125
Nagpur, *India* (21°N, 79°E) 122
Nahanni N. P. (nah HAHN ee), *Northwest Terr.* (62°N, 126°W) 44
Nairobi, *Kenya* (1°S, 37°E) 110
Najd, *region of Saudi Arabia* (25°N, 43°E) 115
Nakhon Ratchasima (NAH KAWN rah CHAH sih MAH), *Thailand* (15°N, 102°E) 123
Nakina, *Ontario* (50°N, 87°W) 46
Nakuru (nah KOOR oo), *Kenya* (0°, 36°E) 110
Nam Dinh (NAHM DEEN), *Vietnam* (20°N, 106°E) 123
Namib Desert, *Africa* (22°S, 14°E) 106
Namibia, *country in Africa* (20°S, 17°E) 107
Nampa, *Idaho* (44°N, 117°W) 60
Nampo, *North Korea* (39°N, 125°E) 125
Namtu (NAHM TOO), *Myanmar* (23°N, 97°E) 123
Nan Ling (NAHN LIHNG), *mts. in China* (25°N, 112°E) 124
Nanaimo (nuh NY moh), *British Columbia* (49°N, 124°W) 44
Nanchang (nahn chang), *China* (29°N, 116°E) 124
Nancy, *France* (49°N, 6°E) 98
Nanjing, *China* (32°N, 119°E) 124
Nanning (NAHN NING), *China* (23°N, 108°E) 124
Nantes (nants), *France* (47°N, 2°W) 98
Nantucket I., *Atlantic O.* (41°N, 70°W) 73
Nantucket Sound, *Mass.* (42°N, 70°W) 73
Nanyuki (nahn YOO kee), *Kenya* (0°, 37°E) 110
Naococane, L., *Quebec* (53°N, 71°W) 47
Napa, *Calif.* (38°N, 122°W) 58

Naperville, *Ill.* (42°N, 88°W) 65
Napier, *New Zealand* (39°S, 177°E) 131
Naples, *Fla.* (26°N, 82°W) 69
Naples, *Italy* (41°N, 14°E) 99
Napo R. (NAHP oh), *South America* (3°S, 73°W) 90
Naracoorte (na ra KOO tee), *Australia* (37°S, 141°E) 133
Narbonne, *France* (43°N, 3°E) 98
Narmada R., *India* (23°N, 74°E) 122
Narragansett Bay, *R.I.* (41°N, 71°W) 73
Narvik, *Norway* (68°N, 17°E) 96
Nashua (NASH uh wuh), *N.H.* (43°N, 71°W) 73
Nashville, *Tenn.* (36°N, 87°W) 70
Nasik, *India* (20°N, 74°E) 122
Naskaupi R., *Newfoundland* (54°N, 62°W) 47
Nass R., *British Columbia* (55°N, 129°W) 44
Nassau, *Bahamas* (25°N, 77°W) 85
Nasser, L., *Africa* (23°N, 33°E) 115
Natal (nuh TAHL), *Brazil* (6°S, 35°W) 89
Natashquan R., *Canada* (52°N, 62°W) 47
Natchez (NACH ez), *Miss.* (32°N, 91°W) 68
Natchitoches (NAK uh TAHSH), *La.* (32°N, 93°W) 67
Natron, L. (NAY truhn), *Africa* (2°S, 36°E) 110
Natuna Is., *South China Sea* (4°N, 108°E) 123
Nauru, *country in Pacific O.* (1°S, 167°E) 135
N'Djamena (ehn JAHM uh nuh), *Chad* (12°N, 15°E) 107
Nebraska, *state in U.S.* (42°N, 100°W) 64-65
Nechako R., *British Columbia* (54°N, 125°W) 44
Neenah, *Wis.* (44°N, 89°W) 63
Negro R. (NAY groh), *Argentina* (39°S, 66°W) 88
Negro R., *South America* (1°S, 65°W) 90
Neisse R. (NEES), *Europe* (51°N, 15°E) 99
Nejanilini L., *Manitoba* (60°N, 98°W) 45
Nelson, *British Columbia* (50°N, 117°W) 44
Nelson, Cape, *Australia* (38°S, 142°E) 133
Nelson R., *Manitoba* (56°N, 97°W) 45
Nelspruit (NEHL SPROYT), *South Africa* (25°S, 31°E) 109
Neman R., *Belarus and Lithuania* (55°N, 23°E) 95
Nemuro (NEHM uh ROH), *Japan* (43°N, 145°E) 125
Nemuro Strait, *Japan* (44°N, 145°E) 125
Nen R., *China* (47°N, 124°E) 124
Neosho R. (nee OH shuh), *U.S.* (38°N, 95°W) 64-65
Nepal, *country in Asia* (28°N, 84°E) 122
Nesselrode, Mt., *North America* (59°N, 134°W) 44
Netherlands, *country in Europe* (52°N, 5°E) 90
Netherlands Antilles, *overseas part of Netherlands* (12°N, 68°W) 90
Neuse R. (NOOS), *N.C.* (35°N, 77°W) 71
Nevada, *state in U.S.* (39°N, 118°W) 58
New Albany, *Ind.* (38°N, 86°W) 70
New Amsterdam, *Guyana* (6°N, 58°W) 90
New Bedford, *Mass.* (42°N, 71°W) 73
New Bern, *N.C.* (35°N, 77°W) 71
New Braunfels (BROWN fulz), *Tex.* (30°N, 98°W) 66
New Britain, *Conn.* (42°N, 73°W) 73
New Britain, *Papua New Guinea* (5°S, 152°E) 131
New Brunswick, *N.J.* (41°N, 74°W) 72
New Brunswick, *prov. in Canada* (46°N, 66°W) 47
New Caledonia, *poss. of France* (22°S, 166°E) 131
New Castle, *Pa.* (41°N, 80°W) 72
New Delhi (DEHL ee), *India* (28°N, 77°E) 122
New Glasgow (GLAS goh), *Nova Scotia* (46°N, 63°W) 47
New Guinea, *island in Pacific O.* (5°S, 141°E) 130
New Hampshire, *state in U.S.* (44°N, 72°W) 73
New Haven, *Conn.* (41°N, 73°W) 73
New Iberia, *La.* (30°N, 92°W) 67
New Ireland, *island in Bismark Sea* (3°S, 152°E) 130
New Jersey, *state in U.S.* (40°N, 74°W) 72
New London, *Conn.* (41°N, 72°W) 73
New Madrid, *Mo.* (37°N, 90°W) 65
New Mexico, *state in U.S.* (35°N, 107°W) 59
New Orleans, *La.* (30°N, 90°W) 67
New Providence I., *Bahamas* (25°N, 77°W) 69
New R., *Va.* (37°N, 81°W) 71
New Siberian Is., *Russia* (75°N, 140°E) 100
New South Wales, *state in Australia* (31°S, 145°E) 133

New York, *state in U.S.* (43°N, 78°W) 72-73
New York, *N.Y.* (41°N, 74°W) 72
New Zealand, *country in Indian O.* (40°S, 175°E) 131
Newark, *Del.* (40°N, 76°W) 71
Newark, *N.J.* (41°N, 74°W) 72
Newark, *Ohio* (40°N, 82°W) 71
Newburgh, *N.Y.* (42°N, 74°W) 72
Newcastle, *Australia* (33°S, 152°E) 133
Newcastle, *New Brunswick* (47°N, 66°W) 47
Newcastle upon Tyne, *England* (55°N, 2°W) 98
Newfoundland, *island in Gulf of Saint Lawrence* (48°N, 56°W) 41
Newfoundland, *prov. in Canada* (53°N, 60°W) 43
Newport, *Oreg.* (45°N, 124°W) 60
Newport, *R.I.* (41°N, 71°W) 73
Newport News, *Va.* (37°N, 76°W) 71
Newton, *Kans.* (38°N, 97°W) 64
Nezpique R. (NEHZ peek), *La.* (30°N, 93°W) 67
Ngangerabeli Plain (eng GAHNG uhr uh BEHL ee), *Kenya* (2°S, 40°E) 110
Nguru Mts. (eng GOO roo), *Tanzania* (6°S, 38°E) 110
Nha Trang (NYA TRAHNG), *Vietnam* (12°N, 109°E) 123
Niagara Falls, *city in N.Y.* (43°N, 79°W) 72
Niagara Falls, *city in Ontario* (43°N, 79°W) 44
Niagara Falls, *waterfall in North America* (43°N, 79°W) 53
Niamey (nyah MAY), *Niger* (14°N, 2°E) 107
Niangua R. (ny ANG gwuh), *Mo.* (38°N, 93°W) 65
Nias, *island in Indian O.* (1°S, 99°E) 130
Nicaragua, *country in Central America* (13°N, 86°W) 85
Nicaragua, L., *Nicaragua* (11°N, 86°W) 83
Nice (NEES), *France* (44°N, 7°E) 98
Nichicun, L., *Quebec* (53°N, 71°W) 47
Nicobar Is. (NIHK uh BAHR), *Bay of Bengal* (9°N, 93°E) 122
Nicosia (NIHK uh SEE uh), *Cyprus* (35°N, 33°E) 115
Niger (NY juhr), *country in Africa* (17°N, 10°E) 107
Niger Delta, *Nigeria* (5°N, 6°E) 108
Niger R., *Africa* (12°N, 4°E) 108
Nigeria, *country in Africa* (10°N, 7°E) 108
Niigata (nee GAHT uh), *Japan* (37°N, 139°E) 125
Niihau (NEE HOW), *island in Pacific O.* (22°N, 160°W) 57
Nile R., *Africa* (38°N, 31°E) 106
Nimes (NEEM), *France* (44°N, 4°E) 98
Nimule (NEE moo LAY), *Sudan* (4°N, 32°E) 110
Ninnescah R. (NIN ehs kah), *Kans.* (37°N, 97°W) 64
Niobrara R., *U.S.* (42°N, 103°W) 64
Nipigon, *Ontario* (49°N, 88°W) 46
Nipigon, L., *Ontario* (50°N, 89°W) 46
Nipissing, L., *Ontario* (47°N, 80°W) 46
Nis (NISH), *Yugoslavia* (43°N, 22°E) 99
Nive, *poss. of New Zealand* (20°S, 167°E) 135
Nizhniy Novgorod (NIZH nee NAHV guh RAHD), *Russia* (56°N, 43°E) 97
Nodaway R., *U.S.* (41°N, 95°W) 65
Nogales (noh GAL uhs), *Ariz.* (32°N, 111°W) 59
Nogales, *Mexico* (31°N, 111°W) 84
Nome, *Alaska* (65°N, 165°W) 57
Norfolk, *Nebr.* (42°N, 97°W) 64
Norfolk, *Va.* (37°N, 76°W) 71
Norfolk I., *Tasman Sea* (29°S, 168°E) 130
Norfolk L., *U.S.* (36°N, 92°W) 67
Norilsk, *Russia* (69°N, 88°E) 100
Normal, *Ill.* (41°N, 89°W) 65
Norman, *Okla.* (35°N, 97°W) 67
Norman, L., *N.C.* (36°N, 81°W) 71
Norman Wells, *Northwest Terr.* (65°N, 128°W) 42
Normandy, *region of France* (49°N, 0°) 98
Norris L., *Tenn.* (36°N, 84°W) 70
Norrkoping (NAWR CHUHP ing), *Sweden* (59°N, 16°E) 96
North America, *continent* 7
North Battleford, *Saskatchewan* (53°N, 108°W) 45
North Bay, *Ontario* (46°N, 79°W) 46
North Canadian R., *U.S.* (36°N, 99°W) 52-53
North Cape, *New Zealand* (34°S, 174°E) 130
North Cape, *Norway* (71°N, 25°E) 95

Name (Pronunciation), *Description* (Lat., Long.)	**Page**
North Carolina, *state in U.S.* (36°N, 82°W)	**70-71**
North Cascades N.P., *Wash.* (48°N, 121°W)	60
North Channel, *L. Huron* (46°N, 83°W)	46
North Channel, *Scotland and Northern Ireland* (55°N, 6°W)	98
North Charleston, *S.C.* (33°N, 80°W)	69
North China Plain, *China* (34°N, 115°E)	124
North Dakota, *state in U.S.* (47°N, 100°W)	62
North Fork., *r. in Texas* (34°N, 102KW)	66
North I., *New Zealand* (37°S, 175°E)	130
North Korea, *country in Asia* (40°N, 127°E)	125
North Little Rock, *Ark.* (35°N, 92°W)	67
North Loup R. (LOOP), *Nebr.* (42°N, 100°W)	64
North Mount Lofty Ranges, *Australia* (33°S, 139°E)	133
North Platte, *Nebr.* (41°N, 101°W)	64
North Platte R., *U.S.* (42°N, 104°W)	64
North Saskatchewan R., *Canada* (53°N, 110°W)	**44-45**
North Sea, *Europe* (57°N, 3°E)	94
North West, *prov. of South Africa* (27°S, 26°E)	109
North West Cape, *Australia* (22°S, 113°E)	130
North York, *Ontario* (44°N, 79°W)	46
Northampton, *Mass.* (42°N, 73°W)	73
Northern Cape, *prov. of South Africa* (30°S, 21°E)	109
Northern Dvina R. (duh vee NAH), *Russia* (64°N, 43°E)	95
Northern European Plain, *Europe* (52°N, 10°E)	94-95
Northern Indian L., *Manitoba* (57°N, 97°W)	45
Northern Ireland, *part of United Kingdom* (55°N, 7°W)	98
Northern Mariana Is., *commonwealth of U.S.* (17°N, 145°E)	134
Northern Terr., *Australia* (18°S, 133°E)	131
Northern Transvaal, *prov. of South Africa* (24°S, 29°E)	109
Northfield, *Minn.* (44°N, 93°W)	63
Northumberland Strait, *Gulf of Saint Lawrence* (46°N, 63°W)	47
Northwest Territories, *Canada* (67°N, 120°W)	**42-43**
Norton, *Kans.* (40°N, 100°W)	64
Norton Sound, *Alaska* (64°N, 165°W)	57
Norwalk, *Conn.* (41°N, 73°W)	73
Norway, *country in Europe* (60°N, 8°E)	**96-97**
Norwegian Sea, *Arctic and Atlantic Oceans* (64°N, 0°)	94
Norwich, *Conn.* (41°N, 72°W)	73
Norwich (NAWR ich), *England* (53°N, 1°E)	98
Notre Dame Mts. (NOH truh DAHM), *Quebec* (47°N, 70°W)	47
Nottaway R., *Quebec* (51°N, 78°W)	46
Nottingham, *England* (53°N, 1°W)	98
Nouakchott (nwahk SHAHT), *Mauritania* (18°N, 16°W)	107
Nova Iguacu (EE gwuh SOO), *Brazil* (23°S, 43°W)	89
Nova Scotia, *prov. in Canada* (44°N, 63°W)	47
Novaya Zemlya (noh vuh yuh ZEM lee uh), *islands in Kara Sea* (72°N, 55°E)	95
Novi Sad (NOH vee SAHD), *Yugoslavia* (45°N, 20°E)	99
Novokuznetsk, *Russia* (54°N, 87°E)	100
Novorossiysk (NOHV uh ruh SEESK), *Russia* (45°N, 38°E)	100
Novosibirsk, *Russia* (55°N, 83°E)	100
Nowra, *Australia* (35°S, 151°E)	133
Nubian Desert, *Africa* (21°N, 33°E)	106
Nueces R. (noo AY suhs), *Tex.* (28°N, 99°W)	66
Nueltin L., *Nunavut* (60°N, 100°W)	45
Nuevo Laredo, *Mexico* (28°N, 100°W)	84
Nullarbor Plain, *Australia* (32°S, 125°E)	130
Nunavut (NOON uh VOOT), *terr. in Canada* (65°N, 95°W)	**40-41**
Nunivak I., *Alaska* (60°N, 166°W)	57
Nurnberg (NOORN behrg), *Germany* (49°N, 11°E)	99
Nyasa, L., *Africa* (13°S, 35°E)	106

O

| Oahe, L. (oh WAH hee), *U.S.* (45°N, 101°W) | 62 |
| Oahe Dam, *S. Dak.* (44°N, 100°W) | 62 |

Name (Pronunciation), *Description* (Lat., Long.)	**Page**
Oahu, *island in Pacific O.* (22°N, 158°W)	57
Oak Ridge, *Tenn.* (36°N, 84°W)	70
Oakland, *Calif.* (38°N, 122°W)	58
Oaxaca (wah HAH kah), *Mexico* (17°N, 97°W)	84
Ob Bay, *Russia* (67°N, 72°E)	100
Ob R., *Russia* (64°N, 67°E)	100
Oba, *Ontario* (49°N, 84°W)	46
Obregon (OH bruh GOHN), *Mexico* (28°N, 110°W)	84
Ocala (oh KAL uh), *Fla.* (29°N, 82°W)	69
Ocean City, *Md.* (38°N, 75°W)	71
Oceanside, *Calif.* (33°N, 118°W)	58
Ocmulgee R. (ohk MUHL gee), *Ga.* (32°N, 84°W)	69
Oconee L. (oh KOH nee), *Ga.* (33°N, 83°W)	69
Oconee R., *Ga.* (33°N, 83°W)	69
Odense (OH thehn seh), *Denmark* (55°N, 10°E)	99
Oder R., *Europe* (53°N, 14°E)	99
Odessa (oh DES uh), *Russia* (46°N, 31°E)	97
Odessa, *Tex.* (32°N, 102°W)	66
Ogbomosho (AHG buh MOH shoh), *Nigeria* (8°N, 4°E)	108
Ogden, *Utah* (41°N, 112°W)	59
Ogdensburg, *N.Y.* (45°N, 76°W)	72
Ogeechee R. (oh GEE chee), *Ga.* (32°, 81°W)	69
Ogoki Res. (oh GOH kee), *Ontario* (51°N, 88°W)	46
Ogoki R., *Ontario* (52°N, 86°W)	46
Ogooue R. (oh guh WAY), *Gabon* (1°S, 10°E)	108
Ohio, *state in U.S.* (40°N, 83°W)	**70-71**
Ohio R., *U.S.* (40°N, 81°W)	**70-71**
Oil City, *Pa.* (41°N, 80°W)	72
Oise R. (WAHZ), *France* (49°N, 2°E)	98
Oita (oh ih TAH), *Japan* (33°N, 132°E)	125
Ojos del Salado (oh hohz dehl suh LAHD oh), *mt. in South America* (27°S, 69°W)	88
Oka R., *Russia* (55°N, 41°E)	95
Oka-Don Plain, *Russia* (54°N, 43°E)	95
Okanagan L. (oh kuh NAHG uhn), *British Columbia* (50°N, 120°W)	44
Okanogan, *Wash.* (48°N, 120°W)	60
Okanogan, R., *North America* (49°N, 120°W)	60
Okayama (oh kuh YAHM uh), *Japan* (35°N, 134°E)	125
Okeechobee, L., *Fla.* (27°N, 81°W)	69
Okefenokee Swamp (OH kuh fuh NOH kee), *Ga.* (31°N, 82°W)	69
Okhotsk, Sea of, *Asia* (55°N, 150°E)	119
Oki Is., *Sea of Japan* (36°N, 133°E)	125
Okinawa, *island in East China Sea* (26°N, 128°E)	119
Oklahoma, *state in U.S.* (35°N, 99°W)	**66-67**
Oklahoma City, *Okla.* (35°N, 98°W)	67
Oland (UHR LAND), *island in Baltic Sea* (57°N, 17°E)	99
Olathe (oh LAY thuh), *Kans.* (39°N, 95°W)	65
Old Crow, *Yukon Terr.* (67°N, 140°W)	42
Old Hickory L., *Tenn.* (36°N, 87°W)	70
Olduvai Gorge (OHL duh VY), *Tanzania* (3°S, 35°E)	110
Olean (OH lee AN), *N.Y.* (42°N, 78°W)	72
Olenek R., *Russia* (68°N, 110°E)	119
Olifants R., *Africa* (24°S, 31°E)	109
Olifants R., *South Africa* (32°S, 19°E)	109
Olt R. (AWLT), *Romania* (45°N, 24°E)	99
Olympia, *Wash.* (47°N, 123°W)	60
Olympic Mts., *Wash.* (48°N, 124°W)	60
Olympic N.P., *Wash.* (48°N, 124°W)	60
Olympus, Mt., *Greece* (40°N, 22°E)	99
Olympus, Mt., *Wash.* (48°N, 124°W)	52
Omaha, *Nebr.* (41°N, 96°W)	64
Oman, *country in Asia* (20°N, 56°E)	115
Oman, Gulf of, *Arabian Sea* (25°N, 59°E)	115
Omdurman, *Sudan* (16°N, 32°E)	107
Omineca Mts. (oh mih NEHK uh), *British Columbia* (57°N, 126°W)	44
Omsk, *Russia* (55°N, 73°E)	100
Onega, L., *Russia* (62°N, 35°E)	95
Onega R., *Russia* (64°N, 39°E)	95
Oneida L., *N.Y.* (43°N, 76°W)	72
O'Neill, *Nebr.* (42°N, 99°W)	64
Oneonta, *N.Y.* (42°N, 75°W)	72
Onitsha (oh NIHCH uh), *Nigeria* (6°N, 7°E)	108

Name (Pronunciation), *Description* (Lat., Long.)	**Page**
Ontario, *Calif.* (34°N, 118°W)	58
Ontario, *Oreg.* (44°N, 117°W)	60
Ontario, *prov. in Canada* (50°N, 90°W)	**46-47**
Ontario, L., *North America* (44°N, 77°W)	72
Ootsa L., *British Columbia* (54°N, 126°W)	44
Opinaca R. (oh PIHN uh KAW), *Quebec* (52°N, 78°W)	**46-47**
Opiscoteo L. (oh PISK oh TEE oh), *Quebec* (53°N, 68°W)	47
Oradea (aw RAHD yah), *Romania* (47°N, 22°E)	99
Oraibi (oh RY bee), *Ariz.* (36°N, 110°W)	59
Oral, *Kazakhstan* (51°N, 51°E)	97
Oran, *Algeria* (36°N, 1°W)	114
Orange, *Australia* (34°S, 149°E)	133
Orange Free State, *prov. of South Africa* (28°S, 25°E)	109
Orange R., *Africa* (28°S, 18°E)	109
Orangeburg, *S.C.* (33°N, 81°W)	69
Ore Mts., *Europe* (51°N, 13°E)	99
Oregon, *state in U.S.* (44°N, 123°W)	60
Orel, *Russia* (53°N, 36°E)	97
Orem, *Utah* (40°N, 112°W)	59
Orenburg, *Russia* (52°N, 55°E)	97
Orinoco R., *South America* (8°N, 66°W)	90
Orizaba, *mt. in Mexico* (19°N, 97°W)	82
Orkney Is., *Atlantic O.* (59°N, 3°W)	98
Orlando, *Fla.* (29°N, 81°W)	69
Orleans, *France* (48°N, 2°E)	98
Ormond Beach, *Fla.* (29°N, 81°W)	69
Osage R. (oh SAYJ), *U.S.* (38°N, 94°W)	65
Osaka, *Japan* (35°N, 136°E)	125
Osceola (ah see OH luh), *Iowa* (41°N, 94°W)	65
Oshawa, *Ontario* (44°N, 79°W)	46
Oshkosh, *Wis.* (44°N, 88°W)	63
Osijek (OH see YEK), *Croatia* (46°N, 19°E)	99
Oslo, *Norway* (60°N, 11°E)	96
Ossa, Mt., *Tasmania* (42°S, 146°E)	130
Ostrava (AW struh vuh), *Czech Republic* (50°N, 18°E)	99
Ostrowiec (aw STRAW vyets), *Poland* (51°N, 21°E)	99
Osumi Is. (OH suh MEE), *East China Sea* (30°N, 131°E)	125
Osumi Strait, *Philippine Sea* (31°N, 131°E)	125
Oswego (ah SWEE goh), *N.Y.* (43°N, 76°W)	72
Oti R., *Africa* (10°N, 0°)	108
Otish Mts., *Quebec* (52°N, 70°W)	47
Otoskwin R., *Ontario* (52°N, 89°W)	46
Otranto, Strait of, *Mediterranean Sea* (40°N, 19°E)	99
Ottawa, *Canada* (45°N, 76°W)	47
Ottawa R., *Canada* (46°N, 78°W)	**46-47**
Ottumwa (uh TUHM wuh), *Iowa* (41°N, 92°W)	65
Otway, Cape, *Australia* (39°S, 144°E)	133
Ouachita, L. (WAHSH uh TAW), *Ark.* (35°N, 93°W)	67
Ouachita Mts., *U.S.* (35°N, 95°W)	67
Ouachita R., *Ark.* (33°N, 93°W)	67
Ouagadougou (wah guh DOO goo), *Burkina Faso* (12°N, 2°W)	108
Ouargla (WAHR gluh), *Algeria* (33°N, 5°E)	114
Oudtshoorn (OHTS HAWRN), *South Africa* (34°S, 22°E)	109
Oueme R. (WEHM uh), *Benin* (9°N, 3°E)	108
Oujda (ooj DAH), *Morocco* (35°N, 2°W)	114
Oulu (OW loo), *Finland* (65°N, 26°E)	97
Outardes R. (oo TAHRD), *Quebec* (51°N, 69°W)	47
Outer Hebrides, *island group in Atlantic O.* (58°N, 7°W)	98
Ouyen, *Australia* (35°S, 142°E)	133
Overland Park, *Kans.* (39°N, 95°W)	65
Owasco L. (oh WAHS koh), *N.Y.* (43°N, 77°W)	72
Owen Sound, *Ontario* (44°N, 81°W)	46
Owens L., *Calif.* (36°N, 118°W)	58
Owensboro, *Ky.* (38°N, 87°W)	70
Owyhee Mts. (oh WY ee), *Idaho* (43°N, 117°W)	60
Owyhee R., *Oreg.* (43°N, 118°W)	60
Oxford, *England* (52°N, 1°W)	98
Oxford, *Miss.* (34°N, 90°W)	68
Oxford, *Ohio* (39°N, 85°W)	70

Name (Pronunciation), *Description* (Lat., Long.)	Page
Oxnard, *Calif.* (34˚N, 119˚W)	58
Ozark Plateau, *U.S.* (37˚N, 94˚W)	65
Ozarks, L. of the, *Mo.* (38˚N, 93˚W)	65

P

Paarl (PAHRL), *South Africa* (34˚S, 19˚E)	109
Pacific Ocean	7
Pacific Range, *mts. in British Columbia* (51˚N, 126˚W)	44
Pacific Rim N.P., *British Columbia* (49˚N, 126˚W)	44
Padang (PAHD AHNG), *Indonesia* (1˚S, 100˚E)	121
Padre I., *Tex.* (27˚N, 97˚W)	67
Padua (PAD yoo uh), *Italy* (45˚N, 12˚E)	99
Paducah (puh DOO kuh), *Ky.* (37˚N, 89˚W)	70
Pahala (puh HAH luh), *Hawaii* (19˚N, 155˚W)	57
Pailolo Channel (py LOH LOH), *Hawaii* (21˚N, 157˚W)	57
Painted Desert, *Ariz.* (36˚N, 111˚W)	59
Paita (pah EET uh), *Peru* (5˚S, 82˚W)	90
Pakistan, *country in Asia* (30˚N, 70˚E)	122
Palatka, *Fla.* (30˚N, 82˚W)	69
Palau (pah LOW), *country in Pacific O.* (8˚N, 135˚E)	134
Palawan, *island in Sulu Sea* (10˚N, 119˚E)	119
Palembang, *Indonesia* (3˚S, 105˚E)	131
Palermo, *Sicily* (38˚N, 13˚E)	99
Palk Strait (PAWK), *Asia* (10˚N, 80˚E)	122
Palm Springs, *Calif.* (34˚N, 117˚W)	58
Palma, *Balearic Is.* (40˚N, 3˚E)	114
Palmas, Cape, *Africa* (4˚N, 8˚W)	108
Palmer I., *Antarctica* (72˚S, 63˚W)	137
Pamir Mts. (puh MIHR), *Asia* (38˚N, 73˚E)	100
Pamlico Sound, *N.C.* (35˚N, 76˚W)	71
Pampa, *Tex.* (36˚N, 101˚W)	66
Pampas, *plain in Argentina* (34˚S, 62˚W)	88
Pamunkey R. (puh MUHNG kee), *Va.* (38˚N, 77˚W)	71
Panama, *country in Central America* (8˚N, 82˚W)	85
Panama, Gulf of, *Pacific O.* (10˚N, 80˚W)	83
Panama, Isthmus of, *North America* (10˚N, 80˚W)	83
Panama Canal, *North America* (10˚N, 80˚W)	8
Panama City, *Fla.* (30˚N, 86˚W)	68
Panama City, *Panama* (9˚N, 80˚W)	85
Pantelleria Is. (pan TEHL uh REE uh), *Mediterranean Sea* (37˚N, 12˚E)	99
Panuco R. (PAHN uh koh), *Mexico* (22˚N, 99˚W)	82
Papua, Gulf of, *Coral Sea* (9˚S, 145˚E)	130
Papua New Guinea, *country in Pacific O.* (5˚S, 143˚E)	131
Paracel Is. (PAR uh SEHL), *South China Sea* (17˚N, 112˚E)	123
Paraguay, *country in South America* (23˚S, 58˚W)	89
Paraguay R., *South America* (19˚S, 57˚W)	88
Paramaribo, *Suriname* (6˚N, 55˚W)	90
Parana R., *South America* (23˚S, 54˚W)	88
Parent, *Quebec* (48˚N, 75˚W)	47
Paricutin Volcano (puh REE kuh TEEN), *mt. in Mexico* (19˚N, 102˚W)	82
Parinas, Point (puh REEN yuhs), *Peru* (5˚S, 81˚W)	90
Paris, *France* (49˚N, 2˚E)	98
Paris Basin, *region of France* (49˚N, 2˚E)	98
Park Falls, *Wis.* (46˚N, 90˚W)	63
Park Range, *Colo.* (40˚N, 107˚W)	59
Parker Dam, *U.S.* (34˚N, 114˚W)	58
Parkersburg, *W. Va.* (39˚N, 82˚W)	71
Parma, *Italy* (45˚N, 10˚E)	99
Parma, *Ohio* (41˚N, 82˚W)	71
Parnaiba R. (PAHR nuh EE buh), *Brazil* (7˚S, 45˚W)	89
Parronatta, *Australia* (34˚S, 151˚E)	133
Parry Sound, *Ontario* (45˚N, 80˚W)	46
Pas, The (PAH), *Manitoba* (54˚N, 101˚W)	45
Pasadena, *Calif.* (34˚N, 118˚W)	58
Pasadena, *Tex.* (30˚N, 95˚W)	67
Pascagoula R. (PAS kuh GOO luh), *Miss.* (31˚N, 89˚W)	68

Name (Pronunciation), *Description* (Lat., Long.)	Page
Pasco, *Wash.* (46˚N, 119˚W)	60
Pasto, *Colombia* (1˚N, 77˚W)	90
Patagonia, *plateau in Argentina* (48˚S, 71˚W)	88
Paterson, *N.J.* (41˚N, 74˚W)	72
Pathfinder Res., *Wyo.* (42˚N, 107˚W)	61
Patna, *India* (26˚N, 85˚E)	122
Patos Lagoon, *Brazil* (31˚S, 51˚W)	88
Patras, *Greece* (38˚N, 22˚E)	99
Patuxent R., *Md.* (39˚N, 77˚W)	71
Pau (POH), *France* (43˚N, 0˚)	98
Paulo Afonso Falls, *waterfall in Brazil* (9˚S, 38˚W)	88
Pawtucket, *R.I.* (42˚N, 71˚W)	73
Payette R., *Idaho* (44˚N, 116˚W)	60
Pea R., *Ala.* (31˚N, 86˚W)	68
Peace River, *city in Alberta* (56˚N, 117˚W)	44
Peace R., *Canada* (57˚N, 117˚W)	44-45
Peace R., *Fla.* (27˚N, 82˚W)	69
Pearl Harbor, *Oahu, Hawaii* (21˚N, 158˚W)	57
Pearl R., *Miss.* (32˚N, 90˚W)	68
Pec (PEHCH), *Yugoslavia* (43˚N, 20˚E)	99
Pechora Basin, *Russia* (67˚N, 56˚E)	95
Pechora R., *Russia* (67˚N, 53˚E)	95
Pecos (PAY kuhs), *Tex.* (31˚N, 104˚W)	66
Pecos R., *U.S.* (31˚N, 103˚W)	52
Pecs (PAYCH), *Hungary* (46˚N, 18˚E)	99
Pee Dee R., *U.S.* (34˚N, 79˚W)	53
Pegu, *Myanmar* (17˚N, 97˚E)	123
Peipus, L., *Russia* (58˚N, 28˚E)	95
Pelee, Mt. (puh LAY, mawn), *Martinique* (15˚N, 61˚W)	83
Pelly Bay, *Nunavut* (69˚N, 90˚W)	43
Pelly Crossing, *Yukon Terr.* (63˚N, 137˚W)	42
Pelly Mts. (PEHL ee), *Yukon Terr.* (62˚N, 134˚W)	44
Pelly R., *Yukon Terr.* (62˚N, 132˚W)	44
Peloponnesus (PEHL uh puh NEE suhs), *peninsula in Greece* (37˚N, 22˚E)	99
Pemadumcook L., *Maine* (46˚N, 69˚W)	73
Pematangsiantar, *Indonesia*, (3˚N, 99˚E)	123
Pemba, *island in Indian O.* (5˚S, 40˚E)	110
Pembina (PEHM buh nuh), *N. Dak.* (49˚N, 97˚W)	62
Pembina R., *North America* (49˚N, 97˚W)	62
Pembroke, *Ontario* (46˚N, 77˚W)	46
Pemigewasset R. (PEHM ih juh WAHS uht), *N.H.* (43˚N, 72˚W)	73
Pend Oreille, L. (PAHN duh RAY), *Idaho* (48˚N, 116˚W)	60
Pend Oreille R., *U.S.* (48˚N, 117˚W)	60
Pendleton, *Oreg.* (46˚N, 119˚W)	60
Pennines (PEH NYNZ), *mts. in England* (54˚N, 2˚W)	98
Pennsylvania, *state in U.S.* (41˚N, 79˚W)	72
Penobscot Bay, *Maine* (44˚N, 69˚W)	73
Penobscot R., *Maine* (45˚N, 69˚W)	73
Penrith, *Australia* (33˚S, 151˚E)	133
Pensacola, *Fla.* (31˚N, 87˚W)	68
Penticton, *British Columbia* (50˚N, 120˚W)	44
Penza, *Russia* (53˚N, 45˚E)	100
Peoria, *Ill.* (41˚N, 90˚W)	65
Peribonca R. (PEHR uh BAWNG kuh), *Quebec* (51˚N, 71˚W)	47
Perm, *Russia* (58˚N, 57˚E)	100
Perpignan (PEHR pee NYAHN), *France* (43˚N, 3˚E)	98
Perry L., *Kans.* (39˚N, 96˚W)	65
Persian Gulf, *Arabian Sea* (28˚N, 51˚E)	115
Perth, *Australia* (31˚S, 116˚E)	131
Perth Amboy, *N.J.* (41˚N, 74˚W)	72
Peru, *country in South America* (8˚S, 75˚W)	89
Perugia (puh ROO juh), *Italy* (43˚N, 12˚E)	99
Peshawar (puh SHAH wuhr), *Pakistan* (34˚N, 27˚E)	122
Peter Pond L., *Saskatchewan* (56˚N, 109˚W)	45
Peterborough, *Australia* (33˚S, 139˚E)	133
Peterborough, *Ontario* (44˚N, 78˚W)	46
Petersburg, *Va.* (37˚N, 78˚W)	71
Petitsikapau L. (PEHT ee SIHK uh POW), *Newfoundland* (55˚N, 67˚W)	47
Petrified Forest N. P., *Ariz.* (35˚N, 110˚W)	59
Petropavlovsk-Kamchatskiy, *Russia* (53˚N, 159˚E)	101

Name (Pronunciation), *Description* (Lat., Long.)	Page
Phenix City (FEE niks), *Ala.* (32˚N, 85˚W)	68
Philadelphia, *Miss.* (33˚N, 89˚W)	68
Philadelphia, *Pa.* (40˚N, 75˚W)	72
Philippine Sea, *Pacific O.* (15˚N, 135˚E)	119
Philippines, *country in Asia* (13˚N, 123˚E)	121
Phnom Penh (nawm pehn), *Cambodia* (12˚N, 105˚E)	121
Phoenix (FEE niks), *Ariz.* (33˚N, 112˚W)	59
Pickwick L., *U.S.* (35˚N, 88˚W)	70
Pico Bolivar (PEE koh buh LEE vahr), *mt. in Venezuela* (9˚N, 71˚W)	90
Pico Duarte, *mt. in Dominican Republic* (19˚N, 71˚W)	83
Piedmont Plateau (PEED MAHNT), *U.S.* (35˚N, 83˚W)	53
Pierre, *S. Dak.* (45˚N, 100˚W)	62
Pietermaritzburg (PEET uhr MAR uhts BUHRG), *South Africa* (30˚S, 30˚E)	109
Pietersburg (PEET uhrz BURG), *South Africa* (24˚S, 29˚E)	109
Pigeon R., *North America* (48˚N, 90˚W)	46
Pikes Peak, *Colo.* (39˚N, 105˚W)	59
Pikeville, *Ky.* (37˚N, 83˚W)	70
Pinang, *Malaysia* (5˚N, 100˚E)	123
Pinatubo, Mt. (PIHN uh TOO boh), *Philippines* (15˚N, 120˚E)	119
Pindus Mts., *Greece* (40˚N, 21˚E)	99
Pine Barrens, *N.J.* (40˚N, 75˚W)	72
Pine Bluff, *Ark.* (34˚N, 92˚W)	67
Pine Creek Res., *Okla.* (34˚N, 95˚W)	67
Pine Ridge, *S. Dak.* (43˚N, 102˚W)	62
Pines, L. O' the, *Tex.* (33˚N, 95˚W)	67
Ping R., *Thailand* (17˚N, 99˚E)	123
Pipmuacan Res., *Quebec* (50˚N, 70˚W)	47
Piraeus (py REE uhs), *Greece* (38˚N, 24˚E)	99
Pisa (PEE zuh), *Italy* (44˚N, 10˚E)	99
Pit R., *Calif.* (42˚N, 122˚W)	58
Pitt I., *Hecate Strait* (54˚N, 130˚W)	44
Pittsburg, *Kans.* (37˚N, 95˚W)	65
Pittsburgh, *Pa.* (40˚N, 80˚W)	72
Pittsfield, *Mass.* (42˚N, 73˚W)	73
Pitcairn I., *Pacific O.* (25˚S, 130˚W)	135
Piura, *Peru* (5˚S, 81˚W)	90
Plano (PLAY noh), *Tex.* (33˚N, 97˚W)	67
Platte R., *U.S.* (41˚N, 99˚W)	64
Plattsburgh (PLATS BURG), *N.Y.* (45˚N, 74˚W)	72-73
Playgreen L., *Manitoba* (54˚N, 98˚W)	45
Plenty, Bay of, *New Zealand* (36˚S, 177˚E)	130
Pletipi, L. (PLEHT uh pee), *Quebec* (52˚N, 70˚W)	47
Ploiesti (plaw YESHT), *Romania* (45˚N, 26˚E)	99
Plovdiv, *Bulgaria* (42˚N, 25˚E)	99
Plum, *Pa.* (40˚N, 80˚W)	72
Plymouth (PLIHM uhth), *England* (50˚N, 4˚W)	98
Plymouth, *Ind.* (41˚N, 86˚W)	70
Plymouth, *Mass.* (42˚N, 71˚W)	73
Plzen (PUHL zehn), *Czech Republic* (50˚N, 13˚E)	99
Po R., *Italy* (45˚N, 12˚E)	99
Pocatello (POH kuh TEHL oh), *Idaho* (43˚N, 113˚W)	61
Pocono Mts. (POH kuh NOH), *Pa.* (41˚N, 75˚W)	72
Podgorica, *Yugoslavia* (42˚N, 19˚E)	99
Point Pelee N.P. (PEE LAY), *Ontario* (42˚N, 83˚W)	46
Pointe des Monts, *cape in Quebec* (49˚N, 67˚W)	47
Pointe Louis-XIV, *Quebec* (55˚N, 80˚W)	46
Pointe-Noire (PWANT nuh WAHR), *Congo Republic* (5˚S, 12˚E)	107
Poland, *country in Europe* (52˚N, 20˚E)	99
Polar Plateau, *Antarctica* (85˚S, 90˚E)	137
Pomerania (PAHM uh RAY nee uh), *region of Poland* (54˚N, 15˚E)	99
Pomeroy (PAHM roy), *Ohio* (39˚N, 82˚W)	71
Pomme de Terre Res. (pohm dee TEHR), *Mo.* (38˚N, 93˚W)	65
Pomona Res. (puh MOHN uh), *Kans.* (39˚N, 96˚W)	65
Pompano Beach (PAHM puh noh), *Fla.* (26˚N, 80˚W)	69
Ponca City (PAHNG kuh), *Okla.* (37˚N, 97˚W)	67
Ponce (PAWN say), *Puerto Rico* (18˚N, 67˚W)	85
Pontchartrain, L., *La.* (30˚N, 90˚W)	67
Pontiac, *Ill.* (41˚N, 89˚W)	65

Name (Pronunciation), *Description* (Lat., Long.)	Page
Pontiac, *Mich.* (43°N, 83°W)	63
Pontianak, *Indonesia* (0°, 109°E)	131
Pontic Mts., *Turkey* (41°N, 37°E)	115
Poopo, L., *Bolivia* (19°S, 67°W)	88
Poplar Bluff, *Mo.* (37°N, 90°W)	65
Popocatepetl Volcano (POH poh kuh TAY peh tuhl), *mt. in Mexico* (19°N, 99°W)	82
Porcupine R., *North America* (67°N, 145°W)	57
Port Adelaide, *Australia* (35°S, 138°E)	133
Port Alberni, *British Columbia* (49°N, 125°W)	44
Port Angeles, *Wash.* (48°N, 124°W)	60
Port Arthur, *Tex.* (30°N, 94°W)	67
Port-au-Prince, *Haiti* (19°N, 72°W)	85
Port Blair, *Andaman Is.* (12°N, 93°E)	123
Port Elizabeth, *South Africa* (34°S, 26°E)	109
Port Gentil (PAWR zhawng TEE), *Gabon* (1°S, 9°E)	108
Port Harcourt, *Nigeria* (5°N, 7°E)	108
Port Hardy, *British Columbia* (51°N, 127°W)	44
Port Hawkesbury (HAWKS BUHR ee), *Nova Scotia* (46°N, 61°W)	47
Port Hedland, *Australia* (20°S, 119°E)	131
Port Huron (HYOOR uhn), *Mich.* (43°N, 83°W)	63
Port-Louis, *Mauritius* (20°S, 58°E)	107
Port Moresby, *Papua New Guinea* (9°S, 147°E)	131
Port Nolloth, *South Africa* (29°S, 17°E)	109
Port of Spain, *Trinidad and Tobago* (11°N, 62°W)	85
Port Orange, *Fla.* (29°N, 81°W)	69
Port Phillip Bay, *Australia* (38°S, 145°E)	133
Port Pirie, *Australia* (33°S, 138°E)	133
Port Said (sah EED), *Egypt* (31°N, 32°E)	115
Port Saint Lucie, *Fla.* (27°N, 80°W)	69
Port Stephens, *Australia* (33°S, 152°E)	133
Port Sudan, *Sudan* (20°N, 37°E)	107
Port-Vila, *Vanuatu* (18°S, 169°E)	131
Portage, *Ind.* (42°N, 87°W)	70
Portage, *Mich.* (42°N, 86°W)	63
Portage la Prairie (PORT ihj luh PREH ree), *Manitoba* (50°N, 98°W)	45
Portland, *Australia* (38°S, 142°E)	133
Portland, *Maine* (44°N, 70°W)	73
Portland, *Oreg.* (46°N, 123°W)	60
Porto, *Portugal* (41°N, 9°W)	114
Porto Alegre, *Brazil* (30°S, 51°W)	89
Porto-Novo, *Benin* (6°N, 2°E)	108
Porto Velho, *Brazil* (9°S, 64°W)	90
Portsmouth (POHRT smuhth), *England* (51°N, 1°W)	98
Portsmouth, *N.H.* (43°N, 71°W)	73
Portsmouth, *Ohio* (39°N, 83°W)	70
Portsmouth, *Va.* (37°N, 76°W)	71
Portugal, *country in Europe* (37°N, 8°W)	114
Possum Kingdom L., *Tex.* (33°N, 99°W)	66
Pothole Res., *Wash.* (47°N, 119°W)	60
Potomac R., *U.S.* (38°N, 77°W)	71
Potosi, *Bolivia* (20°S, 66°W)	89
Potsdam, *Germany* (52°N, 13°E)	99
Potsdam, *N.Y.* (45°N, 75°W)	72
Poughkeepsie (puh KIHP see), *N.Y.* (42°N, 74°W)	72
Powder R., *U.S.* (45°N, 106°W)	61
Powder River Basin, *U.S.* (45°N, 106°W)	61
Powell, L., *U.S.* (37°N, 111°W)	59
Powell River, *city in British Columbia* (50°N, 125°W)	44
Poyang L., *China* (29°N, 116°E)	124
Poznan, *Poland* (52°N, 17°E)	99
Prague, *Czech Republic* (50°N, 14°E)	99
Prairie Dog Town Fork, *r. in U.S.* (35°N, 101°W)	66
Prairie du Chien (PRER ee duh SHEEN), *Wis.* (43°N, 91°W)	63
Pratt, *Kans.* (38°N, 99°W)	64
Prescott, *Ariz.* (35°N, 113°W)	59
Presque Isle (preh SKYL), *Maine* (47°N, 68°W)	73
Pretoria, *South Africa* (25°S, 28°E)	109
Pribilof Is. (PRIB uh LAWF), *Bering Sea* (57°N, 170°W)	57
Price, *Utah* (40°N, 111°W)	59
Prieska (PREE skuh), *South Africa* (30°S, 23°E)	109

Name (Pronunciation), *Description* (Lat., Long.)	Page
Primrose L., *Canada* (55°N, 110°W)	45
Prince Albert, *Saskatchewan* (53°N, 106°W)	45
Prince Albert N.P., *Saskatchewan* (54°N, 106°W)	45
Prince Edward Island, *prov. in Canada* (47°N, 63°W)	47
Prince Edward I. N.P., *Prince Edward Island* (46°N, 63°W)	47
Prince Edward Is., *Indian O.* (47°S, 38°E)	106
Prince George, *British Columbia* (54°N, 123°W)	44
Prince of Wales I., *Arctic O.* (73°N, 99°W)	40
Prince of Wales I., *Gulf of Alaska* (56°N, 133°W)	57
Prince Patrick I., *Arctic O.* (77°N, 120°W)	40
Prince Rupert, *British Columbia* (54°N, 130°W)	44
Prince William Sound, *Alaska* (61°N, 147°W)	57
Princess Royal I., *Hecate Strait* (53°N, 129°W)	44
Princeton, *Ind.* (38°N, 88°W)	70
Principe, *island in Gulf of Guinea* (2°N, 8°E)	108
Pripyat Marshes, *Europe* (53°N, 26°E)	95
Pripyat R., *Europe* (52°N, 28°E)	95
Pristina (PRISH tih NAH), *Yugoslavia* (43°N, 21°E)	99
Providence, *R.I.* (42°N, 71°W)	73
Provo, *Utah* (40°N, 112°W)	59
Prudhoe Bay, *Alaska* (70°N, 148°W)	57
Prut R., *Europe* (47°N, 28°E)	99
Przemysl (puh SHEHM ish uhl), *Poland* (50°N, 23°E)	99
Pskov (puh SKAWF), *Russia* (58°N, 28°E)	97
Puebla, *Mexico* (19°N, 98°W)	84
Pueblo, *Colo.* (38°N, 105°W)	59
Puerto Montt, *Chile* (42°S, 73°W)	89
Puerto Rico, *commonwealth of U.S.* (18°N, 67°W)	85
Puerto Vallarta (PWAIR tuh vuh YAHR tuh), *Mexico* (19°N, 105°W)	84
Puget Sound (PYOO jeht), *Wash.* (48°N, 123°W)	60
Pukaskwa N. P., *Ontario* (48°N, 86°W)	46
Pullman, *Wash.* (47°N, 117°W)	60
Pune (POO nuh), *India* (19°N, 74°E)	122
Punta Arenas, *Chile* (53°S, 71°W)	89
Punta Gorda (PUHN tuh GAWR duh), *Fla.* (27°N, 82°W)	69
Purgatoire R. (PUHR guh TWAHR), *Colo.* (37°N, 104°W)	59
Purus R. (puh ROOS), *Brazil* (6°S, 65°W)	90
Pusan, *South Korea* (35°N, 129°E)	125
Putumayo R., *South America* (2°S, 74°W)	90
Pymatung Res. *U.S.* (42°N, 81°W)	71
Pyongyang, *North Korea* (39°N, 126°E)	125
Pyramid L., *Nev.* (40°N, 119°W)	58
Pyrenees, *mt. range in Europe* (43°N, 0°)	98

Q

Name (Pronunciation), *Description* (Lat., Long.)	Page
Qaidam Basin, *China* (37°N, 95°E)	124
Qandahar (KAN duh hahr), *Afghanistan* (32°N, 66°E)	120
Qaraghandy, *Kazakhstan* (50°N, 72°E)	100
Qatar (KAH tahr), *country in Asia* (25°N, 51°E)	115
Qattara Depression, *lowland of Egypt* (29°N, 27°E)	115
Qilian Shan, *mt. range in China* (39°N, 98°E)	124
Qingdao, *China* (36°N, 120°E)	124
Qinghai L. (zhing hy), *China* (37°N, 100°E)	124
Qiqihar, *China* (47°N, 124°E)	124
Qom (KOHM), *Iran* (34°N, 51°E)	115
Qu'Appelle R. (kwa PEHL), *Canada* (50°N, 102°W)	45
Quebec, *prov. in Canada* (50°N, 70°W)	46-47
Quebec, *Quebec* (47°N, 71°W)	47
Queen Adelaide Archipelago, *Chile* (52°S, 75°W)	88
Queen Bess, Mt., *British Columbia* (51°N, 123°W)	44
Queen Charlotte Is., *British Columbia* (53°N, 132°W)	44
Queen Charlotte Sound, *British Columbia* (51°N, 130°W)	44
Queen Charlotte Strait, *British Columbia* (51°N, 128°W)	44
Queen Elizabeth Is., *Arctic O.* (76°N, 100°W)	40-41
Queen Maud Gulf, *Nunavut* (68°N, 100°W)	40
Queen Maud Land, *region of Antarctica* (73°S, 30°E)	137

Name (Pronunciation), *Description* (Lat., Long.)	Page
Queensland, *state in Australia* (22°S, 145°E)	131
Quelimane (kehl uh MAHN uh), *Mozambique* (18°S, 37°E)	107
Quesnel (kuh NEHL), *British Columbia* (53°N, 122°W)	44
Quesnel L., *British Columbia* (53°N, 121°W)	44
Quetta, *Pakistan* (30°N, 67°E)	122
Quezon City (KAY sohn), *Philippines* (15°N, 121°E)	121
Qui Nhon (kwee NYAWN), *Vietnam* (13°N, 109°E)	123
Quinault R., *Wash.* (47°N, 124°W)	60
Quincy, *Ill.* (40°N, 91°W)	65
Quincy, *Mass.* (42°N, 71°W)	73
Quito (KEE toh), *Ecuador* (0°, 78°W)	90

R

Name (Pronunciation), *Description* (Lat., Long.)	Page
Rabat, *Morocco* (34°N, 7°W)	114
Race, Cape, *Newfoundland* (47°N, 52°W)	41
Racine, *Wis.* (43°N, 88°W)	65
Radom, *Poland* (51°N, 21°E)	99
Raft R., *Idaho* (42°N, 113°W)	61
Rainier, Mt. (ruh NEER), *Wash.* (47°N, 122°W)	60
Rainy L., *North America* (49°N, 93°W)	63
Rainy R., *North America* (49°N, 94°W)	63
Raipur (RY POOR), *India* (21°N, 42°E)	122
Rajang R. (RAHJ ahng), *Malaysia* (3°N, 113°E)	123
Rajkot (RAHJ KOHT), *India* (22°N, 71°E)	122
Raleigh, *N.C.* (36°N, 79°W)	71
Ramsey L., *Ontario* (47°N, 82°W)	46
Ranchi, *India* (23°N, 85°E)	122
Rangeley L. (RAYNJ lee), *Maine* (45°N, 71°W)	73
Rangoon, *alternate name for Yangon* (17°N, 96°E)	123
Rapid City, *S. Dak.* (44°N, 103°W)	62
Rappahannock R., *Va.* (38°N, 77°W)	71
Raquette R. (RAK uht), *N.Y.* (44°N, 75°W)	72
Ras Dashen, *mt. in Ethiopia* (13°N, 38°E)	106
Rasht, *Iran* (37°N, 50°F)	115
Rathbun Res., *Iowa* (41°N, 93°W)	65
Raton, *N. Mex.* (37°N, 104°W)	59
Ratz, Mt., *British Columbia* (57°N, 132°W)	44
Rawalpindi (RAH wuhl PIHN dee), *Pakistan* (34°N, 72°E)	122
Rawlins, *Wyo.* (42°N, 107°W)	61
Reading (REI ID ing), *Pa.* (40°N, 76°W)	72
Recife (reh SEE fuh), *Brazil* (8°S, 35°W)	89
Recife, Cape , *South Africa* (34°S, 25°E)	109
Red Bluff L., *U.S.* (32°N, 104°W)	59
Red Deer, *Alberta* (52°N, 114°W)	44
Red Deer R., *Canada* (51°N, 112°W)	44-45
Red L., *Minn.* (48°N, 95°W)	53
Red Lake R., *Minn.* (48°N, 96°W)	62
Red R., *Asia* (23°N, 105°E)	119
Red R., *North America* (50°N, 97°W)	53
Red R., *U.S.* (34°N, 99°W)	66-67
Red River Valley, *U.S.* (47°N, 97°W)	62
Red Sea, *Africa and Asia* (19°N, 40°E)	115
Redding, *Calif.* (42°N, 122°W)	58
Redwood N. P., *Calif.* (41°N, 124°W)	58
Regensberg, *Germany* (49°N, 12°E)	99
Reggio di Calabria (REHJ oh DEE kuh LAHB ree uh), *Italy* (38°N, 16°E)	99
Regina (ruh JY nuh), *Saskatchewan* (51°N, 105°W)	45
Reidsville, *N.C.* (36°N, 80°W)	71
Reims (REEMZ), *France* (49°N, 4°E)	98
Reindeer L., *Saskatchewan* (57°N, 102°W)	45
Rend L., *Ill.* (38°N, 89°W)	65
Renmark, *Australia* (34°S, 141°E)	133
Rennes (REHN), *France* (48°N, 1°W)	98
Reno, *Nev.* (40°N, 120°W)	58
Republican R., *U.S.* (40°N, 101°W)	64
Resistencia, *Argentina* (27°S, 59°W)	89
Resolute, *Nunavut* (75°N, 95°W)	43
Restigouche R. (REHS tih GOOSH), *Canada* (48°N, 67°W)	47
Reunion, *overseas state of France* (21°S, 56°E)	107
Revelstoke, *British Columbia* (51°N, 118°W)	44
Revillagigedo Is. (rih VIHL uh guh GEED oh), *Pacific O.* (18°N, 111°W)	82

Name (Pronunciation), *Description* (Lat., Long.)	**Page**
Rexburg, *Idaho* (44 °N, 112 °W)	61
Reyes, Point, *Calif.* (38 °N, 123 °W)	58
Reykjavik (RAY kyuh VEEK), *Iceland* (64 °N, 22 °W)	96
Rhine R., *Europe* (52 °N, 7 °E)	99
Rhinelander, *Wis.* (46 °N, 89 °W)	63
Rhode Island, *state in U.S.* (42 °N, 71 °W)	73
Rhodes, *island in Mediterranean Sea* (36 °N, 28 °E)	99
Rhodope Mts. (RAHD uh pee), *Europe* (42 °N, 25 °E)	99
Rhone R., *Europe* (44 °N, 4 °E)	98
Rice Lake, *Wis.* (46 °N, 92 °W)	63
Richland, *Wash.* (46 °N, 119 °W)	60
Richlands, *Va.* (37 °N, 82 °W)	71
Richmond, *Ind.* (40 °N, 85 °W)	70
Richmond, *Va.* (38 °N, 77 °W)	71
Ridgecrest, *Calif.* (35 °N, 118 °W)	58
Riding Mt. N. P., *Manitoba* (51 °N, 100 °W)	45
Riga (REE guh), *Latvia* (57 °N, 24 °E)	97
Riga, Gulf of, *Baltic Sea* (58 °N, 23 °E)	99
Rigolet (RIHG uh LEHT), *Newfoundland* (54 °N, 58 °W)	47
Rijeka (ree YEHK uh), *Croatia* (45 °N, 14 °E)	99
Rimini, *Italy* (44 °N, 13 °E)	99
Rimouski (rim OO skee), *Quebec* (48 °N, 69 °W)	47
Rio Atrato (uh TRAHT oh), *r. in Colombia* (7 °N, 77 °W)	90
Rio Branco, *Brazil* (10 °S, 68 °W)	90
Rio Bravo del Norte (REE oh BRAHV oh dehl NORT ee), *r. in Mexico and U.S.*, (29 °N, 108 °W)	82
Rio de Janeiro (REE oh day zhuh NAIR oh), *Brazil* (23 °S, 43 °W)	89
Rio de la Plata, *r. in South America* (35 °S, 57 °W)	88
Rio Gallegos, *Argentina* (52 °S, 69 °W)	89
Rio Grande (REE oh GRAN day), *r. in U.S. and Mexico* (28 °N, 100 °W)	52-53
Rio Hondo, *r. in N. Mex.* (34 °N, 104 °W)	59
Rio Madre de Dios (MAHD ree DAHD ee OHS), *r. in South America* (12 °S, 68 °W)	90
Rio Muni (REE oh MOO nee), *region of Equitorial Guinea* (2 °N, 10 °E)	108
Rio Rancho, *N. Mex.* (35 °N, 107 °W)	59
Riverina, *Australia* (35 °S, 146 °E)	133
Riverside, *Calif.* (34 °N, 117 °W)	58
Riverton, *Wyo.* (43 °N, 108 °W)	61
Riviera (RIHV ee EHR uh), *region of Europe* (44 °N, 7 °E)	99
Riviere-du-Loup (ree vee EHR duh LOO), *Quebec* (48 °N, 70 °W)	47
Riyadh (ree AHD), *Saudi Arabia* (25 °N, 47 °E)	115
Roanoke, *Va.* (ROH uh NOHK), (37 °N, 80 °W)	71
Roanoke R., *U.S.* (36 °N, 77 °W)	71
Robson, Mt., *Canada* (53 °N, 119 °W)	44
Rochester, *Minn.* (44 °N, 92 °W)	63
Rochester, *N.H.* (43 °N, 71 °W)	73
Rochester, *N.Y.* (43 °N, 78 °W)	72
Rock Hill, *S.C.* (35 °N, 81 °W)	69
Rock Island, *Ill.* (41 °N, 90 °W)	65
Rock R., *U.S.* (42 °N, 90 °W)	65
Rock Springs, *Wyo.* (42 °N, 109 °W)	61
Rockall, *island in Atlantic O.* (58 °N, 14 °W)	96
Rockford, *Ill.* (42 °N, 89 °W)	65
Rockhampton, *Australia* (23 °S, 151 °E)	131
Rocklands Res., *Australia* (37 °S, 142 °E)	133
Rockville, *Md.* (39 °N, 77 °W)	71
Rocky Mount, *N.C.* (36 °N, 78 °W)	71
Rocky Mountain N.P., *Colo.* (40 °N, 106 °W)	59
Rocky Mts., *North America* (45 °N, 111 °W)	36
Roebuck Bay, *Australia* (19 °S, 120 °E)	130
Rogue R. (ROHG), *Oreg.* (42 °N, 123 °W)	60
Rojo, Cape, *Mexico* (21 °N, 97 °W)	82
Rolla (RAHL uh), *Mo.* (38 °N, 92 °W)	65
Rolling Fork, *r. in Ky.* (38 °N, 86 °W)	70
Romaine R., *Quebec* (50 °N, 64 °W)	47
Romania, *country in Europe* (46 °N, 25 °E)	99
Rome, *Ga.* (34 °N, 85 °W)	68
Rome, *Italy* (42 °N, 13 °E)	99
Rome, *N.Y.* (43 °N, 75 °W)	72
Ronne Ice Shelf, *Antarctica* (78 °S, 65 °W)	137
Roraima, Mt., *South America* (5 °N, 61 °W)	90
Rosario, *Argentina* (33 °S, 61 °W)	89
Roseburg, *Oreg.* (43 °N, 123 °W)	60
Ross Barnett Res., *Miss.* (32 °N, 90 °W)	68
Ross Bay Junction, *Newfoundland* (53 °N, 66 °W)	47
Ross Ice Shelf, *Antarctica* (82 °S, 180 °)	137
Ross L., *Wash.* (49 °N, 121 °W)	60
Ross Sea, *Antarctica* (75 °S, 180 °)	137
Rossignol L., *Nova Scotia* (44 °N, 65 °W)	47
Rostock, *Germany* (54 °N, 12 °E)	99
Rostov-na-Donu (ruh STAHV nah DAH noo), *Russia* (47 °N, 40 °E)	97
Roswell, *Ga.* (34 °N, 84 °W)	69
Roswell, *N. Mex.* (33 °N, 105 °W)	59
Rotterdam, *Netherlands* (52 °N, 4 °E)	98
Rouen (roo AHN), *France* (49 °N, 1 °E)	98
Rough River Res., *Ky.* (38 °N, 86 °W)	70
Round Rock, *Tex.* (31 °N, 98 °W)	67
Rouyn-Noranda (ROO uhn nuh RAN duh), *Quebec* (48 °N, 79 °W)	46
Rub al Khali (ROOB al KAHL ee), *region of Saudi Arabia* (22 °N, 53 °E)	115
Rubeho Mts., *Tanzania* (7 °S, 36 °E)	110
Ruby Mts., *Nev.* (40 °N, 116 °W)	58
Rufiji R. (roo FEE jee), *Tanzania* (8 °S, 37 °E)	110
Rugen (ROO guhn), *island in Baltic Sea* (54 °N, 14 °E)	99
Ruiz, Mt. (roo EEZ), *Columbia* (5 °N, 75 °W)	90
Rukwa, L. (RUHK wuh), *Tanzania* (8 °S, 32 °E)	110
Rupert R., *Quebec* (51 °N, 79 °W)	46
Ruse (ROO say), *Bulgaria* (44 °N, 26 °E)	99
Rushmore, Mt., *S. Dak.* (44 °N, 103 °W)	62
Russell, *Manitoba* (51 °N, 101 °W)	45
Russia, *country in Europe and Asia* (60 °N, 60 °E)	100-101
Rutland, *Vt.* (44 °N, 73 °W)	73
Ruvuma R. (ruh VUH mah), *Africa* (11 °S, 40 °E)	110
Rwanda, *country in Africa* (2 °S, 30 °E)	110
Rybinsk Res., *Russia* (59 °N, 38 °E)	95
Ryukyu Is. (ree OO kyoo), *Pacific O.* (26 °N, 128 °E)	121

S

Name (Pronunciation), *Description* (Lat., Long.)	**Page**
Sabah (SAHB ah), *region of Malaysia* (5 °N, 116 °E)	123
Sabine L. (suh BEEN), *U.S.* (30 °N, 94 °W)	67
Sabine R., *U.S.* (32 °N, 95 °W)	67
Sable, Cape, *Fla.* (25 °N, 81 °W)	69
Sable, Cape, *Nova Scotia* (44 °N, 65 °W)	47
Sable I., *Atlantic O.* (43 °N, 59 °W)	41
Sacandaga Res. (SAK uhn DAI guh), *N.Y.* (43 °N, 74 °W)	72
Sachigo L., *Ontario* (54 °N, 92 °W)	46
Sachigo R., *Ontario* (55 °N, 89 °W)	46
Sachs Harbour, *Northwest Terr.* (72 °N, 125 °W)	42
Sacramento, *Calif.* (39 °N, 122 °W)	58
Sacramento Mts., *U.S.* (33 °N, 106 °W)	59
Sacramento R., *Calif.* (40 °N, 122 °W)	58
Sacramento Valley, *Calif.* (40 °N, 122 °W)	58
Sado (SAHD oh), *island in Sea of Japan* (38 °N, 138 °E)	125
Safi, *Morocco* (32 °N, 9 °W)	114
Sagar (SAHG uhr), *India* (24 °N, 79 °E)	122
Saginaw (SAG uh NAW), *Mich.* (44 °N, 84 °W)	63
Saginaw Bay, *Mich.* (44 °N, 84 °W)	63
Saguaro N.P., *Ariz.* (32 °N, 111 °W)	59
Saguenay R. (SAG uh NAY), *Quebec* (48 °N, 71 °W)	47
Sahara, *desert in Africa* (24 °N, 10 °E)	114-115
Sahel, *region of Africa* (14 °N, 10 °E)	106
Saimaa, L. (SY MAH), *Finland* (61 °N, 28 °E)	95
Saint-Augustin R. (sant OH goos TEEN), *Canada* (51 °N, 59 °W)	47
Saint Augustine, *Fla.* (30 °N, 81 °W)	69
Saint Catharines, *Ontario* (43 °N, 79 °W)	46
Saint Clair, L., *Ontario* (43 °N, 83 °W)	46
Saint Clair R., *Ontario* (48 °N, 82 °W)	63
Saint Cloud, *Minn.* (46 °N, 94 °W)	62
Saint Croix R. (KROY), *North America* (45 °N, 69 °W)	73
Saint Croix R., *U.S.* (45 °N, 93 °W)	63
Saint Elias, Mt. (ee LY uhs), *North America* (60 °N, 141 °W)	57
Saint Elias Mts., *Yukon Terr.* (61 °N, 138 °W)	44
Saint Etienne (SAN tay TYEHN), *France* (45 °N, 5 °E)	98
Saint Francis R., *North America* (47 °N, 69 °W)	47
Saint George, *Utah* (37 °N, 114 °W)	58
Saint George's Channel, *Ireland and Wales* (52 °N, 6 °W)	98
Saint Helena, *island in Atlantic O.* (15 °S, 5 °W)	107
Saint Helena Bay (HEL uh nuh), *Atlantic O.* (33 °S, 18 °E)	109
Saint Helens, Mt., *Wash.* (46 °N, 122 °W)	60
St. Ignace I. (IHG nuhs), *L. Superior* (49 °N, 88 °W)	46
Saint Jean, L. (SAN ZHAHN), *Quebec* (49 °N, 72 °W)	47
Saint Joe R., *Idaho* (47 °N, 116 °W)	60
Saint John, *New Brunswick* (45 °N, 66 °W)	47
Saint John R., *Canada and U.S.* (47 °N, 69 °W)	47
Saint John's, *Newfoundland* (48 °N, 53 °W)	43
Saint Johns R., *Fla.* (30 °N, 82 °W)	69
Saint Johnsbury (JAHNZ BER ee), *Vt.* (44 °N, 72 °W)	73
Saint Joseph, *Mich.* (42 °N, 87 °W)	63
Saint Joseph, *Mo.* (40 °N, 95 °W)	65
Saint Joseph I., *L. Huron* (46 °N, 84 °W)	46
Saint Joseph, L., *Ontario* (52 °N, 91 °W)	46
Saint Joseph R., *U.S.* (41 °N, 85 °W)	63
Saint Kitts and Nevis (NEE vihs), *country in Caribbean Sea* (17 °N, 63 °W)	85
Saint Laurent (SAN luh RAHN), *Quebec* (46 °N, 74 °W)	47
Saint Lawrence, Gulf of, *Atlantic O.* (48 °N, 62 °W)	47
Saint Lawrence I., *Bering Sea* (63 °N, 170 °W)	57
Saint Lawrence Is. N. P., *Ontario* (44 °N, 76 °W)	47
Saint Lawrence R., *Canada and U.S.* (48 °N, 70 °W)	47
Saint Louis, *Mo.* (39 °N, 90 °W)	65
Saint-Louis (SANG loo EE), *Senegal* (16 °N, 16 °W)	108
Saint Louis R., *Minn.* (47 °N, 93 °W)	63
Saint Lucia, *country in Caribbean Sea* (14 °N, 61 °W)	85
Saint Malo (SAN muh LOH), *France* (49 °N, 2 °W)	98
Saint Malo, Gulf of, *France* (49 °N, 3 °W)	98
Saint Mary's R., *U.S.* (41 °N, 85 °W)	70
Saint Matthew I., *Bering Sea* (60 °N, 172 °W)	57
Saint Maurice R. (SAN moh REES), *Quebec* (48 °N, 74 °W)	47
Saint Paul, *Minn.* (45 °N, 93 °W)	63
Saint Paul I., *Indian O.* (39 °S, 78 °E)	9
Saint Peters, *Mo.* (39 °N, 91 °W)	65
Saint Petersburg, *Fla.* (28 °N, 83 °W)	69
Saint Petersburg, *Russia* (60 °N, 30 °E)	97
Saint Pierre, *island in Atlantic O.* (47 °N, 56 °W)	41
Saint Pierre and Miquelon (MIK uh LAHNG), *terr. of France* (47 °N, 56 °W)	43
Saint Vincent, Cape, *Portugal* (37 °N, 9 °W)	114
Saint Vincent and the Grenadines, *country in Caribbean Sea* (13 °N, 62 °W)	85
Sainte Foy, *Quebec* (47 °N, 71 °W)	47
Sainte Genevieve (sant JEHN uh veev), *Mo.* (38 °N, 90 °W)	65
Sainte-Marguerite R. (mahr GREET), *Quebec* (50 °N, 67 °W)	47
Sajama, Mt., *South America* (18 °S, 69 °W)	88
Sakai, *Japan* (35 °N, 135 °E)	125
Sakakawea, L., *N. Dak.* (48 °N, 102 °W)	62
Sakhalin I., *Russia* (50 °N, 143 °E)	119
Salado R., *Argentina* (26 °S, 64 °W)	88
Salado R., *Mexico* (27 °N, 100 °W)	84
Salalah, *Oman* (17 °N, 54 °E)	115
Salekhard, *Russia* (66 °N, 67 °E)	100
Salem (SAYL uhm), *Oreg.* (45 °N, 123 °W)	60
Salem, *Mass.* (43 °N, 71 °W)	73
Salerno, *Italy* (41 °N, 15 °E)	99
Salina (suh LY nuh), *Kans.* (39 °N, 98 °W)	64
Salinas (suh LEE nuhs), *Calif.* (37 °N, 122 °W)	58
Salisbury (SAWLZ BEHR ee), *Australia* (35 °S, 138 °E)	133
Salisbury, *Md.* (38 °N, 76 °W)	71

Name (Pronunciation), *Description* (Lat., Long.) — Page

Salisbury, *N.C.* (36°N, 81°W) — 71
Salluit, *Quebec* (62°N, 75°W) — 43
Salmon (SAM uhn), *Idaho* (45°N, 114°W) — 61
Salmon Creek Res., *Idaho* (42°N, 115°W) — 61
Salmon R., *Idaho* (46°N, 116°W) — 60-61
Salmon R. Mts., *Idaho* (44°N, 115°W) — 61
Salonika (suh LAWN ih kuh), *Greece* (41°N, 23°E) — 99
Salt Basin, *Tex.* (32°N, 105°W) — 66
Salt Fork, *r. in U.S.* (35°N, 100°W) — 66
Salt Lake City, *Utah* (41°N, 112°W) — 59
Salt R., *Ariz.* (34°N, 112°W) — 59
Salt R., *Ky.* (38°N, 86°W) — 70
Salt R., *Mo.* (40°N, 92°W) — 65
Salta, *Argentina* (25°S, 65°W) — 89
Saltillo (sahl TEE yoh), *Mexico* (25°N, 101°W) — 84
Salto, *Uruguay* (31°S, 58°W) — 89
Salton Sea, *Calif.* (33°N, 116°W) — 58
Saluda R. (suh LOOD uh), *S.C.* (34°N, 82°W) — 69
Salvador, *Brazil* (13°S, 38°W) — 89
Salween R., *Asia* (18°N, 97°E) — 118-119
Salzburg, *Austria* (48°N, 13°E) — 99
Sam Rayburn Res., *Tex.* (31°N, 94°W) — 67
Samara, *Russia* (53°N, 50°E) — 97
Samarqand, *Uzbekistan* (40°N, 67°E) — 100
Samoa, *country in Pacific O.* (10°S, 172°W) — 135
Samos (SAY mahs), *island in Aegean Sea* (38°N, 27°E) — 99
Samothrace (SAHM uh THRAHK ee), *i. in Aegean Sea* (40°N, 26°E) — 99
Samsun (sahm SOON), *Turkey* (41°N, 36°E) — 115
San Ambrosio Island, *Pacific O.* (26°S, 80°W) — 88
San Andres I., *Caribbean Sea* (13°N, 82°W) — 83
San Angelo (san AN juh loh), *Tex.* (31°N, 100°W) — 66
San Antonio, *Tex.* (29°N, 98°W) — 66
San Antonio, Cape, *Argentina* (37°S, 57°W) — 88
San Antonio R., *Tex.* (29°N, 97°W) — 67
San Bernardino, *Calif.* (34°N, 117°W) — 58
San Blas, Cape, *Fla.* (30°N, 86°W) — 68
San Carlos L. (KAHR luhs), *Ariz.* (33°N, 110°W) — 59
San Clemente (kluh MENT ee), *island in Pacific O.* (33°N, 119°W) — 58
San Cristobal, *Venezuela* (8°N, 72°W) — 90
San Diego, *Calif.* (33°N, 117°W) — 58
San Felix I., *Pacific O.* (26°S, 80°W) — 88
San Fernando, *Venezuela* (4°N, 68°W) — 90
San Francisco, *Calif.* (38°N, 123°W) — 58
San Joaquin R., *Calif.* (38°N, 121°W) — 58
San Joaquin Valley, *Calif.* (37°N, 121°W) — 58
San Jorge, Gulf of, *Atlantic O.* (46°S, 67°W) — 88
San Jose (SAN hoh ZAY), *Calif.* (37°N, 122°W) — 58
San Jose, *Costa Rica* (10°N, 84°W) — 85
San Jose I., *Mexico* (25°N, 111°W) — 82
San Juan (san HWAHN), *Argentina* (32°S, 68°W) — 89
San Juan, *Puerto Rico* (19°N, 66°W) — 85
San Juan Is. (san WAHN), *Puget Sound and Strait of Georgia* (48°N, 123°W) — 60
San Juan Mts., *U.S.* (38°N, 107°W) — 59
San Juan R., *Nicaragua and Costa Rica* (11°N, 85°W) — 83
San Juan R., *U.S.* (39°N, 108°W) — 59
San Lucas, Cape, *Mexico* (23°N, 110°W) — 82
San Luis, *Argentina* (33°S, 66°W) — 89
San Luis Obispo (san LOO uh suh BIS poh), *Calif.* (35°N, 121°W) — 58
San Luis Potosi, *Mexico* (22°N, 101°W) — 84
San Marcos (san MAHR kuhs), *Tex.* (30°N, 98°W) — 66
San Marino, *country in Europe* (44°N, 12°E) — 99
San Mateo, (san muh TAY oh), *Calif.* (38°N, 122°W) — 58
San Matias, Gulf of, *Atlantic O.* (42°S, 64°W) — 88
San Miguel R. (san muh GEHL), *Colo.* (38°N, 108°W) — 59
San Pedro R. (san PAY droh), *Ariz.* (33°N, 111°W) — 59
San Pedro Sula, *Honduras* (15°N, 88°W) — 84
San Rafael (SAN ruh FEHL), *Calif.* (38°N, 123°W) — 58
San Salvador, *El Salvador* (14°N, 89°W) — 84

San Salvador I., *Atlantic O.* (24°N, 75°W) — 83
San Sebastian, *Spain* (43°N, 2°W) — 98
Sanaa (sah NAH), *Yemen* (Sana) (15°N, 44°E) — 115
Sanaga R., *Cameroon* (5°N, 12°E) — 108
Sand Hills, *Nebr.* (42°N, 102°W) — 64
Sandakan (san DAHK uhn), *Malaysia* (6°N, 118°E) — 123
Sandspit, *British Columbia* (53°N, 132°W) — 44
Sandusky, *Ohio* (41°N, 83°W) — 70
Sandusky R., *Ohio* (41°N, 83°W) — 70
Sandy City, *Utah* (40°N, 112°W) — 59
Sanford, *Fla.* (29°N, 81°W) — 69
Sanford, *Maine* (43°N, 69°W) — 73
Sanford, *N.C.* (35°N, 79°W) — 71
Sangamon R. (SANG guh muhn), *Ill.* (40°N, 90°W) — 65
Sangre de Cristo Mts., *U.S.* (38°N, 106°W) — 59
Santa Ana, *Calif.* (34°N, 118°W) — 58
Santa Barbara, *Calif.* (35°N, 120°W) — 58
Santa Barbara Channel, *Calif.* (34°N, 120°W) — 58
Santa Catalina, *island in Pacific O.* (33°N, 118°W) — 58
Santa Clarita, *Calif.* (34°N, 118°W) — 58
Santa Cruz (sant uh KROOZ), *Bolivia* (18°S, 63°W) — 89
Santa Cruz, *Calif.* (37°N, 122°W) — 58
Santa Cruz, *Canary Is.* (28°N, 15°W) — 114
Santa Fe, *N. Mex.* (36°N, 106°W) — 59
Santa Margarita I., *Mexico* (24°N, 112°W) — 82
Santa Maria, *Brazil* (30°S, 54°W) — 89
Santa Maria, *Calif.* (35°N, 120°W) — 58
Santa Maria, *Colombia* (11°N, 74°W) — 90
Santa Rosa, *Calif.* (38°N, 123°W) — 58
Santander, *Spain* (43°N, 4°W) — 98
Santarem, *Brazil* (3°S, 55°W) — 90
Sante Fe (SAN tuh FAY), *Argentina* (32°S, 61°W) — 89
Santee R., *S.C.* (33°N, 80°W) — 69
Santiago, *Chile* (34°S, 71°W) — 89
Santiago de Cuba, *Cuba* (20°N, 76°W) — 85
Santiago del Estero, *Argentina* (27°S, 64°W) — 89
Santo Domingo, *Dominican Republic* (19°N, 70°W) — 85
Santos, *Brazil* (24°S, 47°W) — 89
Sao Francisco R. (SOWN frahn SEE skoo), *Brazil* (14°S, 44°W) — 88
Sao Luis (SOWN loo EES), *Brazil* (3°S, 44°W) — 89
Sao Paulo (SOWN POW loo), *Brazil* (24°S, 47°W) — 89
Sao Tome (SOWN taw MEH), *island in Gulf of Guinea* (0°, 7°E) — 108
Sao Tome, *Sao Tome & Principe* (0°, 7°E) — 108
Sao Tome and Principe (PREEN see puh), *country in Gulf of Guinea* (1°N, 7°E) — 108
Saone R. (SOHN), *France* (46°N, 5°E) — 98
Sapporo, *Japan* (43°N, 141°E) — 125
Saragossa, *Spain* (42°N, 1°W) — 114
Sarajevo (SAHR uh YAY voh), *Bosnia and Herzegovina* (44°N, 18°E) — 99
Sarasota, *Fla.* (27°N, 82°W) — 69
Saratoga Springs, *N.Y.* (43°N, 74°W) — 72
Saratov, *Russia* (52°N, 46°E) — 97
Sarawak (suh RAH wahk), *region of Malaysia* (2°N, 112°E) — 123
Sardinia, *island in Mediterranean Sea* (40°N, 9°E) — 99
Sargodha (suhr GOHD uh), *Pakistan* (32°N, 73°E) — 122
Sarh, *Chad* (9°N, 18°E) — 107
Sarnia, *Ontario* (43°N, 82°W) — 46
Saskatchewan, *prov. in Canada* (54°N, 106°W) — 45
Saskatchewan R. (SAS KACH uh WAHN), *Canada* (53°N, 104°W) — 45
Saskatoon, *Saskatchewan* (52°N, 107°W) — 45
Sassandra R. (suh SAN druh), *Côte d'Ivoire* (7°N, 7°W) — 108
Sassari (SAHS uh ree), *Sardinia* (41°N, 9°E) — 99
Satilla R., *Ga.* (31°N, 82°W) — 69
Satu Mare (SAHT oo MAHR uh), *Romania* (48°N, 23°E) — 99
Saudi Arabia, *country in Asia* (24°N, 44°E) — 115
Sault Sainte Marie (SOO SAYNT muh REE), *Mich.* (46°N, 84°W) — 63
Sault Sainte Marie, *Ontario* (47°N, 84°W) — 46
Sava R., *Europe* (46°N, 15°E) — 99

Savannah, *Ga.* (32°N, 81°W) — 69
Savannah R., *U.S.* (33°N, 82°W) — 69
Savannakhet (suh VAHN uh KEHT), *Laos* (17°N, 105°E) — 123
Savu Sea, *Indian O.* (9°S, 122°E) — 130
Sawatch Range, *Colo.* (39°N, 106°W) — 59
Sayan Mts., *Russia* (53°N, 95°E) — 118-119
Saylorville Res., *Iowa* (42°N, 94°W) — 65
Scandinavia, *region of Europe* (61°N, 12°E) — 94-95
Scarborough, *Ontario* (44°N, 79°W) — 46
Schefferville (SHEF uhr VIL), *Quebec* (55°N, 67°W) — 47
Schenectady (skuh NEK tuh dee), *N.Y.* (43°N, 74°W) — 72
Schleswig (SHLEHS veeg), *Germany* (55°N, 10°E) — 99
Schreiber, *Ontario* (49°N, 87°W) — 46
Scioto R. (sy OHT uh), *Ohio* (40°N, 83°W) — 70
Scotia Sea, *Atlantic O.* (55°S, 50°W) — 137
Scotland, *part of United Kingdom* (57°N, 5°W) — 98
Scottsbluff, *Nebr.* (42°N, 104°W) — 64
Scottsdale, *Ariz.* (34°N, 112°W) — 59
Scranton, *Pa.* (42°N, 76°W) — 72
Sea Is., *Atlantic O.* (32°N, 81°W) — 69
Seaford, *Del.* (39°N, 76°W) — 71
Seal R., *Manitoba* (59°N, 95°W) — 45
Seattle, *Wash.* (48°N, 122°W) — 60
Sebago L. (suh BAY goh), *Maine* (44°N, 71°W) — 73
Sebastian Vizcaino Bay, *Baja California* (28°N, 115°W) — 82
Second Cataract, *waterfall in Sudan* (22°N, 31°E) — 115
Sechelt, *British Columbia* (49°N, 123°W) — 44
Sedalia (sih DAYL yuh), *Mo.* (39°N, 93°W) — 65
Seine R. (sayn), *France* (49°N, 1°E) — 98
Sekondi-Takoradi (sehk uhn DEE TAK uh RAHD ee), *Ghana* (5°N, 2°W) — 108
Selenge R. (SEHL ung GAH), *Mongolia* (49°N, 102°E) — 124
Selkirk, *Manitoba* (50°N, 97°W) — 45
Selma, *Ala.* (32°N, 87°W) — 68
Selvas (SEL vuhz), *forest region in Brazil* (5°S, 65°W) — 90
Semarang (suh MAHR ANG), *Indonesia* (7°S, 110°E) — 131
Semey, *Kazakhstan* (50°N, 80°E) — 100
Seminoe Res., *Wyo.* (42°N, 107°W) — 61
Seminole, L. (SEHM uh NOHL), *U.S.* (31°N, 85°W) — 68
Sendai (sen DY), *Japan* (38°N, 141°E) — 125
Seneca L. (SEN ih kuh), *N.Y.* (42°N, 77°W) — 72
Senecaville Res., *Ohio* (40°N, 81°W) — 71
Senegal, *country in Africa* (15°N, 15°W) — 108
Senegal R., *Africa* (16°N, 14°W) — 108
Senneterre (sehn TEHR), *Quebec* (48°N, 77°W) — 46
Seoul (sohl), *South Korea* (38°N, 127°E) — 125
Sept-Iles (set EEL), *Quebec* (50°N, 66°W) — 47
Sequoia N. P., (sih KWOY uh), *Calif.* (36°N, 119°W) — 58
Serasun Strait, *Malaysia* (2°N, 109°E) — 123
Serbia, *republic of Yugoslavia* (44°N, 21°E) — 99
Serengeti Plain (SEHR uhn GEHT ee), *Tanzania* (3°S, 35°E) — 110
Sergino, *Russia* (63°N, 66°E) — 100
Serrai (SEHR ray), *Greece* (41°N, 24°E) — 99
Seul, L. (SOOL), *Ontario* (50°N, 93°W) — 46
Sevastopol, *Ukraine* (44°N, 33°E) — 97
Severn R., *Ontario* (55°N, 89°W) — 46
Severnaya Zemlya, *islands in Arctic O.* (80°N, 95°E) — 100
Sevier Bridge Res. (suh VIR), *Utah* (38°N, 112°W) — 59
Sevier L., *Utah* (39°N, 113°W) — 58-59
Sevier R., *Utah* (38°N, 112°W) — 58-59
Seville, *Spain* (37°N, 6°W) — 114
Seward, *Alaska* (60°N, 150°W) — 57
Seward Pen. (SOO uhrd), *Alaska* (65°N, 165°W) — 57
Seychelles (say SHEHL), *country in Indian O.* (5°S, 55°E) — 107
Sfax, *Tunisia* (35°N, 11°E) — 114
Shache, *China* (38°N, 77°E) — 124
Shackleton Ice Shelf, *Antarctica* (65°S, 105°E) — 137
Shanghai, *China* (31°N, 121°E) — 124

Name (Pronunciation), *Description* (Lat., Long.)	Page
Shannon R., *Ireland* (53°N, 9°W)	98
Shark Bay, *Australia* (25°S, 113°E)	130
Sharpe, L., *S. Dak.* (44°N, 100°W)	62
Shasta L., *Calif.* (41°N, 122°W)	58
Shasta, Mt., *Calif.* (42°N, 122°W)	58
Shatt al Jarid, *seasonal lake in Africa* (33°N, 9°E)	114
Shawnee, *Okla.* (35°N, 97°W)	67
Sheboygan, *Wis.* (44°N, 88°W)	63
Sheffield, *England* (53°N, 1°W)	98
Shelburne, *Nova Scotia* (44°N, 65°W)	47
Shelby, *N.C.* (35°N, 82°W)	71
Shelbyville, *Tenn.* (35°N, 86°W)	70
Shelbyville, L., *Ill.* (39°N, 89°W)	65
Shellharbour, *Australia* (35°S, 151°E)	133
Shenandoah N. P., *Va.* (39°N, 78°W)	71
Shenandoah R., *Va.* (39°N, 78°W)	71
Shenyang, *China* (42°N, 123°E)	124
Sherbrooke, *Nova Scotia* (45°N, 62°W)	47
Sherbrooke, *Quebec* (45°N, 72°W)	47
Sheridan, *Wyo.* (45°N, 107°W)	61
Sherman, *Tex.* (34°N, 97°W)	67
Shetak, L., *Minn.* (44°N, 96°W)	62
Shetland Is., *North Sea* (61°N, 2°W)	98
Sheyenne R. (shy EN), *N. Dak.* (48°N, 99°W)	62
Shiawassee R. (SHY uh WAWS ee), *Mich.* (43°N, 84°W)	63
Shijiazhuang (shihr jah wahng), *China* (38°N, 115°E)	124
Shikoku, *island in Sea of Japan* (34°N, 134°E)	125
Shinyanga (sheen YAHNG guh), *Tanzania* (4°S, 33°E)	110
Shiraz, *Iran* (30°N, 52°E)	115
Sholapur (SHOH luh POOR), *India* (18°N, 76°E)	122
Shreveport, *La.* (33°N, 94°W)	67
Sialkot (see AHL kohT), *Pakistan* (33°N, 74°E)	122
Siberia, *Asian Russia* (65°N, 120°E)	118-119
Sibu (SEE boo), *Malaysia* (2°N, 112°E)	123
Sichuan Basin (sich oo ahn), *region of China* (30°N, 105°E)	124
Sicily, *island in Mediterranean Sea* (37°N, 14°E)	99
Sidi-Bel-Abbes (SEE dee BEHL uh BEHS), *Algeria* (35°N, 1°W)	114
Sidi Ifni, *Morocco* (29°N, 10°W)	114
Sidney, *Nebr.* (41°N, 103°W)	64
Sidra, Gulf of, *Mediterranean Sea* (32°N, 19°E)	114
Sierra Leone, *country in Africa* (8°N, 12°W)	108
Sierra Madre del Sur, *mt. range in Mexico* (27°N, 100°W)	82
Sierra Madre Occidental, *mt. range in Mexico* (28°N, 107°W)	82
Sierra Madre Oriental, *mt. range in Mexico* (28°N, 102°W)	82
Sierra Maestra, *mt. range in Cuba* (20°N, 77°W)	83
Sierra Nevada, *mt. range in U.S.* (38°N, 120°W)	58
Sierra Vista, *Ariz.* (32°N, 111°W)	59
Sikeston (SYK stuhn), *Mo.* (37°N, 90°W)	65
Sikote-Alin Mts. (SEE kuh TAY uh LEEN), *Russia* (44°N, 135°E)	119
Silver City, *N. Mex.* (33°N, 108°W)	59
Silver Spring, *Md.* (39°N, 77°W)	71
Silvies R. (SIHL veez), *Oreg.* (44°N, 119°W)	60
Simard, L., *Quebec* (48°N, 79°W)	46
Simcoe, L., *Ontario* (44°N, 79°W)	46
Simeulue (SEE muh LOO uh), *island in Indian O.* (3°N, 96°E)	123
Simpson Desert, *Australia* (26°S, 137°E)	130
Sinai Pen. (SY ny), *Asia* (29°N, 33°E)	115
Singapore, *country in Asia* (1°N, 104°E)	123
Sinuiju (SHIHN ee JOO), *North Korea* (40°N, 125°E)	125
Sioux City (soo), *Iowa* (43°N, 96°W)	64
Sioux Falls, *S. Dak.* (44°N, 97°W)	62
Sipiwesk L., *Manitoba* (55°N, 98°W)	45
Sisseton, *S. Dak.* (46°N, 97°W)	62
Sitka, *Alaska* (57°N, 135°W)	57
Sivas (sih VAHS), *Turkey* (40°N, 37°E)	115
Siwah Oasis (SEE wuh), *Egypt* (31°N, 25°E)	115
Sixth Cataract, *waterfall in Sudan* (16°N, 33°E)	115
Sjaelland (SHEHL luhn), *island in Kattegat* (56°N, 12°E)	99

Name (Pronunciation), *Description* (Lat., Long.)	Page
Skagerrak, *strait between Norway and Denmark* (57°N, 9°E)	98
Skagit R. (SKAJ uht), *Wash.* (48°N, 122°W)	60
Skagway, *Alaska* (60°N, 135°W)	57
Skaneateles L. (SKAN ee AT luhs), *N.Y.* (43°N, 76°W)	72
Skeena Mts., *British Columbia* (57°N, 130°W)	44
Skeena R., *British Columbia* (55°N, 128°W)	44
Skopje, *Macedonia* (42°N, 22°E)	99
Skunk R., *Iowa* (41°N, 91°W)	65
Slave Coast, *region of Africa* (6°N, 2°E)	108
Slave Lake, *Alberta* (55°N, 115°W)	44
Slave R., *Canada* (60°N, 111°W)	44-45
Sligo (SLY goh), *Ireland* (54°N, 8°W)	98
Slovakia, *country in Europe* (49°N, 19°E)	99
Slovenia, *country in Europe* (46°N, 15°E)	99
Smallwood Res., *Newfoundland* (54°N, 64°W)	47
Smith, *Alberta* (55°N, 114°W)	44
Smith Mountain L., *Va.* (37°N, 80°W)	71
Smithers, *British Columbia* (55°N, 127°W)	44
Smoky Hill R., *U.S.* (39°N, 100°W)	64
Smoky R., *Alberta* (54°N, 119°W)	44
Smolensk, *Russia* (55°N, 32°E)	100
Smyrna (SMUHR nuh), *Ga.* (34°N, 85°W)	68
Snake R., *U.S.* (47°N, 118°W)	60-61
Snake River Plain, *Idaho* (43°N, 114°W)	61
Society Is., *Pacific O.* (17°S, 152°W)	10
Socorro (suh KAW roh), *N. Mex.* (34°N, 107°W)	59
Socotra, *island in Arabian Sea* (12°N, 54°E)	115
Sofia, *Bulgaria* (43°N, 23°E)	99
Sogne Fiord (SAWNG nuh FYAWRD), *Norway* (61°N, 6°E)	98
Sohag, *Egypt* (27°N, 32°E)	115
Sokode (soh KOH day), *Togo* (9°N, 1°E)	108
Sokoto (SOH kuh TOH), *Nigeria* (13°N, 5°E)	108
Solomon Islands, *country in Pacific O.* (9°S, 160°E)	131
Solomon R., *Kans.* (39°N, 98°W)	64
Solomon Sea, *Pacific O.* (8°S, 154°E)	130
Somali Pen., *Somalia* (10°N, 50°E)	106
Somalia, *country in Africa* (5°N, 47°E)	107
Somerset, *Ky.* (37°N, 85°W)	70
Somerset I., *Arctic O.* (73°N, 93°W)	41
Sondags R., *South Africa* (33°S, 25°E)	109
Songhua R., *China* (46°N, 125°E)	124
Songkhla, *Thailand* (7°N, 101°E)	123
Sonoran Desert, *U.S. and Mexico* (33°N, 113°W)	58-59
Soroti (soh ROH tee), *Uganda* (2°N, 33°E)	110
Souris R. (SOOR uhs), *U.S. and Canada* (49°N, 102°W)	62
South Africa, *country in Africa* (30°S, 25°E)	109
South America, *continent*	7
South Australia, *state in Australia* (28°S, 133°E)	133
South Bend, *Ind.* (42°N, 86°W)	70
South Carolina, *state in U.S.* (34°N, 80°W)	69
South China Sea, *Asia* (15°N, 115°E)	119
South Dakota, *state in U.S.* (45°N, 100°W)	62
South Georgia, *island in Atlantic O.* (54°S, 37°W)	8
South Henik L., *Nunavut* (62°N, 97°W)	45
South Hill, *Va.* (37°N, 78°W)	71
South I., *New Zealand* (45°S, 170°E)	130
South Korea, *country in Asia* (36°N, 128°E)	125
South Loup R. (LOOP), *Nebr.* (41°N, 100°W)	64
South Orkney Is., *Atlantic O.* (60°S, 45°W)	137
South Pass, *Wyo.* (43°N, 109°W)	61
South Platte R., *U.S.* (41°N, 104°W)	59
South Saskatchewan R., *Canada* (51°N, 110°W)	44-45
South Shetland Is., *Atlantic O.* (62°S, 60°W)	137
South Sioux City (SOO), *Nebr.* (43°N, 96°W)	64
Southampton, *England* (51°N, 1°W)	98
Southampton I., *Hudson Bay* (64°N, 84°W)	41
Southern Alps, *New Zealand* (45°S, 169°E)	130
Southern Indian L., *Manitoba* (57°N, 99°W)	45
Soweto, *South Africa* (26°S, 28°E)	109
Spain, *country in Europe* (40°N, 5°W)	114
Spanish R., *Ontario* (46°N, 82°W)	46
Spartanburg, *S.C.* (35°N, 82°W)	69
Spencer, *Iowa* (43°N, 95°W)	65

Name (Pronunciation), *Description* (Lat., Long.)	Page
Spencer Gulf, *Indian O.* (35°S, 137°E)	133
Split, *Croatia* (43°N, 16°E)	99
Spokane (spoh KAN), *Wash.* (48°N, 117°W)	60
Spokane R., *Wash.* (48°N, 118°W)	60
Spoon R., *Ill.* (41°N, 90°W)	65
Sporades (SPAWR uh deez), *islands in Aegean Sea* (37°N, 27°E)	99
Sprague R. (SPRAHG), *Oreg.* (42°N, 122°W)	60
Spratly Is., *South China Sea* (9°N, 112°E)	123
Spree R. (SHPRAY), *Germany* (52°N, 14°E)	99
Spring Hill, *Fla.* (29°N, 83°W)	69
Springbok, *South Africa* (30°S, 18°E)	109
Springdale, *Ark.* (36°N, 94°W)	67
Springfield, *Ill.* (40°N, 90°W)	65
Springfield, *Mass.* (42°N, 73°W)	73
Springfield, *Mo.* (37°N, 93°W)	65
Springfield, *Ohio* (40°N, 84°W)	70
Springfield, *Oreg.* (44°N, 123°W)	60
Springfontein (SPRING fawn TAHN), *South Africa* (30°S, 26°E)	109
Sri Lanka, *country in Asia* (8°N, 81°E)	122
Srinagar, *India* (34°N, 75°E)	122
Stamford, *Conn.* (41°N, 74°W)	72-73
Stanley, *N. Dak.* (48°N, 102°W)	62
Stanovoy Mts. (STAN uh VOY), *Russia* (55°N, 125°E)	101
State College, *Pa.* (41°N, 78°W)	72
Statesville, *N.C.* (36°N, 81°W)	71
Staunton, *Va.* (38°N, 79°W)	71
Stavanger, *Norway* (59°N, 6°E)	96
Steamboat Springs, *Colo.* (40°N, 107°W)	59
Steens Mt., *Oreg.* (42°N, 119°W)	60
Steinbach (STYN BAK), *Manitoba* (50°N, 97°W)	45
Steppes, *plains in Europe and Asia* (50°N, 40°E)	100
Sterling, *Ill.* (42°N, 90°W)	65
Steubenville, *Ohio* (40°N, 81°W)	71
Stevens Point, *Wis.* (44°N, 90°W)	63
Stewart, *British Columbia* (56°N, 130°W)	44
Stewart I., *Pacific O.* (47°S, 168°E)	130
Stikine R. (stik EEN), *British Columbia* (58°N, 131°W)	44
Stillwater, *Okla.* (36°N, 97°W)	67
Stockholm, *Sweden* (59°N, 18°E)	96
Stockton, *Calif.* (38°N, 121°W)	58
Stockton L., *Mo.* (38°N, 94°W)	65
Stockton Plateau, *Tex.* (30°N, 102°W)	66
Stoke-on-Trent, *England* (53°N, 2°W)	98
Stone Mt., *Ga.* (34°N, 84°W)	69
Storm Lake, *Iowa* (43°N, 95°W)	65
Stornoway, *Scotland* (58°N, 6°W)	98
Strasbourg (STRAHS BOORG), *France* (49°N, 8°E)	98
Stratford-upon-Avon, *England* (52°N, 2°W)	98
Stuart L., *British Columbia* (55°N, 125°W)	44
Stuttgart, *Germany* (49°N, 9°E)	99
Subotica (SOO buh TEET suh), *Yugoslavia* (46°N, 20°E)	99
Sucre (SOO kray), *Bolivia* (19°S, 65°W)	89
Sudan, *country in Africa* (13°N, 30°E)	107
Sudbury, *Ontario* (47°N, 81°W)	46
Sudd, *region of Sudan* (8°N, 30°E)	106
Suez (soo EHZ), *Egypt* (30°N, 33°E)	115
Suez Canal, *Egypt* (31°N, 33°E)	115
Suffolk, *Va.* (37°N, 77°W)	71
Sukhona R., *Russia* (60°N, 43°E)	95
Sukkur (SOOK uhr), *Pakistan* (28°N, 69°E)	122
Sulaiman Range (SOOL eye MAHN), *Pakistan* (69°N, 30°E)	122
Sulphur R., *Tex.* (33°N, 95°W)	67
Sulu Sea, *Asia* (8°N, 120°E)	119
Sumatra, *island in Indian O.* (0°, 102°E)	119
Sumba, *island in Savu Sea* (9°S, 120°E)	130
Sumbawa (soom BAH wuh), *island in Flores Sea* (8°S, 117°E)	130
Summerside, *Prince Edward Island* (46°N, 64°W)	47
Sumter, *S.C.* (34°N, 80°W)	69
Sunnyvale, *Calif.* (37°N, 122°W)	58
Superior, *Wis.* (47°N, 92°W)	63
Superior, L., *North America* (48°N, 88°W)	63
Surabaya, *Indonesia* (8°S, 113°E)	130
Surat (SOOR uht), *India* (21°N, 73°E)	122

Name (Pronunciation), *Description* (Lat., Long.)	**Page**
Surat Thani (SOOR aht AN ee), *Thailand* (9°N, 99°E)	123
Suriname, *country in South America* (4°N, 56°W)	89
Surrey, *British Columbia* (49°N, 123°W)	44
Surtsey I. (SURT see), *Atlantic O.* (63°N, 21°W)	94
Susah, *Tunisia* (36°N, 11°E)	114
Susquehanna R., *U.S.* (40°N, 76°W)	72
Sutton L., *Ontario* (54°N, 85°W)	46
Suwanee R., *Fla.* (30°N, 83°W)	69
Suwon, *South Korea* (37°N, 127°E)	125
Suzhou (soo joh), *China* (31°N, 121°E)	124
Svalbard, *poss. of Norway* (77°N, 20°E)	100
Swan Hill, *Australia* (35°S, 144°E)	133
Swan Hills, *Alberta* (55°N, 116°W)	44
Swan River, *Manitoba* (52°N, 101°W)	45
Swanson Res., *Nebr.* (40°N, 101°W)	64
Swaziland, *country in Africa* (27°S, 32°E)	107
Sweden, *country in Europe* (60°N, 15°E)	96-97
Sweetwater R., *Wyo.* (42°N, 108°W)	61
Swift Current, *Saskatchewan* (50°N, 108°W)	45
Switzerland, *country in Europe* (47°N, 8°E)	99
Sydney, *Australia* (34°S, 151°E)	133
Sydney, *Nova Scotia* (46°N, 60°W)	47
Syktyvkar (sik tif KAHR), *Russia* (62°N, 51°E)	97
Syr Darya, *r. in Kazakhstan* (46°N, 65°E)	100
Syracuse, *N.Y.* (43°N, 76°W)	72
Syria, *country in Asia* (35°N, 38°E)	115
Syrian Desert, *Asia* (32°N, 39°E)	115
Szczecin (SHCHET SEEN), *Poland* (53°N, 15°E)	99
Szeged (SEG ed), *Hungary* (46°N, 20°E)	99

T

Name (Pronunciation), *Description* (Lat., Long.)	**Page**
Tabessa, *Algeria* (35°N, 8°E)	114
Table Rock L., *U.S.* (36°N, 93°W)	65
Tabora, *Tanzania* (5°S, 33°E)	110
Tabriz, *Iran* (38°N, 46°E)	115
Tabuk (tuh BOOK), *Saudi Arabia* (28°N, 37°E)	115
Tacoma, *Wash.* (47°N, 123°W)	60
Taconic Mts. (tuh KAHN ihk), *N.Y.* (42°N, 74°W)	72-73
Tadoule L., *Manitoba* (59°N, 98°W)	45
Tadoussac (TAD uh SAK), *Quebec* (48°N, 70°W)	47
Taegu (TAG oo), *South Korea* (36°N, 129°E)	125
Taejon (tah JAWN), *South Korea* (36°N, 127°E)	125
Tagus R., *Europe* (40°N, 4°W)	114
Tahat, Mt., *Algeria* (24°N, 6°E)	114
Tahiti, *island in Pacific O.* (20°S, 150°W)	10
Tahoe, L., *U.S.* (39°N, 120°W)	58
Taichung (TY CHOONG), *Taiwan* (24°N, 121°E)	124
Taipei (TY PAY), *Taiwan* (25°N, 122°E)	124
Taiwan, *country in Asia* (24°N, 121°E)	124
Taiwan Strait, *Taiwan and China* (24°N, 120°E)	124
Taiyuan (TY yoo AHN), *China* (38°N, 112°E)	124
Tajikistan, *country in Asia* (38°N, 69°E)	100
Tajumulco (TAH hoo MOOL KOH), *mt. in Guatemala* (15°N, 92°W)	82
Takamatsu, *Japan* (34°N, 134°E)	125
Taklimakan Desert, *China* (38°N, 80°E)	124
Taku R., *North America* (59°N, 134°W)	44
Talara, *Peru* (5°S, 82°W)	90
Tallahassee, *Fla.* (31°N, 84°W)	69
Tallinn, *Estonia* (59°N, 25°E)	97
Tamanrasset, *Algeria* (23°N, 7°E)	114
Tambora, Mt. (TAHM buh ruh), *Indonesia* (8°S, 118°E)	130
Tamesi R., *Mexico* (23°N, 98°W)	82
Tampa, *Fla.* (28°N, 82°W)	69
Tampa Bay, *Gulf of Mexico* (28°N, 82°W)	69
Tampere (TAHM puh RAY), *Finland* (61°N, 24°E)	97
Tampico, *Mexico* (22°N, 98°W)	84
Tana, L., *Ethiopia* (12°N, 37°E)	115
Tana R., *Kenya* (0°, 40°E)	110
Tanana R. (TAN uh NAW), *Alaska* (65°N, 148°W)	57
Tanezrouft (TAH nehz ruhft), *region of Algeria* (24°N, 1°E)	114
Tanga, *Tanzania* (5°S, 39°E)	110
Tanganyika, L., *Africa* (7°S, 30°E)	110
Tangier (tan JEER), *Morocco* (36°N, 6°W)	114

Name (Pronunciation), *Description* (Lat., Long.)	**Page**
Tanimbar Is., *Arafura Sea* (8°S, 131°E)	130
Tanzania, *country in Africa* (5°S, 35°E)	110
Taos (TAH ohs), *N. Mex.* (36°N, 106°W)	59
Tapajos R., *Brazil* (6°S, 57°W)	90
Tar R., *N.C.* (36°N, 78°W)	71
Tarakan (TAHR uh KAHN), *Indonesia* (3°N, 118°E)	123
Taranto, *Italy* (40°N, 17°E)	99
Taranto, Gulf of, *Ionian Sea* (40°N, 17°E)	99
Tarim Basin, *China* (40°N, 85°E)	124
Tarim R., *China* (41°N, 81°E)	124
Tashkent, *Uzbekistan* (41°N, 69°E)	100
Tasman Sea, *Pacific O.* (30°S, 165°E)	133
Tasmania, *state in Australia* (42°S, 147°E)	131
Tatar Strait, *Sea of Japan and Sea of Okhotsk* (50°N, 142°E)	101
Taunton (TAWNT uhn), *Mass.* (42°N, 71°W)	73
Taurus Mts. (TAW ruhs), *Turkey* (37°N, 33°E)	115
Tawakoni, L., *Tex.* (33°N, 96°W)	67
Taylor, Mt., *N. Mex.* (35°N, 108°W)	59
Taylorville, *Ill.* (40°N, 89°W)	65
Taymyr Pen., *Russia* (75°N, 105°E)	100
Tayshet, *Russia* (56°N, 98°E)	100
Tbilisi (tuh BIHL uh see), *Georgia* (42°N, 45°E)	100
Tegucigalpa (tuh GOO see GAHL puh), *Honduras* (14°N, 87°W)	85
Tehachapi Mts. (tuh HACH uh pee), *Calif.* (35°N, 119°W)	58
Tehran, *Iran* (36°N, 51°E)	115
Tehuantepec, Gulf of (tuh WAHN tuh PEHK), *Pacific O.* (16°N, 95°W)	82
Tehuantepec, Isthmus of, *Mexico* (17°N, 95°W)	82
Tel Aviv, *Israel* (32°N, 35°E)	115
Teles Pires R. (TEL uh SPIR uhs), *Brazil* (7°S, 58°W)	90
Tema (TAY muh), *Ghana* (6°N, 0°)	108
Temagami, L., *Ontario* (47°N, 80°W)	46
Temiscaming (tuh MIHS kuh ming), *Quebec* (47°N, 79°W)	46
Tempe (tem PEE), *Ariz.* (33°N, 112°W)	59
Temple, *Tex.* (31°N, 97°W)	67
Temuco, *Chile* (39°S, 73°W)	89
Tennessee, *state in U.S.* (36°N, 88°W)	70-71
Tennessee R., *U.S.* (35°N, 87°W)	70
Tennessee Tombigbee Canal, *Miss.* (35°N, 88°W)	68
Tepic (tay PEEK), *Mexico* (22°N, 105°W)	84
Teresina, *Brazil* (5°S, 43°W)	89
Terminos Lagoon, *Bay of Campeche* (19°N, 92°W)	82
Terrace, *British Columbia* (55°N, 129°W)	44
Terre Haute (TER uh HOHT), *Ind.* (39°N, 87°W)	70
Terrebonne Bay (TEHR uh BAHN), *Gulf of Mexico* (29°N, 91°W)	67
Teslin R., *Canada* (61°N, 133°W)	44
Tessalit, *Mali* (21°N, 1°E)	107
Teton Range (TEE TAHN), *Wyo.* (44°N, 111°W)	61
Tetouan (tay TWAHN), *Morocco* (36°N, 6°W)	114
Texarkana, *Ark. and Tex.* (33°N, 94°W)	67
Texas, *state in U.S.* (32°N, 100°W)	66-67
Texas City, *Tex.* (29°N, 95°W)	67
Texoma, L., *U.S.* (34°N, 97°W)	67
Thailand (TY land), *country in Asia* (17°N, 100°E)	123
Thailand, Gulf of, *South China Sea* (10°N, 102°E)	123
Thames (tehmz), *r. in England* (51°N, 1°E)	98
Thames R., *Ontario* (43°N, 82°W)	46
Thana (TAHN uh), *India* (19°N, 73°E)	122
Thasos (THAY SAHS), *island in Aegean Sea* (41°N, 25°E)	99
Thayetmyo, *Myanmar* (19°N, 95°E)	123
Theodore Roosevelt L., *Ariz.* (34°N, 111°W)	59
Theodore Roosevelt N.P., *N. Dak.* (47°N, 104°W)	62
Thermopolis (thuhr MAHP uh lus), *Wyo.* (44°N, 108°W)	61
Thief River Falls, *Minn.* (48°N, 96°W)	62
Thies (TY ehs), *Senegal* (15°N, 17°W)	108
Thika, *Kenya* (1°S, 37°E)	110
Thimphu (thim PYOO), *Bhutan* (28°N, 90°E)	122
Third Cataract, *waterfall in Sudan* (20°N, 30°E)	115
Thohoyandou (tuh HOY AHN doo), *South Africa* (23°S, 30°E)	109

Name (Pronunciation), *Description* (Lat., Long.)	**Page**
Thomasville, *Ga.* (31°N, 84°W)	69
Thompson, *Manitoba* (56°N, 98°W)	45
Thompson R., *British Columbia* (51°N, 121°W)	44
Thon Buri (tuhn BOO ree), *Thailand* (14°N, 100°E)	123
Thousand Is., *St. Lawrence R.* (44°N, 76°W)	72
Three Points, Cape, *Ghana* (5°N, 2°W)	108
Three Sisters, *mts. in Oreg.* (44°N, 122°W)	60
Thule (TOO lee), *Greenland* (78°N, 70°W)	37
Thunder Bay, *city in Ontario* (48°N, 89°W)	46
Tianjin, *China* (39°N, 117°E)	124
Tiber R., *Italy* (42°N, 12°E)	99
Tibesti Mts., *Africa* (22°N, 18°E)	106
Tibet, Plateau of, *China* (34°N, 90°E)	124
Tiburon I., *Gulf of California* (29°N, 112°W)	82
Tien Shan, *mt. range in Asia* (42°N, 78°E)	124
Tierra del Fuego (tih EH ruh dehl foo AY go), *archipelago of South America* (54°S, 70°W)	88
Tifton, *Ga.* (31°N, 84°W)	69
Tigris R., *Asia* (35°N, 43°E)	115
Tijuana (tee WHAN uh), *Mexico* (33°N, 117°W)	84
Tiksi, *Russia* (72°N, 129°E)	100
Tillamook, *Oreg.* (45°N, 124°W)	60
Tillery, L., *N.C.* (35°N, 80°W)	71
Timbuktu, *Mali* (17°N, 2°W)	107
Timisoara (TEE mish WAHR uh), *Romania* (46°N, 21°E)	99
Timmins, *Ontario* (48°N, 81°W)	46
Timor, *island in Timor Sea* (9°S, 125°E)	130
Timor Sea, *Indian O.* (11°S, 125°E)	130
Tims Ford L., *Tenn.* (35°N, 86°W)	70
Tippecanoe R., *Ind.* (41°N, 87°W)	70
Tirana (tih RAH nuh), *Albania* (41°N, 20°E)	99
Tisza R. (TIHS aw), *Hungary* (47°N, 20°E)	99
Titicaca, L., *South America* (16°S, 70°W)	88
Titusville (TY tuhs VIL), *Fla.* (29°N, 81°W)	69
Tobique R., *New Brunswick* (47°N, 68°W)	47
Tobolsk, *Russia* (58°N, 68°E)	100
Tobruk (TOH BROOK), *Libya* (32°N, 24°E)	115
Tocantins R. (TOH kuhn TEHNS), *Brazil* (10°S, 48°W)	88
Tofino (toh FEE noh), *British Columbia* (49°N, 126°W)	44
Togo, *country in Africa* (8°N, 1°E)	108
Tok, *Alaska* (6°N, 14°W)	57
Tokelau, *poss. of New Zealand* (8°S, 176°W)	135
Tokyo, *Japan* (36°N, 140°E)	125
Toledo, *Ohio* (42°N, 84°W)	70
Toledo Bend Res., *U.S.* (32°N, 94°W)	67
Toluca (tuh LOO kuh), *Mexico* (19°N, 100°W)	84
Tomah (TOH muh), *Wis.* (44°N, 90°W)	63
Tombigbee R., *U.S.* (32°N, 87°W)	68
Tomsk, *Russia* (56°N, 85°E)	100
Tonawanda, *N.Y.* (43°N, 79°W)	72
Tonga, *country in Pacific O.* (20°S, 175°W)	135
Tonkin, Gulf of, *South China Sea* (20°N, 108°E)	123
Tonle Sap (TAHN lay SAHP), *l. in Cambodia* (13°N, 104°E)	123
Tonopah (TOHN uh PAH), *Nev.* (38°N, 117°W)	58
Topeka, *Kans.* (39°N, 96°W)	64-65
Torngat Mts., *Canada* (59°N, 64°W)	41
Toronto, *Ontario* (44°N, 79°W)	46
Toronto Res., *Kans.* (38°N, 96°W)	64
Tororo, *Uganda* (1°N, 34°E)	110
Torrance, *Calif.* (34°N, 118°W)	58
Torrens, L., *Australia* (31°S, 138°E)	130
Torreon, *Mexico* (25°N, 103°W)	84
Torres Strait, *New Guinea and Australia* (10°S, 141°E)	130
Toubkal Mt. (TOOB kuhl), *Morocco* (31°N, 8°W)	114
Touggourt (too GOORT), *Algeria* (33°N, 6°E)	114
Toulon (too LOHN), *France* (43°N, 6°E)	98
Toulouse (too LOOZ), *France* (44°N, 1°E)	98
Tours (TOOR), *France* (47°N, 1°E)	98
Townsville, *Australia* (19°S, 147°E)	131
Towson, *Md.* (39°N, 77°W)	71
Toyama (toh YAHM uh), *Japan* (37°N, 137°E)	125
Trail, *British Columbia* (49°N, 118°W)	44
Tralee (truh LEE), *Ireland* (52°N, 10°W)	98
Trans-Alaskan Pipeline, *Alaska* (67°N, 150°W)	57

Name (Pronunciation), Description (Lat., Long.)	Page
Transvaal Basin (trans VAHL), *South Africa* (23°S, 29°E)	109
Transylvanian Alps, *mt. range in Europe* (45°N, 23°E)	99
Traralgon (truh RAL guhn), *Australia* (38°S, 147°E)	133
Traverse, L., *Minn.* (46°N, 97°W)	62
Traverse City, *Mich.* (45°N, 86°W)	63
Travis, L., *Tex.* (30°N, 98°W)	66-67
Trenton, *N.J.* (40°N, 75°W)	72
Tres Marias Is., *Pacific O.* (21°N, 107°W)	82
Tres Marias Res., *Brazil* (18°S, 46°W)	82
Tres Puntas, Cape, *Argentina* (47°S, 66°W)	88
Trieste (tree EST), *Italy* (46°N, 14°E)	99
Trindade, *island in Atlantic O.* (21°S, 29°W)	88
Trinidad, *Colo.* (37°N, 104°W)	59
Trinidad and Tobago, *country in Caribbean Sea* (11°N, 62°W)	85
Trinity R., *Calif.* (41°N, 123°W)	58
Trinity R., *Tex.* (32°N, 96°W)	67
Tripoli, *Lebanon* (34°N, 36°E)	115
Tripoli, *Libya* (33°N, 13°E)	114
Tripolitania, *region of Libya,* (32°N, 13°E)	114
Trivandrum (truh VAN druhm), *India* (8°N, 77°E)	122
Trois-Rivieres (TRWAH ree VYER), *Quebec* (46°N, 73°W)	47
Trombetas R. (trohm BAY tuhs), *Brazil* (2°N, 56°W)	90
Trondheim, *Norway* (64°N, 10°E)	96
Trondheims Fiord, *Norway* (64°N, 9°E)	94
Trout L., *Ontario* (51°N, 93°W)	46
Troy, *Ala.* (32°N, 86°W)	68
Troy, *N.Y.* (43°N, 74°W)	72
Truckee R., *U.S.* (39°N, 120°W)	58
Trujillo (troo HEE yoh), *Peru* (8°S, 79°W)	90
Truro, *Nova Scotia* (45°N, 63°W)	47
Tsugaru Strait (soo GAH roo), *Japan* (42°N, 140°E)	125
Tsushima (soo SHEE muh), *island in Korea Strait* (34°N, 129°E)	125
Tuamoto Archipelago, *island group in Pacific O.* (20°S, 140°W)	132
Tucson (TOO sahn), *Ariz.* (32°N, 111°W)	59
Tucuman (TOO koo MAHN), *Argentina* (27°S, 65°W)	89
Tucumcari (TOO kum KAHR ee), *N. Mex.* (35°N, 104°W)	59
Tug Fork, *r. in U.S.* (38°N, 82°W)	71
Tugela Falls, *South Africa* (29°S, 29°E)	109
Tugela R. (too GAH luh), *South Africa* (29°S, 31°E)	109
Tula, *Russia* (54°N, 38°E)	97
Tulcan (tool KAHN), *Ecuador* (1°N, 78°W)	90
Tullulah (tuh LOO luh), *La.* (32°N, 91°W)	67
Tulsa, *Okla.* (36°N, 96°W)	67
Tunduru (tuhn DOO roo), *Tanzania* (11°S, 37°E)	110
Tunis (TOO nihs), *Tunisia* (37°N, 10°E)	114
Tunisia, *country in Africa* (34°N, 10°E)	114
Tupelo (TOOP uh LOH), *Miss.* (34°N, 89°W)	68
Turan Lowland, *Kazakstan* (43°N, 60°E)	118
Turin (TOO rihn), *Italy* (45°N, 8°E)	99
Turkana, L., *Africa* (4°N, 36°E)	110
Turkey, *country in Asia and Europe* (39°N, 35°E)	115
Turkey R., *Iowa* (43°N, 92°W)	65
Turkmenistan, *country in Asia* (40°N, 57°E)	100
Turks and Caicos Is., *Atlantic O.* (22°N, 72°W)	85
Turku, *Finland* (61°N, 22°E)	97
Turlock, *Calif.* (37°N, 121°W)	58
Turpan Depression (toor pahn), *China* (42°N, 90°E)	124
Turtle Mts., *N. Dak.* (49°N, 100°W)	62
Tuscaloosa, *Ala.* (33°N, 87°W)	68
Tuttle Creek L., *Kans.* (39°N, 97°W)	64
Tuvalu, *country in Pacific O.* (5°S, 174°E)	135
Tuz, L. (TOOZ), *Turkey* (39°N, 33°E)	115
Tver, *Russia* (57°N, 36°E)	100
Twin Falls, *Idaho* (43°N, 115°W)	61
Twin Falls, *Newfoundland* (54°N, 65°W)	47
Tyler, *Tex.* (32°N, 95°W)	67

Name (Pronunciation), Description (Lat., Long.)	Page
Tyrrhenian Sea (tih REE nee uhn), *Mediterranean Sea* (39°N, 12°E)	99

U

Name (Pronunciation), Description (Lat., Long.)	Page
Uaupes (wow PEHS), *Brazil* (0°, 67°W)	90
Ubangi R., *Africa* (3°N, 23°E)	106
Uberaba, *Brazil* (20°S, 48°W)	89
Ucayali R. (OOK uh YAH lee), *Peru* (7°S, 75°W)	90
Udaipur (oo DY POOR), *India* (25°N, 74°E)	122
Ufa, *Russia* (55°N, 56°E)	97
Ugalla R. (oo GAH lah), *Tanzania* (6°S, 31°E)	110
Uganda, *country in Africa* (2°N, 32°E)	110
Uinta Mts.(yoo IHN tuh), *Utah* (41°N, 110°W)	59
Ujiji (oo JEE jee), *Tanzania* (5°S, 30°E)	110
Ujung Pandang, *Indonesia* (5°S, 119°E)	131
Ukiah (yoo KY uh), *Calif.* (39°N, 123°W)	58
Ukraine, *country in Europe* (49°N, 30°E)	97
Ulaanbaatar (oo lahn BAH tahr), *Mongolia* (48°N, 107°E)	121
Ulan Ude (oo LAHN oo DAY), *Russia* (52°N, 108°E)	124
Uliastay (OOL yoh STY), *Mongolia* (48°N, 97°E)	124
Ulm (OOLM), *Germany* (48°N, 10°E)	99
Ulsan (OOL SAHN), *South Korea* (36°N, 129°E)	125
Ulungur R. (oo loon gyoor), *Asia* (47°N, 85°E)	124
Umlazi (oom LAHZ ee), *South Africa* (30°S, 31°E)	109
Umnak I. (OOM NAK), *Bering Sea* (53°N, 169°W)	57
Umtata (oom TAH tuh), *South Africa* (32°S, 29°E)	109
Unalakleet (UHN uh LAK leet), *Alaska* (64°N, 161°W)	57
Unalaska I. (UHN uh LAS kuh), *Bering Sea* (54°N, 166°W)	57
Ungava Bay, *Hudson Strait* (60°N, 68°W)	41
Ungava Pen., *Quebec* (61°N, 75°W)	41
Unimak I. (YOO nuh MAK), *Bering Sea* (55°N, 164°W)	57
United Arab Emirates, *country in Asia* (24°N, 53°E)	115
United Kingdom, *country in Europe* (55°N, 3°W)	98
United States, *country in North America* (40°N, 100°W)	54-55
University City, *Mo.* (39°N, 90°W)	65
Unzen, Mt. (OON ZEN), *Japan* (33°N, 130°E)	125
Upington, *South Africa* (28°S, 21°E)	109
Upper Arlington, *Ohio* (40°N, 83°W)	70
Upper Arrow L., *British Columbia* (51°N, 118°W)	44
Upper Iowa R., *Iowa* (43°N, 92°W)	65
Upper Klamath L. (KLAM uth), *Oreg.* (42°N, 122°W)	60
Upper Pen., *Mich.* (46°N, 86°W)	63
Upper Red Lake, *Minn.* (48°N, 95°W)	62
Uppsala (UHP suh LAH), *Sweden* (60°N, 18°E)	96
Ural Mts., *Russia* (64°N, 59°E)	95
Ural R., *Europe and Asia* (48°N, 52°E)	95
Uranium City, *Saskatchewan* (60°N, 109°W)	45
Urawa (oo RAH wuh), *Japan* (36°N, 140°E)	125
Urbana (UHR BAN uh), *Ill.* (40°N, 88°W)	65
Urmia, L., *Iran* (38°N, 46°E)	115
Uruguay, *country in South America* (33°S, 56°W)	88
Uruguay R., *South America* (29°S, 57°W)	89
Urumqi, *China* (43°N, 88°E)	124
Usambara Mts. (oo suhm BAHR uh), *Tanzania* (5°S, 38°E)	110
Usangu Flats (oo SAHNG goo), *Tanzania* (8°S, 34°E)	110
Ushuaia (YOO SWAY yuh), *Argentina* (55°S, 68°W)	89
Ussuri R., *Russia* (46°N, 132°E)	101
Ust-Kut, *Russia* (57°N, 106°E)	100
Usumacinta R. (YOO suh muh SINT uh), *North America* (18°N, 92°W)	82
Utah, *state in U.S.* (39°N, 113°W)	58-59
Utah L., *Utah* (40°N, 112°W)	59
Ute Res. (YOOT), *N. Mex.* (35°N, 103°W)	59
Utica (YOO tih kuh), *N.Y.* (43°N, 75°W)	72
Utikuma L., *Alberta* (56°N, 116°W)	44
Utrecht (YOO TREKT), *Netherlands* (52°N, 5°E)	98

Name (Pronunciation), Description (Lat., Long.)	Page
Uwajima (oo wuh JEE muh), *Japan* (33°N, 133°E)	125
Uzbekistan, *country in Asia* (42°N, 63°E)	100

V

Name (Pronunciation), Description (Lat., Long.)	Page
Vaal R. (VAHL), *South Africa* (27°S, 27°E)	109
Vaasa (VAHS uh), *Finland* (63°N, 22°E)	97
Vacaville (VAK uh vil), *Calif.* (38°N, 122°W)	58
Vadodara, *India* (22°N, 73°E)	122
Vaduz (VAH doots), *Liechtenstein* (47°N, 10°E)	99
Vail, *Colo.* (40°N, 106°W)	59
Val-d'Or, *Quebec* (48°N, 78°W)	46
Valdes Pen., *Argentina* (43°S, 64°W)	88
Valdez, *Alaska,* (61°N, 146°W)	57
Valdosta, *Ga.* (31°N, 83°W)	69
Valencia, *Spain* (39°N, 0°)	114
Valencia, *Venezuela* (10°N, 68°W)	90
Valentine, *Nebr.* (43°N, 101°W)	64
Vallejo (vuh LAY oh), *Calif.* (38°N, 122°W)	58
Valletta (vuh LEHT uh), *Malta* (36°N, 15°E)	99
Valley City, *N. Dak.* (47°N, 98°W)	62
Valley Forge, *Pa.* (40°N, 76°W)	72
Valparaiso, *Chile* (33°S, 72°W)	89
Van, L., *Turkey* (39°N, 43°E)	115
Vancouver, *British Columbia* (49°N, 123°W)	44
Vancouver, *Wash.* (46°N, 123°W)	60
Vancouver I., *British Columbia* (50°N, 127°W)	44
Vanderhoof, *British Columbia* (54°N, 124°W)	44
Vanern, L., *Sweden* (59°N, 13°E)	94
Vanuatu (VAH noo AH too), *country in Pacific O.* (19°S, 169°E)	131
Varanasi (vuh RAHN uh see), *India* (26°N, 83°E)	122
Vardar R., *Europe* (41°N, 22°E)	99
Vardo (VAHR DUHR), *Norway* (70°N, 31°E)	97
Varna, *Bulgaria* (43°N, 28°E)	99
Vatican City, *country in Europe* (42°N, 12°E)	99
Vattern, L., *Sweden* (58°N, 14°E)	94
Venezuela, *country in South America* (7°N, 65°W)	90
Venice, *Italy* (45°N, 12°E)	99
Ventura (ven TOOR uh), *Calif.* (34°N, 119°W)	58
Veracruz (VEHR uh KROOZ), *Mexico* (19°N, 96°W)	84
Verde, Cape, *Senegal* (14°N, 18°W)	108
Verde R., *Ariz.* (34°N, 112°W)	59
Verdigris R. (VUHR duh gruhs), *U.S.* (37°N, 96°W)	64-65
Verdun (vuhr DUHN), *France* (49°N, 5°E)	98
Vereeniging (fuh REEN ih KING), *South Africa* (27°S, 28°E)	109
Verkhoyansk (VEHR kuh YANSK), *Russia* (68°N, 133°E)	100
Verkhoyansk Range, *Russia* (70°N, 130°E)	101
Vermilion R., *Ill.* (41°N, 89°W)	65
Vermillion, *S. Dak.* (43°N, 97°W)	62
Vermillion R., *S. Dak.* (43°N, 97°W)	62
Vermont, *state in U.S.* (44°N, 73°W)	73
Vernon, *British Columbia* (50°N, 119°W)	44
Verona, *Italy* (45°N, 11°E)	99
Versailles (vehr SY uh), *France* (49°N, 2°E)	98
Verona, *Italy* (45°N, 11°E)	99
Vesuvius, Mt., *Italy* (41°N, 14°E)	99
Vichy (VISH ee), *France* (46°N, 3°E)	98
Vicksburg, *Miss.* (32°N, 91°W)	68
Victoria, *British Columbia* (48°N, 123°W)	44
Victoria, *Mexico* (24°N, 99°W)	84
Victoria, *Seychelles* (5°S, 56°E)	107
Victoria, *state in Australia* (37°S, 143°E)	133
Victoria, *Tex.* (29°N, 97°W)	67
Victoria Falls, *waterfall in Africa* (18°S, 26°E)	106
Victoria I., *Arctic O.* (74°N, 110°W)	40
Victoria, L., *Africa* (1°S, 33°E)	110
Victoria, L., *Australia* (34°S, 141°E)	133
Victoria Land, *region of Antarctica* (73°S, 160°W)	137
Victoria Nile, *r. in Uganda* (2°N, 31°E)	110
Viedma, *Argentina* (41°S, 63°W)	89
Vienna, *Austria* (48°N, 16°E)	99
Vienne R. (vee EHN), *France* (47°N, 1°E)	98
Vientiane (vyehn TYAHN), *Laos* (18°N, 103°E)	123

Name (Pronunciation), *Description* (Lat., Long.)	**Page**
Vietnam, *country in Asia* (17°N, 107°E)	123
Vijayawada (VIHJ uh yuh WAHD uh), *India* (17°N, 81°E)	122
Villahermosa (VEE yuh ehr MOH zuh), *Mexico* (18°N, 93°W)	84
Vilnius, *Lithuania* (55°N, 25°E)	100
Vincennes (vin SENZ), *Ind.* (39°N, 87°W)	70
Vineland, *N.J.* (39°N, 75°W)	72
Vinh, *Vietnam* (18°N, 106°E)	123
Vinson Massif, *mt. in Antarctica* (79°S, 86°W)	137
Virgin Is., *Caribbean Sea* (18°N, 65°W)	83
Virgin R., *U.S.* (37°N, 114°W)	58
Virginia, *state in U.S.* (37°N, 80°W)	70-71
Virginia Beach, *Va.* (37°N, 76°W)	71
Virginia City, *Nev.* (39°N, 120°W)	58
Visalia (vih SAYL yuh), *Calif.* (36°N, 119°W)	58
Visby (VIHS bee), *Sweden* (58°N, 18°E)	99
Viscount Melville Sound, *Nunavut* (74°N, 110°W)	40
Vishakhapatnam (vih SHAHK uh PUHT nuhm), *India* (18°N, 83°E)	122
Vistula R., *Europe* (43°N, 19°E)	99
Vitoria, *Brazil* (20°S, 40°W)	89
Vladivostok, *Russia* (43°N, 132°E)	101
Voi (VOY), *Kenya* (3°S, 39°E)	110
Vojvodina (VOY vuh DEE nuh), *prov. of Serbia* (45°N, 20°E)	99
Volcano Is., *Pacific O.* (24°N, 141°E)	119
Volga R., *Russia* (48°N, 46°E)	95
Volga R. Delta, *Russia* (46°N, 48°E)	95
Volga Upland, *Russia* (52°N, 45°E)	95
Volgograd, *Russia* (49°N, 44°E)	97
Volgograd Res., *Russia* (50°N, 46°E)	95
Volos (VOH lahs), *Greece* (39°N, 23°E)	99
Volta, L., *Ghana* (7°N, 0°)	108
Vorkuta, *Russia* (67°N, 64°E)	100
Voronezh (vuh RAWN ish), *Russia* (52°N, 39°E)	95
Voyageurs N.P., *Minn.* (49°N, 93°W)	63
Vyatka R., *Russia* (57°N, 50°E)	95

W

Wabasca R., *Alberta* (57°N, 114°W)	44
Wabash R., *U.S.* (38°N, 88°W)	70
Waco (WAY koh), *Tex.* (32°N, 97°W)	67
Waconda L., *Kans.* (40°N, 98°W)	64
Waddington, Mt., *British Columbia* (51°N, 123°W)	44
Wagga Wagga, *Australia* (35°S, 147°E)	133
Wahpeton (WAW puh tuhn), *N. Dak.* (46°N, 97°W)	62
Wailuku, *Hawaii* (21°N, 156°W)	57
Wainwright (WAYN ryt), *Alberta* (53°N, 111°W)	45
Waipahu (wy PAH hoo), *Hawaii* (21°N, 158°W)	57
Wakayama (WAHK uh YAHM uh), *Japan* (34°N, 135°E)	125
Wakkanai (WAHK uh NY), *Japan* (45°N, 142°E)	125
Wales, *part of United Kingdom* (53°N, 4°W)	98
Walla Walla, *Wash.* (46°N, 118°W)	60
Wallis and Futuna, *poss. of France* (13°S, 176°W)	135
Wallkill R., *N.Y.* (41°N, 74°W)	72
Wallowa Mts. (wuh LOW uh), *Oreg.* (45°N, 117°W)	60
Walvis Bay, *Namibia* (23°S, 15°E)	109
Wangaratta, *Australia* (36°S, 146°E)	133
Wappapello L., *Mo.* (37°N, 90°W)	65
Wapsipinicon R. (WAHP suh PIN uh kuhn), *Iowa* (92°N, 43°W)	65
Wapusk N.P., *Manitoba* (58°N, 93°W)	45
Warner Robins, *Ga.* (33°N, 84°W)	69
Warren, *Ark.* (34°N, 92°W)	67
Warren, *Mich.* (43°N, 83°W)	63
Warren, *Ohio* (41°N, 81°W)	71
Warren, *Pa.* (42°N, 79°W)	72
Warrnambool (WAWR nuhm BOOL), *Australia* (38°S, 142°E)	133
Warsaw, *Poland* (52°N, 21°E)	99
Warta R. (VAHRT uh), *Poland* (52°N, 17°E)	99
Warwick, *R.I.* (42°N, 71°W)	73
Wasatch Range, *U.S.* (41°N, 111°W)	59

Wash, The, *bay in England* (53°N, 0°)	98
Washington, *state in U.S.* (47°N, 123°W)	60
Washington, *D.C.* (39°N, 77°W)	71
Washington, Mt., *N.H.* (44°N, 71°W)	73
Washington, *Pa.* (40°N, 80°W)	72
Waskaganish, *Quebec* (52°N, 79°W)	46
Waterbury, *Conn.* (42°N, 73°W)	73
Wateree L. (WAWT uh ree), *S.C.* (34°N, 81°W)	69
Waterford, *Ireland* (52°N, 7°W)	98
Waterloo, *Iowa* (43°N, 92°W)	65
Waterloo, *Ontario* (43°N, 81°W)	46
Waterton Lakes N. P., *Alberta* (49°N, 114°W)	44
Watertown, *N.Y.* (44°N, 76°W)	72
Watertown, *S. Dak.* (45°N, 97°W)	62
Waterville, *Maine* (45°N, 70°W)	73
Watseka (waht SEE kuh), *Ill.* (41°N, 88°W)	65
Watson Lake, *Yukon Terr.* (60°N, 129°W)	44
Watts Bar L., *Tenn.* (36°N, 85°W)	70
Waukegan (waw KEE guhn), *Ill.* (42°N, 88°W)	65
Wausau (WAW saw), *Wis.* (45°N, 90°W)	63
Wauwatosa (WAW wuh TOH suh), *Wis.* (43°N, 88°W)	63
Waw, *Sudan* (8°N, 28°E)	107
Wawa, *Ontario* (48°N, 85°W)	46
Waycross, *Ga.* (31°N, 82°W)	69
Weddell Sea, *Antarctica* (70°S, 45°W)	137
Wei R. (way), *China* (35°N, 106°E)	124
Weirton (WIRT uhn), *W. Va.* (41°N, 81°W)	71
Weiss L., *Ala.* (34°N, 86°W)	68
Welch, *W. Va.* (37°N, 82°W)	71
Welkom (VEL kum), *South Africa* (28°S, 27°E)	109
Welland Canal, *Ontario* (43°N, 79°W)	46
Wellesley Is., *Australia* (16°S, 139°E)	130
Wellington, *New Zealand* (41°S, 175°E)	131
Wellington I., *Pacific O.* (49°S, 75°W)	88
Wemindji, *Quebec* (53°N, 79°W)	46
Wenatchee, *Wash.* (47°N, 120°W)	60
Wentworth, *Australia* (34°S, 142°E)	133
Wenzou (wuhn joh), *China* (28°N, 121°E)	124
West Allis, *Wis.* (43°N, 88°W)	63
West Bank, *terr. in Asia* (32°N, 35°E)	115
West Frisian Is., *North Sea* (53°N, 6°E)	98
West Grand L., *Maine* (45°N, 68°W)	73
West Indies, *island group in Caribbean Sea* (22°N, 78°W)	83
West Jordan, *Utah* (41°N, 112°W)	59
West Lafayette (LAHF ee ET), *Ind.* (40°N, 87°W)	70
West Memphis, *Ark.* (35°N, 90°W)	67
West Palm Beach, *Fla.* (27°N, 80°W)	69
West Plains, *Mo.* (37°N, 92°W)	65
West Siberian Plain, *Russia* (60°N, 75°E)	118
West Virginia, *state in U.S.* (39°N, 81°W)	70-71
Westbrook, *Maine* (44°N, 69°W)	73
Western Australia, *state in Australia* (25°S, 120°E)	131
Western Cape, *prov. of South Africa* (34°E, 20°S)	109
Western Dvina R. (duh vee NAH), *Europe* (56°N, 26°E)	95
Western Ghats, *mt. range in India* (14°N, 75°E)	122
Western Sahara, *adm. by Morocco* (25°N, 13°W)	114
Westport, *New Zealand* (42°S, 172°E)	131
Wetar (WEH TAHR), *island in Banda Sea* (7°S, 126°E)	130
Wetaskiwin (wih TAS kuh WIHN), *Alberta* (53°N, 113°W)	44
Weyburn (WAY buhrn), *Saskatchewan* (50°N, 104°W)	45
Wheaton, *Md.* (39°N, 77°W)	71
Wheeler L., *Ala.* (35°N, 87°W)	68
Wheeler Pk., *Nev.* (39°N, 114°W)	58
Wheeler Pk., *N. Mex.* (37°N, 105°W)	59
Wheeling, *W. Va.* (40°N, 81°W)	71
White L., *La.* (30°N, 93°W)	67
White Mts., *N.H.* (44°N, 71°W)	73
White Nile, *r. in Africa* (14°N, 33°E)	106
White Plains, *N.Y.* (41°N, 74°W)	72
White R., *Ark.* (36°N, 92°W)	67
White R., *Ind.* (39°N, 87°W)	70
White R., *S. Dak.* (43°N, 102°W)	62

White R., *U.S.* (40°N, 109°W)	59
White River, *Ontario* (49°N, 85°W)	46
White Sea, *Russia* (66°N, 40°E)	95
White Sulphur Springs, *Mont.* (47°N, 111°W)	61
White Sulphur Springs, *W. Va.* (38°N, 80°W)	71
White Volta R., *Africa* (13°N, 1°W)	108
Whitecourt, *Alberta* (54°N, 116°W)	44
Whitefish Bay, *L. Superior* (47°N, 85°W)	63
Whitehorse, *Yukon Terr.* (61°N, 135°W)	44
Whitewater R., *U.S.* (39°N, 85°W)	70
Whitney, L., *Tex.* (32°N, 97°W)	67
Whitney, Mt., *Calif.* (37°N, 118°W)	58
Wholdaia L., *Northwest Terr.* (61°N, 104°W)	45
Whyalla, *Australia* (33°S, 138°E)	133
Wichita, *Kans.* (38°N, 97°W)	64
Wichita Falls, *Tex.* (34°N, 98°W)	66
Wichita Mts. (WIHCH uh TAW), *Okla.* (35°N, 99°W)	66
Wick, *Scotland* (58°N, 3°W)	98
Wicklow Mts., *Ireland* (53°N, 6°W)	98
Wiesbaden (VEES BAHD uhn), *Germany* (50°N, 8°E)	99
Wight, Isle of (WYT), *English Channel* (51°N, 1°W)	98
Wilkes-Barre (WIHLKS bair ee), *Pa.* (41°N, 76°W)	72
Wilkes Land, *region of Antarctica* (70°S, 120°E)	137
Willamette R., *Oreg.* (45°N, 123°W)	60
Willapa Bay (WIHL uh PAW), *Pacific O.* (47°N, 124°W)	60
William "Bill" Dannelly Res., *Ala.* (32°N, 87°W)	68
Williams Lake, *city in British Columbia* (52°N, 122°W)	44
Williamsburg, *Va.* (37°N, 75°W)	71
Williamsport, *Pa.* (41°N, 77°W)	72
Williston, *N. Dak.* (48°N, 104°W)	62
Williston L., *British Columbia* (56°N, 123°W)	44
Willmar, *Minn.* (45°N, 95°W)	62
Willow, *Alaska* (62°N, 150°W)	57
Willowlake R., *Northwest Terr.* (63°N, 123°W)	44
Wilmington, *Del.* (40°N, 76°W)	71
Wilmington, *N.C.* (34°N, 78°W)	71
Wilson, *N.C.* (36°N, 78°W)	71
Wilson L., *Ala.* (35°N, 88°W)	68
Wilson's Promontory, *Australia* (39°S, 147°E)	133
Winchester, *Ky.* (38°N, 84°W)	70
Winchester, *Va.* (39°N, 78°W)	71
Wind Cave N.P., *S. Dak.* (44°N, 103°W)	62
Wind R., *Wyo.* (43°N, 109°W)	61
Wind River Range, *Wyo.* (43°N, 110°W)	61
Windhoek (VINT HOOK), *Namibia* (23°S, 17°E)	107
Window Rock, *city in Ariz.* (35°N, 109°W)	59
Windsor, *Ontario* (42°N, 83°W)	46
Windward Is., *Caribbean Sea* (13°N, 62°W)	83
Windward Passage, *Caribbean Sea* (20°N, 74°W)	83
Winisk L., *Ontario* (53°N, 87°W)	46
Winisk R., *Ontario* (55°N, 85°W)	46
Winnebago, L., *Wis.* (44°N, 89°W)	63
Winnemucca, *Nev.* (41°N, 118°W)	58
Winnipeg, *Manitoba* (50°N, 97°W)	45
Winnipeg R., *Canada* (50°N, 96°W)	45
Winnipeg, L., *Manitoba* (53°N, 98°W)	45
Winnipegosis, L. (WIHN uh puh GOH suhs), *Manitoba* (52°N, 100°W)	45
Winnipesaukee, L., *N.H.* (44°N, 71°W)	73
Winona, *Minn.* (44°N, 92°W)	63
Winston-Salem, *N.C.* (36°N, 80°W)	71
Winter Haven, *Fla.* (28°N, 82°W)	69
Wisconsin, *state in U.S.* (45°N, 90°W)	63
Wisconsin Dells, *Wis.* (44°N, 90°W)	63
Wisconsin R., *Wis.* (44°N, 90°W)	63
Wloclawek (vlawt SLAH vehk), *Poland* (53°N, 19°E)	99
Wolf Point, *Mont.* (48°N, 106°W)	61
Wollaston L. (WOOL uh stuhn), *city in Saskatchewan* (58°N, 103°W)	45
Wollongong, *Australia* (34°S, 151°E)	133
Wonsan (WUHN sahn), *North Korea* (39°N, 127°E)	125
Wood Buffalo N. P., *Canada* (59°N, 114°W)	44-45

Name (Pronunciation), Description (Lat., Long.)	Page
Woods, L. of the, *Minnesota and Ontario* (49°N, 95°W)	62
Woodstock, *New Brunswick* (46°N, 68°W)	47
Woodward, *Okla.* (36°N, 99°W)	66
Woomera, *Australia* (31°S, 137°E)	131
Wooster, *Ohio* (41°N, 82°W)	71
Worcester (WOOS tuhr), *Mass.* (42°N, 72°W)	73
Worcester, *South Africa* (34°S, 19°E)	109
Worthington, *Minn.* (44°N, 96°W)	62
Wounded Knee, *S. Dak.* (43°N, 103°W)	62
Wrangel I., *Chukchi Sea* (71°N, 180°)	101
Wrangell Mts. (RANG guhl), *North America* (62°N, 142°W)	57
Wrangell–Saint Elias N. P. (ee LY uhs), *Alaska* (60°N, 141°W)	57
Wright Patman., L., *Tex.* (33°N, 95°W)	67
Wroclaw (VRAWTS lahf), *Poland* (51°N, 17°E)	99
Wu R. (woo), *China* (27°N, 107°E)	124
Wuhan, *China* (31°N, 114°E)	124
Wuxi (woo shee), *China* (32°N, 120°E)	124
Wuyi Shan (woo yih shahn), *mts. in China* (26°N, 116°E)	124
Wuzhou (woo joh), *China* (24°N, 111°E)	124
Wyoming, *Mich.* (43°N, 86°W)	63
Wyoming, *state in U.S.* (43°N, 109°W)	61
Wyoming Range, *Wyo.* (43°N, 110°W)	61
Wytheville (WITH vil), *Va.* (37°N, 81°W)	71

X

Name (Pronunciation), Description (Lat., Long.)	Page
Xanthi (ZAN thee), *Greece* (41°N, 25°E)	99
Xi Jiang R. (shee jee ahng), *China* (24°N, 107°E)	124
Xiamen (shee ah muhn), *China* (25°N, 118°E)	124
Xian (shyee an), *China* (34°N, 109°E)	124
Xiang R. (shee ang), *China* (27°N, 112°E)	124
Xingu R. (sheeng GYOO), *Brazil* (5°S, 53°W)	90
Xuzhou (shyoo joh), *China* (34°N, 117°E)	124

Y

Name (Pronunciation), Description (Lat., Long.)	Page
Yablanovyy Mts. (YAHB luh nuh VEE), *Russia* (53°N, 115°E)	100-101
Yakima (YAK ih MAW), *Wash.* (47°N, 121°W)	60

Name (Pronunciation), Description (Lat., Long.)	Page
Yakima R., *Wash.* (46°N, 120°W)	60
Yakutsk, *Russia* (62°N, 130°E)	100
Yalong R. (yah long), *China* (32°N, 101°E)	124
Yalta (YAWL tuh), *Ukraine* (45°N, 34°E)	100
Yalu R. (yah loo), *Asia* (41°N, 125°E)	125
Yamal Pen., *Russia* (70°N, 70°E)	118
Yamoussoukro (YAHM uh SOO kroh), *Côte d'Ivoire* (7°N, 5°W)	108
Yampa R., *Colo.* (40°N, 109°W)	59
Yamuna R. (YAH muh nuh), *India* (27°N, 78°E)	122
Yangon (yahng GOHN), *Myanmar* (17°N, 96°E)	123
Yangtze R., *China* (31°N, 110°E)	124
Yankton (YANG tuhn), *S. Dak.* (43°N, 97°W)	62
Yaounde (yah oon DAY), *Cameroon* (4°N, 12°E)	108
Yaqui R. (YAH kee), *Mexico* (28°N, 110°W)	82
Yarmouth, *Nova Scotia* (44°N, 66°W)	47
Yaroslavl, *Russia* (58°N, 40°E)	97
Yathkyed L. (YATH ky EHD), *Nunavut* (63°N, 98°W)	45
Yatta Plateau, *Kenya* (2°S, 38°E)	110
Yazoo City, *Miss.* (33°N, 90°W)	68
Yazoo R., *Miss.* (33°N, 89°W)	68
Yekaterinburg, *Russia* (57°N, 61°E)	100
Yellow Sea, *Asia* (36°N, 123°E)	125
Yellowknife, *Northwest Terr.* (62°N, 114°W)	44
Yellowstone L., *Wyo.* (44°N, 110°W)	61
Yellowstone N.P., *Wyo.* (45°N, 110°W)	61
Yellowstone R., *U.S.* (46°N, 109°W)	61
Yemen, *country in Asia* (16°N, 44°E)	115
Yenisey R., *Russia* (68°N, 86°E)	118-119
Yerevan, *Armenia* (40°N, 45°E)	100
Yichang (yee chang), *China* (31°N, 112°E)	124
Yoho N. P., *British Columbia* (51°N, 117°W)	44
Yokohama, *Japan* (36°N, 140°E)	125
Yonkers, *N.Y.* (41°N, 74°W)	72
York, *England* (54°N, 1°W)	98
York, *Pa.* (40°N, 77°W)	72
York, Cape, *Australia* (11°S, 142°E)	130
Yorke Pen., *Australia* (34°S, 138°E)	133
Yorkton, *Saskatchewan* (51°N, 102°W)	45
Yorktown, *Va.* (37°N, 76°W)	71
Yosemite Falls (yoh SEHM ih tee), *Calif.* (38°N, 120°W)	58
Yosemite N.P., *Calif.* (38°N, 120°W)	58

Name (Pronunciation), Description (Lat., Long.)	Page
Youngstown, *Ohio* (41°N, 81°W)	71
Yu R. (yoo), *China* (24°N, 107°E)	124
Yuan R. (yoo ahn), *China* (28°N, 110°E)	124
Yuba City (YOO buh), *Calif.* (39°N, 122°W)	58
Yucatan Channel (YOO kuh TAHN), *Mexico and Cuba* (22°N, 84°W)	83
Yucatan Pen., *Mexico* (20°N, 90°W)	83
Yugoslavia, *country in Europe* (45°N, 20°E)	99
Yukon R., *North America* (64°N, 160°W)	57
Yukon Territory, *Canada* (63°N, 135°W)	42
Yuma, *Ariz.* (33°N, 115°W)	58
Yunnan Plateau (yoo NAHN), *China* (26°N, 103°E)	124

Z

Name (Pronunciation), Description (Lat., Long.)	Page
Zadar (ZAHD AHR), *Croatia* (44°N, 15°E)	99
Zagreb, *Croatia* (46°N, 16°E)	99
Zagros Mts., *Asia* (35°N, 47°E)	115
Zahedan (ZAH hih DAHN), *Iran* (30°N, 61°E)	115
Zambezi R., *Africa* (16°S, 33°E)	106
Zambia, *country in Africa* (15°S, 25°E)	107
Zanesville, *Ohio* (40°N, 82°W)	71
Zanzibar, *city in Tanzania* (6°S, 39°E)	110
Zanzibar, *island in Indian O.* (6°S, 40°E)	110
Zaria (ZAHR ee uh), *Nigeria* (11°N, 8°E)	108
Zaysan, L., *Kazakhstan* (48°N, 84°E)	100
Zhangjiakou (JAHNG zhee ah KOH), *China* (41°N, 115°E)	124
Zhangzhou (jahng joh), *China* (25°N, 118°E)	124
Zhengzhou (jung joh), *China* (35°N, 114°E)	124
Zhytomyr (ZHEE TOH meer), *Ukraine* (50°N, 29°E)	99
Zibo (dzee bwo), *China* (37°N, 118°E)	124
Ziguinchor (ZEE GAN SHOHR), *Senegal* (13°N, 16°W)	108
Zimbabwe, *country in Africa* (20°S, 30°E)	107
Zinder, *Niger* (14°N, 9°E)	107
Zion N. P. (ZY uhn), *Utah* (37°N, 113°W)	58-59
Zouirat, *Mauritania* (23°N, 12°W)	114
Zuni R. (ZOO nee), *U.S.* (35°N, 110°W)	59
Zunyi, *China* (28°N, 107°E)	124
Zurich (ZOO rik), *Switzerland* (47°N, 9°E)	99

Data: Area and population figures are from the most recent official sources available in mid-1993; unless otherwise specified, city populations are for municipalities, not for wider metropolitan areas. For most of the other themes, values are averages over the last three years for which data are available.